# Comics as History, Comics as Literature

# Comics as History, Comics as Literature

*Roles of the Comic Book in Scholarship, Society, and Entertainment*

Edited by
Annessa Ann Babic

FAIRLEIGH DICKINSON UNIVERSITY PRESS
Madison • Teaneck

Published by Fairleigh Dickinson University Press
Copublished with Rowman & Littlefield
4501 Forbes Boulevard, Suite 200, Lanham, Maryland 20706
www.rowman.com

10 Thornbury Road, Plymouth PL6 7PP, United Kingdom

British Library Cataloguing in Publication Information Available

**Library of Congress Cataloging-in-Publication Data**

Comics as history, comics as literature : roles of the comic book in scholarship, society, and entertainment / edited by Annessa Ann Babic.
    pages cm.
    Includes bibliographical references and index.
    ISBN 978-1-61147-556-2 (cloth : alk. paper) -- ISBN 978-1-61147-557-9 (electronic)
    1. Comic books, strips, etc.—Influence on mass media. 2. Comic books, strips, etc.—Cross-cultural
studies. 3. Comic books, strips, etc., in education. I. Babic, Annessa Ann, editor of compilation.
    PN6714.C653 2013
    741.5'9—dc23
                                                                                    2013034608

♾™ The paper used in this publication meets the minimum requirements of American
National Standard for Information Sciences Permanence of Paper for Printed Library
Materials, ANSI/NISO Z39.48-1992.

Printed in the United States of America

For those I've loved and lost along the way
and for those who still love me.

# Contents

# Acknowledgments

The old adage says that success has many owners and failure, one. In compiling this anthology I have little issue taking ownership, or parentage, of what lies forth. I hope that it lies somewhere between the two categories, and on that note, I also gladly admit that writing and compiling a manuscript takes a small army of people for completion.

The editors at the publishing house have been generous and receptive to me and this project. Through a series of delays, everything from human error to Hurricane Sandy, persistence finally won through. I thank them for their time and support, especially Harry Keyishian. I worked most closely with Harry, and I am certain that we are both delighted to see this project come to a successful conclusion. The writers included here were a wonderful lot, taking my slashing of their chapters, rewrite demands, and attempts at humor in stride. Their essays are passionate and entertaining, so much so that in the final phases of edits, I endured nightmares of Wonder Woman becoming a zombie. I thank them for their patience, energy, and commitment.

Leigh Harrell-Williams allowed me to take over her dining room table, den, and spare bedroom on more than one occasion. She never complained about the mass of books, articles, and shreds of paper I traipsed throughout her house. She even digitally retrieved an article for me when I could not. I owe her a huge debt of gratitude for not balking while I terrorized her house in the name of comic scholarly research. Tanfer Emin-Tunç has remained a mainstay in my life since our Stony Brook days. She engages in my random side trails of conversations about comic culture and comic characters appearing in Turkey and ignores the often capricious nature of our conversations when I am deep in research thought. We collaborated on our first book, and while we did not pair up this time, she has certainly remained with me in more ways than one. Jen Zuniga tells me that she will read these works alongside comics to her daughters as a nod to our long-standing friendship and thirst for scholarship. Steve Mccullough also did some light proofing for me. Nick Bloom, who is technically my chair, spends more time reading my e-mail and listening to my rants than we care to admit. Accordingly, our random conversations have been a welcomed aspect to this project. For anyone left out, I apologize . . . after all there is only so much space on the metaphorical page.

That family of mine, whom wishes I would just write about something normal, such as World War II or the Great Depression, deserves its own note here. The Babics have always been a strange lot, and by dent and design, we are an odd combination of error, humor, and comedy. I thank them for their continued support, even when I know they are less than enthused. Toward the final phases of this manuscript, my life changed from a single-jaded gal, accustomed to her own schedule and path, to one shared with someone. Rich Willette tries his best to understand the editing process, and he makes daily points to ask about my work. For his love and support, I deeply thank him. My life is fuller and richer with him in it, and as much as this work is a reflection of me and my writers, it is an image of his compassion, love, and understanding for the wife who never stops working, rarely sleeps, remembers to cook dinner but forgets to turn the coffee pot off, and leaves the dirty laundry for him to wash.

Finally, as with every manuscript I have completed, loss has been associated with it. Sometimes life has dark paths that never fully make sense. For those I have lost in the course and phases of this project, a part of it will always be marked by them and for them.

Annessa Ann Babic
Astoria, New York

# Introduction

Annessa Ann Babic,
New York Institute of Technology

When I was in middle school, my best friend had a disturbingly strong affection for comic books. Okay, so maybe it was not all that disturbing, but I never understood his fascination with the pages and stories of superheroes and villains. I saw his books as pages riddled with comically clad and multicolored figures with unbelievable storylines. Even then, at the not-so-tender age of thirteen or so, I rolled my eyes at the skintight costumes, the fainting women, the body proportions of said women, and, in general, at the comic character. Men in tights and women acting as second chair just did not appeal to me. Yet, Steve continued to push his comics my way, beg me to read them, get frustrated when I just did not get them in the same way that he did, and tell me about them. Steve may have been my comic book connection in middle school, but he was not my only one. My older brother and I had once—or twice—decided to play Wonder Woman and Batman. I, even at younger ages than thirteen, refused to be predictable, and I played Batman. I remember draping a blanket over my shoulders for a cape, and he donned red running shorts and wielded a garbage can lid as his shield, with a rope tied to his hip for a lasso. Jumping off the garage roof landed us in the soft-tilled soil of the garden, so we luckily did not break any bones . . . though a few plants may have met their maker along the way. Even with these moments of comic book glory, I never read comics in my formative years. Instead, I became a comic book reader by default.

While researching female patriotic iconography in graduate school, my paths crossed with Wonder Woman, and I suddenly found myself reading golden age Wonder Woman stories by the dozens. I have now read almost all the issues (from conception to the early 1970s), histories, and general comic book overviews. Yet, in the midst of all this information, comics still remain on the fringes of popular culture, and readers, researchers, and nonreaders are still left to wonder what constitutes comic books, what makes their longevity, and what are the layers within them. In the spring of 2008, I taught an honors course on comic book history, and the question "What is the comic book?" continually peppered our lively conversations. The group of fifteen students ranged from

1

avid comic book fans—mostly of X-Men, Spiderman, and the Justice League characters—to two students who had never picked up a comic in their lives. These students were apt to admit what they did know and did not. I particularly remember when two of them came to class after having visited their first comic book shop—specifically, their glee at what they found. However, they did ask me how I managed the comic shop world with the "comic geeks" and diehard fans. I was brutally honest. Sometimes I boded well inside the deepest bowels of the shops, and sometimes my gender, appearance, and purpose for comics kept me on the edge of the social network within these walls. Yet, within these group conversations, we continually probed the meaning of comics, what makes them, and what they are. These questions and conversations are what brought me to compile this reader, which takes another look at comics—American and European—to put them within a political, social, and constructive context. Chapters on the gendered, racial, and political definitions within comics will bring us one step closer to bridging the gaps in literature and history on this discursive mainstay of popular culture.

The image of the comic book reader still stands as a young teen or socially outcast older individual; the reader is predominantly male; and comic book readers in general are often closely associated with gamers or role-players. Comic shops usually have *Dungeons and Dragons* players who meet weekly or more often, and store regulars can intimidate the novice comic shopper with their knowledge of superheroes, villains, and book editions. The popular comedy *The Big Bang Theory* makes frequent use of comics, with its nerd casted characters, and Penny—the attractive, blonde, non–comic book reading female—reacts with rolled eyes and nonchalant understanding. These observations led to the question, what are comic books' place in history and literature? More so, how much of a place should they have?

## HISTORICAL OVERVIEW

Rudophe Töpffer, a writer from Switzerland, published *The Adventures of Obadiah Oldbuck* in 1837, and his forty-page tale is considered the first known comic book. In 1842, it became the first comic book published in the United States. By the early twentieth century, the genre began to slowly grow, with such titles as *The Yellow Kid in McFadden's Flats* (1897) and *The Blackberries* (1901). In 1934, the industry was born with the publication of a bound volume of comic strips. Yet, the genre did not really blossom until later in the twentieth century, with cheaper printing methods and the growth of child culture. In the 1920s and 1930s, inexpensive forms of entertainment rapidly captured the market—most notably, pulp novels and movies. Movies quickly became a centerpiece of working- and upper-class entertainment, which paved the way for comics.

Beginning with the publication of *Moving Picture World* in 1907, theater owners were encouraged to embrace the new medium, and by 1913, the feature film began in earnest. These early one-hour films focused on the female audience—mostly middle class—because the ideals of social property, refined manners, and impeccable taste danced across the screen. In the early years, women and children dominated attendance at night showings in suburban venues, with men attending downtown shows, and the mass of women attending these movies were dubbed "movie-struck girls." They often found themselves characterized as being fascinated with the onscreen stories and narcissistic absorption of their own image. This atmosphere of grandeur led to a mood of indulgence and relief from society and life. So successful was the movie medium, with its escape from life's troubles, that in 1909 the National Board of Censorship of Motion Pictures began. In the decade that followed, the board reviewed about 85 percent of movies made.[1] Movies—and all their glamour—captivated the public, and even though the subject matter was typically aimed at the rising middle class, lots of the working class flocked to movies for the same sense of escapism. Working-class women in particular used the movies as a medium to judge their fashion and style. Working girls and middle-class women frequently dolled up to see movies, as they were a social affair, a night out, and a chance to be seen.

Alongside movies, pulp novels boomed on the American consumer market. Also closely associated with factory girls at the turn of the century, these novels captivated their audience with romance, wonder, and allure. Not to mention, they were a cheap form of entertainment that the girls often read together over lunch, sharing these books and passing them back and forth until the cheap and flimsy constructions literally fell apart. The dime and pulp novel also circulated alongside the Western and other adventure stories. These tales honed in on the male audience, but by 1937, a distinctly different genre of cheap, accessible, escapism-based fiction emerged.

In 1937, *Detective Comics* launched its first books, with *Action Comics* following suit in 1938. These early comics cost ten cents, and with their regular publication, they quickly became a staple in American fiction. These early writers flourished from their idealism and thirst for creativity, as they were mostly young and hungry artists. With *Detective Comics* launch in 1937, the golden age of comics began. The age—known for its superheroes, tales of vigilante justice, and stories of the common man doing good—officially died in 1954, with the public's outcry about juvenile delinquency. The 1954 debunking of comics stemmed from Dr. Frederic Wertham's *Seduction of the Innocent*. Wertham claimed that *Wonder Woman* comics contained lesbian themes, *Superman* comics encouraged dissociative behavior traits, and comics in general promoted violence, hostility, and delinquent behavior. Post-1954, the silver age took off, with the birth of Flash—actually the rebirth of an earlier character—in DC

Comics' *Showcase #4* and with Marvel Comics following suit with *The Amazing Spider Man #31* in 1965. By the 1960s, U.S. comics were mostly published by large companies because limited rack space at newsstands made it difficult for smaller presses to reach the larger public. Not until the late 1980s and early 1990s did comics move from their inexpensive periodical format to book-bound products. Underground comics also rose, and the 1970s saw direct marketing tactics encouraging distribution to specialty stores. The 1980s saw this specialization of comics support the collection of pamphlet stories to books, the evolution of book stores, and the acquirement of comics by libraries.[2]

Amid this redefining of the market, its growth, and its controversies, the audience remained predominately male. Its creators, a "boys club," manufactured characters of male strength—with the main exception being Wonder Woman—but the 1990s saw the emergence of a female market. Magna, particularly Sandman, captivated the female reader. The *Sandman* series began in 1989—revived by Neil Gaiman from DC Comics' 1970s creation—and quickly become one of DC Comics' best-selling titles. It ended with its tenth trade paperback in 1996, and it was one of the few comics/graphic novels to earn a spot on the *New York Times* best-seller list, the two other titles being *The Watchmen* and *The Dark Knight Returns.*

The life of comics is interesting, but the stories within their pages are more complex than a tale of a hero surpassing a villain. They are political, romantic, and captivating. The stories of comics are also twofold. They work through words and pictures, both of which are needed for understanding and immersion into the fictional world of good versus evil. When examined by themselves, comics have their own history. Debates arise about mass publishers, such as DC Comics and Marvel Comics, monopolizing the market with watered-down text, a single genre within a genre, and preventing independent printers from making a mark. These debates are valid, but they are not the only discourses concerning comics. Political language within comics, their intersection with patriotism and national honor (most notably during World War II), their gender dynamics, and more shape their complex place within literature and history.

## COMIC LITERATURE

In 1985, comic books finally got their own full-length discussion within academic literature in Will Eisner's *Comics as Sequential Art.* Eisner's work looked at comics as art and literary forms with sequential expression. He marked comics as literary forms because their stories bear strong resemblance to those of literature.[3] Douglas Wolk contradicts Eisner by arguing that comics are no more literary than movies or operas, and he denotes scripts for comics as comparable to film scripts. But the finished product of comics is different from that of traditional books and narratives, making it a unique genre. Samuel R. Delaney goes so far as to call comics "paraliterary."

Max J. Skidmore and Joey Skidmore remark that most children of the golden age did not view their comics as propaganda. Yet, comics have repeatedly delved into and embraced the political. Modern comics have evolved with the times and their audiences. Skidmore and Skidmore note that "contemporary comics often reflect this loss of innocence and upon occasion have gone considerable beyond the public predictions." The authors reiterate that Hercules, Beowulf, and Paul Bunyun not only reflect a heroic tradition but mirror popular attitudes. This argument stands for comics. As Arthur Berger argued in 1971, comics parody American culture and art; they provide a fusion and often emotionally gripping genre for reader support.[4] Most notable, Skidmore and Skidmore discuss how U.S. comics grapple with and frequently ignore American civil liberties and rights. In the 1950s, comics began slowly incorporating black and other nonwhite characters. Heroes such as Luke Cage, the first black superhero with his own magazine; Falcon, a sidekick for Captain America; and Black Panther, who was actually seen more with Falcon than Captain America represented some of these shifting elements of American culture. In comics, the reader sees that the nonwhite characters associated most with other nonwhite actors, much as individuals did in their own lives and communities. Hence, comics literally illustrated diasporas of culture without actually addressing social concerns and misconceptions.

In *Comic Books as History: The Narrative Art of Jack Jackson, Art Spiegelman, and Harvey Pekar*, Joseph Witek discusses how American comics are designed with highly developed narratives, grammar, and vocabulary based on an inextricable combination of verbal and visual elements. Witek notes that comic books have typically been aimed at general readership and that, after the golden era, their themes evolved from revolving around escapist storylines to focusing more on the clash of cultures in American history. Key examples that he uses for his discussion on the discursiveness of comic books and their validity for history and scholarship include Art Spiegelman's *Maus*, Harvey Pekar's *American Splendor*, and Jack Jackson's *Los Téjanos, Commanche Moon*. *Maus* dramatically presents itself as a historical narrative set within an autobiographical style; *American Splendor* showcases the pains and trials of working-class life in Cleveland; and *Los Téjanos, Commanche Moon* gives its readers a revisionist tale of the American Southwest with previously excluded figures of U.S. history as centerpieces of the story. Amid this discussion, he notes that comic books, as a distinct genre, took some time to mature. In the 1930s, comic strips found themselves bound in anthologies, often being dubbed *comic books*. As actual comic books began to captivate the market, the distinct formula of characters—particularly superheroes—and art clearly carved its spot in the literature market. More so, part of the unique culture and form of comic books—aside from the obvious, their presentation—is that comic books are voluntary purchases, as opposed to comic strips, which are included inside newspapers. Comic books also use events from real life to glamorize, rally, and even educate. Some of these books—"preachie" comic books, such as *Bible Studies for Young Folk*—are targeted at religious youth audiences. In 1948, the Democratic National Committee gave away copies of *The Story of Harry S. Truman* to help the presidential campaign and educate the public about the president, and the Federal Reserve Bank of New York encouraged the use of checking accounts by teaching readers how to use them with *The Story of Checks*.[5]

Bradford W. Wright's *Comic Book Nation* continues the discussion of Witek and Skidmore and Skidmore by not only tracing the history of the American comic book industry but bringing its parallelism and complex place within U.S. culture to the center of his dialogue. Wright shows that comic books epitomize the accessibility and disposability of consumer culture. The perennial lowbrow status of comic books allowed them to develop outside of critical, aesthetic, and commercial criteria of "mature culture." Keys to the success of comics lie in the appealing formulas that endure: they serve as source for perception of ourselves; they function as portal of young people; and they work as cultural representations of the reader.[6]

Other works have dealt with the dark side of comic books, particularly the birth of the comics code in 1954 following Wertham's *Seduction of the Innocent*. Amy Nyberg's *Seal of Approval: The History of the Comics Code* looks at adult concerns about comics stemming from bounds of traditional authority and failures to understand cultural appeals. Nyberg and numerous others discuss social conceptions that children should be constructive and not leisurely. These concerns littered the discourse. Responding to these growing criticisms, the industry passed its own code in October 1954, which initially appeased and pacified critics. Before television, comics performed as a major form of entertainment for children, and the irony cannot be missed about the legacy of censorship crusades and new and popular genres of entertainment. Campaigns sought to ban and clean up dime novels and their romance scenes, Westerns and their gun fights, and so forth. But the First World War halted critics, as troops devoured comics for their cheap and accessible means of entertainment. In 1915, an attempt was made to censor films, and throughout the 1920s and 1930s, the industry performed self-censorship. Yet, comics took a different place within the minds of critics because of the "content," which translates to action scenes and women acting outside of traditional roles of domesticity. The debates became so hostile that newspapers refused to print strips because of their association with comic books. The claim rested on the assertion that publishers stole money from the hands of babes (more than $1 million annually). Children flocked to the medium for its price, color, allusion, escapism, and adventure; the industry denounced the complaints of adults, saying that comics remained too literal. [7]

As the industry rapidly grew, new terms emerged, which set the growth and popularity of the genre. For instance, the term *superhero* was not minted until several years after Superman's first appearance. The coining of the term, alongside the staggering sales numbers, established comics' rebirth for each generation. This newfound desire for comics derived from the growing social anxieties of war: fathers gone, moving homes, working mothers, and shortages. Throughout the campaign to censor and curb comic distribution, corporate greed and irresponsibility toward children consistently played a central role in the discourse. Yet, these arguments yielding predictions of societal downfall, disfigured gender roles, and mass children embracing violence as a natural mechanism of communication failed to note that adult readership soared alongside that of children. Children clearly sucked in the storylines at a larger rate than that of adults, but adults—especially soldiers on the front lines—fueled themselves on the junkets of their favorite superheroes. [8]

Reacting to the growing criticism and fearing economic repercussions from unchecked disparagements, the industry created its own code of conduct. The major comic publishers felt that their established "in-house" system sufficed—as it temporarily quelled disputes on comic subjects— and they used it as a mechanism to distance themselves from the smaller publishers of the industry. Officially, the Association of Comics Magazine Publishers adopted the first code in 1948. [9] The code was revised with each generation/decade—much like the characters in the comics—as it reflected society, political movements, and civic rights and codes. The 1948 code echoed McCarthyism and Cold War ideology (as did the British campaign), ditto for 1954; the code of 1971 mirrored the Vietnam War, women's liberation, and other civil rights movements of the era; and 1989 emulated the undercurrents of the ending Cold War, Reagan and Bush conservatism, and the glass-ceiling debate of the 1970s and 1980s.

Peter Coogan's *Superhero: The Secret Origin of a Genre* looks at the world of comics through the eyes of the superhero. Coogan says,

> Superheroes stand as metaphors for freedom—the freedom to act without consequences and the freedom from the restrictions from the restrictions of gravity, the law, families, and romantic relationships. Perhaps this is why so many superheroes are free of their families as unmarried adult orphans. Superheroes are also a metaphor for efficacy—they can accomplish anything they set out to do—and they are often used in this sense in advertising. [10]

His work looks at why superheroes are so adaptable to the large screen, what makes them so popular, and the nature of their costumes. Specifically, he examines how the costumes identify the characters. [11] Coogan's work is slightly different from the growing breadth of literature on comics. Instead of focusing on the storylines or a list of characters, he brings out the point of what makes a comic book unique.

Scot McCloud's *Understanding Comics: The Invisible Art* deliciously examines the actual art and function within comics. McCloud takes his readers/viewers through a chapter-by-chapter analysis of the form and functions of comics, the sequential nature of their art, mood setting through color, the language and usage of the gutter, and the vocabulary of comics. Aside from clearly deconstructing the anatomy of comic books, he demonstrates the importance of a unified language within an often misunderstood medium. McCloud states, "A single unified language deserves a single unified vocabulary. Without it, comics will continue to limp along as the 'bastard child' of words and pictures. Several factors have conspired against comics receiving the unified identity the genre needs." [12]

## INTERNATIONALLY COMIC

The language and discourse of comics extends beyond the large and well-known American market. Just as comics represent and mirror social and cultural conceptions within the U.S. framework, they interact with modernity, revolution, and national honor elsewhere. In nearly every case, comics have taken a backseat to other forms of historical documentation and literature revelations. Yet, the continual rise in scholarship shows how they serve as markers for dialect, gender, nationalism, and highbrow discourse.

Anne Runenstein's *Bad Language, Naked Ladies, and Other Threats to the Nation: A Political History of Comic Books in Mexico* discusses the role of comics in Mexico's desire to form a national culture, as scholars agreed by the 1940s that the nation did not have one. Yet, core ideological issues peppered the debate and evolution of national culture, as tradition did not precede modernity and modernity did not displace tradition. In the case of Mexico, media outlets and comics acted as a modernity force by using language and the image of the urbanite to push culture forward. Even as comics served the national center, the Mexican state established a censorship office in 1944 as a means to protect the reader. [13] Popular mind-set had the average reader as semiliterate, and the Mexican censorship campaign works in similar manner to the comics code in the United States and elsewhere. By the 1970s, dialogues began arguing that comics brought growth to the city because they showed contrast and progress to rural life, namely through gender interpretation by focusing on modern versus traditional women.

John Lent's 1999 anthology *Pulp Demons* focuses on international censorship campaigns and comics throughout much of the 1950s. Key works from the volume come from studies of U.S., British, and Australian comics. Each account discusses the comic's purpose and origin, as well as issues of a democratic state. The height of the debate fell postwar with Wertham's *Seducation of the Innocent*. These allied powers—still aligned for Cold War sensibilities and seemingly foes of communist states—all viewed comics as portals for political corruption of youth.[14] Clearly, with imposed codes for comic conduct (albeit self-imposed by each industry to deflect public rebuttal) show that the public already knew what scholarship is just now getting around to: discussing comics' reflection and shaping of culture in similar manners as plays, film, and novels.

In contrast to the ambiguity shown in American scholarly discourse concerning the place of the comic in history and literature, French critics have long referred to the comic as the "ninth art." Comics discourse continually borrows language to discuss the medium, just as comics borrow from others to create their products. Yet, for the most part, comics are not about art. They are about the style and story within their pages.[15]

Joel Vessels's *Drawing France: French Comics and the Republic* provides a sophisticated account of the political life of *bande dessinée* (BD), exploring the shifting political and cultural place of the image and BD through a combination of social discourse, governmental policy, and popular culture. Moreover, Vessels examines the place of BD in French culture and the external construction of Frenchness itself. Vessels notes, "In France, language competence, and even more, literacy allow access to the national cultural space and are also the tools by which the particularities of various cultural signifiers are managed so as to transform a potential 'battleground of meaning' into 'a shared point of departure.'" Accordingly, BD already has two strikes against it: first, it is difficult to sell because it is not considered art; second because it is not art, it must be a form of communication. Yet, BD is deficient for communication because of its reliance on crude and exaggerated drawings. Fears of illiteracy and corruption of the youth sometimes permeated French culture—as it did in Britain and the United States—and accusations that comics would breed fascism colored the discourse; however, the adoption of the comics code in the United States helped halt the debate in France about the medium.[16] Specifically, the role of BD in national politics and identity shapes the stories and life of BD within French culture.

## COMIC FORMS

Even with this breadth of scholarship, comics still fall into the gutters of placement, research, and understanding. They are hiding in the white matter among the respectable, acceptable, educational, and academic. This anthology takes another step in bridging the gap of scholarly resources and documents, bringing comics closer to the center of the academic debate. The forms of comics have morphed into graphic novels, which, while a different genre per se, attest to the popularity and credibility of comics themselves. *The 9/11 Report, Comic Encyclopedia, History of the World, The Watchmen,* and *Persepolis* are just some examples of the power of comics to change the way that we look at popular culture products. *The 9/11 Report* and *The Watchmen* both deal with political moments—real and fictionalized—and their texts capture a sense of American racism, hatred, care, and concern.[17] These books grapple with terrifying and compelling subjects, making them readily available, and in a roundabout way, they make political turmoil understandable. Along these lines, Marisa Acocella Marchetto's *Cancer Vixen* and Marjane Satrapi's *The Complete Persepolis* weave female narratives, subject matters, and political turmoil into the pages of their captivating tales. *Cancer Vixen* puts the breast cancer battle of a freelance cartoonist into a perspective of humor, fight, and her love of pretty shoes. Its pages make reference to health insurance access, but the story really focuses on the battle with cancer through laughter and living life. Satrapi's narrative tells the story of a young girl in Iran, the failed Iranian revolution, her parents' desire to protect her by sending her off to boarding school, her marriage and divorce, and the quest for freedom of expression.[18] These brutal and poetic tales illustrate the story of life and history, much like comic books have been doing since their inception in 1837.

## LOOKING AT COMICS

This anthology hosts a collection of works examining the role of comics as portals for historical and academic content while keeping the approach on an international market versus the American one. Few resources currently exist showing the cross-disciplinary aspects of comics.[19] This study begins with chapters examining French comics, an area growing substantial ground within academic discourses. Henri-Simon Blanc-Hoàng provides an intriguing study of *Astérix*, created in 1961. His apt study of French nationalism grapples with the "resistance myth against U.S. cultural hegemony" and the longing for lost days of imperial glory. Additionally, he uses *Alix* and *Taranis* (a Marxist counterpart to the other two storylines) to frame his study. The three comics base their storylines following Julius Caesar's conquest of Gaul, with their tales centering on cultural assimilation verses resistance. They show a stark parallel to the postwar discourse in France concerning the growth of international markets (primarily American) and so-called lost national honor from World Wars I and II. Following this discussion, Guillaume de Syon examines French comics in the 1970s. He focuses on "Les Histoires de l'Oncle Paul" (Histories from Uncle Paul), questioning why the strip rose to popularity and became a standard for the genre. The decade saw a renewed interest in nineteenth-century history (via popular culture) and both World Wars. Nostalgia and popular (and imagined) memories of richer and simpler times permeated national discourse and culture. Finally, to end the French section, Annick Pellegrin uses a McDonald's ad campaign with a closing scene from *Astérix* as a portal for her examination of comics, nationalism, and consumer culture. Here, she discusses *Astérix*'s creators' connection with the United States. In turn, her analysis shows that a U.S.–France connection existed long before the 2010 ad campaign. Moreover, her chapter grapples with the recurrent theme of cultural assimilation versus resistance.

Continuing a national theme, Melanie Huska delves into comics books as political education in Mexico. She looks at *México: Historia de un Pueblo* and *Episodios Mexicanos* (published between 1980 and 1982). These books merge fact and fiction to narrate significant political events and periods in Mexican history, such as the Spanish conquests, the colonial era, the Wars of Independence, and the Mexican Revolution. She contends that the Mexican government latched onto comics as a form of civic education to raise the literacy rate and boost national honor. The books, as in so many other cases, were easy reads and consumed by the average individual. More so, they portrayed a state-approved image to circumvent the reality of economic and educational stagnation.

Bending from an international perspective, the following chapters focus on U.S. comics. Peter Lee looks at Wonder Woman and uses the "golden age" of World War II as his primary portal of discussion. Here, he is unique in that, instead of examining the many layers and almost undefinable realm of Wonder Woman, he pays close examination to her alter ego, Diana Prince. In lay terms, Diana Prince is the woman that Wonder Woman is when she is not in costume. Her almost mousy demure and less-than-fashionable attire, complete with large eyeglasses, make her a sore spot for feminists: she is not assertive; she holds a traditional woman's secretarial job; and she longs and agonizes for Steve Trevor's affections. As Lee notes, she is missing from the current DC Comics storyline, but her history is key to understanding the legacy and longevity of Wonder Woman herself. My own chapter looks at the popular comic book heroine Wonder Woman alongside Rosie the Riveter and common advertisements to argue that, not only did she stand for honor and nationalism during World War II, but her postwar legacy continued to teach feminism and promote the changing face of the patriotic female in the Cold War and after. J. C. Lethbridge takes the dark code of comics in tow within the postwar era, discussing hysterical fear that comics would breed commies and degenerates in America's youth by the sheer nature of their being a subversive genre. Yet, this genre captivated nearly 80 percent of army camp readers during World War II. Firmly placing his discussion within the bounds of postwar fears, he discusses the ironies of redefining the guidelines of comics for fear that too much creativity and liberty would lead to unchecked social bounds without constraint. A lack of constraint would obviously, in this case, lead to the destruction of the U.S. power hold. In a postwar world where Americans literally competed with the USSR for the "best" housewife, subverting the genre of comics seemed only prudent. Pitted with Wonder Woman and Cold War culture in this section is Lynda Goldstein's provocative essay on September 11 in graphic narration. She uses Art Spiegelman's *In the Shadow of No Towers*, Alissa Torres's *American Widow,* and the graphic adaptation of *The 9/11 Commission Report*, by Sid Jacobson and Ernie Colón, to convey her notations on memory, meaning, and social purpose. As she examines the narratives for their versions of a realist portrait of the events, she concludes by pondering how the continued aftermath of September 11 can be shown in a realist portrayal. The question at the center of so many of these chapters focuses on how the comic represents national fears, hopes, and aspirations. Goldstein's account of September 11 comic discourse hits this dilemma of comics as forms of scholarship on the figurative graphic page. Just as Pellegrin questions the reasoning behind French anger concerning the *Astérix* strip in a McDonald's advertisement, Goldstein uncovers the layers of complexity of capturing an event and how the reality and truth will continue to have a multiplicity of layers, designs, and conventions.

Rounding out this study brings the final two sections, on so-called morality and aspects of dark logic. Kara Kvaran provides a provocative look at a frequently overlooked area of comics . . . the gay superhero. She uses Marvel Comics' the Rawhide Kid, originally created in the 1950s and killed off in 1979, to discuss the complexities of progress and sexuality. The Rawhide Kid posed a problematic connection of a homosexual who still excelled in the hypermasculine world of the Old West cowboy and gunslinger. Not surprising, he drew criticism from both sides, saying that he promoted gay stereotypes and that he was a degenerate. In the postwar years, he drew criticism for derailing youth from a moral path, particularly after Wertham's *Seduction of the Innocent*. Yet, Kvaran notes that in more recent decades, DC and Marvel comics have made more attempts to address the LGBT (lesbian, gay, bisexual, and transgender) market. The gay superhero still remains within the gutters of the mainstream comic market, as lessons on morality and the national image of a traditional family unit permeate social and political discourse. Of course, a discussion on gay comic book heroes would not be complete without a look at masculinity and the family structure. Micah Rueber parallels Dr. Doom and the Fantastic Four against the 1955 novel *The Man in the Gray Flannel Suit* to provide another examination into perceptions of the male, his role within society and the home, and how he reflects social ambitions. In this chapter, Rueber pits Dr. Doom against the comics code, showing that while he did not violate it per se, he did lurk around its borders while the Fantastic Four worked as a group, thriving on its subversive nature but creating a cohesive element. This element parallels the subversive elements lingering in the pages of 1950s rhetoric on masculinity (even national honor). Christina Dokou completes this section by showing us that portraying the graphic novel or comic onscreen, as in Frank Miller's *Sin City*, alters the story, as the viewer no longer has to imagine the actions on the page. Yet, while a simplistic part is lost, a new layer is gained through the visual imagery moving and morphing on the screen. Hence, as much as the comic can reflect social politics and trends, placing it on the silver screen reshapes it to the era of the film.

Finally, the last two chapters show us the dark logic inside comics, the industry, and their reproduction. Faiz Sheikh uses, parallel to the real tales slightly fictionalized in comics, *The Walking Dead*'s stories of a zombie apocalypse to question the state of nature and the fears of a social/political revolution. Using Hobbes as his probe for this discussion, he shows that the world of hyperindividuality that is the cornerstone of Hobbes's state of nature permeates modern political and popular discourse. Last, Beatrice Skordili's theoretical study of *Logicomix* builds on the concept that comics must fit within a predefined category. Here, she focuses on the complexities of the storyline, that logic is a development of human nature, and that representation of a subject shapes its meaning, purpose, and memory. She also uses the widely popular *Persepolis* and *Palestine* to exemplify her discussion that comics merely act as another layer of documents to uncover the truths of the world around us and tell the figurative and literal stories of our lives.

## NOTES

1. Shelley Stamp, *Movie-Struck Girls: Women and the Motion Picture Culture after the Nickelodeon* (Princeton, NJ: Princeton University Press, 2000).

2. Douglas Wolk, *Reading Comics: How Graphic Novels Works and What They Mean* (New York: Da Capo Press, 2007), 4–11, 43–45.

3. Will Eisner, *Comics as Sequential Art* (Tamarac, FL: Poorhouse Press, 1985).

4. Max J. Skidmore and Joey Skidmore, "More Than Mere Fantasy: Political Themes in Contemporary Comic Books," *Journal of Popular Culture* 17, no. 1: 84–55.

5. Joseph Witek, *Comic Books as History: The Narrative Art of Jack Johnson, Art Spiegelman and Harvey Pekar* (Oxford: University of Mississippi Press, 1989), 3–4, 6–7, 13.

6. Bradford W. Wright, *Comic Book Nation: The Transformation of Youth Culture in America* (Baltimore: The Johns Hopkins University Press, 2001), xiv–xvii.

7. Amy Kiste Nyberg, *Seal of Approval: The History of the Comics Code* (Jackson: University of Mississippi Press, 1998), xiii, x, 2–4, 14.

8. Nyberg, *Seal of Approval*, 16, 19–21, 27.

9. Nyberg, *Seal of Approval*, 104–6.

10. Peter Coogan, *Superhero: The Secret Origin of a Genre* (Austin, TX: Monkey Brain Books, 2006), 14–15.

11. Coogan, *Superhero*, 33.

12. Scott McCloud, *Understanding Comics: The Invisible Art* (New York: Kitchen Sink Press, 1993), 47.

13. Anne Rubenstein, *Bad Language, Naked Ladies, and Other Threats to the Nation: A Political History of Comic Books in Mexico* (Durham, NC: Duke University Press, 1998), 41–44.

14. John A. Lent, ed., *Pulp Demons: International Dimensions of the Postwar Anti-comics Campaign* (Madison, WI: Fairleigh Dickinson University Press, 1999).

15. Wolk, *Reading Comics*, 14–16, 36. In reference to the definitions of art from the French, the first six are architecture, music, dance, sculpture, painting, and poetry. The seventh and eighth are film, photography, television, cuisine, or fireworks, depending on who you ask.

16. Joel Vessels, *Drawing France: French Comics and the Republic* (Jackson: University of Mississippi Press, 2010), 7–8, 12–14.

17. Sid Jacobson and Ernie Colón, *The 9/11 Report: A Graphic Adaptation* (New York: Hill & Wang, 2006), and Alan Moore, *The Watchmen* (New York: DC Comics, 1986–1987).

18. Marisa Acocella Marchetto, *Cancer Vixen* (New York: Knopf, 2006), and Marjane Satrapi, *The Complete Persepolis* (New York: Pantheon, 2003).

19. Since there is no standard manual for citing comic books, I have followed the "established" precedent set by other scholars. Also, since DC Comics has gone by different names, I simply refer to it as DC Comics, and I do not give page numbers for comic book entries, because not every issue had page numbers. Last, comic book makers generally postdate their material to extend shelf life; thus, the date of entry refers to that printed on the cover and not the date that the comic book entered the market. See Wright, *Comic Book Nation*, xviii–xix.

# ONE

## Antiquity and *Bandes Dessinées*

*Schizophrenic Nationalism between Atlanticism and Marxism*

### Henri-Simon Blanc-Hoàng, Defense Language Institute

Accounts of the foundational myth of the French nation-state usually begin with the Roman invasion of Gaul. The diversity of perspectives in the swords-and-sandals genre of comics reveals the country's struggle to identify legitimate ancestors and grapple with the issue of defining/redefining national identity. Three rival political movements — sovereignism, Atlanticism, and international communism — have influenced these comics' productions, thereby endeavors creating a sense of schizophrenia within post–World War II French nationalist discourse. This schizophrenic attitude is illuminated in three *bandes dessinées,* set during and after Julius Caesar's conquest of Gaul: René Goscinny's *Astérix le Gaulois,* Jacques Martin's *Alix,* and Victor Mora's *Taranis, fils de la Gaule.* Each series targets three areas of readership: the youth, a highly educated audience, and consumers of popular culture. Yet, the narratives each support a different contemporary ideology, creating a dynamic discourse within its pages. *Astérix* sides with the Gaullists/sovereignists; *Alix* embraces the Atlanticist/globalist camp; and *Taranis* favors international communism. In each work, the main character — when dealing with Roman/foreign presence on Gallic soil — chooses cultural assimilation or resistance. Their characters' decisions create entertaining and complex examinations reflecting the shifts in social and political milieus. This brief study argues that the comics' historical setting serves as a substitute for the latter twentieth century as the French struggled with concepts of U.S. cultural hegemony and lost days of imperial glory.

René Goscinny's *Astérix* takes place in 50 B.C. Astérix and his side-kick, Obélix, are two friends from the last village in occupied Gaul resisting Roman invasion. Its inhabitants have successfully thwarted Julius Caesar's best legions thanks to the superhuman strength that they receive from drinking their druid's mysterious beverage. This invigorating series debuted in the comic magazine *Pilote* in 1961 and became an instant best seller. Literary critic Lois Davis Vines attributes *Astérix*'s success to the Belgian model of distribution.[1] However, Goscinny's work owes its popularity more to its unique content than to a normative marketing strategy. For instance, Anthea Bell noted that readers of various ages interpreted *Astérix*'s narrative differently.[2] In addition to Bell, Hélène Cassou Yager suggested that its references to popular culture are responsible for its success.[3] In this way, Goscinny's work not only incorporates many characteristics of children's literature but encompasses popular and high culture. By appealing to a wide demographic of readership—from educated adults to young children—Goscinny produced an accessible text to disseminate a national identity and dispense ideas of cultural heritage.

To attract a wide audience, Goscinny utilized various narrative techniques directed toward specific groups of readers. For younger readers, *Astérix* presents as a folktale employing cartoon-style humor. Several critics and authors have examined the most successful techniques used within this comical storyline. Literary critic Matthew Screech, for example, scrutinized the comic's folktale structure, based on Vladimir Yakovlevich Propp's analytical study.[4] Frédéric Maguet, in contrast to Screech, analyzed Goscinny's use of myths, based on Claude Lévi-Strauss's theory.[5] In terms of the comic's visual style, there are two traditions in the Franco-Belgian school of comics: realism and caricature. André Uderzo, *Astérix*'s illustrator, is associated with the latter school.[6] Critics Bart Eerden and Charles Forceville suggested that Uderzo's caricaturist style has much in common with cartoon traditions and is apt for expressing humor.[7]

While children are easily amused by the stories and art of comics, *Astérix* contains many references to popular and elite culture. In some accounts, Goscinny plays with literary theory's attempt to explain the system of comics. In *Astérix et Cléopâtre* (1965), for instance, a strip shows a master engraver making a portrait of the queen. When Cleopatra asks for an engraving of her face instead of the usual profile, the artist replies, "You know how I feel about modern art."[8] Ironically, in this book, the only two-dimensional art form that characters can admire—and not drawn exclusively from their profiles—appears inside the occasional intradiegesis. Indeed, the comic strips in the daily *Pharaon-Soir* (read by one of the characters) appear to have a metatextual function.[9] By imagining that the rivalry between tradition and innovation already existed in

50 B.C., Uderzo suggests that comics—as a literary genre—suffer the same prejudices from reactionary critics as contemporary art.

For educated adults, the real humorous elements in this series come from the decontextualization of famous works of classical Latin and French literature, ancient and modern history, and art history. Throughout the series, several Roman characters quote classical authors, but these quotes are frequently and deliberately used out of context. The more literary-savvy readers would understand and enjoy this highbrow humor, but these clever references—targeted at the educated reader—invoke laughter. For instance, several strips involve scenes with Julius Caesar and his adopted son Brutus. In *Astérix Gladiateur* (1964), the crowd in the arena applauds Caesar before the games. As the dictator realizes that Brutus is the only one not clapping, he says to him directly in Latin, "Tu quoque filii!" (You too my son!). In the Francophone world, only those acquainted with Caesar's death at Brutus's hands would fully appreciate Goscinny's twisting Caesar's last words.[10] Indeed, the quote "Tu quoque filli" is actually an eighteenth-century translation from Ancient Greek (καί σύ τέκνον) to Latin by French Latinist Charles François Lhomond. In 1779, Lhomond published his *De Viris Illustribus Urbis Romae* (The Famous People of Rome), a textbook for first-year students of Latin that is still used today in French schools. This textbook was in fact a compilation of simplified Latin texts. One of Lhomond's sources for his chapter on the life of Caesar is Suetonius's original work, in which the dying dictator utters his famous last words in Ancient Greek.

> Atque ita tribus et uiginti plagis confossus est uno modo ad primum ictum gemitu sine uoce edito, etsi tradiderunt quidam Marco Bruto irruenti dixisse: καί σύ τέκνον.
> [And in this wise he was stabbed with three and twenty wounds, uttering not a word, but merely a groan at the first stroke, though some have written that when Marcus Brutus rushed at him, he said in Greek, "You too, my child?"][11]

Since Lhomond presumed that first-year Latin students would not know Greek, he not only simplified Suetonius's text but also translated the Roman author's Greek quote into Latin: "Quum Marcum Brutum, quem loco filii habebat, in se irruentem vidisset, dixit: 'Tu quoque fili mi!'" (When he saw Marcus Brutus, whom he had treated like a son, rush at him, he said: "You too, my son!"). Goscinny recycles this quote in the series every time that Caesar and Brutus are together. In the English-speaking world, Latinists are more familiar with Shakespeare's Latin translation of Suetonius's original Greek quote—"Et tu, Brute?"—from *Julius Caesar*. Thus, English translations of the graphic novel use the Shakespearian version. Nevertheless, the effects are the same in both languages. For the English translation, only educated readers (who have read Shakespeare) would get the joke. For the original French text, only readers who took Latin in secondary school and used Lhomond's text-book would laugh.

In another example of highbrow humor, in *Astérix chez les Belges* (1979), the inhabitants of Astérix's village take offense when they learn that Caesar considers "the Belgians the bravest people in Gaul."[12] To prove him wrong, Astérix and Obélix must travel to the province of Belgium. A well-versed reader of Latin literature would immediately connect Ceasar's phrase to the first page of the *Commentarii de Bello Gallico*:

> Gallia est omnis divisa in partes tres, quarum unam incolunt Belgae, aliam Aquitani, tertiam qui ipsorum lingua Celtae, nostra Galli appellantur. Hi omnes lingua, institutis, legibus inter se differunt. Gallos ab Aquitanis Garumna flumen, a Belgis Matrona et Sequana dividit. Horum omnium *fortissimi sunt Belgae*.
> [All Gaul is divided into three parts, one of which the Belgae inhabit, the Aquitani another, those who in their own language are called Celts, in our Gauls, the third. All these differ from each other in language, customs and laws. The river Garonne separates the Gauls from the Aquitani; the Marne and the Seine separate them from the Belgae. Of all these, *the Belgae are the bravest*.] (emphasis added)[13]

Of course, the joke derives from the decontextualization of this famous quote by Caesar. He intended this account for educated Latin speakers, which certainly did not include the recently conquered Gauls, who had not been Romanized. A final example of Goscinny playing with words is his use of Caesar's famous line "Vini, vidi, vici" (I came, I saw, I conquered). In *Astérix en Hispanie* (1969), the Roman dictator never finishes this sentence because the rebellious village does not lose. Goscinny also makes intertextual connections with famous works of French literature, including Molière, Jean-Jacques Rousseau, Victor Hugo, and Raymond Rostrand.[14]

*Astérix* also incorporates direct references to popular culture, such as politics, sports, radio, television, and cinema. Whereas Goscinny's amused educated readers with classical literature, artist Uderzo caricatured facets of popular culture through his art. Throughout his adventures, Astérix meets numerous characters, whose facial features caricature famous artists, singers, athletes, and politicians. In *Le tour de Gaule* (1965), for instance, Astérix and Obélix receive help from a group of Marseillais who organize a game of *pétanque* in an effort to prevent the Romans from pursuing the rebellious Gauls.[15] This strip evokes a scene from *César* (1936), a film by French director Marcel Pagnol, where the main character would rather disrupt a streetcar than disturb his game of *pétanque*.[16] In another episode—*Le domaine des Dieux* (1971)—Caesar orders the destruction of the forest surrounding Astérix's village. However, thanks to his mysterious powers, the village's druid manages to replant—in a single night—the trees destroyed by the Roman legionnaires. In retaliation, Caesar imports Numidian slaves (i.e., African slaves) to do the job of his legionnaires.[17] As Andrew Clark points out, the origin of these substitute workers is no coincidence, since "Numidia is the Roman name for the area roughly covering Algeria."[18] Accordingly, Caesar's actions could be interpreted as a comment on the treatment of Maghrebian immigrants in France. Indeed, in the early 1970s, the country's "new racial minorities" from the former colonial empire became more visible, heightening social and racial tensions.[19]

Despite the comic's critique of French attitudes toward their former colonies, this series provides an ambiguous depiction of African characters. *Astérix* denounces injustice against immigrants while perpetuating racist stereotypes, and Goscinny's work includes numerous attempts at humor at the expense of nonwhite people. During their various trips by sea, Astérix and Obélix always encounter a group of pirates with a black sailor sporting an African accent. For example in *Astérix aux jeux olympiques* (1968), the African pirate's speech is transcribed phonetically when he says, "Galè'e d'oit devant!"[20] (Galley right ahead!). A French-speaking audience would understand that the sailor really wants to pronounce "Galère droit devant!" In European French, /r/ is pronounced as an uvular fricative (commonly known as the guttural /r/). However, in parts of Francophone Africa and the Caribbean, this consonant is usually pronounced like a trilled /r/. In *Astérix*, every time that the African pirate speaks, his dialogue imitates the accent of nonwhite peoples in the former French colonies.[21] In some English versions of *Astérix*, when this character speaks, the balloons incorporate a Sambo-stereotyped spelling, but others do not.[22] Furthermore, in the same graphic novel, when the pirate crew is abandoned on a raft, the black sailor suggests cannibalistic tendencies when he proposes to "draw straws."[23] Ironically, Goscinny's most famous comic series provokes a public dialogue about racial discrimination while perpetuating stereotypes. However, this is not necessarily a contradiction. Christopher Pinet notes, "What we learn from *Astérix* . . . is that popular culture conserves traditional values and the status quo, though it may well begin . . . as a form which seems to question and challenge established values."[24] The same holds true for Jacques Martin's *Alix*. The series progressively addresses social ills but adheres to other traditional faults.

Along with Hergé (*Tintin*) and Edgar P. Jacobs (*Blake et Mortimer*), Jacques Martin initiated the realist tradition in the Franco-Belgian school of comics, especially his use of what critics later called the *ligne claire* style.[25] Like Goscinny's *Astérix*, Martin's comic series is named after his main character. Alix is a young Gaul who has grand adventures throughout the Mediterranean world around the year 50 B.C. More pointedly, Alix's earlier escapades occur during the Roman civil war between Caesar and Pompeus. In terms of the plot, however, this is where the similarities between *Astérix* and *Alix* end. Contrary to Goscinny's rebellious Gaul, this character does not resist the invaders. Rather, he embraces Roman culture.

*Le Journal de Tintin* published the initial serialized episode of Alix in 1948.[26] Subsequently, the complete stories were sold as hardcover books in newsstands and bookstores. As an adventure narrative, *Alix* was reminiscent of the *roman scout* (the French preadolescent literature of the 1930s), albeit transposed in 50 B.C.[27] Indeed, this series embraced moral values also promoted by the Boy Scout movement: rectitude, courage, fidelity to the nation, and sense of duty. Literature prompting these attributes was particularly embraced in post–World War II France, as the state struggled to regain its identity and sense of normalcy after the occupation. Martin's upholding patriotism as a core value allowed this *bande dessinée* to pass state and local censorship. This control meant that before the war, in comics such as *Tintin*, even the bad guys could not get killed. They could only be knocked out, sedated, and incarcerated. No blood could be drawn. Of course, any expression of sexuality, whether straight or gay, was out of the question. In the case of *Alix*, however, this kind of censorship produced an opposite effect.

Ironically, the figures of Alix and Enak (the hero's younger Egyptian companion) became icons of the French gay community in later years. Older generations of gay men in France remember becoming aware of their sexuality through reading *roman scout* titles such as Serge Dalens's *Le Prince Eric* and Jacques Martin's *Alix*.[28] French minister of culture Frédéric Mitterrand recalled a similar experience in *La mauvaise vie* (1995).[29] In fact, Martin has never given a "straight" answer when asked about his heroes' sexual orientation:

> [I] always wanted my readers to enjoy what they wanted to taste. Obviously, I am not going to discriminate between my heterosexual and homosexual readers, without wanting to shock one group or the other. Regarding this issue, I am very flexible.[30]

When asked by the same reporter why so many readers see Alix and Enak as a couple, the author simply said,

> [A] tandem like Alix and Enak was totally normal during Antiquity. In present day, they could be viewed as controversial. Nevertheless, I am not going to change Antiquity only to satisfy prudish people who have trouble identifying with the distinguishing characteristics of a distant time period.[31]

Even as the author embraces clichés about the Roman lifestyle, such as putting emphasis on the decadent habits of the patricians, he anchors his stories on literary sources. For instance, in *Le fils de Spartacus* (1976) a corrupt governor swims in the company of naked boys. This scene is a clear reference to Suetonius's *Life of Tiberius*. Emperor Tiberius had a similar habit.

> Maiore adhuc ac turpiore infamia flagravit, vix ut referri audirive, nedum credi fas sit, quasi pueros primae teneritudinis, quos pisciculos vocabat, institueret, ut natanti sibi inter femina versarentur ac luderent lingua morsuque sensim adpetentes.
>
> [He acquired a reputation for still grosser depravities that one can hardly bear to tell or be told, let alone believe. For example, he trained little boys, whom he termed tiddlers, to crawl between his thighs when he went swimming and tease him with their licks and nibbles.][32]

Martin is not the only one to have recycled Suetonius's text. In *Caligula* (1979), film director Tinto Brass also exploits this anecdote.

Additionally, some of the comic's anachronisms extrapolate hypothetical situations based on inventions and theories that first appeared in ancient Greece. Two clear examples are a rudimentary steam engine and the creation of faux gold. In *L'Île maudite* (1951), a group of surviving Carthaginians travel by steamship, which provides an allusion to Hero of Alexandria's rudimentary rotary steam engine (which was more like a spinning ball driven by steam jets).[33] In *L'enfant grec* (1979), Democritus's theory of the atom is put into practice to make artificial gold.[34] The uses show the seamless weaving of highbrow and lowbrow culture, creating a diverse literary space.

Before starting work on further adventures of Alix, Martin spent considerable time researching art and architectural history. Specifically, the author found new uses for artifacts familiar to art connoisseurs. At times, ancient relics become central elements of the plot, thus contributing to their historical fascination. In *Le tombeau étrusque* (1967), Martin depicts the famous sarcophagus of an Etruscan couple, now housed in the Louvre.[35] In this story, however, the sarcophagus cover hides a secret passage to an underground network. Another work of art appears in *Le dieu sauvage* (1969), where Martin includes the statue *Apollo of Piombino*, which here contains magical powers that eventually destroy a city.[36] Another example occurs in *Le Prince du Nil* (1973), where art historians can identify the wall painting of Nut, the Egyptian goddess of the sky. In his reproduction of the divinity, Martin carefully adds a few falling stars to the original work to signify an impending meteor shower; the prophecy promptly comes true. Because of its pictorial nature, it is no coincidence that Goscinny and Martin both exploit ancient Egyptian art to indirectly discuss comic theory.

As in *Astérix*, references to popular culture in *Alix* mirrored the historical context of the post–World War II period. Martin's work, in this respect, echoes contemporary French and American foreign policies. Moreover, while Goscinny relies mostly on icons of French popular culture, Martin finds his inspiration in Hollywood. Contrary to *Astérix*, whose storyline reflected a national popular culture, Martin's young hero experienced globalization *avant la lettre* as he meandered the Mediterranean world—fitting for Alix, whose nation constituted the superpower of the ancient world, or for a French reader experiencing global Americanization after 1945. In particular, Martin borrows the filmic plots of *Ben Hur* (1925) and *Spartacus* (1960) in his stories. Any reader who is familiar with the motion picture *Ben Hur* would recognize *Alix l'intrépide* (1948) as a remake of Fred Niblo's sword-and-sandals film. Claude Aziza notes that Martin's drawings "even imitate the director's shots."[37] Of course, the main character in this case is a young Gaul, not a Jew. Martin also transcribes scenes from *Ben Hur* in his tales, such as the episode involving the galley slaves. In the film, after being sentenced to the galley, Ben Hur must walk, in chains with other criminals, through the desert to reach the harbor. Jesus appears near a well, where the prisoners are allowed to rest and quench their thirst. Although Ben Hur is forbidden from drinking from the well, Jesus hypnotizes the lead Roman so that the poor lad can have some water. In contrast, in *Le tombeau étrusque* (1967), Alix transforms into a Christ-like figure—minus the beard—and also gives water to chain-gang prisoners, against the direct orders of their guard.[38]

Even the title *Le fils de Spartacus* (1974) sounds like a sequel to Stanley Kubrick's film. In the Hollywood classic, after the final battle between Spartacus's army and the Roman legions, the only survivors escaping reenslavement or crucifixion are the hero's wife and son. Martin's "sequel" begins when young Spartaculus, son of Spartacus, reaches puberty. The Roman Senate wants to kill this teenage boy. Indeed, because of the legacy of his father, Spartaculus could become the leader of a new revolt of slaves. Maia, Spartaculus's mother, begs Alix to take her son to a safe haven beyond the mountains of Helvetia, out of reach of Roman power. Alix accepts this mission because if Spartacus's son were to be captured, it is Pompeus, the enemy of Caesar, who would receive the credit. In the history of the Roman republic, the fictional account occurs when the rivalry between Pompeus and Caesar had created irreconcilable differences. Alix—one of Caesar's faithful friends—is willing to keep Pompeus from rising in popularity and possibly usurping the Senate.

Readers familiar with the plot of a tragedy will notice that Aristotle's ideas about this genre coincide with Martin's narration (and sequential art) for several of his graphic novels. Since the plot of a tragedy must involve an evil deed, the tragic hero must make this act easier to happen, do it unwillingly (like Oedipus), or perform it willingly (like Antigone). Consequently, Martin ends neither his sequel nor his remake with happy culminations. Whatever choice the tragic hero selects, he eventually loses. Our hero Alix fully embraces his Roman citizenship (contrary to Ben Hur) in *Alix l'intrépide*. Sadly, he betrays his people—the Gauls—with this decision. With another theme of betrayal, in *Le fils de Spartacus*, Spartaculus becomes the tragic hero after he chooses to take refuge beyond the mountains of Helvetia. Whereas he traveled beyond the reach of Roman power, his son would never be able to perpetuate the legacy of his father. There is no more hope for the oppressed slaves in the Roman Republic. Furthermore, if Spartaculus escaped death, he stood to certainly lose his mother. This element of the plot echoes the example that Aristole gives in his *Poetics*, when he quotes the Tydeus of Theodectes: "I came to find my son, and I lose my own life." [39]

According to Claude Aziza, "Alix lives in a world of balloons where contemporary politics hides behind Gallo-Roman fiction." [40] These stories mimicked the political events of the day, albeit masking international unrest through the guise of accessible entertainment. An interesting case is the plot of *La tiare d'Oribal* (1955) and *La tour de Babel* (1981). In these two adventures, Alix goes on a special mission to the imaginary Middle Eastern kingdom of Zur-Bakal. If we take into account what happened in Iran in the mid-1950s and the late 1970s, it is not a coincidence that twenty-six years separate the two volumes. In *La tiare d'Oribal* (1955), Alix helps the legitimate young monarch of Zur-Bakal regain his throne. [41] Not surprising, this story first appeared two years after the 1953 U.S.-backed coup in Iran, where the CIA played a significant role at helping the shah impose an authoritarian rule to Westernize his country by encouraging a secular lifestyle and promoting industry. However, the Islamic Revolution in 1979 put an end to his project. Alix's sixteenth adventure, *La tour de Babel* (1981), was published two years after this event. Here, Alix must return to Zur-Bakal. The young Gaul learns that the promising young king (and his friend) tragically failed to convince his people to accept the Greek and Roman cultural models. [42] Alix learned, from a secondhand source, that his friend lost his throne because he acted like a tyrant. The similarities with the shah of Iran are abundantly evident.

A contemporary reading of *La tiare d'Oribal* (1955) and *La tour de Babel* (1981) provides a commentary on Iran and the West's involvement in the internal politics of this country, from the ascension of the shah in the 1950s to his political exile in 1979. Martin had to create the kingdom of Zur-Bakal for these two adventures of Alix because he could not use the Parthian empire as a background for this story. During the actual civil war between Caesar and Pompeus, the region of modern-day Iran was not considered an ally of Rome, unlike the imaginary kingdom of Zur-Bakal in the storyline. However, in this case, the art drawn by Martin is more explicit in associating Zur-Bakal with Iran. In the two graphic novels, art historians would recognize the fresco representing Cyrus the Great's ten thousand immortals decorating the walls in the palace of the young king. [43]

Out of Alix's thirty adventures, four occur in the Middle East, and five involve Carthaginian insurgents (geographical ancestors of North African Arabs and Berbers). Since Alix had never raised censorship flags, as it upheld moral values, the temporary ban of its sixth book is ironic.

Initially, reviewers found it to be too far on the right. When *La griffe noire* (1959) was published during the Algerian war of independence, French authorities judged the Ku Klux Klan–look-alike hooded men as too much like the active members of OAS (Organization de l'Armée Secrète), a pro-French Algeria terrorist organization. The legal terminology used for censoring this publication was "violence and incitation to hate." Goscinny (Martin's friend) had to use his connections with the French Ministry of the Interior to lift the ban.[44] As for Martin's depiction of nonwhite people, his sensitivity evolved over time. Despite an anticolonialist stance in *La griffe noire* (1959), his depictions of the peoples in the sub-Saharan region appeared as superstitious and untrustworthy.[45] Ten years later, showing a growth and evolution in thought and scholarship, Martin made a conscious effort to not perpetuate racial stereotypes. In *Le dieu sauvage* (1969), the Cyrenians defy Roman power. Hardly the superstitious lot shown in his previous work, Martin portrays the Cyrenians as a proud and courageous people, who even welcome the remnants of the Greek resistance into their secret city.[46]

According to Aziza, "with the exception of Alix . . . there was only another Gaul who managed to really rival Astérix for a few years: Taranis."[47] In 1976, the editorial board of *Pif Gadget* magazine contracted writer Victor Mora and illustrator Raffaele Marcello to create this Gallic champion who resisted against Caesar. For *Taranis*, World War II France has been transposed to Roman Gaul, and the series became an allegory for the reformation of French identity, with a communist twist. The plot begins during the siege of Alesia in 52 B.C. Just before the Gauls surrender to Caesar, Taranis, a young farmer, sees his family massacred by the enemy, and he inherits the belt of their fallen leader Vercingétorix. This artifact gives the young man the legitimacy that he needs to organize the insurgency against the invaders.[48] Mora and Marcello traced *Taranis's* origins to the underground literature, which built on the mythic importance of the French Résistance against the Nazi occupation.[49] The series ran in *Pif Gadget*, a publication originally aimed at the children and younger siblings of *L'Humanité's* readers, the official daily newspaper of the French Communist Party.

In addition to its adventure stories and humorous strips, two essential features made *Pif Gadget* appealing to a young readership: its "gadget" and its format. Every week, the magazine came wrapped in transparent film to protect a small toy (*le gadget*). The nature of this free trinket varied depending on the theme of the week. A second feature contributing to the success of this comic magazine among young readers was its official policy of publishing only complete stories in each issue. Unlike competing publishers, such as *Le journal de Tintin*, which relied on cliff-hangers, *Pif Gadget* did not make its readers wait for the next issue to find out what happened to their favorite characters. The reason behind this editorial choice was that readers—especially young ones—would grow tired of waiting for each installment and eventually lose interest. *Pif Gadget's* policy lessened this risk for lost readership. Moreover, since each issue contained only complete stories, reprinting a collection of the series as a hardcover book was redundant.[50] While the no-cliffhanger requirement did not pose a problem for authors of short humorous strips, Victor Mora had to write concisely for each *Taranis* episode.

Offering its audience a new gadget every week, along with only complete stories, was more a marketing strategy to gain the loyalty of young readers. Ideologically, it was also important to shape the minds of future adults along a Marxist–Leninist line. Mora and Marcello depicted Taranis's armed insurrection against foreign occupiers, not as a clash between civilizations, but rather as a class struggle. As the Roman presence on Gallic soil becomes permanent, some natives realize that their new masters bring economic advantages, such as a greater market for the sale of goods or opportunities to move up in the newly founded Gallo-Roman administration. Consequently, a class of Gallic collaborators aligns with the emerging Roman power. This new caste of profiteers takes advantage of their privileged position, exploiting their own countrymen. At the same time, Taranis welcomes defectors from Caesar's legions to join his troops. These defectors are seduced by the collectivist lifestyle that the Gallic Résistance defends.[51] In fact, Taranis's freedom fighters include Africans, members of some Germanic tribes, Picts, and Scotts. The war dissolves into a Marxist–Leninist struggle. According to the comic, greed is the cause of fighting. If the workers of the world united, wars between nations would cease because those who own the means of production would become powerless to oppress the masses.

Aside from its economic characteristics, Taranis promotes the Marxist–Leninist idealization of a proatheist stance. In various episodes, the real oppressors are neither the foreign invaders nor their collaborators. Instead, the religious caste becomes the main arena of contention. The comic advances the notion that Gallic druids thrived on superstition and ignorance. Furthermore, these priests enslave the people by taking advantage of their naïveté. Mora justifies his Marxist–Leninist position through selected passages from historical sources. In his *Commentarii de Bello Gallico*, Caesar mentions the human sacrifices practiced by the Gauls' pre-Roman conquest:

> The nation of all the Gauls is extremely devoted to superstitious rites; and on that account they who are troubled with unusually severe diseases and they who are engaged in battles and dangers, either sacrifice men as victims, or vow that they will sacrifice them, and employ the Druids as the performers of those sacrifices; because they think that unless the life of a man be offered for the life of a man, the mind of the immortal gods cannot be rendered propitious, and they have sacrifices of that kind ordained for national purposes.[52]

Here, however, Mora plays fast and loose with historical facts. When the author uses this detail to vilify the religious establishment, he fails to mention that the Romans put an end to this barbaric practice. Instead, "Le poignard des sacrifices" (*Pif Gadget* 536) asserts that the druids who are in favor of human sacrifices are in fact Roman agents, thus removing the religious black mark from the Gallic peoples.[53] Moreover, the druid priest who remains with Taranis's army must work like everybody else, rather than practice his religious ceremonies. However, the druid's old age spares him from physical hard labor, and he serves as a teacher. Of course, Taranis's comrades joke about his teacher's superstitious beliefs, reminding the hero that the gods will not protect him against the Romans.[54] Like Goscinny in *Astérix*, Mora and Marcello advance their political leanings but still maintain vestiges of traditional culture.

*Astérix* presented French national culture as humorous caricature. *Alix* adapted Hollywood epics to create an intersection between American and French popular culture. In *Taranis*, however, popular culture served a well-defined purpose. Since the Gallo-Roman period was part of traditional French history taught in public schools, *Pif Gadget*'s editorial board thought it useful to supplement the readers' education by including didactic articles about pre-Roman Gaul. Moreover, the political orientation of the French Communist Party proved both antinationalistic and anti-Atlanticist. Hence, *Pif Gadget* faced the additional duties of promoting internationalism, antiracism, and environmentalism alongside its Marxist agenda. As a result of these concerted efforts, elements of popular culture in Mora's work are based on the French national heritage and a utopian, international "brotherhood of mankind."

Thus, a reader who picked up a copy of *Pif Gadget* was not solely exposed to the communist propaganda that appeared in the plot of the comics. The form of comics (only complete stories) and the gadget were features well adapted to the short attention span of young readers. Educational articles relating to comics reconciled the French Communist Party's agenda with French national popular culture. For instance, in 1981, the 648th issue of *Pif Gadget* included a Taranis comic, a gadget (*le bracelet de Taranis*) related to the story, and a didactic article about pre-Roman Gaul to historicize Taranis's adventure in that issue. Similarly, an educational article about protecting wildlife in swamps was included in *Pif Gadget* 643, which accompanied a Taranis episode taking place in a French marshland region.

To influence young minds, *Pif Gadget* did not ignore other old-stock French heroes in its adventure/realistic comics to appeal to the readers' patriotism. One of *Pif Gadget*'s early protagonists was Le Grêlé, a member of the French communist resistance fighting the Nazis with the assistance of the Red Army. Later came Fanfan La Tulipe, an eighteenth-century-style French Robin Hood, who protected proletarians against abuses of the nobles. Initially, this procommunist orientation was expressed through plotlines that remained within the limit of the national territory. However, this kind of "in your face" political activism gradually switched to some adventure stories with more of an internationalist twist. Values of the French Communist Party were passed on "not through explicit political references anymore but through the codes of mass culture."[55] These newer international heroes could be Native Americans (Loup Noir, Capitaine Apache), stateless (Rahan, a hero who lived during the Stone Age, before the emergence of nation states), or Arab (Nasdine Hodja). In this new world, even French heroes had to bring an international appeal. Taranis fit this pattern, although his adventures were mostly circumscribed to Gaul. The ethnic diversity of his army gave an internationalist perspective to the story.

To be consistent with the French Communist Party's official internationalist orientation, *Pif Gadget* was also one of the first youth publications to consistently condemn domestic racism. By the 1970s, "guest workers" from the former French colonies were becoming part of the national landscape, and violence against these new "visible" minorities—especially their children—was on the rise. *Pif Gadget* first directed its readers to explicitly take a proactive stance against racial prejudices.[56] Second, the series tried to avoid perpetuating racial clichés, not only in the adventures of its fellow "realistic" (i.e., human) heroes, such as Doctor Justice and Rahan, but also in its portrayals of humoristic anthropomorphized animal characters. In the humoristic "Pif et Hercule" series, after which the magazine took its name, Pif (the dog) and Hercule (the cat) required the help of Professor Belpomme, an African scientist.[57] Therefore, instead of including an African athlete or an Asian scientist among its characters, even humoristic series tried to correct common racial stereotypes.

Realistic heroes (e.g., Nasdine Hodja, Rahan, Dr. Justice) and anthropomorphized animal characters (e.g., Pif and Hercule) both promoted racial tolerance, and almost all the contributors to *Pif Gadget* devised a means of condemning racial stereotypes, including Victor Mora. Mora created Yambo the African, a sidekick to Taranis, after a few episodes. Contrary to Enak (Alix's Egyptian companion), Yambo requires neither guidance nor advice from Taranis. As a matter of fact, the roles reversed. Taranis's immaturity and inexperience led him into trouble, and Yambo usually had to save the day. The series also asserted that racial stereotypes were based on cultural constructions. In one of their earlier adventures, the two heroes help a group of Scots and Picts resist Caesar. Although these new allies paint themselves blue to scare their enemies on the battlefield, their leader is at first prejudiced against the darker-skinned Yambo. By the end of the episode, however, the "Black man" and the "Blue man" become friends. Yambo and Taranis must fight their prejudices and, upon doing so, learn that underneath their war paint, the

Scots are human beings.[58] All parties realize that judging another based on skin color—whether biological or artificial—is irrational.

When considering its relationship to the Roman Empire's legacy, France as a nation-state displays a schizophrenic nationalism. On one hand, the French have twice proclaimed themselves the heirs of Rome by mimicking the early history of the Eternal City. In 1804 and 1852, the "French Empire" replaced the "French Republic." On the other hand, since the nineteenth century, primary school teachers in France have taught students that the Gauls were their ancestors. Thus, while the French celebrate their (Gallo-)Roman heritage, they simultaneously glorify the (failed) Résistance against the Roman invaders.

This tendency to alternately embrace the winning and losing sides of the *Bellum Gallicum* is one that constantly resurfaces in French history when the country faces a foreign invasion (military or cultural), be it the Nazis, international communism, or American cultural imperialism. As a genre, comics of the peplum type ("swords and sandals") become an ideal medium to express this fractured historical identity because of the comics' appeal to a diverse age and educational range of readers. *Astérix* corresponds to a change in the national narrative: from the imperial/colonialist civilizing myth to the resistance myth against U.S. cultural hegemony. *Alix* longs for a lost imperial glory or, barring that, a glory by proxy (i.e., projecting France's imperialism through American expansionism within the Atlanticist alliance). *Taranis* provides a Marxist alternative to the two previous models. It is no coincidence that this last series disappeared at the end of the Cold War; *Pif Gadget* folded in 1993.

The continuing success of *Alix* and *Astérix* suggests that the French still oscillate between the nostalgia of their former status as a world power and a desire to champion the underdogs by leading a new resistance against American cultural imperialism. This internal conflict also reflects postmodern France's mixed treatment of its racial and sexual minorities. While all three series promote a progressive dialogue in some respects, there is clearly plenty of room for present and future comic heroes to challenge the age-old stereotypes still lingering within their pages. The national quest for the ever-elusive utopian goal of absolute equality is an "adventure" with no end in sight.

## NOTES

1. Lois Davis Vines, "Teaching Belgian Cultural Connections with Astérix," *French Review: Journal of the American Association of Teachers of French* 81, no. 6 (2008): 1226. "Cartoons first appeared serialized in magazines, then were sold again as complete episodes in hardcover books with a distribution network that went far beyond the magazine circulation."
2. Anthea Bell, "Translator's Notebook," in *The Signal Approach to Children's Books*, ed. Nancy Chambers (Metuchen, NJ: Scarecrow, 1981), 132.

3. Hélène Cassou-Yager, "Astérix: A Bouillon Cube of French History, Gaullist Politics, and French Attitudes and Prejudices towards Other Countries," in *Selected Proceedings: 32nd Mountain Interstate Foreign Language Conference,* ed. Gregorio Martín and Javier Herrero (Winston-Salem, NC: Wake Forest University, 1984), 85.

4. Matthew Screech, *Masters of the Ninth Art: Bandes Dessinées and Franco-Belgian Identity* (Liverpool, England: Liverpool University Press, 2005), 76. "Following the example set by *Les Aventures de Tintin, Spirou et Fantasio* and Disney, *Astérix* combined humour with Propp's traditional, folk tale structure."

5. Frédéric Maguet, "Astérix, un mythe? Mythogénèse et amplification d'un stéréotype culturel," *Ethnologie Française: Revue Trimestrielle de la Société d'Ethnologie Française* 28, no. 3 (1998): 320. "We are attempting to adapt the Astérix model to the terminology proposed by Cl. Lévi-Strauss for his structural analysis of myths" (translated from the French).

6. Screech, *Masters of the Ninth Art,* 76. "Uderzo's caricatural graphic style recalled Disney and Franquin rather than Hergé: everything was rounded, elastic looking lines and bright, cheerful colours; Astérix, Obélix and the others had bulbous noses and exaggeratedly large feet."

7. According to Charles Forceville, in his analysis of the expression of anger in the *Astérix* series, there are twelve "angry" signs in Goscinny's comic that one would not encounter in the school of realism. These signs are divided into two categories: pictorial runes (i.e., abstract signs) and indexical signs (i.e., concrete signs). The telling signs include bulging eyes, tightly closed eyes, wide mouth, tightly closed mouth, red face, arm/hand position, and shaking. The pictorial runes includes x-mouths, spirals around the head, smoke above the head, bold face, and jagged text-balloon lines. Forceville, "Visual Representations of the Idealized Cognitive Model of Anger in the Asterix Album *La Zizanie,*" *Journal of Pragmatics: An Interdisciplinary Journal of Language Studies* 37, no. 1 (2005): 75–77. Bart Eerden adds two new pictorial runes to Froceville's list: the flying helmet and the smoke just before the explosion of anger. Forceville's indexical sign called the arm/hand position is itself subdivided into three subcategories, to which Eerden adds two additional elements. Furthermore, nobody dies in the caricaturist school: people are only momentarily knocked out. Eerden, "Anger in *Asterix*: The Metaphorical Representation of Anger in Comics and Animated Films," in *Multimodal Metaphor,* ed. Charles J. Forceville and Eduardo Urios-Aparisi (Berlin: Mouton de Gruyter, 2009), 247.

8. René Goscinny and Albert Uderzo, *Astérix et Cléopâtre* (Paris: Editions Dargaud, 1965), 30.

9. Goscinny and Uderzo, *Astérix et Cléopâtre,* 33.

10. In *Astérix gladiateur* (1967), Goscinny suggests looking up quotes in the pink pages of the Larousse dictionary for explanations. However, the author abandoned this practice later in the series. Eerden, "Anger in Asterix ," 247.

11. J. C. Rolfe, trans., *Suetonius: The Lives of the Twelve Caesars* (Loeb Classical Library Edition, 1913–1914), http://penelope.uchicago.edu/Thayer/E/Roman/Texts/Suetonius/12Caesars/Julius*.html.

12. René Goscinny and Albert Uderzo, *Astérix chez les Belges* (Paris: Editions Dargaud, 1979), 10.

13. W. A. McDevitte and W. S. Bohn, trans., *The Gallic Wars: Julius Caesar's Account of the Roman Conquest of the Gauls* (CreateSpace, 2012), 1.

14. In *Astérix chez les Helvètes* (1970), the references to the Roman medical pseudoscience used to diagnose patients are reminiscent of the scam-artist doctors found in Molière's *Le malade imaginaire* (1673). René Goscinny and Albert Uderzo, *Astérix chez les Helvètes* (Paris: Editions Dargaud, 1970), 9. Andreas Stolls has already noted that *Le Devin* (1972) rings a bell with Jean-Jacques Rousseau's play *Le Devin du village* (1752), where an itinerant fortune-teller/scam artist takes advantage of gullible villagers. Andreas Stoll, *Astérix ou l'épopée burlesque de la France* (Paris: Presses Universitaires de France, 1978), 147. In *Astérix chez les Belges* (1979), "Goscinny changed lines from Hugo's poem to fit the battle between the Gauls, Belgians and Romans. The opening

line directs the reader to Hugo's poem [Waterloo]." Vines, "Teaching Belgian," 1229.
"In *Le Cadeau de César* (1974) . . . Astérix takes on a belligerent Roman soldier in the village pub, and as he launches into a swordfight he simultaneously assumes the mantle of Rostand's *Cyrano de Bergerac*, composing a ballade as he fights." Bell, "Translator's Notebook," 138.

15. René Goscinny and Albert Uderzo, *Le tour de Gaule d'Astérix* (Paris: Editions Dargaud, 1965), 32.

16. Screech, *Masters of the Ninth Art*, 81. "When he heard about the scene, Pagnol quipped, 'Maintenant, je sais que mon oeuvre est éternelle.'"

17. If we rely on Rouvière's psychoanalysis of this album, the enslaved pirates, along with other *uprooted* slaves, must *uproot* the trees of the forest that surrounds Astérix's village. Therefore, "Caesar's goal is to cause the community to lose its roots" (translated from the French). Nicolas Rouvière, "Astérix et les Pirates ou l'Obsession Que le Pire Rate: la Conjuration d'un Naufrage de l'Histoire," in *Témoignages de l'Après-Auschwitz dans la Littérature Juive-Française d'Aujourd'hui: Enfants de Survivants et Survivants-Enfants*, ed. Annelise Schulte (Paris : Presses Universitaires de France, 2006), 152.

18. Andrew Clark, "Imperialism in Asterix," *Belphégor: Littérature Populaire et Culture Médiatique* 4, no. 1 (2004): 10.

19. Clark, "Imperialism in Asterix," 11. "It is possible that this is a reflection of the treatment of migrant workers in France—many come from former colonies in countries such as Algeria and can be subjected to ill-treatment, especially by those who claim that they are taking jobs and money away from the indigenous population."

20. René Goscinny and Albert Uderzo, *Astérix aux jeux olympiques* (Paris: Editions Dargaud, 1968), 20.

21. Catherine Delesse and Bertrand Richet, *Le Coq Gaulois à l ' Heure Anglaise: Analyse de la Traduction d'Astérix* (Arras, France: Artois Presses Universitaires, 2009), 303. According to Delesse, the "phonetic" transcription of the trilled /r/ is the "only distinctive sign of this character. Indeed, there is no added mark of lexical or grammatical deficiency. In other words, he does not speak *petit nègre*" (translated from the French).

22. Bell, "Translator's Notebook," 136. "The black pirate employs the accent of the people of the former French colonies, omitting the letter 'r.' This is acceptable and funny in France, but years ago we decided that it was not acceptable to make a comic feature of a similar mode of speech in English, and ever since we have been substituting other jokes for that lost 'r'."

23. Nicolas Rouvière, "Astérix et les Pirates," 156.

24. Christopher Pinet, "Astérix, Brassens, and Cabu: The ABC's of Popular Culture," in *Popular Traditions and Learned Culture in France: From the Sixteenth to the Twentieth Century*, ed. Marc Bertrand (Saratoga, CA: Anma Libri, 1985): 286.

25. Dandridge, "Producing Popularity: The Success in France of the Comics Series "Astérix le Gaulois" (master's thesis, Virginia Polytechnic Institute and State University, 2008), 21. "The 'école belge,' led by Hergé, revolutionized the style of French comics. Hergé's clean lines, deliberate strokes, clear color, and use of few shadows, all typified the adventure series 'Tintin,' greatly influenced the next generation of Francophone BD artists."

26. Eliza Bourque Dandridge, "Producing Popularity," 22. According to Bourque Dandridge, "as one of the only strips published in high-quality album format during the immediate post-war years, 'Tintin' was able to maintain its strong presence on the market, as was the journal by the same name."

27. Martin later wrote and drew *Lefranc*, a new series of adventures that takes place in contemporary times. Not only does *Lefranc* take on all the characteristics of the *roman scout* genre but includes a boy scout as the main character's sidekick.

28. Martin's work (along with Serge Dalens's illustrated *roman scout*) was the only media where a very "close" suggested relationship between two male characters was seen as normal, at a time (the late 1940s and the 1950s) when any expression of sexuality (gay or straight) was highly repressed in "children" literature.

29. Frédéric Mitterrand, *La Mauvaise Vie* (Paris: Editions Robert Laffont), 36, 42. Mitterrand remembers the first boys with whom he fell in love as a preteen and how some of them reminded him of Alix: "Raoul, the lonely blond boy who has just arrived from New Caledonia and whose dry and muscular body looks like Alix's; I saw him a few years later, in the company of an older man who was certainly not his godfather." He even confesses to fantasizing with some of his friends about Prince Eric: "We also loved book covers. Bob Morane was very beautiful. He looked like Prince Eric, in a more modern version" (translated from French).

30. "Le Tandem Alix/Enak et la Rumeur de l'Homosexualité: un Duo Libre, Fier et Esthétiquement Réussi," http://www.tcomt.fr/Sitealix/Dossiers/07Interview/interview04.html.

31. "Le Tandem Alix/Enak."

32. Rolfe, *Suetonius*.

33. Jacques Martin, *L'Ile Maudite* (Paris: Editions Le Lombard, 1957), 39.

34. Jacques Martin, *L'Enfant Grec* (Paris: Editions Casterman, 1979), 23–24.

35. Jacques Martin, *Le Tombeau Étrusque* (Paris: Editions Casterman, 1967), cover page.

36. Jacques Martin, *Le Dieu Sauvage* (Paris: Editions Casterman, 1969), cover page.

37. Claude Aziza, *Guide de l'Antiquité Imaginaire* (Paris : Editions Belles Lettres, 2008), 129.

38. Martin, *Le Tombeau É trusque*, 13–14.

39. S. H. Butcher, trans., *Poetics*, by Aristotle, http://classics.mit.edu/Aristotle/poetics.mb.txt

40. For Aziza, other books echo France's collaboration with the Nazi régime: "An old leader pitifully justifies his surrender of the hostages to the invaders, under the pretense of choosing a lesser evil. Doesn't he recall the cowardly allegations of Pétain's collaboration?" (quote translated from French). Aziza, *Guide de l'Antiquité Imaginaire*, 131.

41. Jacques Martin, *La tiare d'Oribal* (Paris: Editions Le Lombard, 1958), 64.

42. Jacques Martin, *La Tour de Babel* (Paris: Editions Casterman, 1981), 23–24.

43. Jacques Martin, *La tiare d'Oribal* (Paris: Editions Le Lombard, 1958), 1.

44. "Rencontre avec un grand de la bande dessinée," http://perso.wanadoo.fr/erato.pagesperso-orange.fr/horspress/martin.htm.

45. Jacques Martin, *La griffe noire* (Paris: Editions Le Lombard, 1959), 50.

46. Martin, *Le Dieu Sauvage*, 40.

47. Aziza, *Guide de l'Antiquité Imaginaire*, 135.

48. Victor Mora and Raffaele Marcelo, "Taranis, Fils de la Gaule: Complot Contre César," *Pif Gadget* 510 (January 1979): 19.

49. "Its aim was to tell the story of 'la Résistance' and to give young readers a content that was less violent, more humanistic than the other illustrated magazines." Aziza, *Guide de l'Antiquité Imaginaire*, 135.

50. Some selected episodes of *Taranis*, however, were later compiled in a two-volume omnibus.

51. Victor Mora and Raffaele Marcelo, "Taranis, Fils de la Gaule: Le Poignard des Sacrifices," *Pif Gadget* 536 (July 1979): 39–40.

52. Edward Brooks Jr., trans., *Caesar's Commentaries on the Gallic War* (Chicago: Farquhar and Albrecht, 1896), 202–3.

53. Brooks, *Caesar's Commentaries*, 46.

54. Mora and Marcelo, "Taranis, Fils de la Gaule," 20–21.

55. Pierre Bruno, "Chronique culture jeune. Pif Gadget: qu'est-ce qu'un périodique progressiste pour la jeunesse?" *Le français aujourd'hui* 161, no. 2 (2008): 127–32.

56. *Pif Gadget* 526 (April 1979): 31–33. This issue included a three-page article explaining racism to children.

57. Even when Professor Belpomme did not appear in an episode, he was still drawn on the cover of the magazine. In *Pif* 536, for example, the African scientist was shown giving to Pif and Hercule a tour of the Kourou Space Center in French Guyana.

58. Victor Mora and Raffaele Marcelo, "Taranis, fils de la Gaule: Les hommes bleus," *Pif Gadget* 526 (April 1979): 40.

# TWO

## Did You Learn Your Strip?

### *The History of France as Comic Fad in the 1970s*

Guillaume de Syon,
Albright College

In 1976, French state television channel FR3 partnered with the publisher
Larousse to produce a twenty-four-volume comic-strip history of France,
sold in news outlets and bookstores, titled *Histoire de France en Bandes
Dessinées* (*HFBD*; History of France in Comic Strips). Though not intended as a replacement for textbooks, the series encountered a stunning
success that prompted two subsequent series from the same publisher on
historical topics, and a slightly revised edition of the original, thirty years
later, sold as a supplement to *Le Monde's* weekend edition.[1] The purpose
of this chapter is to understand why the strip encountered such success
and became a "classic" of the genre, generating numerous emulations,
from the coverage of regional histories to great battles rendered in graphic formats. Though acknowledged as an outgrowth of the comic medium,
the series' significance has not been analyzed, leaving observers of the
field to bemoan the lack of critical understanding surrounding its existence.[2] It also seeks to address the dichotomy that existed at the time,
whereby comic strips were maturing into the "ninth art" in the Francophone world but were still viewed with suspicion by the elite. In so
doing, it suggests that the timing and success of the series' publication
matches a delayed response to the 1968 student rebellion at the official
and mass levels. Indeed, while the series did not innovate by recounting
historical facts, its approach in the form of a grand narrative that was
limited to historical facts reflected an attempt to deal with a conundrum.

The series limited the iconic power of visual images by restricting artists to known events. The series thus raises ideological issues pertaining to national history, especially in the context of pedagogical use of the medium. As such, however, it falls in line with a long tradition of visual culture that accompanied modern history telling.

## EARLY VISUAL CULTURE

The use of imagery to reflect national historical events had antecedents in the nineteenth and early twentieth centuries across Europe. In France notably, the tradition of "Epinal images" had become so widespread as gifts for children and adults that it had passed into common parlance. Printed by the Pellerin family, these small lithographic drawings first represented religious events and scenes of everyday life. However, several hundreds of these images also showed historical events. Uncritical though highly evocative, such pictures spawned a whole tradition of popular illustrations, some of which evolved into postcards and early comic-strip accounts of contemporary events and continued the tradition through to World War I.[3]

Between 1890 and World War I, the collecting of cards from cigarette packs, boxes of cookies, or those purchased at paper stores became both a child's hobby and a popular adult craze.[4] By 1914, deltiology had gained a substantial following and had become one of the most effective means of communicating images in the early-twentieth-century Western world. Such images included historical events, too, and ranged from famous maxims to particular battles, with some illustrations inspired from officially sanctioned art.

In parallel, the use of art reproductions to illustrate history textbooks gained limited acceptance in the interwar years; the practice gained momentum after World War II and matched the rebirth of comic strips in Europe. Of course, it witnessed a struggle between nascent European series and seasoned American comics readily available to publishers buying and translating them. These attractive pieces from overseas occasionally included historically themed stories, such as *Prince Valliant*. Yet, attempts to create strips with historical themes slowly began to take shape, although it would be several years before some met with success.[5]

## COMICS AND CONFLICTS

In that optic, one should mention the peculiar intersection of historical themes and ideology as reflected in some of the works published by the Catholic group Bayard and the communist-controlled Vaillant (no relationship to the American series). Both show clearly that far from being irrelevant, the use of historical themes was considered central as a dual education and entertainment tool.[6] The ideological tension provoked as a result found its way into law.

In the unstable context of France's Fourth Republic (1944–1958), a general malaise consisting of a mix of antiforeign sentiment (primarily against the United States) and wounded national pride (from World War II and the crumbling colonial empire) led to peculiar alliances among political factions. In the realm of youth publications, strange bedfellows came to include French communists, who opposed the Americanization of French culture, and Catholics, who feared the presence of "adult" material in the comics. With the French government and concerned over protectionist issues, they helped put forward the law of July 16, 1949, to further their goals. The law provided for the creation of a surveillance commission that would vet all youth publications, including comic strips.[7] The result had a chilling effect on the development of comics and youth publications in France.[8] While the comic genre slowly built its way to respectability over a four-decade period, it suffered from the need to present noncontroversial topics, lest the commission demand the removal or redrawing of materials before publication.[9] This also affected the presentation of historical topics.

Narrating historical events in comic strips stemmed from earlier image trends described so far, as well as from tradition of using such events to spin off romanticized accounts. These in turn perpetuated myth and created new ones, especially when related to the antiquity.[10] Single volumes also appeared around biographical themes, partly because these were topics deemed "safe" for public consumption.[11] Shorter series that sought to trace an acceptable historical narrative were also tapped as valuable filler for weekly comic magazines. The latter often needed to balance their content between serialized works appearing over many months and complete stories that would suit younger audiences. In that vein, the series "Les Histoires de l'Oncle Paul" (Histories from Uncle Paul) represents a true predecessor of *HFBD*. Appearing as a complete account in the weekly comic magazine *Spirou*, it became an accepted cultural norm. Parents concerned with the quality of what their children read for entertainment could assume that at least some of the "p'tit mikés" (little Mickey Mouses; a moniker deriding comic strips) offered cultural content. Over one thousand such accounts appeared between 1951 and 1982, and some were reprinted in 1970 under the heading "L'histoire en bande dessinée" (History in comics).[12] Not only did the historical episodes appear as factually correct, but their summary and presentation always contained a moral dimension designed to fit a traditional Christian outlook that permeated postwar Francophone comic strips. As such, it also ensured that the all-powerful French surveillance commission, in charge of enforcing the 1949 law designed to protect youth from publications deemed pernicious, would not censor the content. When analyzed, "Les Histoires de l'Oncle Paul" tended to display a "militant Catholicism," especially in covering the late antiquity and the Middle Ages. By the same token, it overlooked some more troublesome aspects of Christianity's history: whereas Father Ferdinand Verhiest or Jean Chappe d'Auterodre, both early modern astronomers, each rated a full episode, Kepler or Galileo, both banned by the Vatican in the sixteenth century, were never even mentioned. By 1968, however, the stories shifted to emphasize episodes from modern European history. Although the nature of all episodes still reflected a peculiar blend of anecdotal and mythical accounts, the series' longevity nonetheless proves that there was a definite readership for a work that combined comic-strip narratives with history. The evolution from 1968 onward, however, requires some clarification because of what the break in events of that year caused in social and cultural terms.

Although critics of 1968 viewed the student movement across Europe as a proverbial storm in a teacup, the cultural aftermath is impossible to ignore, even in the comic-strip tradition. Simply put, 1968 opened new paths of expression in the comic-strip tradition. Cartoonists took on their editors, often cartoonists themselves, and demanded more freedoms. The resulting shift in comic-strip stories included female characters becoming more common and active, while male heroes' portrayal acquired more introspection. The optimism that characterized earlier comic strips became more nuanced, while outright cultural pessimism appeared in several new series.[13] Two seemingly contradictory trends appeared at the time. On one hand, the wide distribution of weekly comic magazines that serialized mainstream series began to diminish because of market saturation as well as the appearance of new entertainment forms (primarily the increase in television viewership). On the other, the comic medium began to beef up its credentials as the ninth art. This came out through early analytical works on the subject, which included art exhibits and pedagogical discussions. In addition, the endeavor to explore new forms of the comic medium signaled what would eventually turn into the next age of Francophone comic strips and include *HFBD*.[14]

## THE PUBLIC LOVE OF HISTORY

*HFBD*'s appearance in 1976 through 1978 coincides with a shift in comics media as well one affecting history media. The decade witnessed a renewed interest in popular historical accounts. Although this trend reflected but a cyclical resurgence traceable to the nineteenth century, visuals were more widespread, and printing and paper quality ensured greater interest. Generally, serialized encyclopedias (purchased weekly and assembled into mail-ordered binders) offered general histories of great men and great episodes, but the historicization of the world wars also saw renewed interest.[15] In parallel, French television began showing regularly scheduled documentaries as well as conferences by professional historians with a flair for public address. Far from rejecting such public fascination, historians welcomed it generally but were soon dismayed by the emphasis on trivial details and "fluff": what was on offer seemed to stress emotion more than rational historical analysis.[16] In this context of increased visual stimulation, a historical comic strip offered a peculiar analytical challenge.

The debate concerning the pedagogical approach to history and comics had been ongoing in France by the time that a new series appeared. The Museum of Decorative Arts at the Louvre had sponsored the first major exhibit and conference on the importance of the comics medium in 1967, and within three year, the French Ministry of Education issued a study on the how to interpret comic semantics.[17] However, the latter's report emphasized the trope of historical teaching that appeared in the nineteenth century and stressed the building of national consciousness.[18] In a country where all strips were to be checked and approved by a review board under the 1949 law, the appearance of a strip such as "The History of France in Comic Strips" was proved a surprise.

To be socially acceptable, even a series with a noble theme needed to pass muster with concerned parents. The producers of the series would offer the necessary guarantees. FR3—the newly created (1972) third of three French television channels—covered regional news and showed documentaries and older movies. As such, it was viewed "safe" by parents concerned with television watching. Its part in the series involved a weekly summary of historical events to take place shortly before 7 pm, as a proverbial "bedtime story." It is unclear how many families watched this show as opposed to cartoons on other channels.[19] As for the publisher, Larousse had a long tradition of printing textbooks and educational materials, and it was most famous for printing dictionaries that generations of French schoolchildren had bought. The dual logo of both producers was slapped on the cover of each issue, and that of Larousse (showing a woman seeding "knowledge") proved particularly important as a quality brand. This mattered because the staff did not include any comic-strip "stars."

The staff chosen to work on *HFBD* was generally unknown to the public yet had considerable writing and illustrating experience. Several had come from *Vaillant*, a magazine owned by the French Communist Party. After a reorganization of the publishing house in the 1970s, several established writers and artists had found themselves unemployed, and the opportunity of such contract work was very much welcome.[20] Some of the artists hailed from France, but many more came from southern Europe. Some were struggling to stay in business and acquired further experience drawing *HFBD* before going on to create their own stories and series, all removed from historical narratives. Paradoxically, a national historical narrative would become the child of illustrators whose social background challenged traditional middle-class rhetoric or who were simply not French. Ferdinando Tacconi, Maurillo Manara, Xavier Musquera, and Enric Sió—among others—would later distinguish themselves with their work during the birth of the second wave of comics as well as in the adult comic-strip tradition.

As for the content, the series followed a staid format that came closest to the classic textbooks of French history that most schools used. Each of the 24 issues centers principally on two main events or characters, each subdivided into three or four parts. Together, however, they are considered part of a grand narrative, and the volume pages are numbered consecutively. A typological analysis suggests that the approach of *HFBD* clearly rests on three elements borrowed from historical methodology, all the while seeking to reconcile history with the need to entertain and inform. The first requirement was to offer a factual restitution of historical events. In so doing, as one observer noted, it became necessary first to have a "scientific comic strip" that is a work as accurate as possible. [21] The next two requirements exacerbate the seeming oxymoron by calling for an account that children may understand (thus demanding a pedagogical strip). Last but not least, the nature of the medium and its marketing (Larousse is a for-profit publisher) expected the comic strip to be entertaining to readers who were not history buffs.

The requirement of perceived historical accuracy meant that *HFBD* storyboards rarely departed from established accounts and generally emphasized major battles and famous quotes. As such, they came across to some as lighter versions of the classic history manuals that generations of French pupils had read. [22] Consequently, *HFBD* lost the edge of fantasy that historically inspired strips featured. Indeed, fictional histories of the antiquity-based *Alix* had mesmerized youth, for it could rely on the dual power of the scenario and associated artistry to inspire the readers, much in the way that comic-strip versions of popular novels did. [23] Jacques Martin, the author of *Alix*, could easily balance fantasy through exquisitely detailed architectural renditions, but none of his images required the background to be instantly recognizable. The storytelling carried the narrative as much as the image did. *HFBD* was bound by the historical record; therefore, to ensure that the visual element remained attractive, it had to retain common images—be they monuments, known figures, or specific actions. This cognitive technique implied reductionism and explicit commentary to convey information rapidly. [24]

The cover pictures chosen were illustrative of this concern. As a commercial enterprise, the series needed to capture future readers' imagination in the store, and it required either action or a reinterpretation of a famous historical image. [25] Battles were obvious choices, but so were certain portraits and symbols. The flamboyant Francis Ist in front of his Chambord castle fit the bill nicely, but so did Danton and Robespierre in front of the shadow of a guillotine. [26] Though noncontroversial, these images were not all celebratory. The cover showing Napoleon the First had the emperor on horse during his armies' retreat from Russia.[27] Most telling perhaps, the cover that discusses World War II, though shying away from the controversies surrounding the Vichy regime, displays the debacle at Dunkirk in 1940. In the latter case, however, a dual interpretation is possible. The absence of French troops in the city as Germans attacked (the drawing shows a destroyed Canadian tank as British troops board ships) could suggest the destruction of the French army, but it could also demonstrate the Allied abandonment of France. Still, the avoidance of a more glorious image such as the liberation of Paris by French troops in 1944 also reflects the nascent debate that would affect French public understanding of the war in the 1980s. Overall then, these covers were obviously meant to elicit emotion (and a desire to purchase the periodical in question), yet how glorified such feelings were rests on an examination of the contents themselves.

Though clearly inspired from established textbooks and thus deterministic in nature, the volumes' contents needed to generalize and restate an ideology of national unity. Volume 1, unsurprisingly, discussed the Gauls (Celtic France) and the "national" hero Vercingetorix, made famous through textbooks as well as the world-famous *Astérix* comic strip. The early volumes all continued to perpetuate the established trope, notably one that cast France as the eldest daughter of the Catholic church. St. Blandine's martyr was evoked, as was of course the crusades of King Louis IX (Saint Louis). In the latter case, although the king's death in 1270 reads like a Catholic school catechism, the scenario nonetheless acknowledges the massacres that crusaders carried out, as well as the destruction of Greco-Roman literature during the plundering of cities.[28] The need for an all-encompassing narrative suggesting the tragedies of human history were but part of a grand scheme and would have likely been taken apart in revised textbooks, but the medium used seems to have upset only some specialists.

The national myth of the French Revolution meant that most notions of dissension on French territory were deemed nonexistent, to the dismay of regional historians. Commenting on volume 7, which included the massacre of the Albigensians in the Middle Ages, southern French historians wondered why the emphasis of the strip acknowledged the penance of Toulouse king Raymond VII, rather than the destruction of a whole region that would be transferred to the crown of France.[29] In so doing, these critics feared that regional memory would fall prey to a national narrative as part of a cultural trend that reflected fascination with the French Middle Ages. This concern about a regional narrative, though common in historiographical debate, gained new energy because of the very medium that exploited the story and its intended audience. It would in fact spawn a reaction that used the very tools of *HFBD* to present other facets of French history. What it did not resolve, however, was the reductionism of all the episodes and the resulting confusions that these sometimes created.

Some narratives proved far too short to be fully understandable without prior knowledge. The volume on the beginnings of France's Third Republic concludes with three pages on the Dreyfus affair. However, the imbroglio of guilty parties would make it difficult for unaware readers to understand its far reaches. In fact, the volume concludes with a noncommittal question mark that wonders whether the real spy had accomplices.[30] In so doing, the writers shy away from making clear that the affair represented in many ways the victory of republican secular values over royalist longings for a return to an authoritarian system. Although such a statement would move away from factual toward analytical affirmation, its nonappearance shows the limits of the narrative beyond simple deduction. The episode also shows the limitation of an educational agenda. *HFBD* was never about replacing textbooks, but its marketing as a kind of educational support likely encouraged lay readers to view it as such.

Reductionism may have also proven dangerous as a step toward stereotyping, but *HFBD* paradoxically did its bit to reduce one particular trend. While stereotypes of Germans in 1970s France remained heavily ensconced in the classical portrayals of World War II movies, *HFBD* representations did not caricature ridiculous-looking Teutons, nor did its text typically assign them an accent the way that humoristic series did.[31] By going against the grain, *HFBD* in fact pioneered a new vision of Germans that fell in line with the efforts initiated since the signing of a Franco-German friendship and cooperation treaty in 1962. Though seeking to mend the image of Germans though an emphasis on factual events that did not dive into stereotype, *HFBD* nonetheless kept the convenient trope of blaming all the ills of both world wars on German invaders.[32] This helped maintain the illusion of a France free of blame in World War II.

The last two volumes of the series, covering World War II and its aftermath, ring hollow. It comes as no surprise in a nation where the famous World War II documentary *The Sorrow and the Pity* (made in 1969), which questions the importance of the French resistance, was banned from French television until the 1982. In both volumes, the writers abandoned the thematic approach that had characterized earlier volumes to offer instead a chronicle of facts without clear linkage. The hodgepodge of facts brings the reader to World War II and suggests that the naval blockade that the Allies initiated in 1939–1940 was about to have its effect when France fell. No criticism of Marshall Pétain, the leader of the collaborationist regime, appears: he shows up in 1940 as the new leader of Vichy France and in 1945 for his trial.[33] Furthermore, any actions that would be on the initiative of Vichy are ascribed to the Nazi gestapo. The most egregious misstep perhaps is the description of the roundup of Jews in Paris in summer 1942: the gestapo is blamed; no mention appears anywhere that this action was entirely at the instigation of the French police.[34] Thus, the series very much shows its age, as it mimics the rhetoric of the "Vichy syndrome," which is the silence on France's role in World War II and the Holocaust.

Ironically, the resistance does not fare much better. While almost twenty depictions appear of resistance actions, the collection of events ranges from young men leaving their families to join the underground, parachute in enemy territory, or seek help from regular army units. While it would be difficult, as was the case in the Dreyfus affair, to clarify the motivation of small groups of resisters, the impression given to the reader involves a cogent force controlled from French headquarters in London and sufficiently strong to matter wherever it strikes. As one historian of the resistance noted with regret, the moral reasoning behind desperate actions disappears in favor of the glorification of wartime leaders, thus complicating further the work of the professional historian.[35]

Still, *HFBD*'s reception did not become a source of concern. Rather, it prompted several observers to consider the value of comic strips as a kind of popular art that would parallel the role of cinema in communicating selected historical events.[36] The twenty-fourth, and final, volume of *HFBD* concludes with the election of President Giscard D'Estaing in 1974 and a brief quote of his assuming the leadership of a nation with great history.[37] In so doing, the authors may have reaffirmed a public longing for nostalgic tradition rather than opening toward future unknowns. By the time that the series appeared, France had experienced the impact of the first oil shock, and a three-decade-long period of economic growth had ended. Alluding to a beginning malaise would have been difficult at best.

Paradoxically, the cultural malaise was also present in the whole Francophone comic-strip tradition. While comics continued to evolve, the 1970s marked new departures for the medium, thus turning *HFBD* into a historical landmark. The end of the series did not affect closure for the association of factual historical narrative with comic art. On the contrary, *HFBD* proved a fountainhead, spawning numerous variations on the very theme of established narrative, and raised new questions about the value of using the comic strip to teach history, due in part to the popular success of the medium.

Note, however, that while *HFBD* clearly inspired the new wave of such accounts, authors of "spin-offs" defended themselves against claims. Justifying the writing of *Il Était une Fois Lugdunum* (Once upon a Time in Ancient Lyon), authors Jean Prost and André Pelletier noted that their endeavor stemmed from the fact that pupils knew little of their hometown and that, whereas *HFBD* took on great events, they insisted on incorporating social history. To them, the approach was a novel departure and a way to move beyond the classic Francophone series that had occasionally served teachers for anecdotal purposes, such as *Astérix* and *Alix*. However, in a nod to the entertainment value of *Astérix*, the characters were drawn in a caricature style, while anecdotal evidence broke the perceived monotony of an event-based history.[38]

The attempts to separate from the *HFBD* example not withstanding, it is clear that the formulaic medium had registered well with many audiences. Much in the manner of certain film tropes, historical comic stripping had inscribed its own kind of tradition as the central good of the national past.[39] The debates that followed *HFBD* in short sequence had less to do with the series itself than with the use of comic strips in general and their historical veracity. "Should we teach history with comic strips," noted a specialized librarian and teacher, "then teachers will need to study true history to oppose it to popular tradition."[40]

Perhaps the strongest answer to the latter critic appeared in 1980 when the French Ministry of Education approached the Rectorate Council (a board of governors that enforces the application of centralized academic programs) and encouraged it to consider developing and cosponsoring historical comic strips based on regional foci. Consequently, five volumes would appear in the series that the bank Crédit Agricole helped pay for out of its educational fund. As for Larousse, fresh from its series on world explorers and on the "Far West," it too would launch a variation on the regional theme. It would also rush into print a series on "great battles" that would include the Falkland war less than two years after its conclusion.[41] These series, though notable for their subject, did not encounter the success of the *HFBD*.

What occurred instead was a kind of balkanization whereby local initiatives favored the limited printing of a targeted story. By 1990, a new wave of such volumes, sponsored by tourism offices, saw some twenty-five volumes devoted to various French cities.[42] Some publishers picked up out-of-print volumes and reprinted them for sale in the very regions they covered. Such histories, though entertaining and enlightening in an anecdotal manner, nonetheless displayed problems similar to *HFBD*'s macrohistorical approach.[43] While the social historical aspect was better presented, it is unclear how much readers could really get out of such coverage. The debate concerning the value of such comic strips then remained unanswered. One further evolution, that which Belgian historian Pierre Stéphany offered, involved a standard historical narrative illustrated with images culled from comic strips.[44] There, however, the medium was reversed, as symbols of the ninth art seemed to take their place in the historical account much in the manner that landscapes and portraits had in traditional textbooks.

## HFBD'S IMAGINING THE PAST

The 2008 reprinting of the *HFBD* series, in hard cover and a continuous format, reflects how mainstream the comic medium has become.[45] Not only does the French Ministry of Education issue regular updates to school and public libraries stating which comic strips are suitable for various grade levels, but in 2010 publisher Casterman picked up the series' concept with a drawn-down, caricatured depiction of French history directed at younger readers. This dual event, the reprinting of the old series and the appearance of a similar-themed, though redirected, series suggests that *HFBD* is now itself a historical artifact to be enjoyed as nostalgia, as much as for the quality of its art as for its pioneering feat. As such, it fits into what comics critic Thierry Groensteen has identified as the reader's dual task: to read comics contemplatively and participatorily.[46] The risk, however, echoes very much the issue of reception that historians have identified as being problematic in historical film: what does the consumer of images choose to adopt as his or her narrative? Sounding a mild alarm, Pascal Ory put it best when he discussed history's communication through visual culture: factual accuracy was as much a chimera as was historical objectivity; when push came to shove, historians should have not the last word but at least a say in the comic historical narrative.[47]

Although the *HFBD* volumes, taken together, reinforced a traditional outlook on French history that glorified selected facts and avoided such controversial issues as Vichy France, they introduced notions of historical doubt through anecdotal remarks and careful artistry. Thus, though generating a kind of escapist nostalgia, the format of the series offered a new evolution in the tradition of history for public consumption. The very fabric of the comic genre that intellectual elites left and right had attacked for decades came to be accepted as a teaching tool. As such, *HFBD* was not so much a decline of historical narrative; rather, it represented a new evolution that would encounter various degrees of success by showing both the potential and the limits of using the drawn comic's image to represent historical facts.

## NOTES

1. Henri Filipini et al., *Histoire de la Bande Dessinée en France et en Belgique* (Grenoble, France: Glénat, 1984 [1979]), 181.

2. Thierry Groensteen, *La Bande Dessinée en France* (Paris: adf, 1998), 34; Michel Porret, ed., *Objectif Bulles: Bande Dessinée et Histoire* (Geneva: Georg, 2009), 31, 40n42.

3. René Perrout, *Trésors des Images d'Epinal* (Strasbourg, France: Gyss, 1985 [1912]), 11, 35, 58.

4. Charlotte Maier, *Weiter-höher-schneller, Verkehrsgeschichte auf Marken und Medaillen* (Munich: Deutsches Museum, 1987), contains examples of such manifestations.

5. Filipini et al., *Histoire de la Bande Dessinée*, 49.

6. Filipini et al., *Histoire de la Bande Dessinée*, 119–29, 131–39.

7. Thierry Crépin, *Harro Sur Le Gangster! La Moralisation de la Presse Enfantine 1934–1954* (Paris: CNRS, 2001), 144–47.

8. Michèle Piquard, "La Loi Du 16 Juillet 1949 et la Production De Livres Et Albums Pour la Jeunesse," in *L'Image Pour Enfants: Pratiques, Normes, Discours*, ed. Annie Renonciat (Rennes, France: PUR/La licorne, 2007), 219–35.

9. Thierry Crépin and Thierry Groensteen, eds., *"On Tue à Chaque Page!" La Loi de 1949 sur les Publications Destinées à la Jeunesse* (Paris: Editions du temps, 1999), 74.

10. A useful summary of this subfield appears in Martin T. Dinter, "Francophone Romes: Antiquity in *Les Bandes Dessinées*," in *Classics and Comics*, ed. George Kovacs and C. W. Marshall (New York: Oxford University Press, 2011), 183–92.

11. Cartoonist Raymond Poïvet, for example, produced at least three biographical comic strips on Christopher Columbus, Napoleon, and World War II general Philipe Leclerc. Poïvet's experience would help him later draw to four volumes of *Histoire de France en Bandes Dessinées* (*HFBD*). See "Raymond Poivet," *Office de Tourism du Chambresis*, http://www.tourisme-lecateau.fr/page-10102-raymond-poivet.html.

12. "Les Oncle Paul," *Tout le Journal de Spirou*, http://www.toutspirou.fr/Lesonclepaul/lesonclepaul.htm; cf. Michel Pierre, "Les Histoires de L'Oncle Paul: Mythologie ou Mystification?" *Histoire et Bande Dessinée, Supplément Bédésup* 10 (October 1979): 51–58.

13. Charles Dierick, ed., *Le Centre Belge de la Bande Dessinée* (Bruxelles, France: Dexia, 2000), 161.

14. Dierick, *Le Centre Belge*, 191.

15. See in particular Maurice Samuels, *The Spectacular Past: Popular History and the Novel in Nineteenth Century France* (Ithaca, NY: Cornell University Press, 2004). The popular monthly *Historia Magazine* came to rely heavily on such fascination, while another monthly, *Connaissances de l'Histoire*, came to rely exclusively on the history of twentieth-century warfare to woo readers.

16. Ute Frevert and Anne Schmidt, "Geschichte, Emotionen und die Macht der Bilder," *Geschichte und Gesellschaft* 37, no. 1 (2011): 7, 10–12.

17. Pierre Couperie et al., *Bande Dessinée et Figuration Narrative* (Paris: Musée des arts décoratifs, 1967); Ministère de l'Éducation Nationale, *Les Bandes Dessinées: Histoire, Langage, Mythes*, 2 vols. (Bordeaux, France: CRDP, 1978 [1970]).

18. Jeanne Cappe, *Contes Bleus Et Livres Roses* (Bruxelles, France: Editions des artistes, 1940), 126–28.

19. Charles Sansonetti produced the show airing every Friday; "Vercingétorix, César," *HFBD* 1 (Larousse, October 1976), 49.

20. Gilles Ratier, *Avant la Case: Histoire de la Bande Dessinée Francophone du XXE Siècle Racontée par les Scénaristes* (Sangam, 2005), 60, 161.

21. Jean Prost and Alain Pelletier, "A Propos de 'Il Était une Fois Lugdunum' (T. 1 de l'Histoire de Lyon en Bande Dessinée)," *Histoire et Bande Dessinée, Supplément Bédésup* 10 (October 1979): 30.

22. The most famous of these, still available as background reading, was Jules Isaac's *Histoire de France* (Paris: Hachette, 1922). The book went through multiple editions until 1996.

23. Christian Alberelli, "Du Roman à la Bande Dessinée: Scénario pour une Adaptation," in *L'Histoire . . . par la Bande. Bande Dessinée, Histoire et Pédagogie*, ed. Odette Mitterrand and Giles Ciment (Paris: Syros, 1993), 23–24, 30.

24. Matthew P. McAllister, Edward H. Sewell Jr., and Ian Gordon, eds., *Comics and Ideology* (New York: Lang, 2001), 3–4.

25. *HFBD* covers may be reviewed at http://www.bedetheque.com/serie-3850-BD-Histoire-de-France-en-bandes-dessinees.html.

26. "Louis XI, François 1er," *HFBD* 10 (Larousse, July 1977), and "La Révolution," *HFBD* 15 (Larousse, December 1977).

27. "Napoléon," *HFBD* 17 (Larousse, February 1978). A reprint of this volume in 1983 displayed a different cover, showing Napoleon 1st in exile on St. Helena's island.

28. "Les Croisades," *HFBD* 5 (Larousse, February 1977), 208, 216, 231.

29. "La chevalerie," *HFBD* 7 (Larousse, April 1977); Joseph Dovetto and Raymond Roge, "La Croisade Contre les Albigeois dans la Bande Dessinée," *Histoire et Bande Dessinée, Supplément Bédésup* 10 (October 1979): 36.

30. "La Commune, la IIIeme République," *HFBD* 20 (Larousse, May 1978): 958–60.

31. "1942–1974," *HFBD* 24 (Larousse, September 1978): 1117. Only once was the use of a "Germanized" French applied when referring to exclamations about sabotage by the resistance.

32. Albert Barrera Vidal, "Les Relations Franco-Allemandes dans la BD D' Expression Française, ou L' Histoire Revue et Non Corrigée," *Histoire et Bande Dessinée, Supplément Bédésup* 10 (October 1979): 86–94.

33. "La second guerre mondiale," *HFBD* 23 (Larousse, August 1978), 1088; "1942–1974," *HFBD* 24 (Larousse, September 1978), 1131.

34. "La second guerre mondiale," 1102. The Holocaust is also described inaccurately as taking place in Germany exclusively.

35. Jean Arrouye, "Bandes à Part," *Histoire et Bande Dessinée, Supplément Bédésup* 10 (October 1979): 116–17.

36. Jean Hervé Lacoste, "Les Maîtres du Château de Bonaguil et Leurs Problèmes," *Histoire et Bande Dessinée, Supplément Bédésup* 10 (October 1979): 48.

37. "1942–1974," 1152.

38. Prost and Pelletier, "A Propos de "Il Était une Fois Lugdunum," 31.

39. Andrew Higson, "Representing the National Past: Nostalgia and Pastiche in the Heritage Film," in *Fires Were Started: British Cinema and Thatcherism*, 2nd ed., ed. Lester D. Friedman (London: Wallflower, 2006), 96.

40. Jean Claude Faur, "Bande Dessinée ou Histoire? Caligula dans l'Imagerie Populaire," *Histoire et Bande Dessinée, Supplément Bédésup* 10 (October 1979): 22.

41. Georges Castellar et al., *Missiles et Sous-Marins. Le Conflit des Malouines* (Paris: Larousse, 1984).

42. Jean-Frédéric Minery, "La BD et les villes de France et DOM/TOM," http://www.bedetheque.com/serie-13296–BD-Histoire-des-villes-Collection.html.

43. See, for example, Gilbert Bouchard, *L'Histoire de la Haute Savoie en BD* (Grenoble, France: Glénat, 2002 [1988]). A crucial defeat in 1602 that explains the weakening of the Savoy region's autonomy goes unnoticed in favor of the forced conversion campaign of St-Francis of Sales.

44. Pierre Stéphany, *Histoire de la Belgique au Fil de la BD de 1830 à Nos Jours* (Bruxelles, France: versant Sud, 2005).

45. Eight volumes regrouping the original 24 appeared, each with a new historical preface, and published by France's newspaper of record, *Le Monde*, as a weekend supplement that readers could buy separately.

46. Thierry Groensteen, *La Bande Dessinée, Mode d'Emploi* (Bruxelles, France: Les impressions nouvelles, 2007), 190.

47. Pascal Ory, "Historique ou Historienne?" in *L'Histoire . . . par la Bande. Bande dessinée, Histoire et Pédagogie*, ed. Odette Mitterrand and Giles Ciment (Paris: Syros, 1993), 96.

# THREE

## "Ils sont fous ces Gaulois!"

### Astérix, Lucky Luke, *Freedom Fries, and the Love–Hate Relationship between France and the United States*

### Annick Pellegrin,
### The University of Sydney

René Goscinny était à la bande dessinée ce que la tour Eiffel est à Paris,
ce que Balzac est au roman français.
[René Goscinny was to *bande dessinée* what the Eiffel Tower is to Paris,
what Balzac is to the French novel.][1]

In 2010, McDonald's France created an advertising campaign with the slogan "Venez comme vous êtes" (Come as you are). This campaign showcased a variety of well-known characters, such as Cinderella and Darth Vader, eating at a McDonald's restaurant. Among the posters used during this campaign was also one depicting characters from the comic series *Astérix*. The poster made use of the usual closing banquet scene from *Astérix*, a choice that caused an outrage in France.[2] Who is this Astérix, and why the outrage?

Created in 1959 by Albert Uderzo and René Goscinny, *Astérix* is a famous French comic series set in 50 bc recounting the adventures of its eponymous hero and his sidekick, Obélix.[3] It was created specifically for the magazine *Pilote*, upon the request of the magazine's founder, François Clauteaux. The latter wanted his children to be able to "éprouver du plaisir à lire des rubriques didactiques sur les événements essentiels de notre propre patrimoine culturel" (take pleasure in reading didactic columns on key events of our own cultural heritage).[4] Thus, from the start, it was understood that Uderzo and Goscinny would create something spe-

47

cifically French for *Pilote*, and Uderzo recounts that when they found out
that their first idea for a story was already taken, they had a brainstorm-
ing session where they went through different periods of French history
until they came up with the idea of the Gauls.[5]

The two protagonists of the series live in the last Gaulish village free
from Roman control, and Astérix is perceived as an essentially French
hero who resists the imperial invader.[6] Thus, the first album of the series
is titled simply and unsurprisingly *Astérix le gaulois* (Astérix the Gaul).
Despite its apparently ancient setting, *Astérix* regularly includes refer-
ences to present-day situations so that the resistance of the village against
the Roman Empire has been interpreted as a metaphor not only of the
French resistance against the Nazis but also of Charles de Gaulle against
U.S. imperialism.[7] As Matthew Screech states, "the Romans can be the
Americans from whom de Gaulle . . . desired greater independence. . . .
Plenty of . . . evidence can be found to suggest that Astérix is a French
David to America's Goliath."[8] In light of Screech's observation, it is inter-
esting that *Astérix* was created to be not only French but also a French
comic, as opposed to U.S. comics. Indeed, Uderzo comments that while
the choice of a French perspective for the series

> peut sembler un peu Chauvin et xénophobe . . . il faut se remettre dans
> le contexte de l'époque : hormis certains journaux comme *Vaillant*,
> d'obédience communiste, et certains autres d'obédience catholique, la
> majorité de cette presse est envahie . . . par les séries américaines.
> [may seem a little chauvinistic and xenophobic . . . one needs to put it
> back into the context of the time: apart from some magazines such as
> *Vaillant*, of communist allegiance, and some others of Catholic persua-
> sion, the majority of this press is essentially . . . invaded by American
> series].[9]

As a result of the success and the French theme of the series, *Astérix* has
become "part of France's cultural heritage."[10] As Aymar du Chatenet and
Caroline Guillot put it, "en quatre ans à peine, non seulement cette série
s'impose . . . , mais elle devient aussitôt emblématique de son pays, de sa
population et de ses coutumes" (In just four years, not only does this
series make a name for itself, but it also immediately becomes emblematic of its country, of its population and customs).[11] In more recent times,
the Patrouille de France paid homage to *Astérix* by drawing the hero's
head and writing "50 ans" (50 years) in the sky, to mark the fiftieth
anniversary of the series.[12] Before drawing Astérix's head, the skywriters
drew blue, white, and red stripes in the sky, in honor of the French
tricolor flag. Not only is this homage a great honor, but it also serves to
exemplify how iconically French *Astérix* is. After all, the Patrouille de
France "participe au rayonnement de l'armée de l'air en France, mais
aussi à l'étranger où le rôle diplomatique est parfois mis en exergue"
(contributes to the influence of the air force in France but also overseas

where its diplomatic role is sometimes brought out).[13] Given *Astérix*'s cultural iconicity and the context of its creation, it is certainly no coincidence that José Bové—best known for destroying a McDonald's fast-food restaurant in Millau, France, on August 19, 1999, and for taking part in the so-called Battle of Seattle (protests against the World Trade Organization meeting held there in 1999)—is often referred to as a real-life Astérix.[14]

From reading Astérix as a representation of de Gaulle resisting U.S. hegemony to Bové dismantling a McDonald's restaurant, it comes as no surprise that the use of *Astérix* to promote the very same fast-food chain was perceived as treason.[15] Nonetheless, the U.S.–France love–hate relationship is well illustrated and exemplified in the life, work, and legacy of Goscinny. How appropriate, then, is the reaction to the use of *Astérix* by McDonald's? Are these Gauls crazy? I begin this chapter by introducing the concepts of McDonaldization and Disneyization. I continue with an exploration of the iconicity of McDonald's and *Astérix*, as well as their symbolically antagonistic history. From there, I discuss the evolution of the U.S.–France relationship in general and as seen in Goscinny's life and work, especially *La grande traversée* (The great crossing).[16] The discussion then focuses on the McDonaldization and Disneyization of *Astérix* in an attempt to answer the guiding question of this chapter.

## MCDONALDIZATION AND DISNEYIZATION

*McDonaldization* is a term that is very much associated with George Ritzer, editor of *McDonaldization: The Reader*. While he coined the term from McDonald's, Ritzer specifies that his book is not on that fast-food chain or fast food in general but is rather a study of a process that is well exemplified by McDonald's:[17] "the process by which the principles of the fast-food restaurant are coming to dominate more and more sectors of American society as well as of the rest of the world."[18] Four characteristics, according to Ritzer, have brought about McDonald's success: *efficiency*, in terms of satisfying hunger for customers and having clearly defined tasks for employees; *calculability*, the quantity:price ratio and the time that it takes customers to obtain food; *predictability*, the invariability of the taste of each menu item and the content of the customer–employee interactions across outlets; and *control,* using technology to regulate the way that orders are placed and consumed (fast!) and the amounts of food and drink in each serving.[19] The process of McDonaldization is not so much a process of spreading McDonald's restaurants across the globe as it is the adoption of this efficiency–calculability–predictability–control model in other fast-food chains as well as other types of franchises, such as Toys "R" Us, Blockbuster, The Body Shop, and Ikea.[20]

While George Ritzer seems to suggest that Disneyland is another McDonaldized company, Alan Bryman, for his part, sees McDonald's as a "Disneyized institution."[21] Indeed, although the latter agrees that "Disney theme parks and all theme parks modeled on them provide *predictable* tourist entertainment, exert considerable *control* over their guests (including control through the use of nonhuman technologies), and are highly *efficient* in their processing of guests," he has some reservations. His concerns focus on "whether the parks emphasize quantity at the expense of quality," and he is not convinced that the *calculability* factor applies to them.[22] Bryman's Disneyization model, created as a response to Ritzer's McDonaldization model, also has its own set of characteristics, which are exemplified by the Disneyland parks *theming*, "the use of a narrative that is consciously imposed on a particular sphere and which envelops consumers"; *dedifferentiation of consumption*, "the general trend whereby the forms of consumption associated with different institutional spheres become interlocked with each other and increasingly difficult to distinguish"; *merchandising and emotional labor*, "control over the employee so that socially desired emotions are exhibited during service transactions."[23] According to Bryman, the four characteristics of Disneyization can be observed in McDonald's restaurants, and of particular interest here is the dedifferentiation of consumption. Bryman draws attention to the fact that, first, there are a number of toys and collectibles that are made available at McDonald's—including Disney toys—as part of the Happy Meal and, second, this practice has made McDonald's "the greatest distributor of toys in the world." Another aspect of dedifferentiation of consumption is the presence of McDonald's outlets in a variety of places where other products are sold—for example, the grounds of theme parks.[24]

Rather than attempt to debate whether McDonald's is Disneyized or Disneyland is McDonaldized, I suggest that Ritzer's and Bryman's approaches show that there is an element of McDonaldization in Disneyland and an element of Disneyization in McDonald's. This perspective is in fact the one adopted by Bryman in another work, where he says that these two "can be viewed as parallel processes [in] that both can legitimately be viewed as signals of globalization."[25] In light of these links, it is perhaps unsurprising that Max Gallo put theme parks and fast food together when he made the following comment about the opening of Disneyland in France: "Le parc bombarde la France de créations importées qui sont à la culture ce que le *fast food* est à la gastronomie" (The park bombards France with uprooted creations that are to culture what fast food is to gastronomy).[26] Although Ritzer's work on McDonaldization has been criticized as an elitist rejection of mass culture—a point I return to later—both McDonaldization and Disneyization are useful concepts here, as will become evident as the chapter progresses.[27]

## THE WAR ON ICONS

Not only does Bryman show that the processes of McDonaldization and Disneyization are interlinked, but he also points out that McDonald's and Disney are two prominent brands in globalization. He states that "one could hardly disregard the golden arches of McDonald's or Mickey's ears and [Walt Disney's] signature as involved in the global travels of brand names."[28] José Bové himself is very much aware of the iconicity of McDonald's, and in an interview with Gilles Luneau, he stated that "we didn't want McDonald's to be seen as the prime target. It's merely a symbol of economic imperialism."[29] Be that as it may, following his antiglobalization actions, José Bové soon came to be known as a real-life *"anti-McDonald's 'Astérix.'"*[30]

In addition, beyond globalization and economic imperialism, McDonald's symbolically stands for the United States. This posture is well illustrated by the decision to close McDonald's regional offices in the United States following the attacks of September 11, 2001. The reason that was given for this decision was that "the perpetrators were obviously attacking America directly, and since McDonald's represented America, company offices were highly vulnerable."[31] In relation to the September 11 attacks, it is somewhat ironic that the tensions between France and the United States were again expressed through (fast) food in the following two years. Indeed, and as pointed out by the *bande dessinée* blogger who goes by the penname Laureline Karaboudjan, 2010 was not the first time that Astérix joined forces with McDonald's: at the end of 2001, it was announced that Astérix would replace Ronald McDonald as the face of the fast-food chain in France in early 2002. If for Astérix this was part of the promotion for the film adaptation of *Astérix et Cléopâtre* (Astérix and Cleopatra), the BBC reported that with this campaign, "the company [was] hoping to appease anti-American feeling which [had] dogged McDonald's in France."[32] While this first association also sparked controversy in France, the irony of using Astérix for such purposes did not escape the French magazine *Télérama*, which commented, "By capturing our very heritage, McDonald's has achieved a striking revenge over Bové."[33] In addition, two years after the September 2001 attacks, then-president Jacques Chirac's decision to veto the war in Iraq and to abstain from sending French troops to war resulted in the renaming of "french fries" as "freedom fries."[34] On a side note, a similar phenomenon occurred with sauerkraut and hamburgers during World War I, when they were renamed "liberty cabbage" and "liberty sandwiches," respectively.[35] These cases suggest that much importance is placed on certain food items as part of U.S. culture, and it is particularly striking that the typical food associated with McDonald's—burgers and fries—are among those that were renamed in times of war.

From the current discussion, it would seem that the outrage in reaction to the use of an iconic scene (the banquet scene) from an iconic French comic series (*Astérix*) is rather consistent with previous uses of Astérix and McDonald's (or the type of food served by this restaurant) to express discontent on either side of the Atlantic Ocean. However, the relationship between France and the United States is more complex than José Bové's dismantling of a McDonald's restaurant or France's veto on the war in Iraq. In the next section, I cover some of the ups and downs of this love–hate relationship between the two countries.

## DES AMOURS ET DES DÉSAMOURS
## (OF LOVES AND OF FALLING-OUTS)

Just as there have been periods of tension between France and the United States, there have also been moments and eras when the two countries maintained friendly relations. In his brief overview of two centuries of a love–hate relationship, Jean-Michel Demetz lists some key dates of this relationship, starting with the trade agreement signed between France and the British North American colonies in 1778. Later examples of some key moments of friendship are France's gift of the Statue of Liberty in 1886 and the arrival of U.S. troops in Normandy in 1944. These moments of friendly diplomatic relations are counterbalanced with moments of tension, such as de Gaulle's demand that the United States close its military bases in France in 1966, as well as the aforementioned veto on the part of Chirac. To these moments of tension, one might add the Dominique Strauss-Kahn scandal as the latest key moment of a tumultuous relationship.[36] Strauss-Kahn, the director of the International Monetary Fund, was accused of sexual assault and attempted rape on the person of Nafissatou Diallo and was arrested on May 15, 2011, in New York.[37] The French may well have expressed disbelief that this had happened, and the charges against Strauss-Kahn may have been dismissed, but the image of France in the United States was tarnished with this scandal and with the other charges pressed against him by Tristane Banon, in a snowball effect of the scandal that started in the United States.[38] The words used by Banon to describe Strauss-Kahn — "a rutting chimpanzee" — were taken up, for example, in *The New Yorker*'s digest of the Strauss-Kahn scandal.[39] In this digest, Will Oremus lists a series of quotes to illustrate the various reactions to the scandal, one of which is "It's humiliating for the IMF and humiliating for our country," attributed to Bernard Debré, "a French politician from President Sarkozy's party."[40] The scandal indeed did not do much to present France in a positive light, and the anonymous article published in the *Wall Street Journal* of August 25, 2011, provides an example of the perception of the French during that time: "French citizens may not mind their leaders acting out their Louis XIV fantasies with impunity, but Manhattan isn't Paris."[41] It is no accident that in June 2011 the magazine *L'Express* published a dossier titled *Ce que les Américains pensent des Français* (What the Americans think of the French), in which the Strauss-Kahn scandal is a recurring topic of concern across several articles.[42]

Yet, there has been love in this love–hate relationship between France and the United States. The reason why I draw attention to the friendlier moments in the relationship is that both René Goscinny and Albert Uderzo have not only demonstrated a more positive perception of the United States in their work but also maintained connections with the United States. Through their work, Goscinny and Uderzo have shown their interest in the United States in several ways. First, they collaborated to create a series known as *Oumpah-Pah*, with an eponymous hero who is generally regarded as Astérix's big brother. This choice of words does not mean that *Astérix* is a spin-off of *Oumpah-Pah* but rather that *Oumpah-Pah* is a precursor of *Astérix*.[43] *Oumpah-Pah* is of interest here because it takes place at the time of colonial settlement, in the part of the Americas that would later become the United States—although the settlers in this series are in fact French.[44]

Moreover, *Oumpah-Pah* is not the only U.S.-based series written by Goscinny. He also wrote several scripts for *Lucky Luke*, a series created in 1946 by the Belgian Maurice de Bevere—better known by his pen name Morris.[45] If, when he created *Lucky Luke*, Morris took care of both the story and the drawings, starting from 1955, it was Goscinny who was entrusted with the scripts, while Morris was responsible for the graphic side of the series. This collaboration continued until Goscinny passed away in 1977, and the period of the Morris–Goscinny tandem is considered to be the golden age of the series.[46] *Lucky Luke* continues to enjoy significant success, as new adventures are regularly added to the series, and film adaptations continue to be made, not to mention the existence of two spin-off *bande dessinée* series.[47] Of relevance to the discussion on French–U.S. relations here is the fact that Lucky Luke—the hero of the series—is a "poor lonesome cowboy" living in the Wild West. The series shows a recurring concern with the conquest of the West, and its plots are typically centered on the life of settlers, the creation of local newspapers, or the building of the rail network. Additionally, the typical "cowboys and Indians" fight scenes from Westerns pepper the pages, and several legendary figures of the Wild West—such as Billy the Kid and Calamity Jane—are given a prominent place in the series. Although Goscinny used the series as a parody, both he and Morris had conducted considerable research on the Wild West and were aficionados of the Western genre.[48] Thus, Goscinny's work, be it with Uderzo or with Morris, demonstrates that the creators of *Astérix* viewed U.S. culture as appealing and entertaining.

Besides the importance given to the United States in Uderzo and Goscinny's collaborative creations, it is interesting that the United States had
a significant impact on their lives and careers. For instance, in terms of
the graphic quality, note that Morris and Uderzo both greatly admired
Walt Disney's work.[49] In fact, Uderzo still finds Walt Disney's drawings
fascinating, and he says that he aspired to be "the French Walt Disney."
This admiration was so great that early in his career, he used the pseudo-
nym Al Uderzo in an effort to give himself a U.S. identity so that readers
would think that he was from the United States.[50] As for Goscinny, he
made his comics debut in the United States, working with those who
would later create *MAD* magazine. In fact, du Chatenet and Guillot argue
that it is in that environment that Goscinny acquired the type of humor
that we can find in his oeuvre.[51] Given the place that the United States
has in the early careers of both Goscinny and Morris, it is perhaps unsurprising that they first met when they were both living in the United
States.[52] As an aside, it is also worth noting that this meeting between
Morris and Goscinny took place in the context of Morris's travels to the
Americas with his colleagues André Franquin and Jijé (Joseph Gillain), as
well as the latter's family. The journey undertaken by these three men,
who were nothing less than the "stars" of the *bande dessinée* weekly *Spirou*, has been so important to Franco-Belgian *bande dessinée* that part of it
has recently been recounted in *bande dessinée*.[53]

Furthermore, beyond Goscinny and Uderzo's relationship with the
United States, these two men gave it a significant place in *Astérix* itself, on
one occasion in the case of Goscinny and on two occasions in the case of
Uderzo. The first of these occasions is in the album *La grande traversée*; the
second is in a more recent album created by Uderzo alone, after Goscinny's death: *Le ciel lui tombe sur la tête* (The falling sky). In the first of these
two albums, Astérix and Obélix visit two countries, the first of which can
quite easily be understood as a representation of the United States. For
example, upon their arrival, the starved Astérix and Obélix roast what
the latter calls "glouglous" (gobblers), that is, turkeys. This not only gives
an indication of the type of fauna found in this land, but it can also be
seen as a reference to Thanksgiving.[54] A second indication of the intended location of this land is Astérix's reflection, "On dirait un autre
monde" (It's like a new world).[55] Yet another source of information is the
culture and actions of the indigenous people. Indeed, while Obélix and
Astérix have difficulty identifying them as a people, the indigenous people have painted bodies, wear feather ornaments, live in teepees, have
totems, and say "ugh!"[56] These are all stereotypical representations of
"Indians," and the reader might also say that they very much echo the
sort of representations of Indians found in *Lucky Luke* and *Oumpah-Pah*.
Moreover, the geographical location is marked through a particular arrangement of the stars that normally serve to demonstrate a character
being hit, startled, or hurt. Indeed, instead of multicolored stars random-

ly placed around a character, in this album Uderzo arranged stars in such a way that they are a barely veiled reference to the United States. In the first instance, upon being punched by Obélix, an indigenous character is shown with neatly aligned white stars near the upper part of his body. These stars are placed against the blue backdrop of the sky to resemble the U.S. Navy jack.[57] In a second instance, another character, who has just been punched by Obélix, is depicted as surrounded by stars designed like the insignia used on U.S. military aircraft.[58] The most obvious reference, however, is when "Astérix strikes a pose that resembles the Statue of Liberty" immediately after Obélix declares that he wants to stay *libre*.[59] One should bear in mind that Astérix is a typical French hero—so much so that the first French satellite was named *A1* in honor of the series—and that it is possible to see a parallel between the Roman Empire and U.S. imperialism, as suggested by Matthew Screech.[60] However, I suggest that the reference to the Statue of Liberty here is intended as a reminder of the French–U.S. friendship, given that the statue was a present from France, with an internal structure created by none other than Gustave Eiffel, whose name is better known for the Eiffel Tower.

The second *Astérix* album that gives the United States an important place is the thirty-third album of the series: *Le ciel lui tombe sur la tête*. In this story, set in the village, the Gauls are visited by Toune (from the star *Tadsylwine*, or Tadsilweny in English) and Nagma, whose names are veiled references to U.S. "toons" and Japanese "mangas," respectively. The references to the United States also abound in this album, such as the superclones whose costume resembles that of Superman and who have a caricature of Arnold Schwarzenegger for a face. Another hint is to be found in Toune's words when he talks about his home: "Nous arrivons tout droit d'une galaxie formée de cinquante étoiles dont chacune vit en paix avec sa voisine!" (We are from a galaxy of fifty stars, all of them at peace with their neighbors).[61] The fifty stars clearly hark back to the fifty states that are represented by the fifty stars on the American flag. Many more references to the United States are present in this album, but for reasons of space limitation, I mention only one more, for its use of another iconic food item: the "chien chaud" (hot dog) that Toune offers the Gauls as the favorite food of the Tadsilwenyans.[62] In this rather unusual *Astérix* adventure—where Nagma is presented in a negative light, Toune is shown to have (literally) an inflated ego, and both visitors ultimately have equal powers—one might wonder what Uderzo's stance is in this album.[63] He makes clear his intentions in a dedication printed at the end of the album:

> Avec cet album, je voudrais rendre hommage au grand Tadsylwien . . . pardon, au grand Walt Disney qui, de fameux et prodigieux druide qu'il était, nous a permis, certains confrères et moi, de tomber dans la marmite d'une potion dont il détenait seul le grand secret.

[In this book I would like to pay my tribute to the great creations of Tadsilweny . . . sorry, I mean the great creations of Walt Disney who, famous and amazing druid that he was, allowed some of his colleagues, myself included, to fall into the cauldron of a potion of which he alone knew the magical secret.] [64]

## THE CASE OF PARC ASTÉRIX

*Astérix* was created per a specific request for a French alternative to U.S. comics. However, based on the content of Goscinny's and Uderzo's various albums and their lives, as explored so far in this chapter, it is not fair to say that the series is inherently opposed to the United States. [65] After all, Obélix himself says in an early album that his distant cousin Amérix is "the big success in our family," and Obélix shows much devotion to his relative before even meeting him. [66] In fact, Goscinny and Uderzo have both given the United States a prominent place in their work, including, as stated earlier, a potent reminder of the friendship between France and the United States in the form of a reference to the Statue of Liberty. In the case of Uderzo, this is reiterated even more explicitly in the dedication to Walt Disney at the end of the thirty-third album. On this basis, the reaction to the McDonald's poster seems unjustified. However, it may be argued that details of the authors' lives and their work in other series are not necessarily associated with *Astérix*. While that may be so, there is one place that is very much linked with the oeuvre of *Astérix* itself and more readily accessible to the general public: Parc Astérix.

Opened a mere two years after Disneyland Paris in the Ile de France region, Parc Astérix—as its name suggests—is a theme park centered on the world of Astérix. While Uderzo recounts that the request for permission to build an interchange to Parc Astérix was met with a "Ne vous prenez pas pour Disney tout de même!" (Really, don't take yourself for Disney!), he does recount that he formed the idea of creating a theme park precisely after visiting Disneyland in California. [67] The park is quite successful, and according to Aymar du Chatenet and Caroline Guillot, "Seul le petit Gaulois parvient à rivaliser avec les Américains, défiant avec son parc d'attractions (2 millions de visiteurs par an) le géant Disneyland" (Only the little Gaul is able to compete with the Americans, defying the giant Disneyland with his amusement park [2 million visitors a year]). [68] Thus, the Frenchness of the park and the series is constructed in contraposition to the Americanness of Disney and Disneyland. Paradoxically, the oppositional Frenchness of Astérix is constructed through models originating in the United States, and I argue that Parc Astérix is in fact as Disneyized as it is McDonaldized.

All the aspects of Disneyization as identified by Bryman and discussed earlier in this chapter can be found at Parc Astérix. For instance, to enter and leave the park, visitors must walk along an alley replicating the buildings drawn by the architect Numérobis in *Astérix et Cléopâtre*. These instantly recognizable architectural feats host shops filled with licensed products, from magnets to mugs, and there are a few other shops in the park that stock more licensed items, such as plush toys, T-shirts, and writing sets. Aside from serving the purpose of merchandising, these buildings are part of the theming feature, which is present everywhere in the park. However, theming is first and foremost visible in the gigantic sculpture of Astérix that overhangs the park and functions as a lightning conductor. This ensures that the visitor can see the figurehead of the series and Parc Astérix before reaching it, but it is also a very clever reference to the series. Indeed, in the series, Abraracourcix—the chief of the Gaulish village—fears nothing but the possibility of the sky falling on his head, and the sculpture of Astérix literally prevents lightning from falling on anyone's head. There are several other instances of such clever theming in the various rides available in the park, and one may encounter signage such as "Travaux d'Héraclès" or "Défense de nourrir les Vikings."[69] In terms of emotional labor, while I encountered fewer costumed employees at Parc Astérix than at Disneyland Paris, Parc Astérix does offer a photo service with characters from the series, and the masks that these employees wear have smiles. The costumed employees also use body language to make the visitor smile or laugh for photographers (figure 3.1). Last but not least, dedifferentiation of consumption is particularly interesting in the case of Parc Astérix because it links fast food and collectibles much in the way that Alan Bryman describes how McDonald's and Disney join forces in the Happy Meal toy distribution. The fast-food outlet Aux Fastes de Rome serves as an example of this dedifferentiation of consumption. The name of the restaurant translates as "At the Splendors of Rome," and it is part of the integral theming throughout the park. However, the name of the food shop is also a pun on "fast," from "fast food," and the menu items resemble those on the McDonald's menu. The venue also offers items such as reusable and collectible Astérix drinking cups as part of meal deals. Besides showing the characteristics of Disneyization, the outlet shows the same characteristics that Ritzer associates with McDonald's and McDonaldization—efficiency, calculability, predictability, and control.[70]

Further evidence that Parc Astérix is a Disneyized park can be drawn from the 2011 advertising campaign for the theme park. A few posters comparing Disneyland and Parc Astérix were released, but only one poster needs to be analyzed to showcase this point. The poster in question consists mainly of large text, accompanied by some images of the main characters from *Astérix* and the logo of Parc Astérix. The text states, "Là-bas les belles dorment ici elles font la fête" (Over there, beauties sleep; here, they party). The slogan subtly refers to Disneyland—the park where one can find Sleeping Beauty—and suggests that Disneyland is

**Figure 3.1.    Astérix & Obélix at Parc Astérix. Les Editions Albert René / Goscin-ny-Uderzo.**

somewhat boring, since it is sleep inducing. The positioning of the Parc Astérix logo on the bottom right corner of the poster makes it appear as a complement to the statement, like an explanation added between brackets or as a footnote. Moreover, the contraposition of "over there" and "here" includes the reader as an interlocutor, suggesting that he or she is "here"—that is, in Parc Astérix or at least France—with the person who is making the statement. In other words, the reader is welcome into an "us" of Parc Astérix, as opposed to the "them" of Disneyland.

Such a campaign is double-edged and illustrates well the process of Disneyization. By making such a comparison, Parc Astérix recognizes that there is enough common ground between it and Disneyland that they can be compared. Yet, while recognizing this common ground, it highlights the contrast between the two parks, suggesting that one park is boring and external to "us," whereas the other park is fun and internal to "us."[71] What the two parks have in common is their structure, meaning that Parc Astérix is Disneyized but is not Disneyland or Disneyworld itself. This concept is indeed what Uderzo says was his idea in creating the park: "pourquoi ne tenterions-nous pas de trouver des investisseurs pour créer également, sur notre territoire, un parc à thème *dans l'esprit de celui de chez Disney*?" [why not attempt to find investors to also create, on our territory, a theme park *in the spirit of Disneyland*?].[72]

## PAS SI FOUS, CES GAULOIS! (NOT SO CRAZY, THESE GAULS!)

While it is true that, thematically, *Astérix* is very much concerned with French matters and stands as an icon of Frenchness and French resistance, one should not forget that in terms of structure, it has had much in common with U.S. models from the beginning. From the strong influence of the United States on the work and lives of Goscinny and Uderzo to the Disneyization and McDonaldization of the series very much visible in Parc Astérix, *Astérix* had already embraced a model that originated in the United States long before the poster for McDonald's was created. Thus, I suggest that the public outrage against the McDonald's poster, while understandable in terms of its iconoclastic nature, is not necessarily justified when we take into consideration the structural similarities. We could even say that this is in fact a logical continuation of Disneyization and McDonaldization. Indeed, if Astérix is a local counterpart to Disney and if the collaboration between McDonald's and Disney has been so successful in the United States, the reasons for wishing to collaborate with *Astérix* in France seem obvious. What is more, it seems that history may be set to repeat itself and that the links between this series and the United States will continue for some time, as Uderzo announced in October 2012 that his successor as the artist behind *Astérix* would be Didier Conrad, who—among many other things—briefly collaborated on the short-lived *Kid Lucky*, a spin-off of *Lucky Luke*.[73] A former employee of DreamWorks, Conrad currently lives in the United States and has used U.S. film and animation techniques in his previous work in *bande dessinée*.[74]

On the question of the use of the terms *McDonaldization* and *Disneyization*, Alan Bryman aptly remarks that "one of the problems with tying the names of these systems to well-known icons of popular culture—McDonald's and Disney—is that it is easy to make the mistake of lapsing into a discussion of just McDonald's and Disney."[75] Thus, a detailed study of the spread of McDonald's restaurants or Disneylands across the globe does not necessarily address McDonaldization or Disneyization but rather the glocalization of the two companies.[76] He further suggests,

> Disneyization and McDonaldization are potentially more insidious processes because they are far less visible and immediately obvious in their emergence than the appearance of golden arches or of magic kingdoms on nations' doorsteps.[77]

I suggest that this is precisely what has happened in the case of *Astérix*. Indeed, while "Disney was given a decidedly gallic [*sic*] cold shoulder among intellectuals in France when Disneyland Paris was in the planning stage," it appears that little attention has been paid to the Disneyization of *Astérix* in its own theme park, let alone the fact that there is also McDonaldization within this same park.[78] Instead, Parc Astérix is still being presented as part of an "us," and it is the explicit association with McDonald's that caused an uproar. After all, and as the copyright holders of *Astérix* pointed out, when they joined forces with Quick (a Franco-Belgian fast-food chain) for an advertising campaign in 2009, "cela n'avait pas pris les mêmes proportions" (things had not reached such proportions).[79]

In his critical work, Martin Parker warns against the dangers of falling into cultural elitism and conservativism in criticizing McDonaldization.[80] He draws our attention to the fact that Ritzer is focused on a sense of cultural decline through the process of McDonaldization and offers economic wealth as a means of escaping this process.[81] My aim has not been to condemn a supposed decline in French culture or lament the loss of *Astérix*'s Frenchness. Quite the contrary, I argue that *Astérix* continues to be understood as essentially French, which explains the reaction to the McDonald's advertisement as well as the effectiveness of the 2011 advertising campaign for Parc Astérix.

In a world of icons, everyone is at liberty to interpret, reinterpret, or even "misinterpret" their meaning, and this includes McDonald's. Parker says of the fast-food chain, "We could never summarise what McDonald's is or does, simply because we make it and remake it every time we enter a restaurant or write an essay."[82] The same can be said of *Astérix* and Parc Astérix, and I have sought to point out the various ways in which *Astérix* and its creators were already linked with McDonaldization, Disneyization, and the United States before the creation of the McDonald's advertisement. However, we might ask whether the McDonaldization and Disneyization of *Astérix* are really "insidious processes."[83] That is to say, if the French do not appear to perceive these processes as dispossessing *Astérix* of its essential Frenchness, then does it not remove the power of "Americanization" or "standardization" that Bryman suggests such processes might have?

## ACKNOWLEDGMENT

Chaque texte a sa propre personnalité et celui-ci a décidément la vocation du voyage. Le travail de recherche et la rédaction du ce chapitre ont été réalisés alors que j'étais dans diverses villes du monde : Sydney, Manchester, Liège, Bruxelles, Dubaï, Adélaïde . . . et surtout Paris. Pierre et Marie Rose Pellegrin, mon oncle et ma tante de Paris, ont eu la très grande gentillesse de me recevoir chez eux à plusieurs reprises au fil des ans et je tiens à les en remercier, ainsi que mon cousin Gilles. Merci de m'avoir reçue et gâtée tant de fois, de m'avoir accompagnée à diverses expositions liées à la bande dessinée, de m'avoir aidée à obtenir le matériel requis pour rédiger ce chapitre et de m'avoir fait découvrir le Parc Astérix. Mille mercis, enfin, pour votre patience et votre compréhension quand il m'a fallu m'enfermer pour rédiger le chapitre que vous avez sous les yeux. Je vous le dédie.

[Each piece of writing has its own personality, and this one is obviously destined for travel. It was researched and written while I was in various cities across the globe: Sydney, Manchester, Liège, Brussels, Dubai, Adelaide . . . and above all Paris. Pierre and Marie Rose Pellegrin, my uncle and aunt in Paris, have been very kind to have me stay with them on several occasions over the years, and it is very important to me to thank them, as well as my cousin Gilles. Thank you for having me over and spoiling me so many times, for accompanying me to various exhibitions related to *bande dessinée*, for helping me obtain some of the material that I needed to write this chapter and for introducing me to Parc Astérix. Finally, many thanks for your patience and your understanding when I had to shut myself away to write the chapter that you have before your eyes. I dedicate it to you.]

## NOTES

1. Aymar du Chatenet and Caroline Guillot, *Goscinny: Faire Rire, Quel Métier!* (Paris: Gallimard, 2009), 94 (from *Le Monde*, November 1977), my translation.

2. "Émoi en France, Astérix Fait la Publicité de McDonald's," *LeDevoir*, August 20, 2010, http://www.ledevoir.com/culture/actualites-culturelles/294661/emoi-en-france-asterix-fait-la-publicite-de-mcdonald-s; Olivier Levard, "Publicité pour Mac Do: Astérix se Défend," *MYTF1News*, August 18, 2010, http://lci.tf1.fr/economie/entreprise/2010-08/publicite-pour-mac-do-asterix-se-defend-6040857.html.

3. Albert Uderzo, *Uderzo se Raconte* (Paris: Stock, 2008), 136–43.

4. Uderzo, *Uderzo se Raconte*, 134 (my translation).

5. Uderzo, *Uderzo se Raconte*, 136–38.

6. René Goscinny and Albert Uderzo, *Astérix le Gaulois*, 6th ed., vol. 1 of *Astérix* (Paris: Hachette, 1999), 3.

7. Diego Agrimbau, "Argentina a los Pies de Asterix," *Sudestada* (July 2008): 15.

8. Matthew Screech, "A Hero for Everyone: René Goscinny's and Albert Uderzo's Astérix the Gaul," in *Masters of the Ninth Art: Bandes Dessinées and Franco-Belgian Identity* (Liverpool, England: Liverpool University Press, 2005), 75–94. "America" and "American" are to be understood here and in any subsequent citations as referring to the United States of America, the citizens thereof, and phenomena pertaining to its society.

9. Uderzo, *Uderzo se Raconte*, 134 (my translation).

10. du Chatenet and Guillot, *Goscinny*, 59 (my translation).

11. du Chatenet and Guillot, *Goscinny*, 72 (my translation).

12. Jean-Philippe Lefèvre, "Spéciale Albert Uderzo, le Dernier des Géants," *Un Monde de Bulles*, July 14, 2011, http://www.publicsenat.fr/vod/un-monde-de-bulles/speciale-albert-uderzo,-le-dernier-des-geants/69227.

13. Athos 6, "Organisation," *Patrouille de France*, June 23, 2011, http://www.patrouilledefrance.net/index.php?option=com_content&view=article&id=24&Itemid=94, my translation.

14. Joe L. Kincheloe, *The Sign of the Burger: McDonald's and the Culture of Power* (Philadelphia: Temple University Press, 2002), 1, 5; Tony Karon, "Why Courts Don't Deter France's Anti-McDonald's 'Astérix,'" *Time*, February 15, 2001, http://www.time.com/time/world/article/0,8599,99592,00.html.

15. Henry Samuel, "Quelle horreur! Asterix Surrenders to McDonald's," *Telegraph*, August 18, 2010, http://www.telegraph.co.uk/news/worldnews/europe/france/7952441/Quelle-horreur-Asterix-surrenders-to-McDonalds.html.

16. René Goscinny and Albert Uderzo, *La Grande Traversée*, 6th ed., vol. 22 of *Astérix* (Paris: Hachette, 1999), passim.

17. George Ritzer, "An Introduction to McDonaldization," in *McDonaldization: The Reader*, ed. George Ritzer (Thousand Oaks, CA: Pine Forge Press, 2006), 4–5.

18. Ritzer, "An Introduction to McDonaldization," 5.

19. Ritzer, "An Introduction to McDonaldization," 14–17.

20. Ritzer, "An Introduction to McDonaldization," 5–8.

21. Alan Bryman, "McDonald's as a Disneyized Institution," in *McDonaldization: The Reader*, ed. George Ritzer (Thousand Oaks, CA: Pine Forge Press, 2006), passim; Ritzer, "An Introduction to McDonaldization," 19.

22. Bryman, "McDonald's as a Disneyized Institution," 55 (my emphasis).

23. Bryman, "McDonald's as a Disneyized Institution," 55.

24. Bryman, "McDonald's as a Disneyized Institution," 59–60.

25. Alan Bryman, "Global Implications of McDonaldization and Disneyization," in *McDonaldization: The Reader*, ed. George Ritzer (Thousand Oaks, CA: Pine Forge Press, 2006), 319.

26. Sébastien Roffat, *Disney et la France: Les Vingt ans d'Euro Disneyland* (Paris: L'Harmattan, 2007), 148; translation by George Ritzer ("An Introduction to McDonaldization," 19).

27. Martin Parker, "Nostalgia and Mass Culture: McDonaldization and Cultural Elitism," in *McDonaldization Revisited: Critical Essays on Consumer Culture*, ed. Mark Alfino, John S. Caputo, and Robin Wynyard (Westport, CT: Praeger, 1998), passim.

28. Bryman, "Global Implications of McDonaldization and Disneyization," 319.

29. José Bové and François Dufour, *The World Is Not for Sale*, trans. Anna de Casparis (London: Verso, 2001), 13; interview by Gilles Luneau.

30. Karon, "Why Courts Don't Deter" (my emphasis).

31. Kincheloe, *The Sign of the Burger*, 4.

32. Laureline Karaboudjan, "Astérix vaut-il mieux qu'un Big Mac?" *Des bulles carrées: Le blog BD de Laureline Karaboudjan*, August 17, 2010, http://blog.slate.fr/des-bulles-carrees/2010/08/17/asterix-vaut-il-mieux-quun-big-mac/; "McDonald's Takes on Astérix," *BBC News*, December 20, 2001, http://news.bbc.co.uk/2/hi/entertainment/1721029.stm.

33. Levard, "Publicité pour Mac Do"; "McDonald's Takes on Astérix."

34. Jean-Michel Demetz, "Deux Siècles d'Amour Vache," *L'Express* (June 21–28, 2011): 58.

35. Gary Gerstle, "Pluralism and the War on Terror," *Dissent Magazine* (spring 2003), http://www.dissentmagazine.org/article/?article=502. In addition, Thomas Bruscino notes that dachshunds were renamed "liberty pups" while frankfurters became "red hots"; Thomas Bruscino, *A Nation Forged in War: How World War II Taught Americans to Get Along*, ed. G. Kurt Piehler (Knoxville: University of Tennessee Press, 2010), 5.

36. Demetz, "Deux Siècles d'Amour Vache."

37. Anonymous, "L'après-DSK," *Le Monde*, May 21, 2011; anonymous, "The Judgement on DSK," *Wall Street Journal*, August 25, 2011.

38. John Riley, "DSK Gets Passport Returned," *Newsday*, August 26, 2011; anonymous, "DSK Arrest a Setup," *Mail Today*, July 5, 2011; Agnes Poirier, "Le Scandale DSK: The Accusation That Dominique Strauss-Kahn Sexually Assaulted a Maid Has Launched a Wave of Soul-Searching among the French Political Class," *Toronto Star*, May 19, 2011. The latest developments in this scandal include the appearance of the initials DSK in an investigation on a prostitution ring in Lille. In addition, following the court dismissal, Ms. Diallo filed a case for damages, and the matter was finally settled when the parties concerned reached a confidential financial agreement on December 10, 2012; see Matthew Kaminski, "DSK's Fall from Grace," *Wall Street Journal*,

November 1, 2011, and Brigitte Dusseau, "Un Accord Financier Confidentiel Clôt l'Affaire DSK à New York," *Public Sénat*, December 10, 2012, http://www.publicsenat.fr/lcp/politique/un-accord-financier-confidentiel-cl-t-laffaire-dsk-new-york-337715.

39. Will Oremus, "The Crisis in a Nutshell: 'A Rutting Chimpanzee,'" May 17, 2011, http://www.newyorker.com/online/blogs/newsdesk/2011/05/the-crisis-in-a-nutshell-a-rutting-chimpanzee.html.

40. Oremus, "The Crisis in a Nutshell."

41. Anonymous, "The Judgement on DSK," 16.

42. See Philippe Coste, "Ce Que les Américains Pensent des Français," *L'Express*, June 22–28, 2011, and Jean-Michel Demetz, "Une Histoire Marquée par la Suspicion," *L'Express*, June 22–28, 2011.

43. du Chatenet and Guillot, *Goscinny*, 61.

44. Lefèvre, "Spéciale Albert Uderzo."

45. Henri Filippini, "Les Quatre vies de Lucky Luke," *dBD* (November 2009): 32.

46. Filippini, "Les Quatre vies de Lucky Luke," 34–35.

47. The latest album was prepublished in six episodes in the magazine *Spirou* from September to October 2012 and published in October 2012; see Pennac, Benacquista, and Achdé, "Cavalier seul (episode 1/6)," *Spirou* (September 26, 2012): 5–12, to "Cavalier seul (episode 6/6)," *Spirou* (October 31, 2012): 14–18, and *Cavalier seul*, vol. 5, *Les aventures de Lucky Luke d'après Morris* (Givrins: Lucky Comics, 2012). The latest film adaptation was released in cinemas in 2009 and on DVD in 2010; *Lucky Luke*, directed by James Huth.

48. du Chatenet and Guillot, *Goscinny*, 28, 38–39.

49. Filippini, "Les Quatre vies de Lucky Luke," 34–35.

50. Frédéric Bosser, "Uderzo: Souvent Copié Jamais Égalé," *dBD* (December/January 2009–2010): 15–17; Uderzo, *Uderzo se Raconte*, 80.

51. du Chatenet and Guillot, *Goscinny*, 31; Guy Vidal, Anne Goscinny, and Patrick Gaumer, *René Goscinny: Profession: Humoriste* (Paris: Dargaud, 2007), 15.

52. Filippini, "Les Quatre Vies de Lucky Luke," 34.

53. Damien Perez, "Bienvenido a los Gringos!" *Spirou* (November 30, 2011): 4. The first installment, *Gringos Locos* (Crazy Gringos), set in Mexico, was prepublished in *Spirou* from November 2011 to January 2012. The publication of the album was delayed until May 2012 due to objections on the part of Jijé's and Franquin's heirs. The next installment, *Crazy Belgians*, set in the United States and featuring Goscinny, has been announced as "coming soon" since January 4, 2012. See Yann and Schwartz, "Gringos Locos (episode 1/6)," *Spirou* (November 30, 2011): 5–15, to "Gringos Locos (episode 6/6)," *Spirou* (January 4, 2012): 12–15; Yann and Schwartz, *Gringos Locos* (Marcinelle, Belgium: Dupuis, 2012); "Lorg: 'Gringos Locos, C'était du Caviar et on Nous a Servi du Poisson Pané,'" *Expressbd*, January 18, 2012, http://expressbd.fr/2012/01/18/lorg-gringos-locos-c-etait-du-caviar-et-on-nous-a-servi-du-poisson-pane/ (interview with Laurent Gillain).

54. Goscinny and Uderzo, *La Grande Traversée*, 17–19.

55. Goscinny and Uderzo, *La Grande Traversée*, 21/5. Translation from René Goscinny and Albert Uderzo, *Astérix and the Great Crossing*, trans. Anthea Bell and Derek Hockridge, vol. 22 of *Astérix* (London: Hodder & Stoughton, 1976), 21/5.

56. Goscinny and Uderzo, *La Grande Traversée*, passim. "Ugh!" is the French equivalent of "How!"

57. The U.S. Navy jack consists of the section of the U.S. flag that is a blue rectangle with white stars.

58. Goscinny and Uderzo, *La Grande Traversée*, 23/6, 25/10.

59. Goscinny and Uderzo, *La Grande Traversée*, 35/6–7; Screech, "A Hero for Everyone," 84. *Libre* (free) has the same root as *liberté* (freedom, liberty) and can thus be seen as a textual reference to the Statue of Liberty here.

60. Screech, "A Hero for Everyone," 87.

61. Albert Uderzo, *Le Ciel Lui Tombe sur la Tête*, vol. 33 of *Astérix* (Paris: Albert René, 2005), 16/2. Translation from Albert Uderzo, *Astérix and the Falling Sky*, trans. Anthea Bell and Derek Hockridge, vol. 33 of *Astérix* (London: Orion Books, 2006), 16/2.

62. Uderzo, *Le Ciel Lui Tombe sur la Tête*, 20/4–5. Translation from Uderzo, *Astérix and the Falling Sky*, 20/4–5.

63. Uderzo, *Le Ciel Lui Tombe sur la Tête*, 16/4, 27, 41–43.

64. Uderzo, *Le Ciel Lui Tombe sur la Tête*, 48. Translation from Uderzo, *Astérix and the Falling Sky*, 48.

65. Uderzo, *Uderzo se Raconte*, 134.

66. René Goscinny and Albert Uderzo, *La Serpe d'Or*, vol. 2 of *Astérix* (Neuilly-sur-Seine, France: Dargaud, 1962), 7/5 and passim. Translation from René Goscinny and Albert Uderzo, *Astérix and the Golden Sickle*, trans. Anthea Bell and Derek Hockridge, vol. 2 of *Astérix* (London: Hodder & Stoughton, 1975), 7/5. The reference to the United States is lost in the English translation as the name Amérix becomes Metallurgix.

67. Uderzo, *Uderzo se Raconte*, 229, 231 (my translation). Uderzo explains that around the same time interchanges and an RER station were authorized and built free of charge for Disneyland Paris.

68. du Chatenet and Guillot, *Goscinny*, 94 (my translation).

69. "Travaux d'Héraclès" (Heracles's works) was used in 2006 in front of a work-site. It is a reference to the twelve labors of Heracles, also known as Hercules. "Défense de nourrir les Vikings" (Please don't feed the Vikings) was planted in a duck pond and refers to the Vikings, whose navigational activities are very much at the forefront in the series.

70. Ritzer, "An Introduction to McDonaldization," 14–17.

71. Palagret makes similar observations on her blog, where one can also find many of these posters. See Catherine-Alice Palagret, "Publicité comparative: avantage au parc Astérix face à Disneyland," *Archéologie du Futur / Archéologie du Quotidien*, July 23, 2011), http://archeologue.over-blog.com/article-publicite-comparative-avantage-au-parc-asterix-face-a-disneyland-80043470.html.

72. Uderzo, *Uderzo se raconte*, 229 (my translation, my emphasis).

73. Didier Pasamonik, "C'est officiel: Didier Conrad est le Prochain Dessinateur d'Astérix," *Actua BD*, October 11, 2012, http://www.actuabd.com/C-est-officiel-Didier-Conrad-est.

74. Damien Perez, "Voyage en Air de Famille," *Spirou* (April 25, 2012): 4.

75. Bryman, "Global Implications of McDonaldization and Disneyization," 320.

76. Bryman, "Global Implications of McDonaldization and Disneyization," 322.

77. Bryman, "Global Implications of McDonaldization and Disneyization," 322.

78. Bryman, "Global Implications of McDonaldization and Disneyization," 320.

79. Levard, "Publicité pour Mac Do: Astérix se défend."

80. Parker, "Nostalgia and Mass Culture," passim.

81. Parker, "Nostalgia and Mass Culture," 9–10.

82. Parker, "Nostalgia and Mass Culture," 14.

83. Bryman, "Global Implications of McDonaldization and Disneyization," 322.

# FOUR

# Image and Text in Service of the Nation

*Historically Themed Comic Books as Civic Education in 1980s Mexico*

Melanie Huska,
Oberlin College

Mention of history curriculum elicits images of dull textbooks and rote memorization for many people. To counter that image and to encourage citizens to embrace their national history, the Mexican Ministry of Public Education (Secretariat of Public Education; SEP) sponsored an intriguing and creative educational initiative in the form of two comic book series: *México: Historia de un Pueblo* and *Episodios Mexicanos*. The two series, published between 1980 and 1982, combine fact and fiction to narrate significant political events and periods in Mexican history, including the Spanish conquests, the colonial era, the Wars of Independence, and the Mexican Revolution. *México: Historia de un Pueblo*, coordinated by acclaimed Mexican writer Paco Ignacio Taibo II, launched in August 1980 with print runs of between fifty thousand and one hundred thousand. Volumes were available for purchase at supermarkets and sidewalk stands for a cost of sixty pesos.[1] *Episodios Mexicanos* first hit newsstands at the end of August 1981, this time at a considerably lower price of three pesos. Historian Guadalupe Jiménez Codinach coordinated an interdisciplinary team in the production of sixty-eight volumes of *Episodios Mexicanos*. Teachers used the comic books as didactic tools, but the texts were primarily designed as public history products that would appeal to young and old readers alike.

Mexican politicians are not alone in employing the past to justify the present; however, the currency of the past is particularly potent in Mexico because it has been marshaled to legitimize the reign of a single party—the Institutional Revolutionary Party (Partido Revolucionario Institucional)—for most of the twentieth century. Following the violent and divisive Revolution of 1910, even the revolutionary camp was left fractured. Drawing on existing triumphant narratives of the revolution as a popular movement, the nascent National Revolutionary Party, the earliest incarnation of the Institutional Revolutionary Party, crafted an official historical narrative of the revolution to unify this fractured political landscape. The subsequent development of the Institutional Revolutionary Party in 1946 further cemented the significance of history to political power and the development of Mexican identity, positioning public history projects such as the didactic comic book series as remarkably potent political tools. This chapter examines two dimensions of the political significance of the series. The first section demonstrates that the SEP's literacy campaigns—during the early and midnineteenth century and then again in the late 1970s—not only sought to teach Mexicans to read and write but were part of a broader campaign to establish a unifying national culture that could be harnessed for political stability. In this context, the SEP's recognition of a persistent literacy crisis in the late 1970s signaled a political failing as well as an educational one. A comparative analysis of *México: Historia de un Pueblo* and *Episodios Mexicanos* reveals that the two projects were quite different, even though they were produced by the same government ministry in the span of less than two years. The historical narratives of each series are more reflective of their coordinators than any government-sanctioned narrative, revealing that the state's claim to a singular official history was not viable.

## CULTIVATING CULTURAL LITERACY

The Mexican government of the 1980s was not new to the culture industry; it had embraced cultural initiatives as tools of statecraft to consolidate the fractured political and social landscape in the wake of the revolution. The SEP, created in 1921, was at the center of this project of constructing national culture, and it embraced not only formal education but also informal means: as minister of the SEP in the 1920s, José Vasconcelos commissioned the creation of a series of murals, which were instrumental in linking radical politics, peasants, workers, and the indigenous past to the postrevolutionary state in the visual imagination of the Mexican public.[2] In the 1930s, the SEP sponsored itinerant puppet troupes to perform in communities across the nation, teaching children and adults about the merits of revolutionary ideals such as work, hygiene, literacy, and cooperation.[3] The SEP further extended its social influence into Mexican homes across the country by broadcasting educational programs focused on literacy, adult learning, and Mexican culture on radio and television.[4]

One of the SEP's earliest cultural projects was its *misiones culturales*, which were launched by its founder and first director, José Vasconcelos, just two years after the SEP was founded. The initial objective of the *misiones culturales* was to bring education to the nation's rural areas. Teachers were dispatched to rural Mexico in three major literacy campaigns between 1922 and 1944. Corps of energetic, often urban, teachers spread out across the country to teach literacy as well as foment a national culture. Alongside classes on reading and writing, teachers extolled the importance of hygiene, modified traditional *corridos* to sing the praises of the revolution, and played a significant role in the organizing of patriotic and civic festivals.[5]

The tenor of the literacy campaigns shifted with the presidency of Lázaro Cárdenas (1934–1940), whose presidency has been widely considered the most radical in the postrevolutionary period, and education was no exception. When Cárdenas assumed the presidency in 1934, he altered article 3 of the Constitution of 1917 to mandate socialist education. In response, teachers shifted their rhetoric to the project of igniting class consciousness, forming unions, and mobilizing for agrarian reform, while maintaining their focus on formal and nonformal education that was highly nationalistic.[6]

Government census records suggest that the SEP campaigns were incredibly successful: starting in 1930, the literacy rate hovered around 33 percent and climbed each successive decade so that by 1970 it had reached nearly 76 percent. What these numbers obscure is the persistent lack of access to grade school and the reality of high rates of semiliteracy. By 1970, for example, less than 10 percent of the population had studied in high school or beyond.[7] Furthermore, meaningful literacy occurred more frequently by greater access to public schools, not literacy campaigns themselves. Nevertheless, the campaigns were not entirely failures. At least two significant contributions were the nationalization of popular culture and the creation of an appetite for reading. The campaigns successfully linked literacy to the revolution and to the nation, making reading a modern, revolutionary, and nationalist act.[8] Reading engaged Mexicans, not only as a functional and modern skill, but also as a dimension of cultural literacy that could open readers to a shared world of Mexican identity. The transformation of comic books into a cultural phenomenon of the masses was made possible by the scores of new readers. Many people learned to read just so that they could read comic books.[9] Given this link between literacy and comics since the 1930s, it is perhaps not surprising that the SEP would turn to comic books to confront a new literacy crisis in the late 1970s.

In 1979, Roger Díaz de Cossío, director of the SEP's Department of Culture and Recreation, reported to education minister Fernando Solana that the literacy campaigns of the 1930s and 1940s had not achieved the level of reading proficiency that had been previously championed. In 1980, there were twenty-seven million Mexicans who had not finished secondary school (of whom nine to twelve million had not attended primary school), sixteen million who were illiterate, and one million who did not speak Spanish.[10] The geographical map of literacy favored urban centers: 60.8 percent of illiterate Mexicans were rural dwellers.[11] The SEP also recognized that the problem of illiteracy was further complicated by a lack of opportunity for the literate to exercise their skills of reading and writing; as a result, literacy deteriorated, and many Mexicans fell into the category of functional illiteracy.[12]

SEP officials viewed the literacy crisis as a broader cultural deficiency linked to the dramatic shortage of books, libraries, and bookstores. Furthermore, they noted that the culture of reading books was limited to the middle and upper classes, likely due to the high cost of books, making them economically inaccessible to the majority of Mexicans.[13] In 1979, the SEP declared the promotion of reading to be one of its seven basic mandates.[14] SEP minister Fernando Solana promised that the resulting SEP initiatives would be accessible and not simply targeted to the intellectual elite. While many believed that the government ought to publish literary greats, such as the works of Virgil or Plato's *Dialogues*, they would never achieve mass success in a country accustomed to the comic book.[15] Within the SEP, the unit charged with the promotion of reading was the Department of Publications and Libraries. The department sought to correct the deficiencies of the publishing industry by undertaking new publications at affordable prices (no more than the cost of one hour of teachers' pay, forty or fifty pesos); by creating reading rooms, libraries, *tianguis culturales* (cultural markets), and efficient bookstores; and by supporting teachers and library staff.[16]

Citing the publishing industry's lack of consistent educational and quality products, the SEP effectively shifted some of the blame for illiteracy and the lack of reading habits onto publishing companies.[17] The SEP claimed that the source of the problems lie in the publishing industry's infrastructure and organization. Ironically, the SEP viewed comic books and photonovelas as a type of "subliterature" that consumed a remarkable portion of the nation's limited paper supply, thereby limiting publication of higher-quality literature. In 1978, Mexico produced five thousand new titles per year, some fifteen million books, with an estimated print run of about three thousand per title. Public reading habits fell into four broad categories: newspapers, journals, and comic books; textbooks and educational books, of which free primary school textbooks, distributed to twenty-one million schools, had the greatest circulation; bestsellers, often produced by companies dedicated to buying the rights to foreign works and then translating and disseminating them in the Mexican market; and specialty works by provincial and small publishers with small print runs, such as Fondo de Cultura Económica and Siglo XX. [18] In response, Guadalupe Jiménez Codinach, coordinator of *Episodios Mexicanos* , observed that in the face of this dismal level of reading, intellectuals had two choices: they could lament and condemn popular reading habits, or they could analyze, study, dignify, and use them as an instrument for the diffusion of positive cultural content. [19] This attitude drew a group of historians, social scientists, writers, scriptwriters, and artists together to do the difficult work of marrying history and comic books.

The most effective means of transmitting culture, according to a 1979 SEP report, was through the education system, mediums of communication (including radio, television, print press, and film), and social organizations, especially family groups.[20] By citing the utility of media, the SEP was doing as it had been for decades: borrowing popular culture formats for public education projects. If its objective was to foster reading habits among the general public, comic books were a wise choice.

## *MÉXICO: HISTORIA DE UN PUEBLO* AND *EPISODIOS MEXICANOS*: AN EDUCATION IN READING AND CIVICS

Mexico is one of the world's largest producers and consumers of comic books. According to a 1977 SEP report, thirty-six million Mexicans read comics; another SEP report estimated the value of comic books distributed in Mexico that same year to be worth three hundred million pesos.[21] They form part of the quotidian visual landscape of modern Mexico. Their audiences are not what many might expect: they are neither the sole purview of young males nor costly forms of art. They are not sold in specialty stores but rather on most street corner newsstands, where their sales frequently exceed those of newspapers and magazines. First appearing in 1934, comic books experienced a boom in the mid-1930s and have remained enormously popular ever since. As a cheap form of entertainment, they offered the advantages of a visual and textual format accessible to the nation's vast semiliterate population.

To meet these goals, the SEP drew on the staggering success of comic books throughout Mexico. Roger Díaz de Cossío, director of the Department of Culture and Recreation, contracted noted comic-book scholar Irene Herner to coordinate the newly inaugurated *Historietas, Folletos y Fotonovelas* (Comic Books, Flyers, and Photonovelas).[22] Herner's subsequent report argued that the market was already saturated with commercial comic books, so she proposed that the SEP approach commercial comic books, such as *Lagrimas y Risas*, by adding an informative insert. This strategy was also more cost-effective: Herner estimated that the project would cost four million pesos.[23] Ultimately, the SEP did not abide

Herner's advice. Instead, Roger Barros Valero, de Cossio's successor as director of the Department of Culture and Recreation, turned to Paco Ignacio Taibo II to coordinate a new SEP series of comics that would examine national identity.[24]

Letters and reports from bureaucrats in the SEP's Department of Culture and Recreation and Department of Publications and Libraries reflect concern that the SEP's image would be sullied by the unsavory reputation of comic books. Department director Gabriel Larrea Richerand mandated that the program maintain a strict concern for the image of the SEP. In the pages of *El Nacional*, professor Victor Hugo Bolaños Martínez wrote to express his belief that comic books held no cultural value, while another scholar called them tools and products of bourgeois ideology and imperialism.[25] Ultimately, the SEP reasoned that its treatment of weighty concerns, such as national identity, would elevate the medium and prevent criticism. [26]

A 1981 proposed budget for the Department of Publications and Libraries allotted *Historietas, Folletos y Fotonovelas* 256 million pesos, a figure greater than all other budget items combined.[27] The production cost of a commercial comic book from roughly the same period was an average of 3.2 pesos, with fluctuations due to varying printing costs.[28] Before it produced the historical series, the SEP experimented with other didactic comic books targeted at different audiences, such as *SNIF* and *Novelas Mexicanas Ilustradas*: the former was targeted at a select group of readers familiar with high-quality international comic books; *Novelas Mexicanas Ilustradas* sought a broader public audience with comic-book remakes of literary classics, such as *El Periquillo Sarniento* (The Mangy Parrot), *Clemencia* (Clemency), *Los de Abajo* (The Underdogs), and *Santa*.[29] According to Jiménez Codinach, the quality of the editions varied. For example, *El Periquillo Sarniento* and *Los de Abajo* were very well done, while others did not lend themselves to translation into comic book form.[30] *México: Historia de un Pueblo* and *Episodios Mexicanos* were the SEP's first attempts to teach history through comic books. This type of project was not a new idea, however; it had been carried out with varied success in France, Italy, Canada, and Spain. [31]

True to the *Historietas, Folletos y Fotonovelas*'s mandate, both resulting comic book series emphasized pride in a glorious shared Mexican heritage. In 1980 *México: Historia de un Pueblo* was the first of the two series to be published, and just a year later it had penetrated the market.[32] The series' primary aim was to "permit reading that [was] accessible, instructive, mild and capable of defining a national identity among children, young people and new readers of the country."[33] The SEP sought the expertise of public intellectuals—albeit in different fields—to coordinate each series.

## THE STATE, INTELLECTUALS, AND THE CHALLENGES TO
## OFFICIAL HISTORY

Since the revolution, many Mexican intellectuals have taken up the task of shaping the historical narrative and reconsidering it in the context of the changing arena of popular politics, and the SEP was a major employer in this endeavor.[34] Politicians likewise benefited from this arrangement, which provided a measure of legitimacy to their policies, particularly after the 1968 massacre of student protesters at Tlatelolco. The administrations of both Luis Echeverría Álvarez and José López Portillo—the governments in power preceding and during the creation of the comic series—faced a nation disillusioned by the violence of the student massacre. To regain the favor of the academic community, these presidents aimed to incorporate intellectuals and increase their access to resources. Lopez Portillo, in particular, was acutely aware of the political power of the left, which included many intellectuals.

For their part, intellectuals working with the government were often financially and politically motivated. The following comment by Mexican cartoonist Abel Quezada offers a telling reflection of the economic realities faced by scholars: "in Mexico, there are very few means for an intellectual to make a living. It is almost impossible to survive on the basis of his [sic] own intellectual work, since books sell so little. It is a physical necessity to choose public office because it the shortest and easiest route to live."[35] For others, work with the government offered the opportunity to shape public policy and fulfill the political and public responsibilities expected of intellectuals. This political duty of Mexican scholars was echoed by one of Mexico's most prominent literary figures and intellectuals, Octavio Paz. He definitively stated, "In Mexico, the intellectual's mission is political action," and he later claimed the intellectual as "the critical conscience of its people."[36]

Certainly, state employment is not simply an innocuous and apolitical arrangement between the government and intellectuals. Reflecting on this relationship in the context of *Episodios Mexicanos*, Cornelia Butler Flores argues that "the cooptive mechanisms of the Mexican state are such that critical intellectuals can be hired to convert their criticism into projects within the comfortable state-private enterprise nexus that is modern Mexico."[37] However, the state's hegemony is certainly not absolute. While the government grants a seal of approval to literary and cultural production, writers and artists (and presumably intellectuals) are not uniformly official spokespeople of government culture.[38] Indeed, the two series reflect the aspirations and objectives of their coordinators more than they reflect a SEP-sanctioned official historical narrative.

The coordinator of the first series, Paco Ignacio Taibo II, aptly fits Paz's characterization of intellectuals as advocating for political change. Taibo is widely recognized as a prominent political activist. Many of his

literary projects reflect his commitment to political activism: a biography
of Ché Guevara, a twenty-year retrospective of the union movement, a
narrative history of the Bolshevik movement in Mexico in the early 1920s,
a novel coauthored with renowned leader of the Zapatista Army of National Liberation (Subcomandante Marcos), a novel about the student
massacre in 1968, and many other works that feature revolutionaries and
anarchists. His best-known fictional character is Héctor Belascoarán, an
incorruptible "pulp detective noir" with an eye patch. Even a cursory
glance at the bibliography of Taibo's more than fifty works reveals his
political commitment and suggests that he believed that fiction offered a
means to mobilize class consciousness. Still, Taibo's audience was largely
the literate and educated classes, and for him, comic books offered a
means of expanding his readership by communicating with the masses of
illiterate and semiliterate Mexicans who preferred comic book readers to
scholarship or even pulp fiction. It is ironic, then, that the series he produced was significantly less accessible—in cost and physical format—
than its subsequent counterpart.[39]

A 2004 comment about the political saliency of history suggests that
Taibo was more committed to the comic book form, including its practi-
tioners—scriptwriters and illustrators—and its pedagogical potential for
consciousness raising: "A people without history is easier to control . . .
for this reason, we must tell histories. But also to tell history, and I am
convinced more and more of sentimental education than of formal education."[40] This focus, instead of the historical narrative, provoked criticism.

A number of notable Mexican historians, including Sergio Carrillo
and Jaime Labastida, denounced *México: Historia de un Pueblo* for its depiction of the nation's history. One of the most outspoken of these critics
was Guadalupe Jiménez Codinach, who ultimately became the coordinator of the subsequent series, *Episodios Mexicanos*. She argued that *México:
Historia de un Pueblo* offered readers a questionable form of "psuedohisto-
ry."[41] On December 17, 1980, the SEP's Department of Publications and
Libraries formed a publishing committee comprising the director and
subdirectors of the department and four other people, including Guadalupe Jiménez Codinach, to oversee the creative process of the new series.
As coordinator, Jiménez Codinach assembled an interdisciplinary team
of collaborators, including a historical advisory committee, three area
coordinators to facilitate the work of historians with specializations in
each area, as well as consultants on social psychology, cultural anthropol-
ogy, communications and popular vernaculars, and comic-book technique and graphics.

Stemming directly from their critique of *México: Historia de un Pueblo*,
which suggested a singular "pueblo mexicano" or a national culture, the
team chose to emphasize the many Mexicos, or the diversity of traditions
and cultures. Furthermore, a comprehensive history of Mexico was simply not possible given the parameters of the genre and the project. In-

stead, the team chose an episodic emphasis, reflected in the series' title, which would stress interesting and significant moments in the history of the nation. It also identified a series of objectives that would guide the project: to reflect the contemporary debates within the discipline of history; to expand the cultural landscape of readers; to demythify history, which had been rewritten to serve political means for decades; to promote national values, instead of translating foreign mentalities and traditions to Mexican culture, getting the readers to identify with their origins; to humanize history—to present protagonists (real and fictitious) as human beings, with doubts, with successes and failures, with weaknesses and strengths. By placing such figures within their historical contexts, the goal was to challenge the notion that they were simply destined to greatness.[42] The team sought to meet these goals while offering an accessible product.

The first two issues of *Episodios Mexicanos* hit newsstands at the end of August 1981. The second issue was offered free with purchase of the first, for three pesos, which was comparable to the cost of a commercial comic book at that time. The price increased to seven pesos starting with issue 46, in part as a response to protests from newsstand vendors who argued that the three-peso price tag left them with little profit. To put this into economic context, during the month of November 1981 (the approximate time of this price increase), the Mexican peso was valued at an average of 25.75 pesos to the American dollar.[43]

Tensions between the collaborators on both series eventually curtailed *Episodios Mexicanos* prematurely. In the end, *Episodios Mexicanos* published sixty-eight volumes, concluding with the signing of the Constitution of 1917. Originally, the series was intended to have eighty issues, ending with the oil expropriation in 1938, but the scriptwriters who were in charge of the postrevolutionary period gave Jiménez Codinach scripts that she refused to publish. For example, historian Lorenzo Mejebo wrote a summary of the oil expropriation of 1938, but after ten weeks of work, the scriptwriters returned with a tale called "The Red Knight of Tampico." It was situated in a brothel and featured the nightlife of Tampico, as well as a complicated plot starring a journalist who rented a room in a shack that housed the archives of the Shell Company. To compound this, according to Jiménez Codinach, Taibo threatened the artists and scriptwriters that if they did not boycott *Episodios Mexicanos*, they would never work again. When the news was leaked to one of Jiménez Codinach's assistants, she contacted Javier Barros, and together they resolved the problem by announcing that the project had run out of funding. The SEP paid the artists, but they preferred not to publish anymore.

The differences between the professional historian Jimenez Codinach and the leftist activist Taibo were clearly reflected in the historical narratives presented on the pages of the two series. An analysis of their representations of the Spanish conquest illustrates that while both stories anchor their historical narratives in love stories, they treat the Spanish and indigenous Mexicans in distinctly different ways. In *México: Historia de un Pueblo*, readers are privy to the romance between Mexicas Moyana and Mazatzin and their relationship with Moyana's grandmother.[44] These characters offer readers an intimate view of the events of the conquest. The couple is pictured planning their wedding, getting married, having a son, and conversing with each other. The death of these two lovers at the hands of the Spanish emphasizes the destruction and injustice inflicted by the Spanish. The grandmother is left to care for the couple's young son when they die, and looking over the destruction of the Mexica's land and lives, she tells him, "Your inheritance is a network full of holes."[45] The grandmother subsequently dies of sadness, and the tale closes with missionaries carrying off the young boy. Responsibility for this tragedy of an inheritance "full of holes" is understood to lie squarely at the feet of the Spanish, thereby positioning the Spanish as villains.

*Episodios Mexicanos* also employs a romantic plotline as a device to evoke empathy, but this series invites readers to relate to the viewpoint of the Spanish. Throughout *Episodios*, readers follow the progression of a relationship between Nuño de Herrera, a member of Cortés' mission, and Citlalli, a Ocuiteca woman who is gifted to Cortés by the Mexicas and then in turn gifted to Nuño. The relationship spans their initial encounter, brief conversations, and having a child together. Nuño appears quite jubilant about the new arrival: he names him Diego, after his own father back in Spain, and tells Diego that he will grow up to be a brave man.[46] The narrative is unclear about Citlalli's feelings for Nuño. When a Mexican soldier castigates her for bearing a child with a Spanish man—"the enemies of our gods"—Citlalli pointedly responds that at least the Spanish do not intend to sacrifice her.[47] Following this pragmatic retort, she immediately runs off to reunite with the Spanish. Nuño's friendship with fellow soldier Francisco also humanizes the Spanish. They discuss their fears about pressing forward toward Tenochtitlán, and Francisco confides that he is from a *campesino* family and that he cannot bear returning to Spain to work the land, still with nothing to eat.[48] These scenes counter images of conquistadors as simply gold thirsty. In *Episodios Mexicanos*, Nuño plays a more central role in the plot than Cortés himself. This may have been a conscious attempt by the writers to elicit empathy for the Spanish, as such compassion was unlikely to be evoked through the character of Cortés.

According to Butler Flores, the state is the most significant sponsor of noncommercial alternative comics and photo novellas. In the case of twentieth-century Mexico, political parties have been a source of significant sponsorship.[49] Comic books continue to be used for didactic and political means. In December 2004, the Ministry of Foreign Relations (Secretaría de Relaciones Exteriores) released *Guía del Migrante Mexicano*, which employed text and simple colorful images in single panels to convey the dangers and appropriate responses of migrants crossing the Rio Grande. Though the ministry claimed that the guide was not intended to encourage illegal behavior, it provoked outrage in the United States. In their political campaigns, conservative leader Vicente Fox and left-of-center Mexico City mayor Andrés Manuel López Obrador turned to comic books as a means of communicating with the popular classes of voters.[50] Given the enormous and historic popularity of comic books in Mexico, it stands to reason that the SEP embraced the medium to teach Mexican history and foment nationalism; it is more surprising that it did not do so sooner.

## NOTES

1. Paul J. Vanderwood, *The Power of God against the Guns of Government: Religious Upheaval in Mexico at the Turn of the Nineteenth Century* (Stanford, CA: Stanford University Press, 1998), 320. Sales in supermarkets were noted by Guadalupe Jiménez Codinach in an interview, Mexico City, Mexico, July 20, 2005.

2. See, for example, Desmond Rochfort, *Mexican Muralists: Orozco, Rivera, Siqueiros* (San Francisco: Chronicle Books, 1993); Desmond Rochfort, "The Sickle, the Serpent, and the Soil: History, Revolution, Nationhood, and Modernity in the Murals of Diego Rivera, José Clemente Orozco, and David Alfaro Siqueiros," in *The Eagle and the Virgin: Nation and Cultural Revolution in Mexico, 1920–1940*, ed. Mary Kay Vaughan and Stephen E. Lewis (Durham, NC: Duke University Press, 2006), 43–57.

3. For more information, see E. J. Albarrán, "Comino Vence al Diablo and Other Terrifying Episodes: Teatro Guiñol's Itinerant Puppet Theater in 1930s Mexico," *The Americas* 67, no. 3 (2011): 355–74.

4. Joy Elizabeth Hayes, "National Imaginings on the Air: Radio in Mexico, 1920–1950," in *The Eagle and the Virgin: Nation and Cultural Revolution in Mexico, 1920–1940*, ed. Mary Kay Vaughan and Stephen E. Lewis (Durham, NC: Duke University Press, 2006), 249; Joy Elizabeth Hayes, *Radio Nation: Communication, Popular Culture, and Nationalism in Mexico,1920–1950* (Tucson: University of Arizona Press, 2000).

5. Mary K. Vaughan, *Cultural Politics in Revolution: Teachers, Peasants, and Schools in Mexico, 1930–1940* (Tucson: University of Arizona Press, 1997), 5.

6. Vaughan, *Cultural Politics in Revolution*; Engracia Loyo, "Popular Reactions to the Educational Reforms of Cardenismo," in *Rituals of Rule, Rituals of Resistance: Public Celebrations and Popular Culture in Mexico*, ed. William H. Beezley, Cheryl English Martin, and William E. French (Wilmington, DE: Scholarly Resources, 1994), 247–60.

7. Anne Rubenstein, *Bad Language, Naked Ladies, and Other Threats to the Nation: A Political History of Comic Books in Mexico* (Durham, NC: Duke University Press, 1998), 15.

8. Rubenstein, *Bad Language*, 15.

9. Armando Bartra, "The Seduction of the Innocents: The First Tumultuous Moments of Mass Literacy in Postrevolutionary Mexico," in *Everyday Forms of State Formation: Revolution and the Negotiation of Rule in Modern Mexico*, ed. Gilbert Michael Joseph and Daniel Nugent (Durham, NC: Duke University Press, 1994), 301–2.

10. In 1979, Roger Díaz de Cossío reported to education minister Fernando Solana that the literacy campaigns of the 1930s and 1940s had not achieved the level of reading proficiency that had been previously championed. Secretaria de Educación Publica, Departamento de Archivo Histórico y Reprografía (hereafter, SEP DAHR), 9213/8 UNESCO report—interview with Roger Díaz de Cossío, 4.

11. In 1978 and 1980, the average number of illiterate Mexicans aged fifteen and older was 25.8 million. The number of rural-dwelling illiterate Mexicans was 60.8

percent of 25.8 million Mexicans. J. Wilkie et al., eds., *Statistical Abstract of Latin America*, 38 vols. (Los Angeles: UCLA Latin American Center Publications, 1962–2002), 19:118, 20:122.

12. SEP DAHR, Subsecretaria de Cultura y Recreación, Director General de Publicaciónes y Bibliotecas, Mexico City, file 9190/26, report sent May 17, 1979, from Max Molina Fuente to Francisco Serrano, "Marco de Referencia: El Concepto de Educación Permanente," 1; SEP DAHR, Subsecretaria de Cultura y Recreación, Director General de Publicaciónes y Bibliotecas, Mexico City, file 9211/1, letter from Javier Barros to Miguel Limon, November 16, 1979, 5.

13. SEP DAHR, "Marco de Referencia," and letter from Javier Barros to Miguel Limon.

14. Other objectives included the protection and preservation of cultural heritage; the promotion of educational, artistic, anthropological, and historical research; cultural activities and recreation; physical education; and the development of sports. SEP DAHR, Subsecretaria de Cultura y Recreación, Director General de Publicaciónes y Bibliotecas, Mexico City, file 9213/18, Publicaciónes y Bibliotecas, 1979–1980, 2.

15. "Mejor Reparto de los Bienes Culturales," *El Informador* (Guanajuato), June 20, 1980, 3A.

16. SEP DAHR, Director General de Publicaciónes y Bibliotecas, file 9213/8, "Presupuesto, Programas y Metas 1978–1982," August 1978.

17. SEP DAHR, Subsecretaria de Cultura y Recreación, file 9211/1, Serie: Sría Particular 1979, 15.

18. Estela Guadalupe Jiménez Codinach, "Historia e Historieta Episodios Mexicanos," in *Los Intelectuales y el Poder en México: Memorias de la VI Conferencia de Historiadores Mexicanos y Estadounidenses. Intellectuals and Power in Mexico: Papers Presented at the VI Conference of Mexican and Unites States Historians*, ed. Roderic Ai Camp, Charles A. Hale, and Josefina Zoraida Vásquez (Mexico City, Mexico: El Colegio de Mexico; Los Angeles: UCLA Latín American Center, 1981): 783–84.

19. Codinach, "Historia e Historieta," 784.

20. SEP DAHR, Subsecretaria de Cultura y Recreación, file 9211/1, 5.

21. SEP DAHR, Subsecretaria de Cultura y Recreación, file 9211/1, 17; SEP DAHR, file 9213/18, letter and report from Patricia Van Rhijn to Roger Diaz de Cossío, August 30, 1979, 9, diagram 5.

22. *Historietas, Folletos y Fotonovelas* (Comic Books, Brochures and Photonovelas). Photonovelas are essentially comic books that use photos instead of drawings. Text balloons are either drawn by hand or typed. For an overview of the history of comic books in Mexico, see Irene Herner de Larrea, *Mitos y Monitos: Historietas y Fotonovelas en Mexico* (Mexico City, Mexico: Editorial Nueva Imagen, 1979), and Harold E. Hinds and Charles M. Tatum, *Not Just for Children: The Mexican Comic Book in the Late 1960s and 1970s* (Santa Barbara, CA: Greenwood Press, 1992).

23. Irene Herner, interview, Mexico City, Mexico, November 19, 2009.

24. SEP DAHR, Subsecretaría de Cultura y Recreación, file 9213/12, letter to Roger Cossío, Subsecretario de Cultura y Recreación de la SEP from Lic. Gabriel Larrea Richerand, Director de Publicaciónes de la SEP, 1979, 13–14.

25. "Poder de Penetración Desaprovechado," *El Nacional*, August 1, 1984, 1.

26. SEP DAHR, Subsecretaría de Cultura y Recreación, file 9213/12, letter to Roger Cossío, 14.

27. SEP DAHR, 9207/4. "Anteproyecto de Presupuesto," 1981, 2.

28. Herner de Larrea, *Mitos y Monitos*, 94.

29. For more information on *Novelas Mexicanas Ilustradas*, see Jacqueline Covo-Maurice, "Lecturas para el pueblo: Novelas mexicanas ilustradas," in *Prensa, Impresos, Lectura en el Mundo Hispánico Contemporáneo: Homenaje à Jean-François Botrel*, ed. Jean-Michel Desvois (Pessac Cedex, France: PILAR, 2005), 239–49.

30. Guadalupe Jiménez Codinach, "Historia e Historieta Episodios Mexicanos," 785.

31. Guadalupe Jiménez Codinach, "Historia e Historieta Episodios Mexicanos," 786.

32. SEP DAHR, 9229/8, Anteproyecto de Presupuesto por Programas: Producción Editorial Dirección General de Publicaciones y Bibliotecas: Para Proyectos que no son de Atención a la Demanda Educativa, 1981, 3.

33. Miriam Martínez Maza, Jorge Tlatelpa Meléndez, and David Zamora Díaz, *Las Historietas en las Colecciones de las Bibliotecas Publicas Mexicanas* (Mexico City, Mexico: Colegio Nacional de Bibliotecarios y Universidad Autónoma de Baja California Sur, 1993), 105.

34. Maza et al., *Las Historietas*, 151–53. A chart illustrating the public and academic career levels of members of the National College from 1943 to 1976 lists none of the historians, artists, scriptwriters, or coordinators of *México: Historia de un Pueblo* or *Episodios Mexicanos*; however, it does suggest that members, if engaged in a public career, are frequently employed by the SEP.

35. Maza et al., *Las Historietas*, 213.

36. Maza et al., *Las Historietas*, 65.

37. Cornelia Butler Flora, "Roasting Donald Duck: Alternative Comics and Photonovels in Latin America," *Journal of Popular Culture* 18, no. 1 (1984): 170.

38. Roderic Ai Camp, *Intellectuals and the State in Twentieth-Century Mexico* (Austin: University of Texas Press, 1986), 213.

39. The volumes in *México: Historia de un Pueblo* reflect visibly higher production costs. The first two volumes of the series were produced for the high cost of 9.5 million pesos. While it measures almost the same dimensions as *Episodios*, *México: Historia de un Pueblo* volumes are thirty pages longer, printed on thicker and better-quality paper, feature multicolored covers and interiors, and include extras, such as an initial title page, a summary of the historical topic, a glossary, a bibliography, and a multicolored portrait of typical Mexican dress and styles from different eras on each back cover. Volumes vary in their use of color; some employ only muted or vibrant colors; others mix bright and muted palates. The more accessible price of *Episodios* is evident in its aesthetic differences: it has fewer pages, and the covers are in color, although the newsprint interiors are monochromatic and simply staple bound. The divergent physical construction and price tags of the two series potentially attracted different readers and/or influenced how those readers interacted with each comic book. Though longer than other comics of the period, *Episodios* is thin enough to be quite portable. It could be folded into a rear pants pocket, and its simple staple binding could withstand the wear and tear of multiple loans (readers). *México: Historia de un Pueblo*, in contrast, with its better-quality paper and more complicated glued binding, was less flexible, perhaps encouraging readers to treat its volumes more as collectibles than everyday reading.

40. David Brooks and Jim Cason, "Reconstruir el imaginario colectivo, meta constante: Paco Ignacio Taibo," *La Jornada*, November 14, 2004, Mexico City, http://www.jornada.unam.mx/2004/11/14/044f2con.php?origen=.

41. Estela Guadalupe Jiménez Codinach, interview, digital recording, Mexico City, Mexico, July 20, 2005.

42. Guadalupe Jiménez Codinach, "Historia e Historieta Episodios Mexicanos," 788.

43. This average is taken from the foreign exchange figures from the *New York Times* for three dates, which roughly correspond to the release dates of issues 45 to 47: November 17, 24, and 30; *New York Times*, November 18, 1981, 16D; *New York Times*, November 25, 1981, 11D; *New York Times*, December 1, 1981, 18D. The cost of *Káliman*, Mexico's most popular comic book, for example, was two pesos, albeit in 1977 (*Káliman*, February 18, 1977); Cornelia Butler Flora, "Roasting Donald Duck: Alternative Comics and Photonovels in Latin America," *Journal of Popular Culture* 18, no. 1 (1984): 170; Herner in "La Cultura de la Imagen," Parte III, *Gaceta UNAM*, 12.

44. Secretaría de Educación Publica, "El sol vencido: La batalla por México-Tenochtitlan," in *México: Historia de un Pueblo*, vol. 3 of 20 vols. (Mexico City, Mexico: Editorial Nueva Imagen and Consejo Nacional de Fomento Educativo, 1980).

45. Secretaría de Educación Publica, "El sol vencido," 78.

46. Secretaría de Educación Pública, "El Encuentro," in *Episodios Mexicanos*, vol. 6 (Mexico City, Mexico: Consejo Nacional de Fomento Educativo, 1981), 41.

47. Secretaría de Educación Pública, "El Encuentro," 46.

48. Secretaría de Educación Pública, "El Encuentro," 2.

49. Anne Rubenstein, personal communication, July 2005.

50. For further information on the comic books discussed in this paragraph, see Bruce Campbell, *¡Viva la historieta!: Mexican Comics, NAFTA, and the Politics of Globalization* (Jackson: University Press of Mississippi, 2009).

# FIVE

## Who Is Diana Prince?

*The Amazon Army Nurse of World War II*

Peter W. Lee,
Drew University

Dr. William Moulton Marston's Wonder Woman is unique among early comic book superheroes. Unlike her golden age contemporaries Superman and Batman, Marston designed Wonder Woman with a higher purpose than to elicit sales; he wanted to use the Amazon princess to usher in social change—specifically, what Marston considered female empowerment in a war-torn "man's world." Over the years, Marston's ambitions have invited criticism and commentary concerning both himself and his creation. In the 1950s, Dr. Fredric Wertham called Wonder Woman "a horror type [who is] physically very powerful, tortures men, has her own female following, is the cruel 'phallic' woman. While she is a frightening figure for boys [and is also] the exact opposite of what girls are supposed to want to be."[1] After implicating the homosexuality of Wonder Woman's sidekicks—the "'Holliday girls,' i.e. the holiday girls, the gay party girls, the gay girls"—Wertham concludes that the Amazon princess "was concocted on a sales formula," and should her "cardboard figure" come to life, "every normal-minded young man would know there is something wrong with her."[2]

Wonder Woman continues to elude a specific definition in recent scholarship, as historians, academics, and feminists debate her contributions to twentieth-century ideals of feminism, sexism, and patriotism.[3] Gloria Steinem gives the most laudatory appraisal of Wonder Woman, labeling her a prototype who injected "into the mainstream: strength and self-reliance for women; sister-hood and mutual support among women; peacefulness and esteem for human life."[4]

Despite Wonder Woman's standing as a cultural icon, few have given her alter ego, Diana Prince, a second glance. Steinem asks, "When she chose an earthly disguise, why did Wonder Woman have to pick such a loser? How could she bear to be like Diana Prince? Did that mean that all women really had to disguise their true selves in weak feminine stereotype in order to disguise?" Steinem dismisses Prince as "a clear steal to Superman's Clark Kent."[5] In 2004, scholar Lillian Robinson adds that, as a youngster, she skipped the panels featuring Prince, in fear of seeing her wake up and "announce that Wonder Woman was only a dream after all."[6] Another critic diagnoses Prince as a "fractured sense of self and the duplicitous social practices necessary to negotiate the maintenance of submissive femininity while participating in the public sphere of wartime society."[7] Prince herself notes that she "certainly [gets] the worst of the deal, every time!" She continues that her love interest, Steve Trevor, "is so busy talking about this 'beautiful angel' *Wonder Woman* that he pays no attention to me whatsoever! I am wondering if I am getting jealous of my other self."[8] Even Marston frankly acknowledges, "Poor Diana doesn't rate when Steve's thinking about *Wonder Woman*."[9] Prince is intolerable to feminists, unimportant to plot, and entirely unreal.

Nevertheless, Diana Prince is relevant in understanding the American woman's wartime experience. During the Second World War, women were undergoing a shift in American society, reflected in the country's cultural venues. In her study of popular magazines, historian Maureen Honey observes that formula fiction in *The Saturday Evening Post* and *True Story* contained "rich sources of information about its readers' most deeply held values, wishes, and fears, for it expresses their innermost dream in a satisfying way."[10] Honey hones in on the War Advertising Council, a group of advertising magnates who mixed patriotism with profit as they drove "to get the issues of the war before the public" through print, radio, and motion pictures.[11] Publishers urged their writers "to make war work look attractive to female readers" by centering on women performing men's work at the front lines or in factories.[12]

Similarly, along the cinematic front, film historian Thomas Doherty notes that since women were the "prime movers" for theaters, studios quickly incorporated the wartime atmosphere, creating a kaleidoscope of cinematic subgenres.[13] Doherty argues that movies sent mixed messages concerning female empowerment. Nevertheless, movies such as *So Proudly We Hail* (1943) were approval by the Army Nursing Corps, the Red Cross, and the War Department as tributes "to female Marines that sets out with suffragette fervor to raise the consciousness of a blowhard male chauvinist"—sentiment similar to Marston's.[14]

While the war allowed women greater freedom, they were still expected to fulfill their domestic duties to shore up the home front. Honey notes that women in *The Saturday Evening Post* who focused on wartime careers were portrayed as "selfish, exploitive neurotics who callously neglected her home for fame and wealth"[15] Historian Nancy Walker agrees that magazine advertising readily promoted women as being homemakers and consumers rather than joining Rosie the Riveter in the workforce.[16] Despite lauding female strength, Marston, too, crafted Prince's coworkers as characters with poor track records. A list of Prince's peers include the following:

*Lila Brown:* Trevor's secretary who harasses Prince at the workplace. After refusing to heed Prince's warning, Brown snatches a sabotaged pen and is blown up. Prince's epithet: "Poor girl, she will never live to disobey my orders again!"[17]

*Eve Brown:* Lila's sister and an "office errand girl" for G2 who is consistently and not inaccurately accused of treason.[18] Brown later enrolls in Holliday College, but her education is constantly blocked by subversive activity.[19]

*Nerva:* Trevor's secretary for one issue. Prince learns that Nerva is a member of the "Third World War Promoters," whose goal is to "set nation against nation in the worst war of all time!"[20]

*Marva Psycho:* a villain's ex-wife who joins the Women's Auxiliary Army Corps (WAAC) as penance and is later promoted to sergeant, but she remains susceptible to her ex-husband's sinister suggestions.

*Three unnamed female agents and Malone:* Prince mistakenly accuses the former of trying to steal Pentagon papers, while the latter is a "G-Girl" whom Prince mistakenly suspects of treason. Wonder Woman later reminds herself not to prejudge women, but the Amazon princess solves Malone's case anyway.[21]

*Elva Dove:* an officer who moonlights as an industrial spy, where she sabotages the government's attempts to procure rubber.[22]

*Olga:* a translator at Army Intelligence but a slave for a spy ring; Carla Swanson is another brainwashed G2 operative.[23]

*Clarice Mystik:* a G2 agent who smuggles Amazonian jewels for the all-female "Villainy, Inc."[24]

*Sally Lee:* a clerk at Army Intelligence who is introduced as an invalid in her army quarters and later sent home to rest.[25]

*Agnes:* the "chief information clerk" at G2. Prince consults Agnes about a mysterious "Beauty Club," and Agnes replies that many army wives go there, but she does not know that the salon is a front for subversive activities.[26]

*Enid Harper:* her obituary states that the "pretty" operative was "brutally murdered."[27]

*Draska Nishki:* director of the "International Spies, Inc." who "borrowed" the "U.S. secret weapon plans" from G2 but never returned them. Nishki later attacks the Amazons' Paradise Island.[28]

Marston was unable to break Prince away from the traditional depictions of womanhood. Wonder Woman's emotions were on full display in her origin issue. After finding a wounded American army officer, Steve Trevor, unconscious on Paradise Island, Princess Diana escorts Trevor home and falls in love with the unconscious solider along the way. Donning the tiara of Wonder Woman, Diana seeks entry into Trevor's hospital to be near him. There, Wonder Woman encounters a distraught nurse, Diana Prince, who longs to join her fiancée in South America, but "he can't send for me because his salary is too small at the moment!" Wonder Woman offers to purchase Prince's identity, explaining, "By taking your place, I can see the man I love and you can marry the man you love!" Prince accepts, and, giving up her name, adds, "You'd better remember that last name, because it'll be yours from now on!"[29] Now as Diana Prince, Wonder Woman assumes the role of nurturer and mother figure, reinforcing her innate womanhood.

Two issues later, Trevor returns to his post in Army Intelligence, and Prince accompanies him to become the secretary to Trevor's commanding officer, Colonel Philip Darnell. Prince was devoted to G2, yet Marston continues to entrench Prince as a woman at heart as she catches Darnell's eye (when Trevor cozies up to Wonder Woman, Darnell sighs, "I wish *Diana Prince* would look at *me* that way!").[30] In addition, Marston continued to stress Prince's role as a caretaker, though no longer an active nurse, as she forms bonds with children. Prince acts as a surrogate mother as she befriends downtrodden children; spins school yard bullies toward new perspectives; sleds with a boy, then gives him money when the sled is destroyed; feeds two starving waifs and rescues their lost brother; helps a youngster rediscover the meaning of Christmas, despite Trevor's warning, "That kid lives in a bad neighborhood, Di—don't you go down there and play Santa Claus!"; and tackles milk prices by appealing the laws of supply and demand to a higher authority: "You've got to stop milk-starving our American children!"[31] At one point, a pair of malicious midgets takes advantage of Prince: pretending to be orphans, they ransack her home.[32] Historians note that the medium provided a sense of empowerment to children; they, too, could identify with the four-colored superheroics in a black-and-white world of the Great Depression and war.[33]

Prince remains devoted to war work and did not reciprocate Darnell's romantic overtures. Nevertheless, Prince conceals a secondary guise, assuming American gender roles while subverting them. With a rank as a second lieutenant, Prince is automatically a patriotic figure. Marston also implied that Prince has an inner strength simmering under her demure appearance. As early as *Sensation Comics #2*, one Gestapo agent declares, "She's no nurse! She's a Jack Dempsey!"[34] The Americanized agitators recognize Prince as far more than a nurse: "She's a Houdini!" and "You're telling me! She's got a right like Joe Lewis!"[35] In *Sensation Comics #31*, society matron "Selfa Modern" hosts a luncheon in Prince's honor, publicly dubbing her "America's no. 1 woman secret agent!" Prince rejects Modern as "another society-climber," but many shared Modern's sentiments.[36] Students at Holliday College dub Prince the "Famous G2 Girl" who "always brings us luck!"[37] In *Sensation Comics #60*, Prince is hailed as "the famous woman of [the] Army Intelligence Service"; in *Sensation Comics #74*, Prince is a "lie detector expert" and has completed a "detail study of counterfeit money."[38] Prince's success underscored an untapped female empowerment during the war effort.

Nevertheless, despite Marston's claims of female superiority, his beliefs never entirely translate to the printed page. In two stories, Marston addresses the wartime attitudes toward women, and both works presented mixed messages concerning women's roles. Marston hints that women should break the bonds of domesticity, often literally depicted as chains in his comics, but he never completely liberates his female characters from social norms. The first story addresses women in the armed forces, and the second examines the role of women at the home front.

## "A WOMAN SHOT ME": FRONTLINE COMBAT

"It seemed unlikely that any brave, loyal, American girl enlisted in the WAACs would shoot a general," Marston begins in *Sensation Comics #21*, "yet the general was shot before Diana's very eyes!" The general in question is "General Standpat," the chief of staff, who suspects sabotage at nearby "Camp Doe," a training camp for "those WAACs—*women soldiers*—bah!" The general's clear attitude toward willing and able women is confirmed when Trevor asks to bring along Lieutenant Prince. "Yes, bring 50 assistants if you like," Standpat shouts. When Trevor introduces a saluting Prince, the general reciprocates with, "'Lieutenant' Prince—you deceived me, Major! I certainly didn't think you were bringing a *woman lieutenant!*"[39]

Trevor protests that "Miss Prince happens to be an expert at detecting sabotage," but Standpat silences him and directs Trevor to bring along his "petticoat staff—but not in *my* car! You and *Lieutenant* Prince will ride with my baggage in the car behind!" During the bumpy ride, Trevor apologizes, but Prince waves it. Upon entering Camp Doe, a shot rings out, and the general gasps, "Ugh! I'm shot—a woman—shot me!" Prince, "forgetting her feminine role," leaps and catches the fallen officer, much to Trevor's astonishment.[40] After Prince feebly explains her feat, Camp Commander Scott deduces that the would-be assassin is "some hysterical

WAAC in Training Company A. . . . I'll place the entire company under arrest!" Prince frisks the company and encounters Marva Psycho, the ex-wife of a villainous psychiatrist turned psychotic and becomes the primary suspect.

After some plot twists that sends Trevor and Prince out of the picture, Wonder Woman and Psycho apprehend the culprit in the end: a Nazi who masqueraded as Scott and shot Standpat because the general "knew the *real* General Scott [a rank change] too well—you kidnapped Scott on his way to take command of this camp and *you* took his place!"[41] The unnamed Nazi attempts a scot-free getaway, but Wonder Woman blows up his plane as "good exercise!" The last panel shows Standpat's redemption, as the sweating, sputtering general presents medals to Wonder Woman and Psycho. "For heroic action, I commend these brave soldiers . . . ahem . . . brave *women*—harrumph!"[42]

Matching Standpat's stammering, Marston's message is equally vague. Standpat recognizes his stalwart saviors, but he clarifies his statement: brave women rather than soldiers. In any event, the recipient is the super heroine, not Diana Prince, who vanishes in the course of the investigation. Likewise, despite Psycho's knowledge of the plot, she, too, needs a Wonder Woman to save herself from military disgrace.

Paradoxically, the heart of this story—male acceptance of women in the military—did not need a Wonder Woman to wow men over. Historian Lorry Lenner narrates that the U.S. Women's Defense Corps, the forerunner of the WAAC, enjoyed public consensus "that women had an equal military responsibility to defend the nation in 'total war' and that statements like 'women's place is in the home . . . sounds too much like Hitler.'"[43] Various media documented that as many as ten thousand women rushed to enlist before Congress officially voted on the corps.[44] The *New York Times* highlighted the House's approved legislation for the enlistment of women with a full front-page spread.[45]

DC Comics shared that sentiment and threw its characters into the war effort. In *All Star Comics #11*, produced after the attack on Pearl Harbor, the opening page depicts the events of December 7, 1941, and DC's premiere team, the Justice Society of America, disbands to enlist. The vigilante Hawkman joins the Army Air Corps and saves a convoy ferrying nurses to the Philippines, including Diana Prince. Hawkman reveals to an astonished Prince that he knows her alter ego: "The Justice Society has managed to learn many things!"[46]

After Hawkman departs, Prince disembarks into the war zone. Assigned to the ambulance corps, she ventures to the front and, like an "angel of mercy," administers aid.[47] Witnessing a Japanese invasion, Prince applauds the Allies as "outnumbered, but not out-fought! I'm proud to be an American! I-I wish there was something I could do to help them!"[48] Prince changes into her patriotic garb and joins the free-for-all. At the end, a military officer prohibits the Justice Society of America from joining the armed forces, fearing potential disharmony among the troops. Honorably discharged, the society create its own battalion and bestows membership on Wonder Woman.[49]

From there on, the super team became the supporters of Americanism throughout the conflict. At one point, the Justice Society of America's all-star lineup makes a stage appearance alongside a melting-pot cast, chanting, "Polish, Irish, or Italian! Catholic, Protestant or Jew! Black or White! Rich or Poor! An American is still an American!"[50] Among the multiethnic performers is one factory worker who declares, "I'm one of the five million women war production workers who are doing men's work in the factories."[51] Marching alongside her are three uniformed women, chanting, "Yes, the women of a unified America, now march step by step with our husbands, brothers, sweethearts—a *WAAC*! A *WAVE*! A *WAF*!" Bringing up the rear is a granny who knits sweaters and a housewife who feeds "our families good, wholesome food [to] keep them strong and healthy!"[52] In *All Star Comics* #22, the Justice Society of America leads an auditorium full of saluting youngsters in the Pledge of Allegiance. At the bottom, Wonder Woman reminds readers, "You know what that means—'Liberty and Justice for all'—*all* regardless of *race, color, or religion*!"[53] Similarly, in *Comic Cavalcade* #3, Trevor describes a new monument that "will pay tribute to our modern woman warriors, the WAAC, the WAVES, the SPARS, the Woman Marines." Prince replies that Wonder Woman will "probably make it her business to be there!"[54] The statue is destroyed by an Axis super weapon, but that the enemy singled out this one monument in Washington, DC, suggested the symbolic threat that the artwork poised to the master racists.

Less threatening, Standpat never graced the comics again, and readers would never know if he fully embraced the idea of female combatants. Wonder Woman has the final word: "Don't forget to kiss us on both cheeks, general—it's a new army regulation for WAACs!" Perhaps Wonder Woman wants to taunt the general, but her self-made rule suggests that soldiers, segregated by gender, are separate but hardly equal. As Standpat sweats out his misogyny, Wonder Woman reinforces his preconceived notions that military women are rooted in feminine attributes. After all, Trevor receives nothing, but he definitely would have been ineligible for a smack from Standpat. This is Wonder Woman's story, but Marston's final point might have been more poignant had Lieutenant Prince received the medal instead of Wonder Woman. Prince respects the chain of command and, having never received a promotion or medal before, may have appreciated the award without offering snippy comebacks. The exonerated Marva Psycho says nothing, and Wonder Woman moves on to greater exploits.

## "CAVEMAN IDEAS": EMPOWERING THE HOME FRONT

While Wonder Woman emerges triumphant at the expense of her alter ego, Diana Prince has claim to legitimacy in her own right. In Wonder Woman's origin story, the Amazon princess encounters army nurse Diana Prince and, seeing Prince in distress, assumes that a perpetual state of mental weakness is the norm for her future alter ego. The original Diana Prince, who sells her soul in the name of true love, is far more than what Wonder Woman suspects. The original Diana Prince appears only once more during Marston's tenure, and she reflects the strength of a nation's women embroiled in war.

"The Return of Diana Prince" in *Sensation Comics #9* opens with Prince and Trevor being rudely interrupted by a disheveled man. "Diana! What do you mean by going out with *another man*?"[55] The stranger claims Prince as his wife and begs her to come home, adding, "Have you forgotten our baby?" While Trevor rids them of this pest, Prince uses her Amazonian memory and identifies her malefactor as Dan White, the original Diana Prince's fianc, now husband and father of her child.

Unfortunately, the Whites are having trouble in paradise. Dan White heads home, and his house-making wife immediately snaps at him over a stove. They feud until Mrs. White realizes that Dan has mistaken Prince for her. She coos, "Dan, dear, I've just thought of somebody who'll give me a nurse's job. *Please* let me go to work, Dan!" Dan refuses, to keep the family unit intact: "*No!* My wife doesn't *have* to work!" The caption asserts that this is "an old argument," as Diana White reveals that "we're down to our last dollar and the baby *must* have food!" Her husband insists on remaining the breadwinner and states that he has an appointment to present his "anti-aircraft disintegrator shell." Diana White halts him: "Stop it, Dan! I've heard all that a hundred times. Your shell won't feed us, so *I've* got to!" Mrs. White, in a nurse outfit, then races out the door. "You can't stop me! Lucky I kept my army nurse's uniforms—I'm going to work!" Dashing to Army Intelligence, White begs Prince, "I can't let my baby starve—won't you *please* give me this job?"[56]

Marston explains that "Diana, the Amazon girl, can never resist the call of human need, no matter the cost to herself." Back to being a full-time Amazon, Diana investigates Dan White's luckless invention. Mr. White, mistaking one Diana for the other, is so desperate to maintain a traditional housewife that he shoves her into a chair and declares, "You'll stay right in this room from now on [because] I'm going to chain you like this every time I go out!" Diana plays along "because it will be fun" and gushes, "How thrilling! I see you're chaining me to the cookstove! What a perfect caveman idea!" When White leaves, Diana grows bored being chained to the stove and leaves. Nearby, Diana White is kidnapped by the "World Peace Society" to encourage White to surrender his invention. Knowing that the World Peace Society is a Nazi front for agitation, Diana changes to Wonder Woman and encounters the society's chief, Dr. I. M. Cue. Diana White spills the beans: "The doctor is a fiend! He is developing disease germs to attack America!" Wonder Woman ends the Nazi's germ warfare, saves Diana White, and unmasks Dr. Cue, and the army buys White's weapon. "Oh, Dan!" Mrs. White sighs, while Wonder Woman holds their nameless newborn. "Now the other Diana can have her job back!" The last panel shows one Diana telling the other, "I am Diana White, and you are Diana Prince from now on. We don't look much alike either with my new hair-do." Prince responds, "I'm happy to get my old position back, but I envy yours, as wife and mother."

On the surface, the conclusion implies that Mrs. White and Prince are both reinforcing women's duties at home, even under a chain-wheeling husband. After all, White surrenders her career to support Dan and his weapon—a double salute to patriotism and patriarchy, as was the standard fare for wartime literature. As the issue made clear, Mrs. White seeks work only to support her baby after her husband could not provide for her. Conversely, White restores the original status quo once White's invention is a hit with the military brass.

That Mrs. White takes charge of her household underscores Marston's views of female strength. Mrs. White lacks Amazonian strength, yet she runs her home with a firm hand while her frustrated husband flops as an arms dealer. Mrs. White's decision to return to the nursing field is certainly apt. One month after Pearl Harbor, *Life Magazine*'s cover photo expressed that need in one blurb—"Wanted: 50,000 Nurses"—and listed the article under its "Handbook for Americans" feature—a basic how-to guide for all in times of national calamity.[57] Historian Barbara Brooks Tomblin documents that the number of army nurses increased from seven thousand to twelve thousand by June 1942, while the number of "general hospitals also experienced phenomenal growth, . . . from fourteen to forty by June 1943."[58] Nevertheless, the armed forces continually needed nurses throughout the war. In 1945, the age limit for nurses was increased from forty to forty-five.[59] Historian Betsy Kuhn notes that the House passed HR 2277, endorsed by the American Nursing Association, which proposed to draft single women between twenty and forty-five.[60] The war ended before the Senate could act; yet, given the demand, White could have kept her job. The wartime environment—the "Rosie the Riveter" and similar campaigns—supported qualified women who wanted to do just that. Nevertheless, that Diana White returns to the role of caregiver is a conscious effort to shore up the home front now that her husband has a role in protecting his castle and country. Mrs. White's decision-making process is what Diana Prince applauds at the end.[61]

This decision to stay as a wife and mother was a hard choice, even for a Wonder Woman. Historian Doris Weatherford observes that with large numbers of women at work during World War II, child care was in infancy, and advice for women juggling jobs and kids was "controversial and contradictory."[62] Public enthusiasm for female enlistment aside, the strongest dissent came from civilian husbands and women who feared that they would be relegated to latrine and laundry duties.[63] Still, Diana White makes her choice concerning her family life, and for all the romantic alludes that Wonder Woman and Trevor partake, the responsibilities of marriage and child rearing are subjects that neither considers. That Diana White does so and takes a stance with husband and hearth as easily as she does with her hair was cause for sincere admiration from Marston's story and Prince's dialogue. Decades later, these sentiments were echoed by television's own Wonder Woman, Lynda Carter.[64]

## BEYOND WORLD WAR II

Diana Prince is not the only non-super-powered heroine in Wonder Woman's comics. Just as Marston was a member of DC Comics' Editorial Advisory Board, fellow member Alice Marble sketched biographies that glorified feminine ingenuity in the subfeature "Wonder Women in History," published among the Amazon's adventures. The first feature showcases Florence Nightingale, whom Marble characterizes as "like Wonder Woman, gave up the birthright of her happy and protected home to save the lives of suffering humanity."[65] As the "Angel of Crimea" Nightingale is more like the World War II Prince's "Angel of Mercy" in administering medicine rather than walloping bad guys. Marble continued these features until Marston's death in 1947.[66] Robinson dismisses these features as "not *real* comics," citing the poorer artwork when compared to Wonder Woman's pages.[67] Still, the feature's longevity, in an industry that rested on current trends, suggests the audience's approval of these stories.

No less did readers accept Diana Prince. After Marston's death, however, writers diluted Marston's message, and Wonder Woman began dispensing dating tips for her younger female readers.[68] Despite the 1950s reputation as a period of homemaking and child rearing for women, visual representations of strong women persisted. Historian Eugenia Katedin argues that the postwar decade was an "active period of consciousness raising for modern American women; women pushing baby carriages still may have time to think."[69] During this time, Betty Friedan would formulate her questionnaire concerning the disease that had no name, the results of which she published in the following decade.

In fact, *Wonder Woman* worked well in the postwar decades with an emphasis on Diana Prince as a strong character. In 1958, DC Comics scripted a new origin story for Prince, in which the Amazon princess assumes a position at G2 to hide from Trevor's romantic posturing. After passing "one grueling test after another"—from written exams to deep-sea scuba diving—Prince beats the other contenders and earns a commission.[70] In 1966, the series reverted to a World War II setting in *Wonder Woman #159*, visually restoring Prince to the 1940s, with artists Ross Andru and Mike Esposito imitating H. G. Peters's "golden age" style.[71] In the 1970s, Lynda Carter's *Wonder Woman* television program also took place during the Second World War. At the same time, comics attempted to update Wonder Woman by dropping the Amazon connections and turned Prince into an espionage adventuress relying on karate rather than Greek mythology. With all the shifts in the series, DC Comics cleaned up its continuity with a major "reboot" in the 1980s. In the new *Wonder Woman* series, "Diana Prince" is mentioned as a possible alter ego for Wonder Woman, and the Amazon rejects the idea. Nevertheless, the 1940s Diana Prince resurfaced in 2007's "Infinite Crisis" storyline, in which the 1940s' Wonder Woman, Prince included, remains alive and vibrant. The upcoming *Wonder Woman* motion picture was rumored to also have a World War II setting.

In the early years, the Amazon princess garnered instantly worldwide recognition for her good deeds in "Man's World"; as a superhero, she was definitely not a typical woman. Conversely, Wonder Woman's depowered alter ego, Diana Prince, despite her surname, is rarely given royal treatment, especially from Trevor. Still, like all patriotic citizens, Lieutenant Prince persisted in the wartime environment. Marston believed in Prince as a representation of strong womanhood and even projected that message into the future. In *Wonder Woman #7*, published in 1943, Marston scripted that Prince, not Wonder Woman, will become the president of the United States in 3004. After beating out Trevor and the "Men's Party" platform, Prince emerges triumphant. "Diana Prince, after many years of faithful service to her country, finally holds its highest office," while readers see her swearing in to faithfully execute her duties.[72] The futuristic setting still cannot escape its past, as the issue's final panel shows Prince representing her country at the "United World" conference (a super United Nations of sorts). After surviving an assassination attempt, Prince assures her peers, "I'm very much alive—*Wonder Woman* saved me!" Nevertheless, Prince muses, "Sometimes I wish she hadn't—I get so sick of wearing these glasses!"[73] Yet, that Prince has worn her glasses for over one thousand years underscores Wonder Woman's recognition of her alter ego's contribution to the evolution of womanhood since her inception in the 1940s. While the World War II Diana Prince does not exist in the current DC Comics' universe, her history demonstrates that Prince is an essential component in understanding Wonder Woman's presence in a figurative man's world.

## NOTES

1. Fredric Wertham, *Seduction of the Innocent* (New York: Main Road Books, 2004), 34.

2. Wertham, *Seduction of the Innocent*, 193, 234–35.

3. See Bradford Wright, *Comic-Book Nation: The Transformation of Youth Culture in America* (New York: The Johns Hopkins University Press, 2003), 21; Gerard Jones, *Men of Tomorrow: Geeks, Gangsters, and the Birth of the Comic Book* (New York: Basic Books, 2005), 211; David Hajdu, *The Ten-Cent Plague: The Great Comic-Book Scare and How It Changed America* (New York: Farrar, Straus and Giroux, 2008), 77–78; Mitra C. Emad, "Reading Wonder Woman's Body: Mythologies of Gender and Nation" *Journal of Popular Culture* 39, no. 6 (2006): 956.

4. Gloria Steinem, "Introduction," in *Wonder Woman* (New York: Holt, Rinehart and Winston, 1972).

5. Gloria Steinem, "Introduction," in *Wonder Woman: Featuring over Five Decades of Great Covers*, ed. Amy Handy and Steven Korté (New York: Abbeville Press, 1995), 9.

6. Lillian S. Robinson, *Wonder Woman: Feminisms and Superheroes* (New York: Routledge, 2004), 11–12.

7. Quoted in Emad, "Reading Wonder Woman's Body," 964–65.

8. *Sensation Comics #3* (New York: DC Comics, 1942), 13.

9. *Sensation Comics #5* (New York: DC Comics, 1942), 13.

10. Maureen Honey, *Creating Rosie the Riveter: Class, Gender, and Propaganda during World War II* (Amherst: University of Massachusetts Press, 1984), 15.

11. Honey, *Creating Rosie the Riveter*, 32.

12. Honey, *Creating Rosie the Riveter*, 42.

13. Thomas Doherty, *Projections of War: Hollywood, American Culture, and World War II* (New York: Columbia University Press, 1999), 153.

14. Doherty, *Projections of War*, 158.

15. Honey, *Creating Rosie the Riveter*, 70.

16. Nancy Walker, *Shaping Our Mothers' World: American Women's Magazines* (Jackson: University Press of Mississippi, 2000), 68–72.

17. *Wonder Woman #5* (New York: DC Comics, 1943), 6D–7D.

18. *Sensation Comics #3*.

19. *Sensation Comics #4* (New York: DC Comics, 1942), 4; *Wonder Woman #3* (New York: DC Comics, 1943), 1A–15A.

20. *Wonder Woman #12* (New York: DC Comics, 1945), 3A–4A.

21. "Battle for Womanhood!" in *Wonder Woman #5* (New York: DC Comics, 1943), 10A–11A; "The Masked Menace!" in *Sensation Comics #16* (New York: DC Comics, 1943), 1–13.

22. *Wonder Woman #4* (New York: DC Comics, 1942), 1C–13C.

23. "Wonder Woman Is Dead!" in *Sensation Comics #13* (New York: DC Comics, 1943), 6–7; *Sensation Comics #4* (New York: DC Comics, 1942), 6.

24. "Villiany, Incorporated!" *Wonder Woman #28* (New York: DC Comics, 1948), 1A–12C.

25. *Sensation Comics #17* (New York: DC Comics, 1942), 1–13; "The Unbound Amazon," in *Sensation Comics #19* (New York: DC Comics, 1943), 1–13.

26. "The Adventure of the Beauty Club" in *Wonder Woman #6* (New York: DC Comics, 1943), 2B.

27. *Sensation Comics #4* (New York: DC Comics, 1942), 2.

28. "Peril in Paradise Island," in *Sensation Comics #42* (New York: DC Comics, 1945).

29. *Sensation Comics #1* (New York: DC Comics, 1942), 8.

30. "Danny the Demon Had Plans!" in *The Big All-American Comic Book* (New York: DC Comics, 1944), 13.

31. *Sensation Comics 23* (New York: DC Comics, 1943), 2; *Wonder Woman 3* (New York: DC Comics, 1943), 2C–3C; *Comic Cavalcade #1* (New York: DC Comics, 1942/

1943), 2–3; "Racketeers Kidnap Miss Santa Claus!" in *Sensation Comics #38* (New York: DC Comics, 1945), 2; *Sensation Comics #6* (New York: DC Comics, 1942), 4–5.

32. *Sensation Comics #48* (New York: DC Comics, 1945), 1–12.

33. See Hajdu, *The Ten-Cent Plague*, 30, 39–47; Amy Kiste Nyberg, *Seal of Approval: The History of the Comics Code* (Jackson: University of Mississippi Press, 1998), 3–15; Kristie Lindenmeyer, *The Greatest Generation Grows Up: American Childhood in the 1930s* (Chicago: Dee, 2005), 156–205, especially 183–85.

34. *Sensation Comics #2* (New York: DC Comics, 1942), 4.

35. *Sensation Comics #2*, 36.

36. "Grown-Down Land," in *Sensation Comics #31* (New York: DC Comics, 1944), 4.

37. *Comic Cavalcade #3* (New York: DC Comics, 1943), 4.

38. See *The Encyclopedia of Comic Book Superheroes*, ed. Michael Fleisher (New York: Macmillan, 1976), 2:219.

39. *Sensation Comics #21* (New York: DC Comics, 1943), 1–2.

40. *Sensation Comics #21*, 3.

41. *Sensation Comics #21*, 11.

42. *Sensation Comics #21*, 13.

43. Lorry Lenner, "Introduction to the Letters," in *An Officer and a Lady: The World War II Letters of Lt. Col. Betty Bandel, Women's Army Corps*, ed. Sylvia J. Bugbee (Lebanon: University Press of New England, 2005), xvii.

44. Lenner, "Introduction to the Letters," see notes 191–92.

45. Lenner, "Introduction to the Letters," xviii.

46. *All Star Comics #11* (New York: DC Comics, 1942), 14.

47. *All Star Comics #11*, 2.

48. Wonder Woman is not an American, but Diana Prince assumes the nationality of her namesake.

49. Prince returns to the United States by the issue's end to receive membership into the Justice Society of America. Perhaps her creators realized that had their heroes remained overseas in real time during the war, they would be susceptible to ensuing events. Had Prince stayed in the Philippines, she would have been included among the nurses captured by the Japanese following the fall of the American defense in March 1942, approximately the same time that this issue hit the newsstands with a summer cover date.

50. "The Justice Society Fights for a United America!" in *All Star Comics #16* (New York: DC Comics, 1944), y.

51. "The Justice Society Fights," z.

52. "The Justice Society Fights," z+.

53. "A Cure for the World," in *All Star Comics #22* (New York: DC Comics, 1945), z.

54. *Comic Cavalcade #3* (New York: DC Comics, 1943), 2–3.

55. *Sensation Comics #9* (New York: DC Comics, 1942), 2.

56. *Sensation Comics #9*, 5.

57. "Aides Relieve Nurse Shortage," *Life Magazine* 12, no. 1 (January 5, 1942): cover, 32–35.

58. Barbara Brooks Tomblin, *GI Nightingales: The Army Nurse Corps in World War II* (Lexington: University Press of Kentucky, 2003), 186.

59. Tomblin, *GI Nightingales*, 200.

60. Betsy Kuhn, *Angels of Mercy: The Army Nurses of World War II* (New York: Antheneum Books, 1999), 82.

61. Uncommented on is Diana White's decision to safeguard Wonder Woman's secret identity. In *Sensation Comics #1*, Wonder Woman approaches Prince to buy her identity. White could now easily piece together that "the other Diana" and her savior are the same, yet she maintains the secrecy. The final parting confirms their unspoken agreement.

62. Doris Weatherford, *American Women and World War II* (New York: Facts on File, 1990), 167.

63. Weatherford, *American Women*, 37–38.

64. Carter writes, "And the Wonder Woman in each of us is even better than the original. For we are also mothers, girlfriends, wives, givers of life and love –roles that Wonder Woman, for all her adventures, was never able to play." Lynda Carter, "Introduction," in *Wonder Woman: The Life and Times of the Amazon Princess—The Complete History,* ed. Les Daniels (San Francisco: Chronicle Books, 2004), 9.

65. "Wonder Women in History," in *Wonder Woman #1* (New York: DC Comics, 1942), 1.

66. Les Daniels, ed., *Wonder Woman: The Life and Times of the Amazon Princess—The Complete History* (San Francisco: Chronicle Books, 2004), 40.

67. Robinson, *Wonder Woman,* 57–58.

68. Susan M. Hartman, *The Home Front and Beyond: American Women in the 1940s* (Boston: Twayne, 1982), 202.

69. Eugenia Katedin, *Mothers and More: American Women in the 1950s* (Boston: Twayne, 1984), 214.

70. Robert Kanigher, Ross Andru, and Mike Esposito, "Top Secret," *Wonder Woman #99* (New York: DC Comics, 1958), 10.

71. The comic-book industry seems to retroactively glorify the World War II era. In the 1960s, after a stalemate in Korea and with the escalating conflict in Vietnam, publishers looked back fondly at World War II as a "good" war. DC Comics' hard-boiled Sgt. Rock meets his match with an army nurse when he is injured and sent to a hospital. When the Nazis advanced, the nurse refuses to abandon her patient. With an Axis tank a mere few feet away, Rock orders her to leave, and she replies, "Don't try to pull rank on a lieutenant, *sergeant!*" See "A New Kind of War!" in *Our Army at War #104* (New York: DC Comics, 1961), 13. Marvel Comics' World War II series *Sgt. Fury and His Howling Commandos* features the hard-boiled Howlers taking on the worst of fascism's fanatics. This testosterone-laden tribute to combat has a soft spot for nurses. In issue 13, one nurse, when called a "gal" by a noncom, replies, "I am a *lieutenant,* not a 'gal!' Kindly, step this way—*corporal!*" See "Fighting Side-by-Side with . . . Captain America and Bucky!" in *Sgt. Fury and His Howling Commandoes #13* (New York: Marvel Comics, 1963), 22. Fury's love interest, Pamela Hawsley, a British officer and nurse, is killed in action after eighteen issues. The series' creators were veterans of the war, which they proudly note in the credits in each issue.

72. "America's Wonder Women of Tomorrow!" in *Wonder Woman #7* (New York: DC Comics, 1943), 13B.

73. "The Secret Weapon!" *Wonder Woman #7* (New York: DC Comics, 1943), 12C.

# SIX

# Wonder Woman as Patriotic Icon

*The Amazon Princess for the Nation and Femininity*

Annessa Ann Babic,
New York Institute of Technology

One of the most recognizable posters of World War II is "Rosie the Riveter." Rosie was meant to represent the ideal American women as beautiful, sexy, alluring, manicured, and supporting her country and man through valiant uncomplaining service to her nation. Comparatively, the popular comic book heroine Wonder Woman also represented foundational gendered elements of U.S. society. She, too, was pretty, manicured, sexy, and alluring. Both these women supported and "protected" the United States in a time of national need through their unfailing service to their country, but society expected them to return to their established gender roles after the war. While Rosie ascended from wartime propaganda and Wonder Woman derives from a fictional incarnation, both female images served a central purpose. They educated and rallied women to the national front, transgressed the bounds of expected behavior, and helped shape a new generation of women.

By using popular culture creations such as *Wonder Woman* comic books, governmental propaganda posters, and popular advertisements, this discussion shows how women reacted, engaged with, and opposed notions of femininity and national pride. Moreover, it puts a seemingly fringe icon such as Wonder Woman at the center of a discursive debate concerning the construction of national memory (even honor). Cultural creations based in popular emotion, desire, and sense of wartime urgency—from a variety of sources with numerous intentions—worked together to help construct and reinforce national ideals of women, particularly the patriotic woman. Rosie, Wonder Woman, and the female worker (white- or blue-collar) lived and acted the part of the patriotic woman, and even though their intentions and desires for (and of) service did not always match the national ideal, they still served their nation through fiction and reality.

## IMAGING MYTHS

Wonder Woman entered the American consumer market in 1941, shortly before the United States officially entered World War II. The *Wonder Woman* comic began as an insert to a larger comic, and when buyers showed a positive reception, creator William Moulton Marston (pen name, Charles Moulton) incorporated her Amazon character and shapely figure into a full-length monthly story. Wonder Woman, clad in red, white, and blue, fought to save "the last arsenal for democracy," and in her first episode, she wore a dress. Quickly, her creators removed her skirt for the hot pants because Marston's team felt that Wonder Woman needed to adhere to feminine attributes, one of those being that a lady would not have her skirt fly over her head, which Wonder Woman would have had occur in her exploits to combat evil. In her early story-line, she longed for Steve Trevor. He often rescued her; she saved him; and their romantic affair helped keep Wonder Woman grounded in feminine roots and customs. Wonder Woman could never wed Steve, because according to Amazon custom, she would have to give up her powers if she married a man. Moreover, the romantic liaisons with Steve Trevor would be revitalized in the 1950s to stave off comic critics.

In contrast to the creation of *Wonder Woman*, the "Rosie the Riveter" campaign is often noted to have been the most successful of World War II.[1] In December 1999, Rosie was nominated for woman of the century. Paula Watson, author of an editorial on Rosie, stated, "Rosie's legacy is one of courage and grace." Also, she symbolized a woman's ability and willingness to do her part.[2] The symbolic effect of Rosie to encourage women to "do their part" also had corrosive effects on female employment and safety measures. Women were instructed to be "soldierettes" on the home front, and propagandists pointed to European women, particularly German women, to exemplify their contentions. Media writers stated that German women worked long and arduous hours at jobs that previously extended beyond the female sphere, they supported their country, and they maintained their feminine attributes.[3]

World War II advertisements proclaiming, "There's a war job in my kitchen," "Who said this is a man's war?" "Wanted: Housekeepers to help the Army and Navy," and "Mother, keep house clean the way Uncle Sam does" show some of the home-front mobilization.[4] These titles drew on the emotions of the female to provide care for her family through cleanliness and well-prepared meals, but the patriotic consumption campaign did not end here. Women were further told that mundane tasks, such as sewing a button onto a shirt when gripper fasteners could not be found, served a patriotic purpose through their mending of torn clothes instead of purchasing new ones.[5] Purchasing news clothes, after all, would lead to waste. Last, the patriotic female could guide her family and self toward a patriotic life through her work and consumption habits, but to fully solidify her role within the national psyche, she had to look her best. Looking her best derived from appearance and fashion, and as Tangee Lipsticks proclaimed, lipstick marked one of the reasons why the United States was fighting in the war. "No lipstick—ours or anyone else's—will win the war," the ad declared. "But [lipstick] symbolizes one of the reasons why we are fighting . . . the precious right of women to be feminine and lovely—under any circumstances."[6] Accordingly, Rosies were the women of the home front who looked fabulous. Wonder Woman, however, was the personality (perhaps hidden within) that urged them on and rallied a force within the generation of women who were born post–World War I, in a nation allowing them suffrage, and who were fully embraced in the pleasures of a booming consumer society.

Wonder Woman's mission, revealed in the first episode of her story, portrays her as a savior of the United States. She is needed to defend "American Liberty and freedom" because "America [is] the last citadel of democracy, and of equal rights for women."[7] She was not chosen to be the "savior" of the United States from her Amazon legacy, being the daughter to the queen of Paradise Island, or because of her looks. Rather, Wonder Woman earned her title, mission, and outfit by defeating other Amazon women in a long and engaging competition of physical strength. When she wins the competition, reveals herself to her mother, and is crowned with the title of "Wonder Woman," her costume is symbolic of her cause and the era that created her. She wears a red corset, with a gold eagle on the chest, blue skirt dazzled with white stars, and red knee-high boots with high heels. Additionally, her outfit flatters her figure, embellishes her femininity, and is symbolic of the American flag. The red corset with the white belt resembles the red and white stripes of the flag, with the skirt—a blue field with white stars—representing the upper-right-hand corner.[8] Her outfit, mission, and later-revealed attraction to Steve Trevor solidify her as a patriotic woman because she gives unconditional service to her adopted country, dons its colors of pride and heritage, and holds the desires that gender codes expected—that she would fall in love and get married. Wonder Woman never marries, but her obvious attraction to a man—a military one at that—elevates her feminine nature to keep her within the realm of "natural and desirable women."

In contrast to this image of feminine strength and power, Wonder Woman has another side: the image that she herself calls her "own rival."

Wonder Woman appears in only her sultry red, white, and blue regalia when she is fighting crime, saving Steve Trevor from harm, or protecting U.S. national security. Thus, when she is an "everyday woman," her persona and clothing reflect her change in attitude, mission, and atmosphere. In her capacity as a "mortal," earthbound woman, Wonder Woman becomes Diana Prince—a mousy woman lacking substantial self-confidence and alluring looks. Diana Prince wears round, black-rimmed spectacles and pins her hair in a neatly formed bun with curls framing her face, and her clothes represent a "plain Jane" style. She usually wears a drab-colored skirt falling three-quarters down her calf, with a white-buttoned blouse. Her heels are the fashion of the period—black with a squared toe and deemed functional. Diana is secretly lusting after Steve Trevor, whom she saved from death on Paradise Island while still under her original identity as Princess of Paradise Island. When he returned to the United States, she worked as his nurse, then later as his secretary and through the continuing story. In the fashion of comics and suspense novels, Steve Trevor does not know that Diana is Wonder Woman, and when she does attempt to reveal her secret identity to him, he believes Diana's confession as nothing more than nonsense.[9] Wonder Woman also provides a paradox to patriotic women and gendered spheres. Novelist and comic book historian Les Daniels remarks that Marston "was convinced that as political and economic equality became a reality, women could and would use sexual enslavement to achieve domination over men, who would happily submit to their loving authority."[10]

Daniels further remarks that feminists of the modern era may have somewhat misinterpreted the situation by suggesting that Wonder Woman was "intended exclusively as a role model who would encourage self-confidence in young girls."[11] While she did show bravado and strength to young girls, she represented the fears and aspirations of the nation. Propaganda continually urged women to join their country in arms, via the home front, while reminding them that their "true" social place remained in the home with children and family—centered by the husband.

Throughout her publications, she has consistently remained against violence, and her villains are never killed—even though lots of ropes and chains are used in their capture. The first villain arrives in the February 1942 book as Dr. Poison, and in true feminist discourse, when Dr. Poison's mask is removed, the doctor becomes a woman—the Japanese Princess Maru. Furthermore, men are often portrayed as "too feeble to be worthy" of Wonder Woman's time, but the peculiar dichotomy of the text remains in the fact that Steve Trevor continually saves her from entrapment. Wonder Woman represents schisms within society concerning social mobility and actions concerning women. Wonder Woman's sidekicks and a regular villain—Baroness Paula von Gunther—provide excellent examples of the unclear intent of the comic books. Her sidekicks, the Holliday Girls, first appear in *Sensation Comics* #2 with Etta Candy as their leader. The Holliday Girls, a group of four coeds from the *all*-girls Holliday College, also wear red, white, and blue outfits. They are often portrayed as playful and giggly girls, with Etta being addicted to candy (hence her name), and they reinforced societal notions of cooperation and unity because they continually put their needs aside to aid Wonder Woman. As for the Baroness, she represented cooperation and education instead of submission. She continually battles Wonder Woman, is sent to Transformation Island, escapes, and eventually turns toward the "side of good" to become an aide and confidant of Wonder Woman. [12]

These perplexities in Wonder Woman directly correlate to advertisements for beauty aids and the war work campaign. These images provoking patriotism were responsive to broader social forces and reflect a larger element of the nation's popular cultures at play in these national contexts. These women faced contradictions with perceptions of acceptable behavior; they faced social stigma when they left their children with day care centers, babysitters, family members, and, sometimes, their other children to work; and women perceived as strong and assertive were often victimized in "witch hunts."

Images mirroring those of Wonder Woman can be seen in a variety of advertisements. Wonder Woman, like Rosie the Riveter, worked for the war effort. Wonder Woman's mortal personality of Diana Prince was a secretary. Marston never directly explained if Diana worked before the war, but since the comic book is published shortly before the attack on Pearl Harbor, a reader could easily connect Diana Prince's employment to wartime service because U.S. society had already begun producing for the war. Moreover, the Holliday Girls acted outside their gender by aiding Wonder Woman in her fight for democracy, and they represented the young and attractive female, sacrificing her idealic youth for the nation. These girls stepped outside of prescribed boundaries only for national honor; therefore, they were not subversive or threats. They fit within the constructed discourse of the era. Advertisements and propaganda posters from the 1940s provide surrounding evidence for the patriotic female's actions and implications for Wonder Woman.

A sampling of such advertisements demonstrates a social desire to perpetually educate the woman on her need for self-sacrifice, national service, and continual support for her man (or for one who has not been found yet). Headlines such as "And I'm No Part-Time Wife!" leave the reader/viewer with clear connotations about the sentiment behind the ad. This one—for Nabisco Shredded Wheat, showing a woman smiling and clearly dressed in U.S. uniform regalia—told the reader that she could work and keep a healthy family. [13] Other ads illustrate these societal sentiments with their message celebrating the female worker and encouraging young women and young/new brides to be "Uncle Sam's Girls."

A 1944 Listerine advertisement declares, "Put it there, Sister!" The ad pictures a young solider outstretching his hand with a hint of a smile on his face. The text of the ad applauds, encourages, and employs women to work in factories and other nontraditional jobs because the wartime nation desperately needed their service. The "punch line" of the piece states, "The more women at war the sooner we'll win." In contrast to asking women to join the labor force, *Good Housekeeping* ran a series of fashion pieces instructing the reader on how to make sensible fashions that would "withstand the test of time," appeal to the male sex, and be sensible in most situations.[14]

Other advertisements that honed in on a woman's "need" to beautify herself for a man were bountiful and unabashed in their use of emotion. Ads for Pond's Cold Cream pictured a young girl in uniform answering phones and serving coffee and donuts in a navy canteen; as the ad boldly proclaimed, she was engaged, serving her country through her civilian service with the navy, and beautiful because she kept up her good looks. To make this tale more compelling, the lower left corner of the ad proclaimed that Jacquelline Proctor (the ad's model) was a real person— from Boston, Massachusetts, engaged to Guy de Brun (of New York and in the U.S. Army at Camp Barkeley), and she was a descendant of James Otis, who signed the Declaration of Independence. Procter represented an ideal patriotic woman because of her engagement, job, and family heritage. Woodbury Facial Soap went so far as to name one of its campaigns "Contact," and it pictured a man and a woman in a deep embrace with the male clearly resembling a sailor. The sweeping lines of the illustration and deep embrace of the reunited lovers are captured in the brief and romantic-laced text of the piece. Woodbury soaps would "guard the skin he loves" and keep a woman's face soft and supple.[15] Each of these ads served the same purpose: to promote a product, inform the reader, reinforce accepted gender codes, and capitalize on elements of patriotism. These were the actual Wonder Women, acting on the daily basis by living their lives and adhering to social ideals. Yet, these real Wonder Women did not stay within defined, expected, or so-called acceptable boundaries.

## IMAGINING THE 1950S

In an effort to counter economic changes post–World War II, the idealization of women, home, and family proliferated. In the 1950s—unlike the World War I and II periods— no central figure representing the modern patriotic woman emerged. Instead, the postwar years relied on social codes, beliefs, and conceptions for womanhood and the family to perpetuate national beliefs about the sex. This lack of a unifying figure for women to adhere to derived from a sense of "normalcy" and return to the home. The promise of suburbia, civil defense, and the rise of a child-centered society made the new image of the patriotic woman that of the housewife and mother. Women did not need a rallying figure to guide and motivate them, because their husbands and families would be their motivation. The previously seen heroines of Lady Columbia, Wonder Woman, and Rosie subsided for the more subtle figure of the mother. Similar to how the advertisement "Mother, when will you stay home again?" promoted the belief that women would only temporarily work for the war effort, advertisements and other forms of expression stated that women in the 1950s would not work. [16]

Following World War II, men faced strong expectations to "pay the bill," and those who could not fulfill their manly duties often encountered accusations of homosexuality and nonconformity. [17] The triumph of the Allied powers and the United States created a belief that manhood had been won in the war, and men were expected to pass on this sense of responsibility and allure to their sons. Men had created a powerful and wealthy nation with the aid of "the greatest destructive force ever imagined," and to prevent a decline in U.S. power and superiority, men had to embrace their manhood and masculinity. [18] To maintain this position of grandeur, men had to contain women because of the fear that equality would destroy this newly formed concept of strength, security, and self-assurance. *Family* became a code word for *constraint*, and the family developed into a constraining factor for individuals. [19] Institutions manipulated images to force obedience and silence from the public. Michel Foucault states that speaking the truth admits fears and faults. These actions recognize the power of community, a power that prevents truth because it implants fear into individuals so that they will not deviate from customary expectations. [20] These silences enabled socially constructed agencies to hold power, and as Betty Friedan remarked in her best seller, these structures facilitated the "feminine mystique," which encouraged women to ignore the question of their identity. [21] Wonder Woman of the 1950s became more focused on—actually obsessed with—Steve Trevor. The storyline spotlighted the Diana–Wonder Woman struggle of identity and so-called feminine desire for marriage, love, and the ideal of security. Much like Wonder Woman herself served as a symbol for women of the war years, her postwar image continued to postulate a symbol for women's identity and expectations. The patriotic female evolved just as Wonder Woman herself did. Most important, the fictional icon of heroism within comic pages came under fire as civil right movements—in this case, women's liberation—captured the nation and forced it to examine itself.

## BRA BURNINGS

The late 1960s and early 1970s saw a plethora of protests that captivated the nation, and some became more volatile than others. Historians have often cited the catalyst for social uproar of the era as the increasing media coverage of the Vietnam War, rising death rates of American draftees, and the Tet Offensive. As with the Korean Conflict, the U.S. Congress never officially declared war with the Vietnamese. Even without an official declaration of war, U.S. forces actively engaged in a militarized zone, and the U.S. military relied on the draft to supply continued manpower.

The decade helps examine the passing and failure of the Equal Rights Amendment, changing perceptions of women, and why the patriotic female further declined from view. Combined and continual actions of protest act as social misdemeanors, leading to major category shifts in national rhetoric and cultural thought. A key aspect of literature from the 1960s is that surging patriotism, seen during earlier war periods, dissipated from soldiers' letters in the Vietnam era—even though media and congressional portrayals demonstrated an urgent need and desire for patriotic impulses. This dichotomy played heavily into patriotic impulses and iconography. Soldiers of the Vietnam War did not have the same emotional pull as men fighting in World Wars I and II, because the Vietnamese had never made a direct threat to the U.S. homeland.[22]

The 1968–1973 Wonder Woman storyline removed her from patriotic dress and superpowers. She became a mortal woman, a woman looking for love and trying to fulfill her role and place within mainstream society. Just like so many other female images of the era, Wonder Woman became average, commonplace, and normal.

In "Wonder Woman's Rival," the beginning of Wonder Woman's superpower decline emerges when villain Alex Block calls her a freak. Labeling her a freak indirectly compared Wonder Woman to females who did not fit the gendered expectations of the era. Marston created Wonder Woman as a valiant female, with heroic powers. Even though he made her valiant through her superpowers and desire to fight villains without violence, her actual intentions are unknown. Individual and consumer beliefs frequently dictate cultural meanings for objects and events, and Wonder Woman clearly took the role of a female heroine, savior, and role model. In 1968, DC Comics drastically changed her appearance and mission. The company stripped her of her powers, making her a mortal. Books 178 and 179 (titled "Wonder Woman's Rival" and "Wonder Woman's Last Battle," respectively) remove Wonder Woman from her patriotic dress and superhero status, making her a student of I Ching, a martial arts specialist who trained Diana (Wonder Woman's "human" name) for the next five years. The premise of Wonder Woman's loss of powers stems from her love for Steve Trevor and from her Amazon home moving to another magical realm. In the story line, the Amazon women had consumed their magic and needed to relocate to another secluded island to rest. Wonder Woman received a message to return home, did so, learned the fate of her sisters, and the Amazon women gave her the choice of staying with them or joining the ranks of citizens as a mortal.

She relinquished her powers because Steve had commented on his attraction for her alter ego, Diana Prince. Wonder Woman removed her patriotic garb, immersed herself in the fashions of the era, and attempted to live the life of a normal woman.[23] In her "civilian role," she continued to appear perfectly manicured, dressed, and mannered.

Wonder Woman's new look placed her in go-go boots, tunics, miniskirts, multicolored and brightly colored outfits, and "chic" fashion of the era. Her long and lustrous hair hung down her back; her eyebrows showed a fashionable arch; and her makeup remained flawless. She represented the women of the 1960s just as Rosie the Riveter represented the needs of World War II society. Rosie also maintained perfectly manicured looks, but her clothing—pants, overalls, and work shirts—represented a national need for women to enter factories, leave their homes, and interact with society in previously unacceptable ways. Propaganda of the 1960s did not need a woman to leave her home or socially interact on the professional or political level as she had in World War II. Even though gender codes relegated women to the home, women still entered colleges and universities, graduate programs, and professional fields in increasing numbers. With female emergence into academic and financial spheres and with higher rates in the 1970s, women became more visible. Fashions slimmed the female figure, and pantsuits gradually became more acceptable.[24]

The premise of the revised *Wonder Woman* story rests on Diana Prince, not Wonder Woman, coming to the aide of Steve Trevor and rescuing him from jail. Trevor has been falsely imprisoned for the murder of Alex Block because Trevor was the last person seen with him. Through a complex story of deceit, the reader learns that Trevor went into a local hippie nightclub, Tangerine Alley, and had a momentary flirtation with a young blonde girl. Throughout the trial, the girl could not be identified, but Diana Prince searches the downtown streets to find the girl's identity— her only clue is a cat-face ring. After a day of searching, she locates the ring at a local thrift store, along with the girl's address, and upon arriving home, she contacts Trevor's friend Roger Seely, who is supposed to be abroad in Europe. He has coincidentally sent her a telegram saying that he is returning from Europe because he heard the news about Trevor. Once Seely arrives at Diana's apartment, he pretends to call the jail warden to alert Steve about the found ring and subsequent location of the girl. They then set out to find the girl and get her, but on the car drive to the jail, Seely pulls out a gun and forces Diana to drive over a cliff, while he attempts to escape in a waiting plane. But Diana releases herself from the car, turns herself into Wonder Woman in midair, stops the car's descent, manhandles Seely's plane to detain him, and later brings him to the proper authorities. The episode ends with Wonder Woman and Trevor, cozy on a couch and discussing the events, and Trevor remarks that he sees Diana in a different light—he must get to know her better.[25] Diana's saving Trevor from jail proves to be her last act as Wonder Woman for some time. The episode ends with the tie-in to her loss of superpowers. Steve's having affection for Diana causes her to shed her legacy. The storyline of Wonder Woman's transformation might seem shaky, but the result of her actions draws out the social references of the day—particularly that of her appearance.

Wonder Woman is jealous that Trevor would have an attraction for Diana, because she is mousy and unattractive, and Diana saves the day by transforming her natural attire into the trendy "chick" fashions of 1968. She adorns herself in go-go boots, lets her long brunette locks down, wears a tunic, and blends in with the "hippie culture." Diana is no longer the mousy, dull-looking woman that Trevor has known for years. She is a young attractive woman, and her alter ego—of valor and determination—is gone. She is a natural woman, looking for and needing a man to love and support her. Wonder Woman's loss of powers reflects the comic industry and media outlets' attitudes concerning women's liberation, dismissing it with a sense of bemusement.[26] This oddly construed transformation of Diana fits in nicely with the social and political struggles of the era—particularly those concerning the national front and women's rights.

Americans had grown tired of sending their boys abroad; they were tired of sacrificing them for the "betterment of the nation"; and they did not desire to continue using their national resources in foreign lands. These belief structures can be easily identified in several popular images from the period to demonstrate discursive threads of thought in 1960s' culture and society. The backdrop of the argument rests on the 1968–1973 Wonder Woman storyline and Luis Jimenez's 1969 *Barfly–Statue of Liberty* sculpture. These images demonstrate elements of unrest, chaos, and misunderstanding that pervaded the era. The 1968–1973 Wonder Woman storyline removed her from patriotic dress and superpowers. She became a mortal woman, a woman looking for love and trying to fulfill her role and place within mainstream society. Just like so many other female images of the era, Wonder Woman became average, commonplace, and normal. In contrast to Wonder Woman, the Jimenez statue's imagery, stark contrast, and relevance to the politics of the era make *Barfly* a mirror and tangible piece of evidence. She is a drunken depiction of the Statue of Liberty, which makes her a drunken image of the nation. The chaotic appearance and disheveled nature of *Barfly* directly correlate to U.S. patriotic women because their public imagery had declined. Women were more vocal about voting, living alone, working alongside men, and demanding equal rights. They had been doing these things for centuries, but the latter half of the twentieth century saw the issues of women's rights capture the public's mind. Thus, women were no longer angelic angels of the home front. Instead, they were drunken barflies looking and waiting for the right moment to enter the scene.[27]

However, in 1975, ABC broadcast its pilot for a *Wonder Woman* series entitled *The New, Original Wonder Woman.* The initial response was weak, as the show met lackluster ratings. It was set in World War II, beginning as the first episode of the comics did with Wonder Woman winning her title on Paradise Island. Lynda Carter, a onetime Miss World USA, took the lead role. At the time, she was a newcomer to Hollywood, and the network balked a bit at her being cast in the lead. But executive producer Douglas Crammer fought for the five-foot-nine brunette to maintain the headline. In doing so, Carter brought Wonder Woman alive to those who had and had not read the books. In turn, her red, white, and blue body-suit made the superhero simultaneously attractive and assertive. The series lasted a year on ABC when the network dropped it, but as the story of Wonder Woman goes, she does not fail. In October 1976, CBS began airing a revamp of the series, with the story based in the 1970s and with Carter and others still in the lead—although Lyle Waggoner, who played Steve Trevor in the first run, came back as Steve's son. This series, which ran for three seasons, transformed the icon of Wonder Woman from comic book character to television star.[28] The image of Carter spinning in a cloud of red smoke to transform into her costume is an image that many still associate with the character itself.

The series paid homage to the comic books while playing notice to the social demands of the day. Just as Wonder Woman's creator removed her skirt for feminine reasons, in the pilot, the queen tells Wonder Woman that the skirt can be removed if it is too cumbersome. Well, she immediately removes it and does not don it again. In the pilot, she is described as "unfeminly pushy," and throughout the series, she keeps her sense of awe and wanderlust—as in the pilot, not knowing or understanding the need for money, and at later points, when she sees an icon to herself and does not comprehend that someone wants to wish her harm.[29] Just as Rosie could flex her arm and not show muscle bulk, the onscreen version of Wonder Woman adhered to what her creators and culture viewed of women's bodies: they were to be statuesque, without muscle bulk, and attractive. Wonder Woman, always the heroine, maintained predescribed bounds of social civility. Of course, there is also that notion that the princess of Paradise Island acts like a prince, with her valiant defeats of enemies to democracy. She is a parody—with the actions of a man but the visual beauty of a woman—that serves the icons of patriotism well.

## CONCLUSION

Devising a conclusion to the story of patriotic women is perplexing at best and a bit aggravating in the least. Unlike traditional events in history, the story of patriotism and gendered iconography has not ended. The study of the patriotic female does not permit concrete boundaries. Instead, the public role of women—and the face of patriotism—continues to perplex and confuse the nation. In 1973, the U.S. military removed the draft, again making its ranks a voluntary force; the Vietnam War ended in 1975; and in 1982, the Equal Rights Amendment failed to reach passage. These events and numerous others have continued to reshape the nature of American patriotism and the way that U.S. society has constructed itself. Most important, the gendered face of patriotism still exists, but this female face is no longer iconic and infiltrated throughout popular culture. Instead, the patriotic female has become an introvert of sorts. She is no longer "Rosie"; the portrait of femininity and beauty seen in Howard Chandler Christy's artistic expressions of the First World War era has faded from the popular mind; and Wonder Woman barely holds her marker among newer comic book characters of Japanese anime and male heroes who fight until the death. Instead, the new woman lies beneath the surface, and her sacrifice and patriotic honor are seen through familial service and key public roles in the nation.

With the 2001 war on terror and the 2003 U.S. invasion of Iraq, the nature of warfare and the face of the military have changed. Propaganda posters have evolved to encourage women to join the services, but controversies about the role that women should play in combat zones still dominate. Much of the debate concerns their ability to handle the job and traditional notions of gender. Political actions correlate to this discussion, as female losses and achievements continue to reflect gendered boundaries: the Equal Rights Amendment's failure and the appointment of the first female Supreme Court justice provide two examples of this new trend in gendered patriotism. The image of the woman as wife, mother, and housekeeper no longer guides society. Instead, the image of the woman as judge, advocate, professional, wife, mother, divorcee, villain, and martyr all structure the female's image in the late twentieth and early twenty-first centuries.

## NOTES

1. The Four Vagabonds, "Rosie the Riveter," *The War Years*, CDC 1046 (Intersound, 1943). The actual image of "Rosie" began in 1942 as a propaganda poster by J. Howard Miller for Westinghouse Corporation, and in 1943 the colloquial name "Rosie" became associated with her because the song "Rosie the Riveter," by the Four Vagabonds, became a national hit.

2. Paula Watson, "All Guts for Old Glory, One Person's Choice for Woman of the Century Is: Rosie the Riveter [editorial]," *Dallas Morning News*, December 29, 1999, K4656.

3. Allison L. Helper, "'And We Want Steel Toes like the Men': Gender and Occupational Health during World War II," *Bulletin of the History of Medicine* 72 (1998): 693, 696–97; Lucia Anderson, "Rosie the Riveter: Rear-Guard Support That Shattered the Male-Only Mindset," *American Legion Auxiliary National News* 87, no. 1 (2007): 8–10, 12, 14.

4. "There's a War Job in My Kitchen," Nabisco, National Biscuit Company, *Good Housekeeping*, September 1942, 101; "Who Said This Is a Man's War?" General Electric, *Good Housekeeping*, October 1942, 82; "Wanted: Housekeepers to Help the Army and Navy," Pepperell Fabrics, *Ladies Home Journal*, August 1943, 66; "Mother Keep House Clean the Way Uncle Sam Does," Lysol Disinfectant, *Good Housekeeping*, April 1942, 69.

5. "It's No Fun . . . but It's Patriotic!" Gripper Fasteners, Scovill Manufacturing Company, *Good Housekeeping*, March 1942, 175; see Annessa Ann Babic, "Buying and Selling a Piece of the American Pie: Uses and Disuses of Patriotic Consumption," in *The Globetrotting Shopaholic: Consumer Products, Spaces, and Their Cultural Places*, ed. Annessa Ann Babic and Tanfer Emin Tunç (Newcastle upon Tyne, England: Cambridge Scholars Press, 2008), 13–29.

6. "War, Women, and Lipstick," Tangee Lipsticks, *Ladies Home Journal*, August 1943, 73; Anne McClintock, *Imperial Leather: Race, Gender, and Sexuality in the Colonial Conquest* (New York: Routledge, 1995), 190, 196.

7. "Introducing Wonder Woman," in *Wonder Woman #8* (DC Comics, 1941–1942).

8. The field of blue with white stars is said to be on the right because, according to *The Flag Code*, the flag elements of the flag are referred to as if the flag were speaking for itself. Another example says that when the flag is displayed, it should be flown with the stars facing the flag's right and to the right of another state or organizational flag. See *The Flag Code*, 36 U.S.C. § 10.

9. Wonder Woman's original name, the title she would have had before earning the title of Wonder Woman on Paradise Island, is never revealed, and she takes on the name of Diana Prince when she delivers Steve Trevor to the hospital. After she deposits Steve at the hospital, she returns to visit him, discovers a nurse who looks like her without glasses on, and offers to buy her name and identity. Wonder Woman claims to also be a nurse. The real Diana agrees because her fiancé is leaving for South America, and she needs the money to accompany him. Wonder Woman and Diana meet again on only one other occasion, in "The Return of Diana Prince," and on the last page of the issue, the two women decide that Wonder Woman will continue to be Diana Prince and that the real Diana Prince will be known as Diana White—taking on her husband's name. The taking of her husband's name, for the original Diana, provides another poignant example of a gendered society—that is, men were not (nor are they in the current era) expected to change their names upon marriage. "Introducing Wonder Woman"; "The Return of Diana Prince," in *Wonder Woman #9* (DC Comics, 1942).

10. Les Daniels, *Wonder Woman: The Life and Times of the Amazon Princess* (San Francisco: Chronicle Books, 2000), 12.

11. Daniels, *Wonder Woman*, 33.

12. Daniels, *Wonder Woman*, 36–37, 64; *Wonder Woman (Sensation Comics) #2* (DC Comics, 1942). Transformation Island was a failed attempt to convert spies and other undesirables because its only detainee—the Baroness—escaped. But the message of education and cooperation remained, as she later aided Wonder Woman. Additionally, on a side note, it can be ascertained that the Baroness represents several European countries that the United States treated as friends during the war because the nation had previously been skeptical, if not outright hostile, toward them.

13. "And I'm No Part-Time Wife!" Nabisco, National Biscuit Company, *Good Housekeeping*, July 1946, 74.

14. "Put It There, Sister!" Listerine, *Good Housekeeping*, June 1944, 3.

15. "She's Engaged! She's Lovely! She Uses Pond's!" Pond's Cold Cream, *Good Housekeeping*, June 1943, 65; "You Were Coming Home, Dear," Jergens Lotion, *Ladies Home Journal*, January 1944, 43; "Contact," Woodbury Facial Soap, *Ladies Home Journal*, February 1945, 91.

16. "Mother, When Will You Stay Home Again?" Adel Manufacturing Company, *Saturday Evening Post*, May 6, 1944, 99.

17. Robert L. Griswold, *Fatherhood in America: A History* (New York: Basic Books, 1993), 189.

18. Susan Faludi, *Stiffed: The Betrayal of the American Man* (New York: Perennial, 2000), 5; Benita Eisler, *Private Lives: Men and Women of the 1950s* (New York: Watts, 1986), 41–42.

19. Tyler Cowen, *In Praise of Commercial Culture* (Cambridge, MA: Harvard University Press, 1998), 197.

20. Michel Foucault, *The History of Sexuality: An Introduction*, trans. Robert Hurley (New York: Random House, 1990): 1:53–54.

21. Foucault, *The History of Sexuality*, 1:26–27, 1:86; Betty Friedan, *The Feminine Mystique*, 20th anniversary ed. (New York: Dell, 1983), 71; Judith Butler, *Gender Trouble: Feminism and the Subversion of Identity* (New York: Psychology Press, 1990), 96.

22. Soldiers' letters home during the Vietnam War still showed love, respect, and longing for their families, but in contrast to World War I and II, they lack the patriotic and emotional pull calling for home-front women to stand strong and wait patiently for their man's return. Instead, many of these letters express disdain for the military, the conditions of the warfront (an element seen in most wartime letters), and perceptions about why the United States should not be in this conflict. For examples of such war letters. see Andrew Carroll, ed., *War Letters: Extraordinary Correspondence from American Wars* (New York: Washington Square Press, 2001), 391–443.

23. Daniels, *Wonder Woman*, 19, 33, 34, 36–37; "Wonder Woman's Rival," in *Wonder Woman #178* (DC Comics, 1968); "Wonder Woman's Last Battle," in *Wonder Woman #179* (DC Comics, 1968).

24. Alice Kessler-Harris, *Out to Work: A History of Wage Earning Women in the United States* (Oxford, England: Oxford University Press, 1982): 300–1, 305; Susan Douglas, *Where the Girls Are: Growing Up Female with the Mass Media* (New York: Three Rivers Press, 1994), 171–72. By the 1960s, women who did not work for wages were steadily entering the workforce, with 29 percent of married women working in 1950, 35 percent in 1965, and 40 percent in 1975. Furthermore, in 1950, one third of married women worked, half at full-time positions, and by 1975 almost half of them worked, with 70 percent at full time. Even with progress, women were still regulated to "women's jobs" (i.e., teacher, secretary, nurse) and discouraged from taking professions. In 1970, fewer women held PhDs than in 1940; women composed 51 percent of the population; and they made half that of men (average yearly income for women at $4,000). In 1960, the median annual income of full-time working women had fallen by 60 percent to that of men.

25. "Wonder Woman's Rival," *Wonder Woman* 178 (September/October 1968): n.p.

26. Bradford Wright, *Comic-Book Nation: The Transformation of Youth Culture in America* (New York: The Johns Hopkins University Press, 2003), 350–51. In 1972, Marvel Comics published *Shanna the She-Devil, Night Nurse,* and *The Cat.* These femme characters and books were crafted from all-female writers. The sales of all three lagged behind other publications, including *Wonder Woman,* and they each only survived for five published episodes.

27. For an image of *Barfly*, see "Exhibitions: Luis A. Jimenez," Plains Art Musuem, http://plainsart.org/exhibits/the-white-album-the-beatles-meet-the-plains/barfly/.

28. Daniels, *Wonder Woman*, 136–46.

29. "Pilot: The New Original Wonder Woman," *The New Original Wonder Woman*, 70:53, 1976, http://www.thewb.com/shows/wonder-woman/pilot-the-new-original-wonder-woman/b6dad16f-4e16-41f0-8534-590f88ef6c44; "The Man Who Could Move the World," *The New Original Wonder Woman*, 46:17, 1977, http://www.thewb.com/shows/wonder-woman/the-man-who-could-move-the-world/fef55001-89f5-42ea-8dff-37225ab9c8f9.

# SEVEN

## Comic Containment

*No Laughing Matter*

James C. Lethbridge,
Bloomfield College

The comic-books medium is one immersed in culture. Much like movies or music, comic books are created to sell, and their popularity is directly dependent on consumer demands and preferences. This concept of supply and demand, while certainly fascinating to a scholar of economics, is also relevant to a historian. As the public makes demands on the comic-book industry, indicating what themes and styles it desires to see, the industry supplies comic books that fulfill these perceived needs. The content desired by the public is reflected clearly within the pages of the comic books themselves.[1] Looking between these pages can provide a glimpse into the attitudes and desires of a culture during any given period in history.

The way in which public desire is reflected by the content of comic books can be seen in the popularity of superhero comics during World War II. During the war, nearly 80 percent of all reading material in army camps was comic books. The troops desired reading that was exciting yet also reinforced the values they were fighting for.[2] This demand resulted in the proliferation of characters such as the infallible Superman and the patriotic Captain America, both of whom were clad in red, white, and blue and fought vehemently against oppression and injustice.

Yet, over time, the demands that the public made of the comic-book industry began to change. Rather than demanding tales outlining the dichotomous struggle of justice versus injustice, the general U.S. public began seeking comic books that more accurately portrayed the gray areas of life. Alan Moore and David Lloyd's *V for Vendetta*—a British creation written during the political upheaval of the 1980s, when the climate verged on radical conservatism—serves as an example of American thirst for new storylines. *V for Vendetta* outlines the exploits of an anarchist who overthrows his conservative/fascist/totalitarian government. This story emanates directly from Moore's fear of fascism in his own government, and its popularity speaks to the fact that it appealed to similar suspicions in readers since its publication in 1988; that is, it has continually sold well, especially on the American market. As one reads in *V for Vendetta* of the nation's undesirables being interred in concentration camps, one can imagine a frightened British public fearing the same thing, which had in reality been suggested by Margaret Thatcher.[3] To read this comic in its historical context—noting the public sentiment and its effect on the content of the supplied comic books—provides an idea of the cultural moods mirrored within its pages.

## VILLAINS AND HEROES: SECURITY AND FEAR

The historical context for comic books in the 1950s is an interesting one. Elaine Tyler May proposes that during the 1950s, American culture was a "containment culture," one in which fear and insecurity could be countered by peace and security if the fears were properly contained: a fear of sexual promiscuity could be properly contained within the unit of marriage; the fear of insecurity at work could be contained within the unit of the home; and the overarching fear of subversion could be contained by relegating subversives to their various units, creating scapegoat groups of communists, homosexuals, and virtually any other social deviants. For May, culture during the 1950s was a dichotomy between fear and security.[4]

The great fears of the decade were often avoided through this method of containment. It is easy, however, to focus on the procurement of security when discussing containment and, in doing so, fail to recognize its implicit notions. To look at social issues during the 1950s in terms of fear versus security without looking at the exact methods in which fear was averted and security attained simply calls attention to the moods of the period, without looking to the exact methods used and the ideologies behind them.

Take, for example, the fear of promiscuity. During the 1950s, a happy married life yielded security, and so a woman—and, to a lesser extent, a man—of dubious sexual character posed a direct threat to that refuge. These women became *bombshells*, a direct reference to the widespread fear of destruction by atomic bombing. The iconic picture of a sexually charged woman became a scapegoat for fear, a breach of familial security, and a representation of the broader fear of atomic holocaust.[5] While matters essential to security were contained within units, objects of fear became scapegoats without. This is the first notion implicit within the concept of containment.

The second notion is more integral to containment, but it is also more subtle. When a source of fear could not be eradicated or was so widespread that eradication was impractical or impossible, it could be sublimated and used to promote positive values rather than negative ones. To look once again to the idea of sexual containment, the aforementioned bombshells were regarded with fear and contempt. However, at the same time, the sexual prowess of these women was advocated within marriage as a means to promote familial security. The powerful sexuality of a woman could be "harnessed for peace" within the confines of a socially acceptable marriage.[6] The notion implied is that common objects of fear could be utilized toward the ends of greater security.

These examples point to much broader steps within the containment process. Three of these steps can be seen clearly in the comic-book industry as one traces its history across the 1950s: fear leading to containment (and oftentimes suppression), containment spurring the creation of scapegoats, and scapegoats themselves being sublimated within their proper societal boundaries—all three phases can be seen distinctly in the comic-book industry during the 1950s. Although not always chronological and oftentimes overlapping, these three phases reflect general attitudes of the American culture of the 1950s.

First is the phase started by fear, which leads to containment. The experts of the late 1940s and early 1950s viewed comic books as the leading cause of juvenile delinquency. By outlining cases where juvenile crime was either directly or indirectly influenced by the objectionable content found in comic books, these experts fostered a fear in the American public that the medium caused moral degeneration in children. Experts continued to foster this dread by drawing correlations between the specific fear of comic books and the general angst of familial breakdown, subversion, and communism. By directing blame on the comic-book industry, Americans attempted to contain these anxieties within a predisposed framework. This phase is outlined by the works of Frederic Wertham, newspaper articles documenting the growth of fear, and the overarching fear of communism and subversion in the United States during the 1950s.

The second phase of containment leads to suppression and the creation of scapegoats. Much in the way that the fear of unrestrained sexual desire was contained within the proper framework and dissipated by creating a scapegoat of the idea of sexually promiscuous women, the American public, joined by experts and government officials, dissipated its fear of subversive comic books by creating a scapegoat of the entire industry. Comic books alone were blamed for juvenile delinquency, as

evidenced by the Senate Subcommittee Hearing into Juvenile Delinquency (SSHJD), which—although in nomenclature a committee dedicated to
finding the cause of juvenile delinquency—focused solely on the influence of comic books, disregarding other possible influences. These hearings and the published works of Dr. Wertham created a moral panic,
resulting in the comic-book industry becoming a scapegoat for juvenile
delinquency.

The third phase is that of the scapegoat becoming sublimated and
utilized to use popularly held negative practices and ideologies to promote positive ones. This occurred as the comic-book industry began to
reevaluate its place in the American public. The SSHJD caused a severe
wane in the popularity of comic books, and to retain a valid business, the
comic-book industry not only turned from its negative practices but utilized them in acceptable ways. Accordingly, the industry increased production of comic books focusing on love and domestic life, seen most
clearly through Chester Gould's *Dick Tracy* stories. Using the popular
crime-story formula, writers were able to provide entertaining stories
using negative ideals, such as crime, kidnapping, and murder, to promote positive ones, such as family, integrity, and fighting for noble
causes. This trend continued with the 1950s war comics, which maintained the popular gore of the negative crime comics. Yet, the trend was
justified by focusing it on U.S. enemies and showing their barbarity and
brutality. The industry also began to promote the educational value of
comic books by first using them to advertise the excitement of education
and then by producing educational comics, such as the award-winning
*Classics Illustrated* series.

## THE COLD WAR CONSENSUS AND THE PSYCHOLOGY OF DEVIANCE

As the United States exited World War II, it entered the Cold War with
the Soviet Union—being fought, not with bullets and firearms, but with
political ideologies and economic practices, all progressing under the
looming fear of impending nuclear war. Being fought on grounds of
ideology, the Cold War caused the United States to form "the Cold War
consensus," a national identity that pitted America directly against Soviet
Union.[7] American capitalism accentuated a free market, whereas Soviet
communism emphasized a controlled market. American government
was opposed to Soviet communism in every respect.

This extreme ideological counterattack resulted in the widespread fear
of communism, exhibited by the practices promoted by Senator Joseph
McCarthy, J. Edgar Hoover, and the House Un-American Committee.
These practices included sustained attacks on and purges of social deviants, including gay men, lesbians, and any persons with suspected ties to

the Communist Party.[8] This was not a fear that could be attacked physically, like the fear of fascism that resulted in World War II. Accordingly, it was expressed as a larger fear of subversion. Matthew Costello, quoting Victor Navasky, states that the House Un-American Committee "hearings were instrumental in developing the US Cold War consensus: 'A major contributor to this . . . was the ex-Communist whose testimony helped create, confirm, and fix the image of the Soviet Union as the *subverted* of American capitalism, to link Soviet imperialism abroad to the 'red menace' at home." This testimony helped persuade Americans that Russians were a greater fear than Hitler.[9] The fear of communism was not a fear of direct attack; rather, it was one of subversion and infiltration from the inside out.

This fear of subversion was not strictly limited to a terror of communism, however, as evidenced by the research of May, mentioned earlier. The fear of subversive communism often took on the identity of some other negative force, from the aforementioned fear of sexuality outside of marriage to the fear of familial breakdown. Historian Matthew J. Costello so aptly notes,

> The popular fear of communists infiltrating the United States and undermining it was manifest in the wide array of popular entertainments. . . . The rhetoric of the government and anticommunist experts—that the family was the bulwark of American values and thus the greatest weapon against the communists—linked the popular fear of communists to fears about the breakdown of the family.[10]

The hysteria of anticommunism often took the form of more general anxieties, which are frequently showcased in 1950s comic books. More so, the critiques of the industry published by Frederic Wertham exacerbated the situation.

Wertham, a psychologist working in Harlem's Lafargue Clinic of the New York Quaker Emergency Service, published an article in 1949 in the *Saturday Review of Literature* entitled "The Comics . . . Very Funny!" In this short article, Wertham rails against the comic-book industry, linking it directly to the juvenile delinquency that he encounters in his clinic. For Wertham, the proliferation of comic books causes "manifestations of brutality, cruelty, and violence "[11] In an article published a year earlier, Wertham attributed the rise of juvenile delinquency to comic books stressing "crime, sex and sadism."[12] Wertham's claims illustrate the first phase of containment: fear.

The next stage involves the containment of this fear, and much like the containment of the aforementioned fear of sexual promiscuity, this containment results in repression. A plethora of newspaper articles focused on Wertham's crusade against the comic-book industry, highlighting the general topic of fear. This anticomic stance began to take on legal implications in 1950, when Dr. Hilde Mosse, a colleague of Wertham, urged lawmakers to follow Canada's lead. He suggested enacting legislation prohibiting the sale of certain comic books on newsstands on the grounds of public health and safety. In 1951, the fire continued to spread and became more legislatively explicit, as Wertham "declared that most of the 80,000,000 comic books sold monthly in the United States caused the psychological mutilation of children." In 1952, no less than six bills were submitted to the New York State Legislature urging censorship. In 1953, these bills were passed into law. [13]

Wertham encouraged the fear of subversion by comic books and managed to bring this hysteria to a peak in 1954, when he published his magnum opus on the subject of comic books: *Seduction of the Innocent*. This four-hundred-page tome outlines—in detail—his grievances with the comic-book industry. This work is the literary predicator to the apex of comic-book censorship: the 1954 SSHJD. A thorough reading of *Seduction of the Innocent* shows the intense concentration and research that Wertham devoted to his study of the genre. He gives page after page of specific quotations and even provides numerous illustrations to elucidate his points of sexuality and violence in the medium. [14] He is certainly exhaustive in his primary research. However, his correlation between the comic-book industry and his research as a clinical psychologist lacks cohesion. For instance, Wertham examines more than twenty-five cases of juvenile delinquency. References to when and where the events occurred, as well as where one could find corroborating evidence, are absent. Furthermore, he makes blanket statements, such as "There is nothing in these 'juvenile delinquencies' that is not described or told about in comic books. These are comic book plots," insinuating a cause-and-effect relationship between comics and children but without any substantial evidence. [15] The data that he does present are merely circumstantial or coincidental, as when he describes a boy who accidentally shot another one: "we came to the conclusion that the fact that he was an inveterate reader of comic books was an important contributing factor. His favorite comic book, read over and over, contained no less than eighty-one violent acts, including nineteen murders." [16] He also refers to studies conducted by himself and his colleagues that are suspiciously omitted from official reference. There is an overall lack of documentation throughout the work, with the only example being a list of comic-book publishers mentioned for their violent publications.

This lack of documentation forces the reader to trust Wertham's personal credibility as an expert in his field, a common trend in the 1950s to reply on so-called experts. The widely popular Dr. Spock books are another example of this cultural phenomenon. This trust, as seen with Dr. Spock and other scientific experts, was extended toward the government and its officials. The line between civilian "experts" and politicians became blurred as civilians, such as novelist Philip Wylie, became members of government boards and committees. [17] As the government began taking a more active role in everyday life, it was implied that proper governmental administration and the appointment of key experts could solve social problems, and civilian experts began to have a great influence over day-to-day American life.[18] This deep trust in experts is important to the discussion of the containment and suppression urged by the SSHJD.

## LEGISLATING CONTAINMENT: THE SSHJD

The SSHJD was a three-day-long hearing held in 1954 and geared toward discovering the roots of juvenile delinquency in the United States. Most notably, it focused on the possible degenerative effects of comic books. This hearing was the American people's attempt to contain its insecurity with juvenile delinquency.[19]

The goals of the committee may have been noble; however, the general fear of communism and subversion permeates the hearing, illustrating how the suppression of comic books goes hand in hand with the repression of communism. For example, take the testifying of one individual about the actions of the American Civil Liberties Union in Minnesota. He quotes Naval Intelligence as saying, "American Civil Liberties Union— this organization is too well known to need description. The larger part of the work carried on by it and its various branches does undoubtedly materially aid communistic objectives." He further quotes Congress as saying, "The American Civil Liberties Union is closely affiliated with communistic movement in the United States and fully ninety percent of its efforts are on behalf of Communists who have come in conflict with the law." By linking the deep American fears of communism with the popularity of comic books, government officials and so-called experts created a new fear, one now centering squarely on the comic-book industry. Describing this process, John Sringhall remarks that "moral panic" arises when media and official outlets (the federal government here) exaggerate the actual threat offered.[20] Can the motive and effects of the SSHJD be more aptly described?

The effects of this suppression were twofold. Creating a scapegoat out of the comic-book medium had far-reaching effects on the comic-book industry itself. Despite the relative brevity of the SSHJD, its impact on the comic-book industry was profound. Suspicion was cast on the enormously successful crime and horror comics, and as a result, comic-book companies began to fold as quickly as their pulp-paged products.[21] The industry was affected primarily in terms of economics, as laws strictly regulated the content of comic books, and concerned parents—made fearful by the statements of Wertham and the SSHJD over the past seven years— began to take a more active role in the suppression of comic books. This is where the third stage begins: sublimation/utilization of scapegoats.

## THE INDUSTRY STRIKES BACK: SUBLIMATION

As early as 1950, the comic-book industry began to conform to the desires of the American public. Although its efforts were either unnoticed or ineffective, as seen by the insistence on censorship throughout the 1950s, the early part of the decade marked a slight departure from the habit of comic-book publishers. A 1950 article proclaims, "Since the ban on crime comics in Ottawa, Canada, Professor Zorbaugh reported that the demand there for 'love and romance themes' was unbounded."[22] Although these kinds of comic books came under fire for promoting implicit sexuality, it is clear that an early attempt was made to placate anxieties and promote a culturally positive subject through this commonly considered negative medium. One example of this conformity to pressure within the industry is displayed in the classic Dick Tracy story *Crewy Lou* (serialized in newspapers from May to November 1951).[23]

Deviating from his usual battles with organized crime, fascism, and gritty violence, writer Chester Gould focused on the home life of Dick Tracy and his new daughter, Bonnie Braids. Special attention is given to the domestic side of Dick Tracy, showing him not only as "an astute detective *and* a fast-shooting lawman" but also as a "tortured father." It portrays the emotional distress of Mrs. Tracy when her daughter disappears, and the tear-filled reunion takes up six silent panels, ending with a lamp shining on a Bible.[24] This story blends the negative subject of crime with the social perceptions and beliefs of sanctity and family, attributes common to the 1950s. The crime is clearly against the family, and as such, drastic measures, including physical violence, are necessary and commendable to preserve that positive concept.

The Dick Tracy story *Model* provides another provocative portal for these concepts. Serialized from January to March 1952, it deals even more explicitly with the fears expressed by parents. *Model* is a love story involving Tracy's adopted son Junior and his first love, Model. However, being a detective comic, it also deals with crime. The crime in *Model*, however, is not the killings by crime syndicates or the subversions of Nazi sympathizers. Instead, the juvenile delinquency of Model's teenage brother takes center stage. Gould directly addresses the fears of the American public that comics promote juvenile delinquency by showing that crime, even juvenile crime, does not pay.[25]

Looking to an even more familiar face, one can trace the containment process in the Superman stories of the 1950s. Mark Waid describes Superman, from his inception in 1938 until the dawn of the 1950s, as "a quick-tempered social activist whose dedication to the ideals of truth and justice apparently put him above the rules and regulations of common society. . . . [He] would have gladly bent the Miranda Laws with his bare hands."[26] The Superman of the 1940s was a scrapper, a hero who would let nothing, not even the American ideals of due process, stand in the way of his quest for true justice. However, in the suppressive climate of the 1950s, the writers of Superman comic books needed to reevaluate his identity. As the culture began to decry violence and crime in comic books, even Superman, the paragon of American justice, would need to be contained. Waid also notes that as the 1950s progressed, "Superman gradually curbed his rebel ways to become more of a super-lawman—a global Boy Scout, if you will."[27] A look to the narratives helps to show-case this transformation—and process of containment—from superhero to super civil servant.

A quick survey of titles of Superman stories from the 1950s shows that he was seemingly no longer interested in fighting heroic battles with the forces of evil. Instead, he focused his superhuman prowess toward more domestic worries. Superman finds himself in "The Menace from the Stars!" battling not a Martian invasion but dangerous weather caused by an incoming asteroid. He rescues beachgoers from an incoming wave and saves a Midwestern farmhouse from destruction in a tornado.[28] These actions are a far cry from "bending the Miranda Laws with his bare hands." They show clear evidence in the shift of comic-book publishers moving away from stories of crime and violence and toward those of everyday issues. The suppression of undesirable influences—in this case, violence and crime—is one of the steps in the containment process, and a Superman relegated to fixing domestic inconveniences evidences the se-vere climate of fear, in which violence, no matter how just, was anathe-ma.

In "The Girl Who Didn't Believe in Superman!" the narrative moves beyond the repressive stage of containment into the stage of sublimation and showcases how even the supreme power of Superman can be con-tained within noble, albeit humble, accomplishments. In this story, the titular hero is "forced into his most puzzling case" by convincing Alice, an unbelieving blind girl, that he indeed exists. Exhibiting the full gamut of his abilities, Superman is unable to convince Alice of his superpowers until he uses his X-ray vision to espy a shard of glass behind her eye. Having made his diagnosis, Superman dons surgical scrubs and heals Alice, then proceeds to take her on a grand tour of the Seven Wonders of the World. He later beats a peeping tom from the rafters of her house. As it turns out, this voyeur is none other than Alice's father, who abandoned his family when he found out his daughter was blinded from a car acci-dent that he caused. Now that Alice's sight has been restored, thanks to Superman, the family is once again whole. Superman leaves them, say-ing, "Nothing I've ever done had made me so glad that I really am a Superman!"[29] The writer of this story contained Superman's powers, pre-viously used in violent acts against all manner of forces of evil, within the units of family and personal well-being. Superman's abilities were show-cased as constructive rather than destructive. His X-ray vision, now contained for domestic endeavors, cures a girl of her blindness, and his superhuman strength rebuilds a broken family.

It is clear that under the repressive influence of Wertham and the SSHJD, even the character of Superman, poster boy for the comic-book industry, was contained. His superhuman feats were restricted to solving everyday problems, and his superhuman abilities were sublimated toward the ends of promoting health and securing family unity. In response to the concerns of the SSHJD, the violence so common to Superman stories in the 1940s was toned down, and his narratives were used to support cultural ideals. Once again, the narrative impulse of comic-book medium was changed to both remain culturally acceptable and to dissipate the fear of subversion by comic books themselves. [30]

To further dispel this fear of subversion, the comic-book industry attempted to promote comic books as educational aids. An ad from 1950, presumably published throughout the decade, features the tagline "The World of Adventure in BOOKS." It depicts two boys perusing their local library, annoyed with the lack of excitement in traditional books. However, three comic-book heroes appear on the scene and relay thrilling exploits, suspense, action, and gallant deeds. The stories they told derived from *Last of the Mohicans, The Adventures of Robin Hood,* and *The Story of King Arthur and His Knights*. The ad ends with one of the boys proclaiming, "Golly! Thanks! We didn't know what we were missing! I'm getting a library card right away!" The text underlying the ad reads, "Published as a public service in cooperation with leading national social welfare and youth-serving organizations, this page appears in more than 10,000,000 magazines of the National Comics Group (Superman-DC Publications)." [31]

What is apparent here is the defense that the comic-book industry took of itself by sublimating the negative into the positive and by turning the subversive comic book into a promoter of education and intellectual growth for children. The heroes and characters that so often were the source of juvenile delinquency are shown as leading children into a world of "exciting" education and reading.

These slight departures were not enough to quell the growing fear of comic books however, and the industry continued to shift its focus throughout the 1950s. The closure of many publishers flooded the comic-book job market with unemployed writers and artists. While a lack of demand and a surplus of supply certainly did not help the economics of the comic-book industry, it did allow the exploration of areas not previously entertained. The need to cater to the desires of the American public greatly diminished, allowing such freedom. This newfound autonomy resulted in the creation of much lighter comic books throughout the mid- to late 1950s, which either were so innocuous as to border on ridiculous or became explicit in their aforementioned sublimation. [32]

A key example of this type of explicit sublimation can be found in the war comics of the 1950s. As mentioned earlier, comic books made up the bulk of wartime reading for the American soldier. During World War II, comics depicting the war effort of America in Europe and the Pacific were extremely popular. They were full of patriotic nationalism, and they promoted Americans as freedom-fighting antifascists.[33] However, with the ending of the war, interest in these wartime comics waned, and the popularity of horror and crime comics rose. In the 1950s, however, fascism was replaced by communism, and America's entrance into the Cold War opened a new medium from which to draw war stories. The Korean War in particular provided writers with vast amounts of material to work with, allowing them to hearken back to their World War II style and use the grittiness of their unpopular crime comics to teach valuable lessons about cultural ideals.

This new type of war comic from the Cold War era allowed the medium to move in a new direction. The "constant threat of infiltration and subversion intensified by the [House Un-American Committee] and Senate hearings . . . made the communists an even more dangerous and insidious enemy than the Nazis."[34] With the fear of communism as a backdrop, comic-book writers could feed off this calamity by using the violence and gore of their crime stories to portray the evil communists. Communists were presented as uncivilized barbarians whose battle tactics flew in the face of any notion of "civilized warfare." Brutal and merciless, resorting to assassinations and torture, they represented the antithesis of American soldiery, standing gallantly against the threat of a Red invasion. The stark sense of good versus evil present in this depiction of the Korean War, as well as the blood and glory common in crime stories, set the stage for war comics portraying the war as a "glorious crusade against the evils of communism."[35]

When looking at war comics in terms of being sublimated and utilized, note the attention given to them during the SSHJD. In a list of criteria for judging the level of "morbid emotionality," a comic book could be considered objectionable if it included stories or illustrations deemed to go against national endeavors.[36] The American government clearly had an interest in promoting its own war efforts, and comic-book writers of the 1950s sublimated their gritty style to promote this very notion.

Another example of explicit sublimation/utilization is the continuation of the educational trend discussed earlier. However, while the comic-book industry in the early 1950s was subtly promoting the general idea of education and educators were slowly beginning to realize the educational potential of comic books, the industry in the mid- to late 1950s made this idea explicit. A 1956 article tells of educators who began to view comic books as an "important track" to childhood education and mental development. Furthermore, comic books in the *Classics Illustrated* received awards for its contributions to children's literature, something of a prodigious achievement given the hostile climate toward the medium during the decade.[37] An early issue of *Classics Illustrated* features a full retelling of Robert Louis Stevenson's *Treasure Island*, complete with a full-page biography of the author, as well as supplemental pages, one describing "pioneers of science" and another telling the story of a heroic dog, showing the explicit goal to use this particular comic book—and the new goal of the industry as a whole—to educate as well as entertain.[38]

## COMIC BOOKS CONTAINED: AN OLD HERO BEHIND A NEW MASK

While the comic-book industry did indeed shift its focus and its methods to remain a viable source of entertainment under the growing power of the SSHJD and the legislative powers that be (as evidenced by the proliferation of romance stories and so-called educational aids), the shift in practices was not always as paradigmatic, as has been shown. The concept of containment, boiled down to its most basic thesis, is this: social orders deemed unsavory by society become contained within certain structures into become culturally acceptable. Sexuality does not need to be eradicated; it simply needs to be contained, within the confines of the family unit. Violence does not need to be done away with; it also needs to be contained, within the unit of patriotic duty against fascism or communism. Similarly, the culturally "unsavory" elements of comic books were not expunged; they were simply contained within units that were deemed socially acceptable.

In comparison with tales written in the preceding decades, those written during the 1950s are just as violent and dark, if not more so. In *Crewy Lou,* there are scenes in which a villain is crushed by a descending elevator, a crying infant is knocked to the floor of a moving vehicle and brutally slapped, and the titular villainess is smoked out of a guard tower before falling to her death.[39] The violence and grittiness that were hallmarks of the *Dick Tracy* series were not eliminated. Instead, they were contained within a culturally acceptable unit—in this case, that of familial loyalty and integrity. The violence condemned by Wertham and the SSHJD in popular crime stories was made acceptable in Dick Tracy by containing it within a narrative arc toward a socially acceptable purpose: to preserve the solidarity of the family.

The sexuality decried by the SSHJD was contained in a similar manner. "Castoff Love," a romance story published in 1954, follows the love life of Nan, a nubile girl who has, since childhood, lived under the shadow of her older sister, Nola. When they were children, Nan always received Nola's castoffs—an old doll, a used dress. Now that they are older and at a marriageable age, Nan, apparently unlucky in her romantic pursuits, receives Nola's castoff boyfriends. At one point, Nola's current squeeze, Bob, follows Nan into the moonlit night after his date with Nola. In an opportune moment, Bob reaches for Nan, kissing her with parted lips "hard against [hers]," leaving Nan with "[her] heart pounding."[40] Nan finds out, however, that she has been played by her sister, who set up the entire encounter to hurt Nan and flatter Bob. Later, after Nola has finished with Bob, she brings home Gene, another man who, even more so than Bob, leaves Nan "breathless." After watching Gene and Nola kiss passionately, Nan runs to her bedroom, where Nola finds her and taunts her with a wedding dress, reminding Nan not to get any "wild ideas about Gene—the way you did with Bob." After several weeks of being drawn to the wedding dress "as if [she] was a moth," Nan flees the house, only to be confronted by Gene, who reveals his undying love for her, sealing it with another open-mouthed kiss. Nan ends her story with the words, "I realized my wildest dream would never end—it would be my whole life."[41]

There are several important things to note in this rather long summary of "Castoff Love." The juxtaposition of Nola and Nan—Nola, the unrestrained woman who changes partners and ruins relationships, and Nan, the pure little sister whose only dream is to be married—embodies the fear of the promiscuous woman mentioned earlier, and she serves as a warning. It is the pure, monogamous girl who has her dreams come true—within the confines of marriage—while the promiscuous woman, who is uncontained, will be forever unfulfilled.

The art in the story also conveys a subtle sexuality, one that is subdued and protected. It is Nola who wears the low necklines and the tight sweaters, while Nan generally appears in high-collared dresses and her work uniform, again juxtaposing the loose woman to the pure virgin. Also, while Nan may be the more modest of the two, she is drawn to be more attractive, superficially and sexually. She has an ample bosom that, while not exposed, is certainly given presence by generous shading. Nan's sexuality is contained within a framework of modesty, one that, according to Elaine Tyler May, creates "the aura of untouchable eroticism . . . warding off sexual contact but promising erotic excitement in the marriage bed."[42] Nan's sexuality has been drawn to be contained, a teasing glimpse of the sexual joys of a properly contained relationship.

Sexuality is certainly present in this story—pounding hearts, hard kisses, men that leave the protagonist short of breath—yet it has been contained within its proper framework: in this case, first in a warning against promiscuous behavior (for women anyway; no thought is given to Bob and Gene necking with two sisters) and second in the promotion of the idea of marriage and the family. Sexuality is not prohibited nor eradicated; it has been contained properly within the structure of marriage.

It is clear then that although the comic-book industry responded to the SSHJD in part by changing its subject matter—turning from the crime and horror stories of the 1940s to the patriotic, educational, and romantic stories of the 1950s—it continued to print stories with similar elements of crime, violence, fear, and sexuality by containing them within story arcs that were culturally acceptable. In this way, the stories were contained within narratives that showcased containment.

To conclude, the changes in the comic-book industry during the 1950s provides a mirror in which to view the prevailing notions of the American public during the decade. One can see clearly the general fears of the time, the methods used to deal with these fears, and the attitude toward these fears. With attention given to these general aspects as seen through the development of the comic-book industry, several conclusions (implications at least) can be drawn. The strong call for censorship seems to point to a higher premium put on safety than on individual rights. The heavy reliance on the advice and opinions of experts seems to point to a general lack of independent thinking among the American public and shows a willingness to unite around key issues almost blindly, all in the name of security. This trend is furthered by the trust placed in government by the American public, a trust that seems relatively unquestioned under the firm belief that the government is looking out for the good of American citizens. These implications and scores of others show the importance of the comic-book medium in deciphering the American past.

## NOTES

1. Ferenc M. Szasz and Issei Takechi, "Atomic Heroes and Atomic Monsters: American and Japanese Cartoonists Confront the Onset of the Nuclear Age, 1945–80," *Historian* 69, no. 4 (2007): 728–52.

2. Johanna Rizzo, "ZAP! POW! BAM!" *Humanities* 27, no. 4 (2006): 28–29.

3. Alan Moore and David Lloyd, *V for Vendetta* (New York: DC Comics, 2005), introduction, 158–61.

4. Elaine Tyler May, *Homeward Bound* (New York: Basic Books, 2008), 11–12.

5. May, *Homeward Bound*, 106–7.

6. May, *Homeward Bound*, 108.

7. Matthew J. Costello, *Secret Identity Crisis: Comic Books and the Unmasking of Cold War America* (New York: Continuum, 2009), 38–50.

8. May, *Homeward Bound*, 12–13.

9. Costello, *Secret Identity Crisis*, 52, emphasis mine.

10. Costello, *Secret Identity Crisis*, 51.

11. Frederic Wertham, "The Comics . . . Very Funny!" *Saturday Review of Literature*, May 29, 1948, 6–10.

12. "Juvenile Delinquency Seen on Increase; Quaker Official Blames New Comic Books," *New York Times*, June 24, 1948.

13. "Urges Comic Book Ban: New York Psychiatrist Says They Pollute Minds of Children," *New York Times*, September 4, 1948, 16; "Psychiatrist Charges Stalling Tactics on Legislation to Control Comic Books," *New York Times*, January 24, 1950, 9; "Health Law Urged to Combat Comics, Legislative Group Is Asked to Offer Bill as Protection against Crime 'Virus,' Licensing Also Proposal, Psychiatrist Says Some Books Are 'Cause of Psychological Mutilation of Children,'" *New York Times*, Decem-

ber 4, 1951; Douglas Dales, "6 State Bills Seek Comic Book Curbs: Censorship before Publication Urged—Industry Expected to Oppose the Program," *New York Times*, February 20, 1952; "Obscene Books Ban Pushed at Albany: Assembly Vote for Bill Giving Police and Sheriffs Broader Powers Is Unanimous," *New York Times*, March 4, 1953.

14. Frederic Wertham, *Seduction of the Innocent* (New York: Rinehart & Company), picture inset between pages 212 and 213, throughout.

15. Wertham, *Seduction of the Innocent*, 155.

16. Wertham, *Seduction of the Innocent*, 168.

17. May, *Homeward Bound*, 29, 93.

18. Costello, *Secret Identity Crisis*, 35.

19. Robert C. Hendrickson, "United States Senate, Subcommittee of the Committee on the Judiciary, to Investigate Juvenile Delinquency," in *The Comic Books*, ed. Jamie Coville, http://www.thecomicbooks.com/clendenen.html.

20. Richard Clendenen, "United States Senate," 39; John Sringhall, "Horror Comics: The Nasties of the 1950s," *History Today* 44, no. 7 (1994): 10.

21. Mike Gold, "Introduction," in *The Greatest 1950s Stories Ever Told* (New York: DC Comics), 7.

22. Madeline Loeb, "Anti-comics Drive Reported Waning: 'Love' Type Found Replacing 'Crime'—Medium Gains as Educational Aid," *New York Times*, January 21, 1950.

23. It may be wondered why, in a work on Wertham and the Senate Subcommittee Hearing into Juvenile Delinquency's influence on the containment of comic *books*, has the discussion here turned to a comic *strip*, namely, Dick Tracy. It is worthy to note that while the Dick Tracy narratives written by Chester Gould were, at their inception, printed in strip form in newspapers, these selfsame stories were then republished in comic book form. Garyn Roberts, author of *Dick Tracy and American Culture: Morality and Mythology, Text and Context*, in an e-mail states, "Many of Chester Gould's 'Dick Tracy' newspaper strips were adapted for Whitman Publishing's Big Little Books (starting in 1932), and then in Black and White over-sized comic book reprints of the strips in the 1930s. These reprints by Dell and by David McKay publishers were forerunners of the standard comic book format of the mid and late 1930s. Dell publishers reprinted Gould's Dick Tracy from then until the late 1940s will little editing and textual change. When Harvey Comic Book Publishers took over reprinting stories in the 1940s and 1950s, Gould's strips were severely compromised and changed. In fact, other artist did the covers and some of the interior art; some of the content (art and storylines) was cut and changed." Any comic book, regardless of its origin, was well within the scope of Wertham and the Senate Subcommittee Hearing. Furthermore, the fact that Dick Tracy comic books published in the 1950s were heavily edited for content further shows the strength and severity of the Senate Subcommittee Hearing and Wertham.

24. Chester Gould, "Crewy Lou," in *The Dick Tracy Casebook*, ed. Max Allan Collins and Dick Locher (New York: St. Martin's Press), 55, 56–103, 103.

25. Gould, "Model," in *The Dick Tracy Casebook*, 105, 106–24.

26. Mark Waid, "Introduction," in *Superman in the 50s*, ed. Mark Carlin (New York: DC Comics, 2002), 5.

27. Waid, "Introduction," 5–6.

28. "The Menace from the Stars!" (1954), in *Superman in the 50s*, 23–34.

29. "The Girl Who Didn't Believe in Superman!" (1955), in *Superman in the 50s*, 35–44.

30. This is a very small sampling of narratives showcasing Superman's containment by domestication. For a more complete survey, one need look no further than the collection of Superman stories in the previously cited *Superman in the 50s*, which contains such scenes as a young Superman training his Kryptonian dog and a love triangle among Superman, Lois Lane, and Lana Lang.

31. "Institutional Ad: The World of Adventure in Books, 1959," in *The Greatest 1950s Stories Ever Told,* ed. Mike Gold (New York: DC Comics), 234.

32. Mike Gold, "Introduction," in *The Greatest 1950s Stories Ever Told*, 8. See "The Masters of the Unknown: The Secrets of the Sorcerer's Box," as it features an Olympic wrestling champion, a master skin diver, a circus daredevil, and a "war hero and fearless jet pilot" as protagonists. Also, "Tommy Tomorrow: Marooned in the Fourth Dimension" features the titular character transported to a dimension in which words are spelled backward, both in *The Greatest 1950s Stories Ever Told*, 259–82, 171–76.

33. D. Melissa Hilbish, "Advancing in Another Direction: The Comic Book and the Korean War," *War, Literature and the Arts: An International Journal of the Humanities* 11 (1999): 210.

34. Hilbish, "Advancing in Another Direction," 210.

35. Hilbish, "Advancing in Another Direction," 211, 215.

36. Richard Clendenen, "United States Senate, Subcommittee of the Committee on the Judiciary, to Investigate Juvenile Delinquency," exhibit no. 6b, 50.

37. "Comic Books Held Aids to Education" *New York Times*, April 3, 1956.

38. Alex Blum, *Treasure Island* (New York: Berkley), 1949.

39. Gould, in *The Dick Tracy Casebook*, 77, 90–93, 99.

40. Frank Giacoia and Pamela Johnson, "Castoff Love, 1954," in *The Greatest 1950s Stories Ever Told*, ed. Mike Gold (New York: DC Comics), 203–4.

41. Giacoia and Johnson, "Castoff Love, 1954," 206–8.

42. May, *Homeward Bound*, 108.

# EIGHT

## Graphic/Narrative/History

*Defining the Essential Experience(s) of 9/11*

Lynda Goldstein,
Penn State Wilkes-Barre

Representing—in a meaningful way—the events commonly referred to in the United States as "9/11" poses a threefold challenge shared by any significant contemporary event: how do we define such an event as "historical"? how do we represent that contemporary historical event for audiences? and how do we do so within a cultural context whose highly mediated visual texts often compete for meaning with more complex discourses about a historical event? Meeting such a challenge necessarily means maintaining the freshness of detail found in documentary reportage (conveyed in the electrifying "now") while simultaneously representing a deeply contextualized historical account (situated in the textured "past"). It means using a form of discourse—of causality, of narrativity, of balance between "objectivity" and "subjectivity"—capable of representing a historical experience that we are collectively still living (although not necessarily collectively remembering). It means communicating to others the simultaneity of personal memory, collective memory, and historical memory. Finally, it means representing for others an experience that captures a sense of *being present in a memory* of an event so significant that we experience "living past," or what Pierre Nora characterized as "the present itself . . . seen as a retrieved, updated past, its presentness . . . rooted in what went before."[1]

What I suggest in this chapter is that three graphic narratives dealing directly with the experiences of 9/11—those terrorist-coordinated airplane attacks intended for New York City and Washington, DC—provide specific and crucial approaches to representing the essential experience(s) of the event. To be considered here, then, are two memoirs—one by Art Spiegelman, *In the Shadow of No Towers* (2004), and the other by Alissa Torres, illustrated by Sungyoon Choi, *American Widow* (2008)—and the graphic adaptation of *The 9/11 Commission Report*, by Sid Jacobson and Ernie Colón (2006). Each uses not only the "graphicness" of the graphic narrative to remediate the overdeterminedness of those well-known, iconic televisual and photographic images but also a "narrativeness" to situate a perspective (individual or collective) that the reader must negotiate actively and often in the present tense, ultimately producing versions of history that provide access to an essential experience of 9/11: being *in* the "true" historical moment. As Hayden White argues, "the conjuring up of the past requires art as well as information."[2] Indeed, White goes on to say, "Anyone wishing to write narrative history in our time would do well to think about the discursive instruments available in the rhetorical tradition for the translation of structures into sequences and the task of giving to histories the look of a novel for purposes of representing not only the truth about the past but also the possible meanings of this truth"[3] Sounds rather like the definition of a graphic narrative, no?

So, let's sketch out some of the theoretic issues to which these narratives address themselves, their unique qualities as graphic narratives, and what it is I mean by "essential experience," "graphicness," "narrativeness," and "overdetermined iconicity." Then we'll look at some ways that these narratives work to provide readers with an essential experience of the contemporary historical event that is "9/11."[4]

## SOME ISSUES OF REPRESENTING CONTEMPORARY HISTORY

As novelist William Faulkner once wrote, "The past is never dead. It's not even past." For "lived" contemporary events, a challenge to representation is that there is no clearly demarcated line that signals "*that* is history" over there and "*this* is now" over here. Because the political, social, cultural, and economic reverberations of the event are not *only* in the past but also in our individual and collective memories, we are not only still living them in the present time but also living with their ramifications in the present and future. No matter how transformed a contemporary historical event may be by subsequent events and by an enriched knowledge of its happening, it remains the event itself and becomes—simultaneously—part of the fabric of that which we consider our everyday lives . . . at least, that is, while there are those who have living memories of the event. Once those who remember are gone—and others of us forget—then contemporary history is much more easily categorized as a kind of "past" history.

A related challenge to representing such a contemporary event of "historic" proportions is how to convey scope. In the case of "9/11," scope is twofold, for not only does it refer to that which is bigger than any individual memory or action or consequence, but it also refers to that which is multiply and complexly formed. After all, what we mean by "9/11"—despite the singularity and abbreviation of that date as a referent—refers to events that took place in multiple locations during a two-hour time frame but were years in the making with years of direct, subsequent repercussions. In addition to the obvious spatial multiplicity (ultimately, three U.S. locations for plane crashes) and temporal expansiveness (the years of terrorist preparation and the years of "Homeland Security" measures subsequent to the two hours of attacks) is the global staging of the attacks. Further are the personal, national, and global responses to them as well as the time frame stretching years before the attacks and, at the moment of this writing, more than a decade (of commemorations) after. Pitched into global relations, "9/11" laps out in ever-expanding rings of time and consequence like a pebble dropped into a lake.

Finally, another significant issue is that so much of our sense of "9/11" as a "historical" and "unprecedented event" is visually sutured to the now iconic live television images and news photography of the second plane incomprehensibly colliding with the second of the World Trade Center's Twin Towers and the subsequent implausible collapse of both.[5] Moreover, there are the other indelible images—of "Falling Man," of fleeing crowds pursued by explosions of debris, of the Twin Towers' skeletal remains amid dust and rubble in the waning light of evening. The very texture of the event for many of us is primarily a visual one (and too often a reductively New York–centric one, leaving out of many of our imaginations and memories the reality of the destruction at the Pentagon and the downed flight in Shanksville, Pennsylvania).

Thus, it is that 9/11's manifestation as a "real" event in memory and history is one spatially and temporally mediated by the documentary visuality of live television and photography archived by news media websites, Google images, and commemorative museum exhibits in perpetuity. This visual mediation remains the case even for those who lived through some aspect of it in "actual" proximity to any of the three physical sites. This being the case, then, a very real question is how one represents an essential experience in such a highly mediated cultural context. This challenge is in some ways similar to representing the "unrepresentable" horrors of a repressive Iranian regime (Marjane Satrapi in *Persepolis*) and the Holocaust (Art Spiegelman in *Maus*). In the case of 9/11, however, there is a simultaneous challenge: to represent the *over*represented, the *over*determined with meaning. (To take one example, Governor George Pataki began calling the rebuilt tower at the site of the World

Trade Center the "Freedom Tower," overly determining the meaning of the replacement building as a symbol for [and only for] the notion of freedom. The Port Authority of New York, which is charged with the construction project, has since been renamed One World Trade Center.) The challenge for these graphic narratives is to visually represent that which is already so indelibly represented through "real" and iconic images while simultaneously attempting to convey stories that provide readers with access to an essential experience of this "lived" personal/ national/global event.

## SOME APPROACHES: GRAPHICNESS, NARRATIVENESS, AND ESSENTIAL EXPERIENCE

There has been no shortage of artistic and analytical responses to 9/11, all of which have had to contend with scope and iconicity. One approach has been to circumvent the visual. We might consider the musical responses of Bruce Springsteen's *The Rising* or John Adams's *On the Transmigration of Souls* or, more recently, Steve Reich's *WTC 9/11* or the dance response choreographed by Paul Taylor in "Promethean Fire" or even some of the literary responses, such as Claire Messud's novel *The Emperor's Children*, in which the event figures as an unanticipated spectral backdrop to the comedy of manners playing out in the months prior to September 11, 2001.[6] Another approach has been to reshape "the real" of these images through metaphoric revision, such as Don DeLillo's *Falling Man* (whose title references Richard Drew's photograph) or the subtle temporal and spatial shifts that Colum McCann achieves in his revisionary use of Philippe Petit's 1972 tightrope walk between the Twin Towers in *Let the Great World Spin*.[7] Most relevant to our discussion is still another approach: using the tacit constructiveness of the hand-drawn image allowed by the graphic narrative format to disrupt the iconicity of the "real" embedded in those iconic mediated images such that the writers'/ graphic artists' subjectivities—their essential experiences—can provide readers with a way of renegotiating those images and recontextualizing the events of 9/11 through specific lived experiences.[8] So, let's consider three ways in which these three graphic narrative texts attempt to meet the challenges of representing contemporary history as sketched above.

## THE CHALLENGE OF CONTEMPORARY HISTORICAL DISCOURSE: GENRE AND RHETORICAL PURPOSE

*The 9/11 Report: A Graphic Adaptation*, by Jacobson and Colón, comes closest to what we might call traditional, or "objective," historiography because, as a distillation of the essential information in the investigative commission report issued by chair Thomas H. Kean and vice chair Lee H.

Hamilton, it is the most concerned with providing the reader with the experience of determining *what happened* so that security measures might be enhanced and such an event *might never happen again*. To make this point explicit, its cover caption states the following in unavoidably stark "comic book" language: "THE NATION WAS UNPREPARED. HOW DID THIS HAPPEN. AND HOW CAN WE AVOID SUCH TRAGEDY AGAIN? Such a purpose, then, is consistent with the tandem explanatory purposes of the bipartisan commission's report. (Indeed, the two cochairs of the 9/11 Commission considered their efforts so accurate that they wrote a brief introduction to the graphic narrative.) These explanatory purposes were foundational to the primary objective of the commission's report: to provide recommendations for corrective action. That is, the aim of the commission's report issued in 2004 was to recommend specific and necessary changes to the U.S. Congress, the president, and the appropriate (federal) agencies so that what happened on 9/11 would *not* happen again, at least not for the reasons explained therein.

Its recommendations were typically targeted toward the various local, state, national, and international levels of responsible (governmental) parties who might act on behalf of the United States and its citizens, particularly relative to emergency response or (air) security protocols. For example, citing "four kinds of failure: in imagination, in policy, in capabilities, and in management" on page 107, the commission issued numerous recommendations, such as fostering a comprehensive coordinated response among police, fire, and port authority personnel; replacing the current position of director of central intelligence with a national intelligence director; and incorporating strategically focused, democratically inclined educational projects and initiatives into our foreign policy. These kinds of recommendations (and the intelligence upon which they were based) are visually and textually represented by Jacobson and Colón.

But most significant for our purposes in thinking about how this text fosters an "essential experience" of 9/11 for its readers is its characterization of private citizens as "first responders" who are encouraged to act accordingly. And I say "most significant" for our purposes because of the way that the graphic adaptation represents its recommendation that civilians be included in the planning and *be prepared* to take appropriate action. In chapter 9, "Heroism and Horror," the analysis section focuses on the level of success in evacuating the Twin Towers. Its first panel is indeed filled with sixteen lines of text to provide context for the subsequent graphic panels of the chapter's analysis. For example, the text explains that of the 2,152 individuals who died in the World Trade Center who were neither rescue workers nor airplane passengers, 1,942 were located at or above the impact zones. Meanwhile, the number of successfully evacuated civilians has been estimated at between 16,400 and 18,800, easily eight times the number killed. The first graphic panel after this text-dense panel thus focuses on those "private-sector civilians," that is, typical occupants of the Twin Towers with whom the reader is most likely to identify. Depicted on page 97 are five (primarily white) office workers attempting to "get out of here!" through a stairwell door as light from an undisclosed source glows upon their backs. This "heroic civilians panel" is followed by a group of ten graphic panels including either overlapping text boxes or inclusive text to portray some of the less successful aspects of the evaluation. The final graphic panel of this analysis section on page 98 concludes that "the lesson of 9/11 for civilians and first responders can be stated simply: in the new age of terrorism, they are the primary targets. The losses that day demonstrated the gravity of the threat and the need to prepare ourselves."

Note the shift of the collective pronoun referring to civilians from "they" to "we." Initially in this chapter, civilians are equated with first responders; here that association is disaggregated as civilians *and* first responders, although not in a way that excludes the possibility that there may be many who will simultaneously occupy both categories of experience. But more to the point is the inclusive shift to "we," clearly suggesting a collective, even national, interest in and responsibility for civilians being prepared *as* the "first responders" who "must plan for the next attack." This is but one example of the ways in which *The 9/11 Report* provides its readers with a rhetorically purposeful means to have an essential experience of 9/11, for we are all—in a post-9/11 world—potentially in a position of civilian/first responder in the event of another attack, which *The 9/11 Report* posits as highly likely (at least to be tried).[9]

## THE CHALLENGE OF SPATIAL MULTIPLICITY AND TEMPORAL ELASTICITY: GRAPHIC NARRATIVITY

Originally published in *Der Spiegel* as sixteen serial sheets in large format, Art Spiegelman's *In the Shadow of No Towers* reproduces some of the experience of reading the original through its extra-large format on heavy-stock paper. We might consider the graphic rendering of memory on page 3 as illustrative of Spiegelman's technique. Laid out vertically over two pages are four stylistically distinct layers of images or graphic narratives, which nevertheless work coherently in a typical gridlike left-to-right, top-to-bottom reading pattern to convey a multilayered narrative about "smoke." Conjoined with the smoke arising from the first plane crash into the North Tower are layered storylines that disrupt one another spatially and temporally. Situated between the twin images of a smoking North Tower on the left and a smoking cigarette mirroring the tower's verticality on the right are three other storylines. The first regards the "present" time of the strip—9:15 am—as Art, wheezing from a two-pack-a-day cigarette habit, and his wife race to find daughter Nadja in high school just four blocks north of the Twin Towers. The second story-line, interrupting the first, is situated in a "future" time in which Spiegel-man's Maus alter ego explains that his daughter's high school became a rescue center (an indication that it was not destroyed in the "present" of the two-pack-a-day storyline and that they likely found her uninjured). Thus, these moments of parental panic are the primary—or at least in-itial—narrative thread of this panel series, but it is immediately resituat-ed to another (and an other's) essential experience: that of Art/Maus's father's experience as graphically told in *Maus*. As such, the second story-line is already conveying the historical weight of the 9/11 experience—even as its ramifications are as yet unknown—through a reference to the difficulties of representing an essential experience of the past: "I remem-ber my father *trying to describe* what the smoke in Auschwitz smelled like" (emphasis added). Lighting a cigarette in this series of eight panels, Art/Maus makes a metonymic narrative connection between the "inde-scribable" smell of Auschwitz with the toxic "witch's brew" of Lower Manhattan's air. But what really makes this storyline work is that by the final two panels, Art/Maus's own cigarette smoking has so filled the pan-els that it is clear his "2-pack-a-day" self is implicated in this toxicity—of the environment and of the necessary work of trying to represent the experience. Disrupting the first "present" storyline of racing to find Nad-ja, this second story line provides a complex historical context that simul-taneously provides a morally disruptive sense of continuity: a smoking line of familial and moral culpability from Art's father, Vladek, to Art to Nadja, from Auschwitz to the Twin Towers, from the Nazis to the 9/11 terrorists, from the Environmental Protection Agency's assurances to Art's smoking habit. There is seemingly no escape from this hazy histo-ry.[10]

The page (at the crease) then reverts to the present-time parental race to find Nadja only to have it again interrupted at the moment of revela-tion that a third plane—this time in Washington, DC—has engulfed a building in flames. At this moment, the high school security guard trans-lates his Spanish-language radio news broadcast for Art: "They saying a plane just bomb into the Pentagon." The translation here is not only from Spanish to English and from "present" to another past—Art's own past at the age of Nadja in 1962—but also from one graphic style to another. For overlaying this panel of the security guard's explanation is a reproduc-tion of a Topp's Inc. bubblegum card from the series entitled "Mars At-tacks" depicting a garishly colored "Washington in Flames." So vivid is this Topps-induced memory card that the narrative space of the "present" storyline is completely infiltrated, overlaying and obscuring a subsequent panel.[11] It is not until two panels later that a boxed caption informs the reader, "He figured the Martians had invaded. That Paris was burning and Moscow was vaporized. His wife stayed more focused" (on finding Nadja).

This present-time parental search storyline ends with a bizarrely banal announcement from the principal that "absolutely *no* students will be allowed outside for lunch!" yet the hazy history graphic narrative is not over. Once again, it is disrupted by a stylistically different image. This image, while sharing a certain retrosensibility with the Topps card, is clearly constructed in an agitprop graphic format. Reprising the images of Dick and Jane from the 1960s' reading primers, it features them wearing respirator masks (making them look like alien anteaters in an atomic-scare science fiction film). Their image is topped with the bold graphic interdiction "NYC TO KIDS: *DON'T BREATHE!*" The narrative trace returns to concerns about air quality due to smoke and takes us *back* up to the eight-panel Art/Maus storyline regarding the smoke of Auschwitz/Lower Manhattan/Art's two-pack-a-day habit. But it also takes us *forward* because it overlays the next and final eight-panel storyline in which Art/Maus rails against the Environmental Protection Agency's certification that the air quality is fine. Here he explains the NYC TO KIDS image is a poster that he designed for a protest at City Hall (one that some parents found "too shrill"). But the explanation is not simply textual in its narrative; it is also graphic in its narrative by showing Art/Maus in this image holding the stake on which the poster is affixed and having the poster overlap the image in which he explains the poster, which happens also to completely obscure the first panel of the final storyline, which ends with Art/Maus lighting a second cigarette and acknowledging that the stress has him smoking even more than usual.

Text and graphic narrative overlay one another simultaneously on the page while also overlaying time—present, past, future—in such a way that the essential experience of this event is inextricably one of memory and history. Describing how the page is laid out and how one would typically read it (acknowledging, of course, that there are multiple paths of reading graphic narratives) is necessarily more tedious than simply reading it for one's self. That is part of the point, of course, that graphic narrative can communicate ideas—and the juxtapositions of those ideas through montage—far more effectively than text *and* must do so with the necessary complicity of the reader.[12] And it is this complicity that helps to achieve the "essential" experience, the "lived" history of the event that we're reminded of in the intertexual, pastiche references to *Maus*, "Washington in Flames," and the eponymous heroes of the Dick and Jane series.

## THE CHALLENGE OF ICONICITY: GRAPHICNESS

One of the distinguishing characteristics of graphic narratives is their hand-drawn illustrations, which provide the reader with a clear and consistent sense of the constructiveness of the narratives; that is, they literally draw attention to the fact that they are produced subjectively (even cosubjectively in the case of *American Widow* and *Graphic Adaptation* with their coauthors) and that they reflect a subjective point of view rather than an illusory "reality" effect so often conveyed by documentary film, television, or photography.[13] This constructiveness, while evoking a "real" referent—that graphic image looks like the Pentagon, or this one resembles secretary of defense Donald Rumsfeld—is also clearly a rendering of the referent, an interpretation filtered through another's sense of the referent. It is, in short, an interpretation. And it is this signaling of interpretation that is also an invitation to the reader to interpret, to decode the image in a more lingering reading than a more "realistic" documentary image whose transparency with the referent is the hallmark of its reality effect but which also can lead to reading the image as an icon with a singular or narrow range of meaning.

Each of these three texts uses the visual syntax of the graphic narrative to convey to its readers its experience of 9/11. While each has a different intentional purpose for his or her work and a different narrative point to be made, each also has in mind some common qualities of the essential experience of 9/11: primarily, this essential experience is characterized by a temporal and spatial simultaneity—of event, of reception, and of interpretation. We'll consider examples from each of the three texts that highlight one of these intentional foci.

The first chapter of *The 9/11 Report* initiates its corrective investigation at the moment of the near-simultaneous attacks of the four planes targeting the World Trade Center, the Pentagon, and the Capitol (although the last will crash en route in a field in Shanksville, Pennsylvania, as a result of passengers attempting to seize control of the aircraft from the hijackers). It does so in the very first panel on page 2 in an elegantly wordless and graphic way: a realistically rendered greenish radar image showing four parallel white blips at staggered positions and a thin yellow sweep is centered on a stark black page. The right-side page 3 extends the blips visually by presenting four generic white airliners in formation above the chapter 1 title "We have some planes . . . ," again on a black background. Thus, the graphic setup on these two pages establishes in stark relief the chapter's parallel structure as it conveys the simultaneous stories of each of the four flights in two separately sequenced timelines. According to the top caption, the first timeline on page 6 shows in twelve pages (six two-page spreads) "the simultaneous histories of the four hijacked airplanes as they began and completed their horrendous missions" drawn against the same stark black background as the preceding pages. Arrayed from top to bottom are flights 11 (7:59), 175 (7:58), 77 (8:10), and 93 (8:00) in the order in which they became airborne.

Divided into four roughly equivalent horizontal sections across two pages, the time markers for moments of significant information or action occur in roughly the same area of each so that images are only present when there is something significant to depict and so that one can read the events as they occur in time for a single flight's timeline horizontally while being able to read the events for multiple flights at roughly the same time vertically. For example, the hijacking of flight 11 occurred at 8:14, and we read across this flight's timeline, at the top of the pages through a series of tightly juxtaposed images and text, some of the details (stabbings, mace, bomb threat) of the hijacking. Because the events of this first fifteen minutes occur fairly quickly, there is a density of visual information here, which is in stark contrast to, say, flight 93 depicted at the bottom of the pages, whereby we receive one large black and yellow panel on page 6 depicting three planes at their respective gates at 8:00 and, on page 7, a text box (white text on black background) informing us that the airplane "had to sit on the ground for 42 minutes." Thus, we can read the simultaneity of flight action, including the hijackings, crashes, passenger rebellion, and responses from air traffic controllers, airline officials, and the Federal Aviation Administration, with near simultaneity across each two-page spread for all four flights and thereby gain an appreciation of the enormity of the communications failure (which is one of the narrative points being made here).[14] In other words, seen collectively on the page, the coordination of these four flights' terrorist mission is obvious, but read singly and sequentially (by two different airlines, multiple air traffic controllers, and an ill-informed Federal Aviation Administration), it is equally obvious how poorly everyone except for the flight crews and passengers read the plot. Armed with information from friends and family via their cell phones (and aided by the forty-two-minute delay), passengers on flight 93 were in a position to "connect the dots" and fight back, downing the plane before it reached the Capitol.

Ok, so what kinds of temporal and spatial simultaneity are we talking about? There is the obvious graphic presentation of what was happening in multiple locations over a two-hour period in a manner that we can grasp visually in milliseconds compared to the "real" time that it took those involved to put these pieces together. The hindsight provided by reconstruction—as acknowledged by the report itself—provides clarity of vision in retrospect that was impossible to see as the event unfolded. And the beauty of Jacobson and Colón's series is that it reconfigures the geographic chaos of those hours into a neat temporal/spatial package that does not diminish the emotional impact of what was happening to those directly involved or for those of us reading about it later. Indeed, it converts the inchoateness of each of these three locations—with the twinned terror of the World Trade Center attacks—into a comprehensive and comprehensible event, which sets the stage for the thrust of the purpose of *The 9/11 Report*: bring clarity, involve all in national security, and restructure our thinking and institutions to act promptly and courageously.

This use of graphicness is in many ways entirely different from that found in Alissa Torres's memoir *American Widow*. While it too provides a timeline, it is one that is more specifically linear, as events unfolded in time, rather than reconstructing it so that we can see events *across* time. In many ways, this would be consistent with how an average person would have experienced the event in real time, so its re-creation fits its rhetorical purpose well: to tell a very personal story from Torres's point of view. It is simultaneously about and to her now dead husband, about and to the son born after his death, and about the construction of her widowhood to herself and to those of us who would necessarily define her through her widowhood.

Far less graphically glossy than *The 9/11 Report*, the memoir opens with the hand-stenciled words "Chapter One," followed by the date "September 11, 2001." The following page is nearly filled by a seemingly crayoned rectangle of pale greenish blue blurring into a border of white. Its subsequent page 4 reprises this coloring with the addition of two abstractly rendered birds (almost checkmarks), one black, one white, reminiscent of seagulls or hawks in hovering, distant flight, so that a reader would most likely read this greenish blue–colored, blur-edged rectangle as a sky (but one that is not, incidentally, colored the crystalline azure blue indelibly marked in most of our memories of that cloudless day on the East Coast). The third full-page image in this chapter, beginning on page 5, moves the reader from the exterior to the interior as we see centered within a hard-edged rectangle an older-model television set depicting the "breaking news" image of the Twin Towers, with the North Tower pouring smoke into the sky. The iconicity of this televised image is surrounded by speech bubbles in various formats (round, elliptical, spiky, with and without tails) in six languages conveying the excited admonishment to "turn on your TV!" There are no diegetic, in-the-frame interlocutors. We see no one depicted as speaking or being spoken to. Language erupts spontaneously and in multiple linguistic registers in a single frame around this iconic image. It captures not only that documentary image we know so well in a simple penciled drawing but does it at the moment of its global reception, of its incitement to make sense of what we are seeing: "The World Trade Center was just hit by a plane."

The following three pages (6–8), laid out sequentially in a left-right-left pattern, comprise panels varying in size and number on each page. For example, there are three on page 6, five on page 7, and six on page 8, all neatly arranged to be read from top to bottom, left to right. These three pages of panels establish the time frame from the instant of the televisual image's global reception on page 5 as well as depict various physical locations from the top image of a pregnant woman (who we retroactively learn is Alissa Torres) seated on the bed in a cramped studio apartment watching the television perched on stacked boxes in New York at 8:50 am to President Bush in Florida, depicted in panel 3 and sandwiched between the 9:02 of the second panel and 9:05 of the fourth initiating the second page of this three-page sequence. From here, title captions inform us of a chronology that moves inexorably forward while also giving the *local* time of the new location. Three of the panels on page 7 take place at 9:10 am eastern standard time, but by depicting television viewers in their respective locations, the captions reveal the *local* times such that the local and global become resonant with each other: Los Angeles, 6:10 am; Tokyo, 10:10 am; and Indianapolis, Indiana, 8:10 am.[15] This second page (8) of the three-page sequence of global reception ends with a page-wide panel set in New York half an hour later, at 9:40 am. Here, numerous people on a sidewalk are informed by a passing taxicab driver that "the Pentagon's just been hit by an airplane," shifting the locus of chronological action (a third plane crashing) while acknowledging the proliferation of the loci of reception for this news (no matter where people are globally, they hear this news at the same time in a virtual "live" moment).

This notion is clearly the setup for the panels set in Los Angeles, Tokyo, and Indianapolis and prepare us for the third page of this global reception sequence. As readers, we can anticipate a chronology that will take us to spatially disparate locales, and indeed that is what occurs in the remaining six panels of the sequence. The first five, equally sized panels mark reception of the news of the Pentagon attack from Kuwait, Colombia, London, and Madrid to Cairo at each location's local time. The final, sixth panel in this sequence shifts us five minutes later to 9:45 am and back to New York as we see a young woman with vaguely Asian features looking out her apartment window identified as in Brooklyn toward the billowing clouds obscuring the skyscrapers in the distance. From the can of brushes in the foreground, we might read this image as representing our illustrator, Sungyoon Choi, separated from Alissa Torres by twelve panels, the East River, and fifty-five minutes but joined to her through the experience of visibly witnessing the first of three plane crashes. That New York will be a central referent is hardly a surprise considering that the first two attacks occur there with our memoirist (and illustrator) residing in (witnessing) proximity to the World Trade Center. And, of course, it is the immediate loss of her husband in that attack that will figure so prominently in the narrative.

The final page of this chapter (9) is immediately to the right of the sympathetic global reception sequence. Here, three vertically oriented trapezoidal panels are juxtaposed in a neatly fitted fashion reminiscent of a three-way mirror in a clothing store dressing room. Each depicts a lightly bearded man going about his business as a New York City cabdriver, convenience store clerk, and father of three, respectively, with a speech bubble from an out-of-frame speaker stating "You're Under Arrest." It is only with the repetition of this phrase that we might begin to read the ethnicity of each of these men as (vaguely) Middle Eastern rather than Italian or Hispanic or Eastern European. The tight juxtaposition of these three panels suggests an almost instantaneous and simultaneous interdiction, yet in relation to the previous pages of the chapter, the time shift is unmarked. Minutes, days, or weeks may have passed from that Brooklyn, New York, 9:45 am panel (8). Such a jump cut in time—after so carefully demarcating every other panel's chronology and synchronicity with others—and skewed/fractured framing of the panels is jarring, forcing the reader to make sense of the narrative logic. It should come as no surprise, then, that Choi is suggesting graphically a critique that Torres makes more explicit later in the text: the national security response of random racial profiling in the wake of global, sympathetic, reception was a (socially) fracturing leap in logic.

Art Spigelman takes a different tack toward using graphicness to represent an essential experience of simultaneity, as we've already seen in the ways that he overlays multiple storylines graphically on the page in "a visual paragraph."[16] Yet another element that *In the Shadow of No Towers* adds is a historicity of New York through the lens of turn-of-the-twentieth-century comic characters, in particular the Katzenjammer Kids, who become sutured in meaning to both Art and his wife, as well as to the Twin Towers of the World Trade Center. Such a New York–centric choice as Rudolph Dirks's *New York Journal* comic strip is at once to evoke the "vital, unpretentious ephemera from the optimistic dawn of the 20th century," as Spiegelman explains in "The Comic Supplement" (11) and to situate his own text within the stability of a history—not only of "comics" themselves but of popular and political cultural critique that they so often offered up with their entertainment. It is to suggest that the instability wrought by 9/11 is consonant with the transitory nature of a hand-drawn newspaper cartoon yet to also suggest that the continuity of the graphic medium is also constant and stable—particularly as Spiegelman's serial was reprinted from its *Der Spiegel* magazine run with richly colored plates on heavy cardboard stock—in a way that feels even more stable than the hard- or soft-bound graphic narratives of either of the others.

### AFTERWARD/AFTERWORD: WHAT HAPPENS AFTER THESE ESSENTIAL EXPERIENCES?

In some ways, this is an entirely unanswerable question. After all, each of us as readers—more than a decade later—will have had very different responses to the event, as well as to the graphic narrative representations of these events offered up by these writers. For Spiegelman and Torres, the work that we've discussed here has remained the only graphic narrative evidence of their essential experience. We might think that their work retains its power because of this. But for Jacobson and Colón, there has very much been an "after" experience. With the 2008 publication of *After 9/11: America's War on Terror (2001–)*, characterized as a "work of graphic journalism," Jacobson and Colón have produced a text that captures the essential *history* of the event: a clear and concise reprise of the specific political context leading to the attacks and the actions taken by the United States and its allies against those identified as the perpetrators and those believed to harbor them. Using substantiated news accounts, Jacobson and Colón provide an accurate graphic account in keeping with the rhetorical purpose of their graphic adaptation of the *9/11 Report*.

If this were all that the text performed for readers—provided an extended context for the attacks and response (up to September 2007)—then we might say that the text enriches the essential experience with more— and more accurate—information about the continuing "war on terror," but *After 9/11* contributes something more than that, I think. In the graphic choices it makes to render this history, it offers a subtle tonal shift in how it defines an essential experience. Whereas the earlier text (certainly Spiegelman's and Torres's) conveys the emotional, psychological, and even traumatic experience of the event, *After 9/11* downplays these in favor of a recurring realism at key moments. [17] To provide one example, consider the rendering of the first anniversary ceremony depicted on page 34. The drawing takes up the entire page but requires a quarter turn of the text to view it. Tightly focused on a representative group of casually dressed Americans in the foreground (some with their backs to our point of view), indistinguishable buildings form the backdrop while Mayor Rudolph Giuliani is shown in inset performing the now traditional solemn reading of names of those known to have been lost in the attacks. The entire scene is washed in shades of blue with a minimum of black to indicate clothing accessories such as hats, belts, or shoulder bags. It is a scene of solemnity and grief, held in the surreality of memory. This is in high contrast not only to the extraordinary colorful reality of a panel on the facing page in which lavender- and orange-clad journalists interview United Nations secretary-general Kofi Annan but to specific moments of *reality* that come up against the misinformation that the Bush administration circulated in the media in the run-up to its response.

The subtle shift in representation that I want to draw attention to is an increasing use of a more realistic style at moments of revelation, that is, at moments when representatives of the United States are shown to have misrepresented the truth or when the consequences of our misguided military response in Iraq and Afghanistan are measured by the reality of increasing numbers of killed and injured American soldiers or the decreasing moral support offered by the world in light of dishonorable conduct perpetrated by the administration.

The first notably more realist rendering is of President George W Bush on page 6 after the capture of Saddam Hussein; this is especially the case when read in juxtaposition to the crayoned and diminished (by overlaid text boxes) sketch of Hussein looking unkempt and distraught. President Bush, on the other hand, is depicted as, well, presidential in a three-quarters realist portrait that one might expect to see hanging in the National Portrait Gallery (except for the text bubble informing the unkempt

Hussein, "Good Riddance! The world is better off without you"). In this case, the relative realism of the portrayal functions to underscore the administration's sense of justification for initiating the war in Iraq, but this "real" justification will soon be undermined by the subsequent realist representations. The first of these comes just two pages later in the depiction of 9/11 Commission chair Thomas Keane, whose dialogue bubble states, "We are telling the Congress and the President what we need in order to do the best possible job." Not only does the realism of this portrait, virtually a mirror image of the Bush portrait on page 68, reinforce the gravity of Governor Keane's declaration, but overlaid on his portrait is a text box stating, "The Commission cited the administration's delay in turning over papers as one reason for their request." This textual explanation tips the balance for how to read these more realistic portraits, I would argue, in favor of moments where the "truth" will countermand the alleged justification for the war in Iraq. That the world is better off without President Hussein might well be the case but not, as Jacobson and Colón remind us, for the reasons that the administration claimed as justification—and not, they suggest, as a reasonable justification for the loss of U.S. military or Iraqi civilian lives or loss of reputation and goodwill in the eyes of the world.

This last point is driven home repeatedly by the use of strategic realist portraits on page 85 of secretary of state Colin Powell, interim prime minister Ayad Allawi, and senator John D. Rockefeller, the last of which declared in October 2004, "We invaded a country, thousands of people have died, and Iraq never posed a grave or growing danger." And as the real evidence piles up—the intelligence lapses, the dysfunction of the Iraqi government, the competing assessments of the surge's success in September 2007—so, too, do the number of realist portrayals, finally ending on page 147 with facing portraits of secretary of defense Robert Gates and senator Jim Webb, the latter of whom had attempted legislation to Ensure that troops "spend as much time at home as on their most recent tour overseas, which ultimately would force an earlier return of our troops from Iraq." Of course, we learn, it (and seven earlier attempts) failed to pass. The grim reality of what we as a nation have wrought in Iraq is inescapable in the use of these realist portraits. Ten years after September 11, 2011, the reality remains a two-front war built on the most tenuous of premises and fought against a continued insurgency in Iraq and against a guerrilla force in Afghanistan that, as General Petraeus observes in the closing statement, handily beat the Soviet Union. After graphically relating the personal and essential experiences of September 11, is our afterword to be a realist portrait of failing to extricate ourselves as a nation from the nightmarish consequences of the war on terror?

## NOTES

1. Pierre Nora, "Between Memory and History," *Realms of Memory* 1:11–12.

2. Hayden White, "Introduction: Historical Fiction, Fictional History, and Historical Reality," *Rethinking History* 9, nos. 2/3 (2005): 149.

3. White, "Introduction," 151.

4. In an article eerily and perhaps inevitably similar in theoretical design, the memory of 9/11, particularly in comics such as *The Amazing Spider Man #36*, is discussed by Cathy J. Schlund-Vials, "Crisis of Memory: Memorializing 9/11 in the Comic Book Universe," *Modern Language Studies* 41, no. 1 (2011): 12–25.

5. Jean Baudrillard, *The Spirit of Terrorism*, trans. Chris Turner (New York: Verso, 2002), 47; he claimed "the collapse of the towers is the major symbolic event."

6. Adams's and Reich's respective album cover designs use versions of Masatomo Kuriya's image of the second plane approaching the Twin Towers. Indeed, Reich's album cover art ignited a firestorm of controversy. The acrimony of the protests might be explained by the expected release date of the album on September 6, 2011, a week before the tenth anniversary of the attacks, and illustrates the power of these images, as well as the power of ritualistic commemorations (anniversaries) of events.

7. This is by no means an exhaustive list—one might include more visual art, such as Eric Fischl's sculpture "Tumbling Woman," for instance—nor is it a privileged list of the "best" examples of some of these types of responses. As such, 9/11 will continue to be a muse for decades to come, and the reader is encouraged to seek out for himself or herself the many fine artistic responses to it. Whether they singly or collectively also produce a "history," I will leave for the reader to determine.

8. For an excellent introduction to how hand-drawn comics convey a sense of particularity, see Scott McCloud, *Understanding Comics: The Invisible Art* (New York: Kitchen Sink Press), 1993.

9. In other words, the text as just discussed reinforces what Robert Scholes would call "narrativity"—the process by which readers actively construct the story—by specifically inviting readers to imagine ourselves as potential first responders like those graphically represented. Robert Scholes, *Semiotics and Interpretation* (New Haven, CT: Yale University Press, 1982).

10. As Herman argues in relation to Alison Bechdel's *Fun House*, "experiential knowledge of life-transforming events is less a thing of the past, than a process that flows across some time frames"; David Herman, "Multimodal Storytelling and Identity Construction in Graphic Narratives," in *Telling Stories: Language, Narrative, and Social Life*, ed. Deborah Schiffrin et al. (Washington, DC: Georgetown University Press, 2008), 204.

11. For a discussion of this overlapping in *Maus* as a strategy for grounding history in the personal, see Charles Hatfield, *Alternative Comics: An Emerging Literature* (Jackson: University Press of Mississippi, 2005), 142; for a discussion of this overlapping in *In the Shadow of No Towers* as a representation of personal traumatic experience, see Chrisophe Dony and Caroline van Linthout, "Comics, Trauma and Cultural Memory(ies) of 9/11," in *The Rise and Reason of Comics and Graphic Literature: Critical Essays on the Form*, ed. Joyce Groggin et al. (Jefferson, NC: McFarland, 2010), 179–83.

12. While some students have reacted with initial confusion and a desire for a more linearly rendered graphic narrative, they come to appreciate White's claim "that to change the form of the discourse might not be to change the information about its explicit referent, but it would certainly change the meaning produced by it." Hayden White, "The Question of Narrative in Contemporary Historical Theory," *History and Theory* 23, no. 3 (1984): 19.

13. For an explanation of the "reality effect" in documentary film, see Bill Nichols, *Representing Reality* (Indianapolis: Indiana University Press, 1991), 28.

14. Robert S. Petersen, *Comics, Manga, and Graphic Novels: A History of Graphic Narratives* (Santa Barbara, CA: Praeger, 2011), 226.

15. Recall Tony Blair's sense of spatial and temporal simultaneity: "we are all Americans now."

16. Joseph Witek, "Interview with Art Spiegelman," in *Comic Books as History: The Narrative Art of Jack Johnson, Art Spiegelman and Harvey Pekar* (Oxford: University of Mississippi Press, 1989), 277.

17. Dana A. Heller, "Memory's Architecture: American Studies and the Graphic Novels of Art Spiegelman," in *Teaching the Graphic Novel,* ed. Stephen E. Tabachnick. (New York: MLA, 2009), 159.

# NINE

# SuperGay

## Depictions of Homosexuality in Mainstream Superhero Comics

### Kara Kvaran,
### University of Akron

The first Marvel Comics' gay superhero to have his own book, *The Rawhide Kid*, drew fire from both pro- and antihomosexual rights groups. Half the opposition felt that a gay superhero would, at the very least, expose youths to homosexuality and, at worst, encourage such behavior. The other half opposed the campy, innuendo-laden *Kid* as a derogative gay stereotype and a step backward for gay rights. *The Rawhide Kid* was created in the mid-1950s as a wholesome clean-cut cowboy hero. The Kid remained popular through the 1960s and 1970s, but he was killed in 1979. In 2003, Ron Zimmerman began writing a new run of *The Rawhide Kid*, with art by the Kid's original artist, John Severin, who was nearly eighty-two years old. The choice of Zimmerman—a comedian, comic author, and contributor to the *Howard Stern Show*—to write the series shows that Marvel attempted to create something fun and campy rather than progressive. The book was filled with unironic camp that invited the reader to laugh at the premise of a gay effeminate cowboy who constantly insinuated that he was homosexual without explicitly stating it and who shocked the supporting characters by being both flamboyant and tough. He was supposed to present a hilarious contraction: a homosexual who excelled at the hegemonically masculine images of the Old West cowboy and gunslinger.

*The Rawhide Kid's* very existence marks a transition from previous attitudes about homosexuality and comic books. In the twentieth century, comic books were often accused of containing homosexual subtexts, which could foster and encourage such deviant behaviors in their young and impressionable readers. In the twenty-first century, homosexuality has become the focus of superhero comic characters and storylines that directly deal with homosexual issues. Times and American attitudes toward homosexuality and comic books have changed. We can gain a deeper understanding of attitudes toward homosexuality within the comic subculture by examining the shift from the perceived homosexual subtext of early superhero comics through the increasingly normative inclusion of gay and lesbian characters into well-known contemporary franchises such as *X-Men* and *Batman*. Many depictions of homosexuality within superhero comics such as *The Rawhide Kid* present insulting stereotypes, while others offer a more realistic view of gay and lesbian issues.

As material manifestations of culture, comic books provide a window into the social attitudes and beliefs of that culture, similar to film, television, and literature. Comic-book historian Bradford Wright explained the link between American culture and comics: "Put simply, formulas that appeal to audience tend to proliferate and endure, while those that do not, do neither. As a means through which changing values and assumptions are packaged into mass commodities, formulas are the consequence of determining pressures exerted by producers and consumers, as well as by the historical conditions affecting them both."[1] In terms of cultural attitudes toward homosexuality, comic books—specifically, mainstream superhero comic books—represent several obstacles, real and imagined, toward gay and lesbian equality. There was, for example, resistance from publishers who felt that homosexual characters did not fit with their key demographic. These publishers were often fearful of offending antigay activists groups and insisted on publishing comics with central gay characters under their adult-only distribution lines. Homosexual superhero equality also faced resistance from fans who adhered to narrow and traditional modes of femininity, masculinity, and sexuality. A thorough examination of the history of gay and lesbian representations in mainstream superhero comics reveals that initial resistance on the part of the big two publishers (Marvel and DC Comics) and self-censorship (through the Comics Code Authority [CCA]) meant that the gay liberation movement of the 1970s bypassed superhero comics. As a result, the industry lagged behind other forms of media in its treatment of homosexuality. This trend has changed in the past decade, as Marvel and DC Comics have both made an effort to include homosexual characters and storylines in their major titles, and in recent years, the depiction of lesbian, gay, bisexual, and transgender (LGBT) individuals in comics has vastly improved.

This chapter details only the history of homosexuality in mainstream superhero comics published by Marvel and DC Comics. While there is a thriving subgenre of independent and queer-orientated comics and graphic novels, this study concerns itself only with the most mainstream comics. While independent comics or those geared toward a homosexual or queer demographic are certainly deserving of study and would contribute to a greater understanding of comics and popular culture, this chapter concentrates on those published by Marvel and DC Comics. This choice was made for several reasons. These two presses control, by far, the largest share of the comic market, and their books are intended for the broadest possible audiences. Finally, examining only their products places a convenient and manageable boundary on this study.

## BATMAN COULD SEDUCE THE INNOCENT: THE CCA AND HOMOSEXUALITY

Superman, the first popular comics superhero, debuted in 1938. Jerry Siegel and Joe Shuster—two middle-class second-generation Jewish Americans—combined their fascination with popular culture, their belief in the American dream, and their adolescent fantasies of strength and power to create the superhero prototype, Superman. In doing so, they ushered in the golden age of comics. In this early period, from the late 1930s to the early 1950s, superheroes multiplied and comic books flourished. The new industry, however, was not without opponents, and by the 1950s, many began to blame comic books for the rise in juvenile delinquency. In 1954, Dr. Frederick Wertham published a scathing indictment of comic books and the negative effects that they have on American youths. In the book *Seduction of the Innocent: The Influence of Comic Books on Today's Youth*, Wertham argued that comic books turned adolescents into violent delinquents and encouraged sexual perversion: "Chronic stimulation, temptation and seduction by comic books is a contributing factor to many children's maladjustment."[2]

*Batman #84*, "Ten Nights of Fear!" included a scene from the everyday life of Batman and his boy sidekick, Robin. "Morning. And it begins like any other routine morning in the lives of millionaire Bruce Wayne and his ward, Dick Grayson," the exposition stated.[3] The corresponding art depicted the two characters in their pajamas waking up in bed together. While most assuredly this act was not intended to be sexualized, this one panel (also published in 1954) is often showcased by those who believe a strong homosexual subtext to superheroes exists. Wertham also points to Batman: "The Batman type of story may stimulate children to homosexual fantasies, of the nature of which they may be unconscious." For Wertham, the sexual connotations of the comic were obvious: "Only someone ignorant of the fundamentals of psychiatry and of the psychopathology of sex can fail to realize a subtle atmosphere of homoeroticism which pervades the adventures of the mature 'Batman' and his young friend 'Robin.'"[4]

Wertham was not the first to attack comics and link them to juvenile delinquency. In 1950, a new U.S. Senate committee, convened to inspect interstate crime, also investigated comics for promoting juvenile delinquency.[5] Then in 1953, with another Senate committee convened to investigate juvenile delinquency, comic books once again came under fire. The hearings continued into 1954, and this time Wertham testified before Congress. He criticized all comics, but he mentioned superhero comics as being particularly damaging to young people.[6] While Wertham did not explicitly mention sexuality in the hearings, the subject did serve as a platform for his ideas.

With *Seduction of the Innocent* gaining in popularity and the Senate committee hearings drawing unfavorable attention to and protest of the comic-book industry, publishers decided to preempt any censorship by creating their own code, similar to the Hays code, which had governed the Hollywood film industry since the 1930s. With this in mind, the Comics Magazine Association of America was founded, and one of its first acts was the establishment of the CCA, which would henceforth endorse every comic before it could be sold. Approved comics would carry a logo from the CCA on their covers to prove that the standards had been met. The code was lengthy and strict. Comic book historian David Hajdu wrote of the CCA, "The Code was an unprecedented (and never surpassed) monument of self-imposed repression and prudery."[7]

There were several provisions in the new CCA that governed sexuality and marriage. Homosexuality is never specifically and emphatically outlawed, but in the parlance of the 1950s, depictions or implications of homosexuality would not to be tolerated. This portion of the code stated, "Illicit sex relations are neither to be hinted at or portrayed. Violent love scenes as well as sexual abnormalities are unacceptable." Furthermore, all sex must lead to marriage, which was, of course, impossible for same-sex couples. According to the code, "the treatment of love-romance stories shall emphasize the value of the home and the sanctity of marriage." Finally—and perhaps most damning for the possible inclusion of any future homosexual characters—the code stated, "Sex perversion or any inference to same is strictly forbidden."[8] Sex perversion was widely understood as including homosexuality. So, if homosexuality was absent before the implementation of the code, it was outlawed afterward. As a result of the CCA, the gay liberation movement sparked by the Stonewall Riots in 1969 and the push for LGBT equality seemed to bypass the world of superheroes.

Homosexual characters were banished from mainstream comics through the 1980s. Indeed, most every aspect of sexuality was virtually absent from mainstream comics in this era. Reinhold Reitberger and

Wolfgang Fuchs analyzed the lack of sexuality in comics in their 1970 study *Comics: Anatomy of a Mass Medium*: "Super-heroes as well as super-villains seem to have absolutely nothing to show underneath their tight-fitting tights; they all appear to be poor androgynous beings—hermaphrodites who lack the primary sexual organs. Jack Kirby's figures who always stand with their feet at least four feet apart, make this lack pretty obvious."[9] They concluded that possible liberalization of the code could happen in the next decade and make mainstream comics more representative of real-life sexuality.[10]

In 1989 a substantial revision to the code finally occurred. In the interim, when homosexual characters did appear, which seldom happened, they were mostly villainous stereotypes. The first mainstream superhero book to feature gay characters was Marvel's *Hulk Magazine* #23, published in 1980. In this story, mild-mannered scientist Bruce Banner, who when sufficiently angered turns into the Hulk, is cornered in the YMCA men's shower by two would-be rapists, Dewey and Luellen. The men push him up against the wall while he is nude. When Banner, with a somewhat worried expression on his face, asks the men what they want, one replies "Umm! You're soft! And all pearly white—And you've got the cutest little cheeks."[11] He then asks Dewey, his fellow would-be rapist, if he thinks Banner will whine. As the attack progresses, Banner surprisingly does not turn into the Hulk, not even when he is on his knees, and Dewey is beginning to undress. Banner, the reader is told, is more afraid of turning into the Hulk than he is of being raped. He manages to escape by threatening to turn into the Hulk, without actually having to transform. After fleeing, however, Banner becomes overwrought with "fear, horror, and revulsion," in a nearby alley and is unable to stop himself from transforming into the Hulk.

That Bruce Banner is overcome by strong emotions in the aftermath of an attempted sexual assault is probably the most realistic and least insulting part of this storyline. The comic was written by Marvel editor-in-chief Jim Shooter and received a largely negative response. It is interesting that Shooter chose a YMCA locker room as the stage for the attempted assault. YMCAs were known at this time, especially in New York City, as an important location of gay cruising culture.[12] This fact was so widely recognized that the musical group the Village People's ode to the YMCA, which was released in 1978, reached number 2 in the U.S. charts in early 1979. On paper, this was one comic character attacking another comic-book character, but it can easily be read as an attack on gay culture. The first openly gay characters in comic books were sexual predators who prowled public showers looking for unsuspecting straight men to rape. Responding to criticism, Shooter claimed that the story was based on an event that happened to him. Few people were convinced.

Comic writer Mike Grell addressed this issue of *Hulk* in an interview:

> The *Hulk* story was badly done, and so blatantly homophobic that I
> think everybody with a brain in his head who read it was embarrassed
> by it. I was embarrassed to be working in an industry that would allow
> something like that to see print in the first place. It was a badly written
> story, with characters who were very badly portrayed. It only had the
> negative aspects, without showing a balance. I thought it was really in
> poor taste.[13]

The storyline was controversial, and it would be years before Marvel
would depict an openly homosexual superhero. Several writers later
claimed that Shooter issued an edict during his tenure as editor in chief
that there were "no gays in Marvel Comics."[14]

## "I AM GAY!" SUPERHEROES VERSUS THE CLOSET

The first gay Marvel superhero was introduced in the mid-1980s. Northstar, a mutant in the X-Men universe had superhuman speed and was
able to fly. Over the course of his superhero career, Northstar was a
member and leader of Alpha Flight, joined the X-Men multiple times, and
worked with fellow Canadian mutant Wolverine. The character even
briefly had a self-titled series in 1994. He was first introduced in the
*Uncanny X-Men # 120* in 1979, as a part of a Canadian superhero team
named Alpha Flight. In 1983, Marvel tapped comic-book writer John
Byrne to write an Alpha Flight series. Byrne later claimed that in his mind
Northstar was homosexual from his inception, though during the time
that Byrne wrote the series, from 1983 to 1985 the only thing to really
imply that Northstar was gay was his lack of interest in women, though
this was not unusual in superhero comics.

   Not everyone was happy with the character or his subtly implied
sexuality. An anonymous self-identified gay comic-book writer summed
up Northstar in 1988:

> Northstar was never openly gay, he used his powers for his own ends
> and was involved in some illegal activities, and he had the most abra-
> sive personality in Marvel Comics, with the possible exception of the
> Hulk. Absolutely nobody in the Marvel Universe liked him, including
> his sister! It may have been impressive for Byrne to say, "I created the
> first gay super-hero," but I think it's more honest for him so say, "I
> created one of the worst gay super-heroes." I don't think he did gays
> any favors with Northstar. I want to be pleased that he created a gay
> character, but the one he created was such a jerk. He wasn't much
> better than the rapists in the *Hulk* story.[15]

Regardless of his likability, the character endured. In 1985, Byrne passed
the series to writer Bill Mantlo, and afterward, Northstar's sexuality became a bit more obvious. Byrne said of new writer, "He's trying to say
the unsayable about Northstar."[16] It turns out he was.

Writer Bill Mantlo never outed Northstar, but over the next two years, he strongly hinted at his sexuality. Then, in 1987, Northstar was stricken by a mysterious illness. Mantlo indicated in interviews that he intended to reveal that Northstar had AIDS. "It [the AIDS storyline] would give me the opportunity to deal with a frightening, sad, and controversial topic in a comic book—which I had always understood Marvel was about."[17] Before the story could be realized, however, Carl Potts, *Alpha Flight*'s editor, stepped in and deemed it inappropriate to have the only generally acknowledged gay character dying of AIDS. Marvel's editor-in-chief Jim Shooter also chimed in and, according to Mantlo, told him that not only could Northstar not have AIDS but that he also could not be gay. As a result of Marvel's demands, Mantlo and Potts changed Northstar's illness mid–story arc. Northstar no longer had AIDS but instead was afflicted with a mysterious magical aliment. Writer Peter David summed up the conclusion of Northstar's storyline by writing, "The declaration was subsequently made that Northstar was, in fact, a magical being, and was dying because he was away from his magical homeland for too long. Yes, that's right . . . he wasn't gay. He was just a fairy. That's muuuuch better. And the protectors of superheroic masculinity breathed a sigh of relief. That was a close one."[18]

Northstar subsequently disappeared to his magical fairy homeland and was never supposed to return. The character did, of course, return, and subsequent authors have simply ignored the storyline completely. Bill Mantlo somewhat bitterly told LGBT magazine *The Advocate* in 1987, "Northstar couldn't live as a gay character in comics, because it was too controversial, and he couldn't die as one because it was too controversial. . . . Quite honestly, I think it's hypocritical and pointless, but that's comics."[19]

During the 1980s, treatment of homosexuality at DC Comics was almost as sporadic and uneven as at Marvel. Of instance, when rumors and speculation persisted that Star Boy of the *Legion of Super-Heroes* was gay, series creator Paul Levitz wrote him a girlfriend to dissuade any speculation about his sexuality. Meanwhile, in the early run of *John Constantine: Hellblazer*, Constantine had a good friend named Ray Monde, who was an English shopkeeper. Monde was an older man who was in a long-term monogamous relationship and remained faithful to his lover even after the man died. His early storyline dealt with discrimination, gay bashing, and HIV. But he was a supporting character with no powers—not a superhero—and he was older; as a result, he was desexualized and nonthreatening.

DC Comics' first real attempt at a gay superhero came in *Millennium*, in early 1988. Born in Peru, magician Gregorio De La Vega was chosen, along with nine other members, for the superhero team the New Guardians. He took the name Extrano, which means "strange" in Spanish, and he had magical powers. While Extrano never officially stated that he was gay, his sexuality was universally recognized. In fact, Extrano embodied nearly every stereotype of a gay man. He was flamboyant and colorful, and he referred to himself in the third person, as "Auntie." Extrano was mainly used as comic relief, and he never had a boyfriend.

When the New Guardians got their own book in 1988, the title was offered to Steve Englehart, who had created the team for *Millennium.* Englehart wanted to continue to use Extrano and to include political and topical issues from the real world. He wanted to do an AIDS story arc. Then editor-in-chief Dick Giordano okayed the story, but Englehart butted heads with the book's editor, Andy Helfer. According to Englehart, Helfer did not want any homosexual characters in the book, and he thought that Extrano was "cured" at the end of *Millennium.*[20] The two men compromised, and Extrano and two straight members of his team were exposed to HIV while fighting an "AIDS vampire," created by white supremacists named Hemo-Goblin.[21]

Extrano was a controversial figure. Some disliked him because he was gay; others disliked him because he was an effeminate stereotype. Comic writer and artist Keith Giffen described Extrano as an "absolute atrocity and set the cause of doing gay characters in comics back at least ten years. It was like hitting one on the head with a hammer."[22] Englehart defended the character, stating, "I don't think I was perpetuating a stereotype. There *are* flamboyant homosexuals. Is doing one perpetuating a stereotype? I reject the argument that he is stereotyped. There are plenty of people like this, and he happens to be one of them. I was just writing a person."[23] Horrific stereotype or not, Extrano was alive, gay, and a superhero at a time when that was a rare combination.

In the late 1980s, some lesbian characters began to appear in the DC Comics universe. A police captain in Superman's Metropolis (Maggie Sawyer), and the Green Arrow's psychologist in Star City were both lesbians. These women were, however, small supporting characters and not superheroes. There were far fewer female superheroes than male at this point in comic history, so the lack of lesbian superheroes at a time when each of the big two publishers had only one gay superhero is understandable.[24] At the same time, Marvel and DC Comics' adherence to the Comic Code Authority meant that they could not utilize lesbians for sexualized and fetishistic purposes. In conjunction, this meant that there were no lesbian superheroes fighting in the big two.

Then, in 1989, the comic code was revised. While still conservative and strict, the code's provisions about sexuality had relaxed considerably. The new code stated, "Scenes and dialogue involving adult relationships will be presented with good taste, sensitivity, and in a manner which will be considered acceptable by a mass audience. Primary human sexual characteristics will never be shown. Graphic sexual activity will never be depicted."[25] Homosexuality could still be outlawed as unacceptable for a mass audience, but the code removed the stricture against "sex perversion." The 1989 revisions to the CCA did not open the flood gates to a slew of new homosexual superheroes, but it did signal, along with the gay characters of the 1980s, that attitudes were changing, albeit slowly.

In 1992, Marvel's gay superhero Northstar was back, no longer a fairy, but the leader of the Canadian superhero team Alpha Flight. Marvel hired new writer Scott Lobdell to take over the *Alpha Flight* book, and he changed comic history. In *Alpha Fight #106*, Northstar proclaimed, "I am gay."[26] It was the first time that a mainstream superhero declared his homosexuality. Lobdell was drawn to the character from the time that he was first offered the title. "Northstar had always fascinated me because he was always so angry. Why was that? Everyone working in comics and many fans knew he was gay—the always talented John Byrne made it very clear in both the comics and in interviews. But no one in the comic book universe seemed to know it," Lobdell explained in an interview.[27]

With Jim Shooter no longer at Marvel, the CCA no longer as strict, and a writer who actually liked the character and supported his homosexuality, the time was right for the first mainstream superhero to come out. And come out he did. Northstar shouted "I am gay!" while fighting a Canadian hero turned villain named Major Mapleleaf, who dressed like a mountie and wanted to kill Northstar's newly adopted baby, who was born with HIV. Response to Northstar's outing was largely positive. An editorial even appeared in the *New York Times* applauding the comic and proclaiming, "Mainstream culture will one day make its peace with gay Americans. When that time comes, Northstar's revelation will be seen for what it is: a welcome indicator of social change."[28]

## THE QUESTION: FINDING A PLACE FOR HOMOSEXUAL SUPERHEROES

Northstar's declaration, as important as it was, did not do much to change the tone and inclusion of homosexual characters in superhero comics. In fact, it was not until the twenty-first century that a marketed rise in the number of homosexual characters in the comics of the big two occurred. The CCA also began to fall apart at this time and lose its hold on the industry. DC Comics and Marvel both had "mature readers" distribution lines, and they did not submit those comics to the CCA for approval. In 2001, Marvel dropped out of the CCA and started to use its own ratings system. Similar to what the Motion Picture Association of America used, the Marvel system assigned a rating based on age groups.[29] Wertham's fears and the impetus behind the *Seduction of the Innocent* occurred at the height of the Cold War and were driven by the McCarthy-era Red scare of the 1950s. By 2001, however, the Cold War had long dissipated, and many of the sociopolitical fears revolving around conformity were more or less forgotten.

In the last decade, DC Comics and Marvel have attempted to increase the number of homosexual characters in their roster of superheroes. Some have been more critically and commercially successful than others. A few, such as the previously discussed Rawhide Kid, are reminiscent of earlier stereotypical attempts at homosexual characters. The campy, innuendo-spouting Kid, who never outright declares his sexuality, is fairly reminiscent of Extrano. There are other characters—lesbian and gay, adults and teenagers—who have finally broken through into mainstream superhero comics. These characters are well rounded and heroic; they are shown dating and fighting crime.

Since 2003, the DC Comics universe has included two lesbians who are notable for their excellent characterization and for storylines that deal with their sexuality with a matter-of-fact tone. Hispanic detective Renee Montoya was first introduced in the televised cartoon *Batman: The Animated Series*, and she is one of the two characters to cross over from that show into the comic universe. She was heavily featured in *Gotham Central*, a comic about the police detectives of Gotham who must live and work in the city while being overshadowed by the city's masked superheroes, such as Batman. In one story arc, Montoya is forcibly outed at work and to her family when someone posts a picture of her kissing her girlfriend. When already-out lesbian police captain Maggie Sawyer, who was introduced in the 1980s, takes her aside to try to offer her advice and understanding, Montoya calls her out on her white privilege and storms away.[30] Rarely, if ever, had sexuality and race been so realistically dealt with in comics. Much of the credit goes to writers Greg Rucka and Ed Brubaker. Rucka stated in an interview that, to him, depicting Montoya as a lesbian was not a matter of rewriting the character: "It was clear the first time I read her. Other people out there wrote her as straight, and every time I read it, I read it that it was 'bearding.' She read to me as gay and in the closet. And I don't know why I saw that in the character, but literally from the moment I laid eyes on that character, I thought, 'Oh, she's in the closet.'"[31]

When *Gotham Central* ended and Rucka, along with writers Geoff Johns, Grant Morrison, and Mark Waid, began to work on DC Comics' epic yearlong *52*, Montoya became a central character. In this series, Montoya becomes a private investigator and eventually takes over the mantle of the superhero the Question from her PI mentor Vic Sage. When Montoya becomes the Question, she is not Question Girl or Question Woman. She is a hero. More so, she does not show her cleavage or wear a short skirt. Whether it is progressive or stereotypical, Montoya, DC Comics' first major lesbian superhero, wears what her predecessor wore: a pinstripe suit.

Montoya is joined in *52* by her sometimes girlfriend Kate Kane, aka Batwoman. Batwoman was first introduced in 1956 as a love interest for Batman to prove his heterosexuality after the release of *Seduction of the Innocent*. The character was not very popular and disappeared in the 1960s. According to Greg Rucka, the 2006 decision to reinvent Batwoman as a lesbian character in *52* was made by DC Comics' editors, not the writers. The change received a lot of press before the first issue was even published. The *New York Times* wrote a story on the push for diversity at both DC Comics and Marvel, in which they described the as-yet-unseen Kane as a "buxom lipstick lesbian" who was "a lesbian socialite by night and a crime fighter by later in the night."[32] Rucka felt that all the early publicity placed too much focus on the character's sexuality. "When things like that happen," Rucka said, "it certainly gives the appearance of sexuality being more important than character. And sexuality is an element of character, not character. Saying the character is gay is like saying that character is white. It's an element, but it isn't the person."[33] The early hype did not hurt sales or diminish interest in Batwoman. She was successful enough to become the first lesbian superhero to get her own title, *Batwoman: Elegy*, which ran as *Detective Comics #854–860* in 2009–2010.

The inclusion of Kate Kane and Renee Montoya came as a part of a concentrated effort made by DC Comics and editor-in-chief Dan DiDio to diversify their characters. "There's a lot of talk about the 'DC agenda,'" Greg Rucka explained. "And you know what, there is an agenda, but that doesn't mean somebody in editorial is walking around saying, 'You, introduce three new black characters, two Arabs and one homosexual.' That's not the way it works. The agenda is, very overtly, to diversify the world of the DC universe because for the longest time, the DC universe was white and male, and that's not representative."[34] While not all these attempts at diversification survived beyond their initial runs, Kane and Montoya's comics were commercially and critically successful.

While Marvel's editorial staff did not make the public declaration in favor of diversity that DC Comics did, it nonetheless released during the same period several new titles that featured homosexual characters, one of which was the *Rawhide Kid*. Despite having no sex, very little violence, and never stating outright that the Rawhide Kid, whose real name was Johnny Bart, was gay, the book came with a notice on the cover stating, "Parental Advisory Explicit Content." The book was also released under Marvel's MAX line, which featured comics that involved explicit content for mature readers. Although the *Rawhide Kid* was a relatively innocuous comic with no explicit content, its inclusion on the MAX label made the lead character's implied homosexuality seem all the more salacious. Many within the gay and lesbian, as well as comic, communities question whether *Kid* represented a step forward for superhero equality or the continued marginalization of homosexual characters.

At the same time, Marvel had two high-profile homosexual teen relationships in major titles. Brian K. Vaughan cocreated and wrote the *Runaways* beginning in 2003. The comic focused on a group of teenagers with assorted powers and abilities who runaway after they discover their parents are supervillians. One member of the group, Karolina Dean, is revealed to be an alien and a lesbian. In the second arc of the title, a new character, Xavin, arrives and declares that he is Karolina's betrothed from a neighboring planet. When Karolina reveals that she is a lesbian, Xavin is not upset and informs her that his species, Skrull, are shapeshifters, and he transforms into a she.[35] Xavin states that among her species, "changing our gender is no different than changing our hair color," and she has no problem being a female to be with Karolina, whom she loves.[36]

Xavin's gender is often questioned, especially by Molly, the youngest of the group. Xavin presents as male more often than female, though he does go back and forth. Karolina even questions Xavin's gender when it is pointed out to her that Xavin presents as male most of the time unless the two of them are alone. When their relationship is questioned in the Young Avengers–Runaways Civil War crossover, Karolina explains, "He's not my boyfriend! She's my girlfriend . . . sometimes. Kind of."[37] She expresses a similar sentiment later and states, "That's my 'betrothed' you're talking about! And when he's a she, she's actually really sweet."[38] Karolina seems to have much more invested in Xavin's gender than Xavin does.

While Xavin's gender is questioned, the issue of his/her sexuality is not really explored. Karolina, as she makes quite plain, identifies as a lesbian, but aside from Xavin professing love for Karolina, he/she does not seem to identify with a specific form of sexuality. If, as Xavin implies, gender is not fixed on his/her planet, then perhaps sexuality is also fluid. Gender theorist Judith Butler argues that there is no link between gender and sexuality, stating, "No correlation can be drawn, for instance, between drag or transgender and sexual practice, and the distribution of hetero-, bi-, and homo-inclinations cannot be predictably mapped onto the travels of gender bending and changing."[39] Butler's theory, however, might not apply to shapeshifting aliens.

In 2005, Marvel released the first issue of *Young Avengers,* created and written by openly gay writer Allan Heinberg. Within the team, two young male heroes—Billy Kaplan (aka Wiccan) and Teddy Altman (aka Hulkling)—are in an established relationship. Hulkling, it is revealed, is able to transform into his version of the Hulk because, like Xavin, he is shapeshifting Skrull alien, albeit one who was half-human and raised on Earth. Hulkling does not have the same attitudes about gender that Xavin does and always presents as a gay male. While some disapprove of the fact that, of the two high-profile homosexual couples in Marvel titles, both involve shapeshifting aliens, writer Allan Heiberg dismissed that criticism, stating in an interview, "It's actually meaningful to me that someone like Hulkling—who has the ability to change shape, to hide, to appear 'normal'—doesn't. He simply is who he is."

Hulkling and Wiccan's relationship has remained in the background of the comic, and the two are rarely seen touching or engaging in displays of affection. They were, however, openly gay. In an early issue, Captain America forces the teens to admit their superhero secret identities to their parents. When Wiccan tries to tell his parents that he is a superhero, they think he is coming out as homosexual. "We've always known," his mom tells him. "And what you have to know is, we love you, we're proud of you." She then hugs both Hulkling and Wiccan and tells them, "We're just so happy you boys found each other."[40] That the two teen's relationship has remained largely unexplored has nothing to do with editorial pressure or fear of public backlash. Heinberg stated that Marvel has given him complete creative control over the characters and their sexuality. "If anything, I've been perhaps a bit too self-censoring, wanting to make sure that I'm not exploiting the characters' sexuality for the sake of pushing mainstream boundaries," Heinberg explained. He added, "My primary goal in all my work is to keep the story moving forward at all times. When you're fighting Kang the Conqueror, it's tough to find time to make out."[41]

Marvel and DC Comics have both shown a willingness and desire to embrace homosexual superheroes in the past decade. The way that LGBT issues are dealt with may have more to do with the individual writers than with any cohesive strategy on the companies' part. Even with Jim Shooter's alleged pronouncement that there were "no gays in Marvel comics" and DC Comics' current attempts to diversify, there does not seem to be a marked difference in the number or portrayal of homosexual characters within the superhero comics of the big two.

## MEANWHILE . . . THE FUTURE OF HOMOSEXUALITY IN SUPERHERO COMICS

In the past, fans could read a subtext of homosexuality in early comics via Batman and Robin or Wonder Woman (who, after all, was from an all-female island), but these characters were not queer identified, and mainstream superhero comics did not actually portray homosexual characters until the 1980s. In recent years, the inclusion of more homosexual superheroes in mainstream comic books coincides with the increased acceptance of LGBT individuals in American culture and the relaxation of the CCA. The establishment of new characters (e.g., the Runaways, the Young Avengers) and the reimagining of older characters (e.g., Batwoman) as homosexuals is a step toward gender and sexual equality in a medium known for embracing hetronormativity, hypermasculinization, and feminization. Some of the characters have been successful, some simply insulting, but their mere existence shows that the comic industry and comic readers are becoming increasingly accepting of homosexuality in superheroes. Superheroes are, after all, supposed to be the best, most idealized, most powerful, most righteous versions of ourselves. If Americans can embrace homosexual superheroes, then American culture and society seem poised to accept homosexuality as merely another possible trait of its citizens, like the ability to fly.

"There are a lot of controversial subjects that aren't handled well in comics," comic author Chuck Dixon told an interviewer in 1988. "Gays are just one segment of a long list. . . . I think comics have a double standard about offending everybody. They don't want to offend the Moral Majority or the Bible Belt, or whoever they think they're going to offend. They think the subject of homosexuality would ring bells all over the country. . . . Homosexuality just seems to be the subject that we may not be ready to approach yet."[42] By 2000, however, comics seemed ready to substantially broach the issue. Northstar—one of the first homosexual superheroes who for years was written into the closet, forced to become a fairy, and killed off several times—once again joined the X-Men, where he dealt with storylines involving homophobia, mentored teen gay superheroes, and even married his boyfriend, in 2012.

Charting the progress of the depictions of homosexual characters in mainstream superhero comics over the decades provides a window into understanding American attitudes about LGTB issues. In the early decades of the industry, the issue was completely ignored; in the postwar period, it was outlawed; and by the 1980s, when gay and lesbian characters did begin to appear, they were villains, insulting stereotypes, or shuffled off into fairyland. In the past decade, however, the big two have made a lot of progress toward including homosexual characters and issues in their books. While advancements have been made, there is still definite room for improvement. "Comics are already well behind mainstream media and advertising in terms of promoting the positive inclusion of gay characters, and I wouldn't look for the industry to be a prominent civil rights beacon anytime soon," comic author Devin Grayson stated. However, she added, "Overall, the trend toward inclusion, although slow, has been steady and positive, and when the right people are in the right places and in the right frame of mind, the medium will be capable of some truly inspiring leaps forward."[43] As mainstream American society has gradually become more accepting of homosexuality, superhero comics have followed suit, though often years, if not decades, behind film and television. If Grayson is correct, then the mainstream comics industry is never going to be a progressive cultural force for sexuality and gender equality. It is still clear, however, that in the past decade, the big two—and some of their writers, artists, and editors—have made an effort to depict homosexual superheroes as well-rounded, fleshed-out characters who are just as realistic as the next superstrong, shapeshifting half-alien.

## NOTES

1. Bradford Wright, *Comic-Book Nation: The Transformation of Youth Culture in America* (New York: The Johns Hopkins University Press, 2003), xv.

2. Frederic Wertham, *Seduction of the Innocent* (New York: Main Road Books, 2004), 52.

3. *Batman #84* (New York: DC Comics, 1954).

4. Wertham, *Seduction of the Innocent*, 189–90.

5. David Hajdu, *The Ten-Cent Plague: The Great Comic-Book Scare and How It Changed America* (New York: Farrar, Straus and Giroux, 2008), 171.

6. Hajdu, *The Ten-Cent Plague*, 264.

7. Hajdu, *The Ten-Cent Plague*, 191.

8. Amy Kiste Nyberg, *Seal of Approval: The History of the Comics Code* (Jackson: University of Mississippi Press, 1998), 168.

9. Nyberg, *Seal of Approval*, 120.

10. Reinhold Reitberger and Wolfgang Fuchs, *Comics: Anatomy of a Mass Medium* (Boston: Little, Brown, 1970), 122.

11. *Hulk Magazine #23*, 1980.

12. John Donald Gustav-Wrathall, *Take the Young Stranger by the Hand: Same-Sex Relations and the YMCA* (Chicago: University of Chicago), 1998.

13. Andy Mangels, "Out of the Closet and into the Comics: Gays in Comics—The Creations and the Creators, Part I," *Amazing Heroes* 143 (June 15, 1988): 40.

14. Mangels, "Out of the Closet, Part I" 43.

15. Mangels, "Out of the Closet, Part I," 43.

16. Peter Sanderson, "The Big Switch," *Amazing Heroes* 76 (1985): 27.

17. Mangels, "Out of the Closet, Part I," 44.

18. Peter David, "When You Wish upon a Northstar," February 14, 1992, http://www.peterdavid.net/index.php/2004/11/23/when-you-wish-upon-northstar/.

19. Mangels, "Out of the Closet, Part I," 44.

20. Andy Mangels, "Out of the Closet and into the Comics: Gays in Comics—The Creations and the Creators, Part II," *Amazing Heroes* 144 (July 1, 1988): 51.

21. Steve Englehart, *The New Guardians #1.1* (DC Comics, 1988).

22. Mangels, "Out of the Closet, Part II," 49.

23. Mangels, "Out of the Closet, Part II," 48.

24. Wonder Woman was the only female comic hero to continuously remain in print, beginning in 1941 and only briefly taking a hiatus in 1986. In 2011, DC Comics relaunched the comic, issuing *Wonder Woman #1*.

25. Nyberg, *Seal of Approval*, 178.

26. Scott Lobdell, *Alpha Flight #106* (New York: Marvel, 1992).

27. Emmett Furey, "Homosexuality in Comics, Part II," *Comic Book Resources News*, July 17, 2007, http://www.comicbookresources.com/?page=article&id=10809.

28. "Editorial," *New York Times*, January 24, 1992, A28.

29. In 2010, DC Comics was one of the last companies still participating in the Comics Code Authority. As of January 2011, all companies have stopped submitting their comics to the authority, and the code is now obsolete.

30. Ed Brubaker and Greg Rucka, *Gotham Central, Book 2: Jokers and Madmen* (New York: DC Comics, 2004).

31. Furey, "Homosexuality in Comics, Part II."

32. George Gustines, "Straight (and Not) out of the Comics" *New York Times*, May 28, 2006, A25.

33. Furey, "Homosexuality in Comics, Part II."

34. Furey, "Homosexuality in Comics, Part II."

35. Brian K. Vaughan, *Runaways #2.7* (New York: Marvel, 2004).

36. Brian K. Vaughan, *Runaways #2.8* (New York: Marvel, 2004).

37. Zeb Wells, *Civil War: Young Avengers and Runaways #1* (New York: Marvel, 2006).

38. Zeb Wells, *Civil War: Young Avengers and Runaways #2* (New York: Marvel, 2006).

39. Judith Butler, *Gender Trouble: Feminism and the Subversion of Identity* (New York: Psychology Press, 1990), xiv.

40. *Young Avengers #2.*

41. Emmett Furey, "Homosexuality in Comics: Part IV," *Comic Book Resources News,* July 19, 2007, http://www.comicbookresources.com/?page=article&id=10809.

42. Mangels, "Out of the Closet, Part I," 53.

43. Furey, "Homosexuality in Comics: Part IV."

# TEN

# The Man in the Gray Metal Suit

*Dr. Doom, the Fantastic Four, and the Costs of Conformity*

## Micah Rueber,
## Mississippi Valley State University

In the 1955 novel *The Man in the Gray Flannel Suit*, author Sloan Wilson contrasts the fears, demands, expectations, and desires of the book's protagonist, Tom Rath—an "everyman" who worries about his wife, his grandmother, his children, his illegitimate son, the condition of the area schools, and the decisions of the local zoning board as much as he frets about his job—with workaholic Ralph Hopkins, president of United Broadcasting Company. While Rath struggles to find a balance between the demands of home and work, Hopkins pushes himself to almost Herculean efforts. Wilson describes in some detail the demands made on Hopkins's time:

> First there were all the people who wanted to see him on company business. . . . There were the executives of the many corporations of which he was a director, and the men and women connected with the good works of which he was a trustee. . . . In addition to that, he was a member of committees and commissions studying, variously, conditions in South India, Public Health in the United states, Racial Segregation, Higher Standards for Advertising, the Parking Problem in New York City, Farm Subsidies, Safety on the Highways, Freedom of the Press, Atomic Energy, the House Rules of the City Club, and a Code of Decency for Comic Books. [1]

Writer Wilson drew up an amazingly representative, if fictional in its specifics, laundry list of the most important issues facing the United States in the mid-1950s.

The last item on the list, the "Code of Decency for Comic Books," though seemingly more trivial than many of the other issues, was an important issue that attracted widespread attention in the decade following the end of the Second World War. As detailed by Bradford W. Wright in *Comic Book Nation*, the 1940s witnessed the publication of comics that pushed the boundaries of good taste. Titles such as *Crime Must Pay the Penalty*, *Murder Incorporated*, and *True Crime Comics* "featured within the space of a few pages images of narcotics sales, drug injections, machine-gunnings, burning bodies, and a hypodermic needle poised to pierce a woman's eye."[2] The issue attracted public attention when a handful of influential clergy and academics, alarmed by an increase in juvenile delinquency in the United States, assigned some portion of the blame to this new breed of lurid comics. A Bavarian-born psychologist, Dr. Fredric Wertham, emerged as a leader of the movement to censor comics after his experience as director of the Psychiatric Clinic at Queens Hospital Center led him to believe that a growing number of impressionable youth drew inspiration from these works. Wertham, whose essays appeared in a number of national periodicals, called for government intervention at the same time that several public entities—including the city of Chicago and the state of New York—attempted, with mixed success, to impose standards on comics. The U.S. Senate eventually became involved, and in response, the comics industry agreed to censorship in 1954 under the guise of the Comics Magazine Association of America. For three decades, the association would remain the arbiter of good taste for America's mainstream comic publishers.[3]

Sloan Wilson might or might not have had his tongue planted in cheek when he inked his description of the dictatorial Hopkins, but less than a decade after the appearance of *Gray Flannel Suit*, the tables had turned. In fiction, Ralph Hopkins battled the menace of lurid comics. In reality, some comics came to battle Ralph Hopkins—or at least the image that he represented: that of the single-minded, driven businessman who ignored his family, his friends, and even his own health in his almost megalomaniacal quest for success. In fact, in these comics the "Hopkins's type" would be portrayed not as a successful, if troubled, overachiever but as the archetype of the supervillain. Put simply, the appearance of Marvel's *Fantastic Four* comic in November 1961 made clear the fact that the heyday of the self-motivated, Horatio Alger–esque individual as the model of success had come to an end. Instead, the group—the Fantastic Four—was portrayed as the appropriate vehicle for success, while its arch nemesis Dr. Doom—born poor, self-made, and, perhaps tellingly, clad in a gray metal suit—was clearly painted as the antithesis of what the comic's readers should aspire to. As such, the *Fantastic Four* serves as an useful historical document that charts this shift away from unfettered individuality.

*Fantastic Four* was produced by Marvel Comics, a longtime publisher that managed to weather the waxing and waning fortunes of the comic industry better than most but had rarely been a leader in the field. By the late 1950s, the company had been reduced to seeking out its existence by offering a limited range of titles, most of them unoriginal derivatives of the more successful offerings of other publishers. Marvel writer and editor Stan Lee—who had entered the family business in 1940 at the age of seventeen and felt increasingly limited by the constraints of the medium—pondered leaving the firm. However, about this time he began collaborating with a young artist, Jack Kirby, and the pair would, within a handful of years, completely revolutionize the comic world. In 1961, Marvel executives, noting the success of DC Comics' new offering *Justice League of America*, asked Lee to create a similar team-based comic for Marvel. Feeling that he had nothing to lose—he was, after all, seriously considering quitting the industry— Lee drafted a short outline for a new comic featuring a team of superheroes. Artist Jack Kirby fleshed out the details, and in the process the Fantastic Four were born.[4]

On the surface, the Fantastic Four resembled most other superheroes. While testing a new spacecraft in an effort to beat the Soviet Union into space, the four members of the troupe—respected scientist Reed Richards; his fiancée, Sue Storm; her teenage brother, Johnny; and Richards's college roommate, war hero and test pilot Benjamin J. Grimm—had been exposed to cosmic radiation that endowed the quartet with strange powers. Richards became Mr. Fantastic, with the Gumby-like ability to stretch his body to almost any length or shape; Sue became the Invisible Girl, and while she could initially turn herself (or other objects) invisible, she eventually gained the useful ability to create invisible force fields; Johnny became the Human Torch, with the ability to turn his body into flame, to control fire, and to fly; and Grimm underwent the most dramatic transformation: in becoming the Thing, his skin became rock hard and orange, endowing him with awesome strength, endurance, and body armor but rendering him incapable of blending into human society because of his appearance.

What distinguished the Fantastic Four from their comic rivals was not their powers—which, if anything, were rather pedestrian by superhero standards (Johnny Storm was actually the second human torch; the first had graced the pages of Marvel comics during the Second World War)— but the fact that despite their amazing abilities, they suffered from the same foibles and failings as their audience. Wright notes, "The heroes' idiosyncrasies often impede their work as a team. They frequently argue and even fight with each other."[5] In his history of comics, Shirrel Rhoads paints a similar picture of the Fantastic Four: "They bickered, they worried about money, they behaved like . . . a family. Stan Lee and Jack Kirby had unknowingly invented a new kind of superhero, a more vulnerable character with human failings."[6]

The readers of the *Fantastic Four* did not need academics to point out that the Marvel team of Lee and Kirby were offering something new. Sales of the new comic surpassed expectations, and Stan Lee and team responded with new titles: *Thor, Spider-Man, Iron Man, Captain America, The Hulk,* and *The X-Men* soon graced the Marvel catalogue. All shared the same premise: superheroes might possess awesome powers, but they were first and foremost humans, with all the accompanying desires, fears, and other emotional baggage. While the humanity of their characters drove the success of these titles, Lee and the Marvel staff took the further step of establishing all their characters within a common universe and chronology. This commonality allowed characters and even storylines to weave in and out of the various titles, a move that reinforced the "reality" of the Marvel world and encouraged readers to buy more comics. Because of these tactics, the Marvel company, once moribund, became the industry leader, a position that it held for more than three decades.

It is this success that makes these works valuable historical documents. Their large sales numbers suggest that something about them resonated deeply with their readers; as such, a close perusal of these works might reveal some otherwise obscured truths about their time. In *Comic Book Nation*, Wright demonstrates how comics mirrored the important issues of the day—be it the Great Depression, World War II, or the Cold War—and how these changed over time. Fittingly, Wright devotes a fair amount of time in his wide-ranging survey to the Fantastic Four. Of the group, he concludes,

> Embodied in the reluctant hero were the celebrated possibilities of American republicanism: virtuous citizens giving to the community without sacrificing their freedom and individuality. The demands of World War II and the Cold war had subverted whatever individuality superheroes . . . had once possessed for the sake of the national consensus. Now the Fantastic Four opened the door for reluctant comic book superheroes to pose an alternative to that consensus.[7]

Wright does not make explicit exactly where that consensus lies, but a close reading of the comics suggests that the "alternative to that consensus" was neither a return to individuality nor blind nationalism but rather a voluntary commitment to a rather smaller group that served to instill the individual members with a sense of identity and purpose. A perusal of the *Fantastic Four* demonstrates that the members' loyalty to the organization—to the Fantastic Four—trumped their personal desires and motivations as well as whatever patriotic ideals they might hold. Although the Fantastic Four provide ample evidence for a variety of conclusions—one could make much of Dr. Doom's iron mask in an era dominated by the Iron Curtain, to say nothing of the fact that the female of the group, introduced roughly one year before the debut of Betty Friedan's *The Feminine Mystique*, escapes trouble (or responsibility?) by turning herself invisible—the most pervasive message is the importance of the group and the subjugation of the individual. Put simply, the Fantastic Four were, to use a phrase popularized by William H. Whyte, Organization Men (and Women).

Whyte's *The Organization Man* appeared in 1956 and became a best seller. Whyte, a journalist working for *Fortune* magazine, sensed—like some of his contemporaries, including Wilson (*Flannel Suit* was published in 1955) and David Riesman (whose *Lonely Crowd* debuted in 1950)—that the pendulum between the individual and the group had swung too far toward the latter. Whyte believed that this new organization dynamic—perhaps most prominently displayed by, but by no means limited to, the executive and management branches of large national and multinational corporations, such as General Electric, Ford, and IBM— crushed rather than facilitated individual initiative and genius. Whyte ranged far and wide, from downtown boardrooms to suburban bedrooms, to make his case and in doing so made it clear that he believed this nascent devotion to the organization shackled American progress and prosperity.[8]

Whyte and Wilson were not alone in their critique of American culture. David Riesman beat both to the punch in 1950 with the publication of *The Lonely Crowd* and its discussion (and introduction to the lexicon) of "inner-directed" and "other-directed" individuals. C. Wright Mills contributed to the debate with two important works: *White Collar* and *The Power Elite*. The trope of individuality, or the lack thereof, has become standard fare for historians of the 1950s, and authors as diverse as David Halberstam and Karal Ann Marling include a discussion of these writers.[9]

Historians of the 1960s have paid less attention to the group, instead focusing on the rise of the counterculture and individualism. However, the popularity of the Fantastic Four suggests that interest in and concern for the group continued into the 1960s, as exemplified by a pair of Western movies that bookended the decade. Although Sergio Leone's "Man with No Name," first portrayed by Clint Eastwood in 1964's *Fistful of Dollars*, has become the iconic Western character of the 1960s, the decade opened and closed with Westerns that, in different ways, demonstrate the importance of the group and the dangers of individuals acting on their own. *The Magnificent Seven*, which premiered in 1960, and *The Wild Bunch* in 1969 both found box office success while warning of the perils of individuality.[10]

The pages of the *Fantastic Four* make it abundantly clear that Whyte was not tilting at windmills. Whether good or ill, Whyte clearly viewed group mind-set in a negative light. The organization ethos had pervaded

American life, right down to its comic books. An examination of the first five years of the *Fantastic Four* makes clear that the heroes subscribe to this new dynamic. When the Four act in the interests of the organization rather than for themselves, they find success: they beat their opponent, save the world, and so on. When they act as individuals, they are easily defeated by their foe. The message is clear: heroes act as a group, in the best interest of the team, and when they do so, they vanquish the bad guys (and girls). Villains, however, are individuals. Whether acting alone or as the undisputed leader of others, their individualism inevitably leads to their downfall at the hands of the organization: the Fantastic Four. Time and again, the group is shown to be more important than the individual.

To be sure, many Marvel titles featured individuals: Captain America, the Hulk, Thor, Iron Man, Spider Man, and so on. However, in these cases, the title character meets with success most often when acting in concert and accord with others. Even Spider Man, who would eventually eclipse the Fantastic Four as Marvel's most popular and valuable entity, demonstrates this concern with the group. Although the "Webbed Crusader" almost always acted alone, the underlying theme of the comic centered on his struggles to find the balance between the group and the individual: remember that it was his selfishness in refusing to aid police in apprehending a fugitive that led to the death of his uncle. Spider Man wanted to belong, to fit in with his family, his classmates, his work colleagues, and various young lovelies, but he feared that revealing his secret would endanger those same loved ones. While *The Fantastic Four* is the story of the group, *Amazing Spider Man* is the tale of a young man who desperately wants to belong but cannot.

Six pages into the *Fantastic Four*'s second issue, the tensions between the individual and the group reach a boiling point. The group discovers than an alien race with the ability to change shape has been committing crimes while impersonating the Four. Reed Richards, the group's leader, counsels patience until he can figure out exactly how to fight the menace. Ben Grimm (the Thing) grows tired of sitting and lashes out. When Richards recommends patience, the Thing explodes: "Wait?? That's all right for you, mister! At least you're human! . . . I won't wait any longer! I'm going out . . . to fight! . . . to smash!" As the Thing lurches off, the remaining members discuss the situation. Sue wonders, "Reed, how much more of this can we take!" Johnny agrees: "We've got to do something about him!" Richards admonishes them: "No! We must be patient!" Tensions again mount after the group escapes from government capture. Later, the group decides to set a trap for the alien imposters, and the Human Torch and the Thing immediately argue about which should act as bait. As the pair come to fisticuffs, Richards comes between them: "This is no time to be fighting among ourselves!" Sue seconds the notion: "We'll just keep destroying ourselves if we keep at each other's throats this way!" The Thing expresses doubt, but Johnny has the last word: "Aw, forget it, Thing—I'm not holdin' any grudges!"[11]

The exchange might have been lifted from Whyte. In *The Organization Man*, Whyte demonstrates how far the group ethos has permeated American culture by examining discipline in schools. There, too, he found group mentality at play: "Like their parents . . . the children already have a degree of social skill. . . . If a child falls out of line, he does not have to subjected to authoritarian structures. . . . He senses the disapproval of the group and . . . learns to discipline himself as much as possible." Thus, this one issue of a comic neatly encapsulates the whole organization dynamic: (*a*) the importance of the group instead of the individual; (*b*) the fact that when one member threatens the integrity of the group, the other members show as much or more concern about the continuing integrity of the group as the feelings and needs of the hostile individual; (*c*) one individual's subversion of personal initiative and creativity to maintain group cohesiveness; and (*d*) a group leader who leads, not by group fiat, but by careful consideration of what action is most likely to benefit the group.[12]

The comic also demonstrates the importance of the group in more subtle ways. In the third issue, Sue designs "colorful costumes" for the team. Richards jests to Sue, "Ever think of working for Dior?" Helping the Thing into his outfit, Sue comments, "Here Thing, this even makes you look glamorous!" But the real message lies in a comment from Sue: "If we're a team, we should look like a team!" Later in the issue, Sue and the Thing encounter the menace that they have been tracking. Preparing for battle, the Thing rips off most of his new accoutrements: "You stay hidden, Sue. . . . As for Me, I'm gettin' out of this monkey suit so I can move!" Stripping down to a pair of blue trunks, the Thing at least matches the outfits of the other team members, but his outfit demonstrates the ambiguity of the individual (the Thing) vis-à-vis the group: the remaining teammates wear full costume while the Thing sports only a pair of modest shorts. The other members are "all in"—and their outfits "all on"—and the Thing's decision to wear only enough of the uniform to protect his modesty is a subtle signal of his investment in the group.[13]

Later, in the same issue, the Thing's ambiguous feelings about his membership in the group play out within the space of a handful of panels. After a spat with Johnny, Grimm reminds him of the spaceflight that endowed the group with its superpowers: "That's when we decided our destinies were all entwined, and so we decided to remain together, as The Fantastic Four!" His touching speech notwithstanding, an irate Thing tries to goad the Human Torch into a fight. Again, Richards intervenes: "Why must we always fight among ourselves? What's wrong with us?" Once more the message is clear: the group is more important than the individual, and—à la Whyte—a properly functioning group finds ways to minimize friction among members.[14]

Unfortunately, the Fantastic Four have clearly not yet found the proper group dynamic. On the final page of the third issue, the Thing takes offense with Richards's suggestion that Johnny had saved the day: "Wait a minute, Reed!! Are you tryin' to give that flaming juvenile delinquent the credit for this caper??" Sue frets: "Oh please! Don't start arguing among yourselves again!! I—I just can't stand any more!" Johnny interjects: "Relax, sis! They're not gonna argue about me any more! I had all the bossin' around I can take! I'm cuttin' out of this combo, right now!" "But you can't quit us, Johnny!" Sue cries as the Torch flies off. Again, in three panels Stan Lee and company have encapsulated the important issues of the organization. One member, the Thing, wants to ensure that he gets proper credit for his contributions; another member, the Human Torch, chafes at authority and his place within the group; finally, a third member, Sue Storm, worries more about the unity of the group than the feelings—whatever their merit—of Torch and the Thing.[15]

Once again, the tension among the group members acts as a dramatic element within the story but also a historical signpost suggesting that the pervasive organizational urge that Whyte identified at play in American culture had actually seeped beyond the well-paneled walls of the boardroom to pervade even such innocuous and lowbrow art forms as the comic book. Whyte's groupthink aphorisms—*"The rough and tumble days are over. . . . Unorthodoxy can be dangerous to The Organization. . . . Ideas come from the group, not from the individual"* (italics in original)—are played out within the covers of the *Fantastic Four*.[16]

The organizational trope, already well established in the first few issues, remained (and remains) a staple of the comic's plotlines and perhaps accounts in part for the fact that the *Fantastic Four* remains in print a half-century after its debut in 1961. As both Rhoades and Wright noted, readers were drawn to the comic precisely because the members of the Four had "real" problems: they bickered and fought among themselves. They, presumably like their readers, wondered how they fit into their chosen group.

The message, repeated ad nauseam, makes abundantly clear the importance of the group: people working together can and do defeat those working alone. When the members act as individuals, they are defeated; when they pull together, they prevail. This lesson is reinforced by the fact that in the majority of issues of the comic, the group is fighting either an individual or an army/group/mob led by a dictatorial villain willing to accept no opposition from his followers. The *Fantastic Four* makes this clear from the first issue, when the Four defeat the mysterious (and rather absurd, even by comics' standards) Mole Man, undisputed and unquestioned leader of a band of "subterraneans." The second issue of the comic repeats the plot, replacing the Mole Man with the Skrulls, a group of shapeshifting aliens. Over the next couple years, the Fantastic Four defeat the Sub-Mariner and his undersea minions, Dr. Doom and his lackeys and robots, the Hate-Monger (a disguised Adolf Hitler?!) and his mob of bigots, Rama-Tut ("the Pharaoh of the Future") and his Egyptians, the Mad Thinker and his Awesome Android, and so on. Over and over the comic—echoing the mantra of *The Organization Man*—makes it abundantly clear that the individual, acting alone and without the checks and balances of the group, is a threat to society. Moreover, the individual is not only a menace but will, in the end, be bested by a properly organized group working toward a shared goal.

However, that the Fantastic Four were an organization whose members were expected to put aside personal differences for the sake of the group does not mean that it was without a leader. To borrow George Orwell's phrase, the Four might have been equals, but some were more equal than others. Scientific genius Reed Richards, who led the group on the spaceflight that bestowed them with their powers, became—apparently with little discussion—the group's leader. Although he almost always acts in the best interests of the group, the comic makes it clear that he is his own man. In issue 14, the group as a whole decides that it should temporarily split—for the good of the group—so that each member can pursue his or her interests. While Sue stars in a movie, Johnny joins the circus, and the Thing becomes a wrestler, Richards accepts a temporary job at "General Electronics in New England." Mr. Fantastic proves to have difficulty fitting neatly into a different organization. In the workshop, Richards uses his ability to stretch his body "to examine my apparatus from the inside as well the outside!" and requests his employer to "forgive me if my methods are a little unorthodox!" His boss admonishes Richards: "This is a laboratory—not a carnival!" Mr. Fantastic decides that he has made a mistake in accepting the employment offer: "I'm just not cut out to work for anyone else! I've got to do things my own way— without interference!"[17]

The dialogue feels lifted from a passage in Whyte's *Organization Man*. In chapter 17, Whyte examines in some detail "the bureaucratization of the scientist." Whyte quotes at length "one young scientist, Walter Roberts": "There is a tremendous difference between science as it is done in the laboratory and science as it is reported. True science is helter-skelter, depending on one's hunches, angers, and inspirations, and the research itself is done in a very personal fashion." Roberts bemoans that fact that "thirty or forty years ago," the results of this chaotic research method would be reported truthfully, but the organizational ethos encourages scientists—and, more often, committees of scientists—to smooth the rough edges off scientific research. Gerald Horton amplifies Roberts's sentiment: "Months of tortuous, wasteful effort may be hidden behind a few elegant paragraphs." "Thus," Whyte concludes, "the organization mystique has grown in science."[18]

However, Whyte also suggests that Mr. Fantastic's defense of his autonomy was, when he penned the book in 1956, the voice of the past.

Whyte uses official data to infer that "less than 4 percent" of the money spent on science by "government, industry, and the universities" goes toward "creative research." Moreover, Whyte estimates that "of the 600,000 people engaged in scientific work . . . probably no more than 5,000 are free to pick their own problems." While in this case Mr. Fantastic appears the exception to the rule, the point remains that the organizational ethos described by Whyte was no mere phantasm but a very real feature of American culture.[19]

Even on the rare moments when Richards loses his temper and flexes his autocratic authority, the comic makes clear that he does so only in the best interest of the group—that leadership is a burden to be borne, if one is capable, rather than an end in itself. And who is better suited to serve as leader than the flexible Mr. Fantastic, who can change leadership styles as easily as he contorts his body? Richards exemplifies the new leader described by Whyte: the leader who can maintain the focus and direction of the group while minimizing conflict among members and acknowledging and encouraging the contributions of each individual. In Whyte's words, the group leader "must not only accept control, he must accept it as if he liked it. . . . He must appear to enjoy listening sympathetically to points of view not his own. . . . It is not enough now that he work hard; he must be a damn good fellow to boot."[20]

For, maintaining the group is not easy, a fact most clearly demonstrated when the Fantastic Four face a group of supervillains. Although the Fantastic Four usually fought an individual—alone or as the leader of others—the cover of issue 36 announced something new. The illustration depicted a quartet—obviously with some kind of superpowers (one is flying, one turning his body to sand, one hanging by her hair, and the fourth wearing an outlandish costume and shooting some sort of gun)—preparing to surprise the Four. The caption announces, "Sooner or later someone was bound to come up with an evil group like this . . . so we thought we'd beat 'em to it!! . . . The Attack of the EVIL F.F.—'The Frightful Four!'" The issue reveals how onetime rival "The Wizard" had gathered fellow previous Four foes Sandman and Trapster as well as newcomer Madam Medusa to form the "Frightful Four." The Frightful Four fight the Fantastic Four to a standstill before mysteriously disappearing, only to reappear in issue 38 to defeat the Fantastic Four and leave the unconscious group to die from the explosion of a powerful "Q-Bomb." The Invisible Girl, Sue Storm, manages to surround the bomb with a force field, but radiation from the blast mysteriously negates the Four's superpowers, forcing them to rely on their native abilities (and the help of friends) to once again thwart Dr. Doom.[21]

The Frightful Four return for a multi-issue arc beginning in issue 41. Although they have bested the Fantastic Four on two occasions, the group eventually unravels as members begin to bicker among themselves. In part, they quarrel about who should lead the group, but tensions are exacerbated as the three male members come to blows about who can claim the affections of Madam Medusa—who, it must be said, encourages the rivalry in her own bid for power. Unable to resolve their inner differences, the Frightful Four finally split, and their example serves once again to underlie the organizational mantra that pervades the comic. The Frightful Four, when able to act as a cohesive group, managed to defeat the Fantastic Four. They, as a collective whole, accomplished a feat that no individual had been able to master. The Frightful Four demonstrate not only the power of the group but also the fact that the group functions only when each member plays his or her assigned role. The lesson is twofold: working as a group requires each member to work for and with the group; while the group can accomplish great things, it calls on the members to exert a certain effort to get along within the group.[22]

The primacy of the group—the properly functioning group, as the example of the Frightful Four makes clear—is reinforced by the fact that the only foes that the Fantastic Four are not able to best are not human (or even superhuman) at all but rather godlike beings possessed of virtually unlimited power. The list is short: the Watcher and Galactus. The Watcher, introduced in issue 13 and making occasional cameos in subsequent issues, belongs to an alien race of advanced, intelligent beings pledged to observe the emergence of other sentient life-forms throughout the cosmos. Although pledged not to interfere with the actions of less-advanced life, the Watcher—evidently sensing some promise in humanity (at least as exemplified by the members of the Fantastic Four)—sometimes stretches his vow of neutrality to tilt the odds in favor of the Four by allowing them to "steal" a needed piece of technology or by revealing an important tidbit of information. Though officially neutral, the Watcher acts as a sort of super (or, perhaps more accurate, extra) human benefactor of the group.

Galactus, however, presents a threat to not only the Fantastic Four but all humanity. Galactus, a cosmic being of unimaginable powers who maintains his power by consuming worlds, targets Earth for his next "feeding." With the help of the Watcher, the Four convince Galactus to set his (or, perhaps better, its) sights elsewhere. Although the Four thwart Galactus's plan, their actions result in "victory" in only the loosest definition of the term. Even though readers might draw any number of conclusions from the fact that the Fantastic Four are bested only by a godlike individual, the contrasting lessons drawn from the examples of the Watcher and Galactus present two obvious conclusions. The example of the Watcher suggests that humanity might eventually gain enough wisdom and insight to act alone, while Galactus acts as a warning: as the ultimate disinterested individual, Galactus, unburdened by allegiance to any group, represents humanity's greatest threat.

Of course, as most every reader of the series knows, the Fantastic Four's arch foe has always been Dr. Doom. Literally the "man in the gray metal suit," Doom's steadfast refusal to subordinate his will to others renders him inimical to the organization mentality. Ruler of the small country of "Latveria"—located "in the heart of the Bavarian Alps"— Doom quite literally reigns with an iron fist, his subjects loyal from fear rather than love of Doom. Born the son of gypsies—his father a healer and his mother some sort of "enchantress"—Doom became orphaned at a young age. Possessed of a formidable scientific genius, Doom attracted the attention of a dean at "State University" who offered the teenager a scholarship. Thus far, the biography of Doom encapsulates the Horatio Alger model of success: penniless orphan makes good through pluck, hard work, and native talent. Doom fulfills that promise, becoming "absolute monarch" of Latveria (exactly how is never made clear) and fulfilling the rags-to-riches dream.[23]

But the creators of the Fantastic Four, writing in the early 1960s, turned Alger on his head, thereby revealing how the United States had changed since the turn of the century. While Alger clearly intended for his heroes to serve as models for their young readers, Dr. Doom, though quite clearly a success, is portrayed as the face of evil rather than a paragon of virtue. Where Alger's characters found success through hard work and sacrifice, Marvel's achieved happiness through identification with a group.

Moreover, despite his successes, Doom is neither happy nor, at least when facing the Four, successful, and the *Fantastic Four* suggests that this is due, in no small part, to the fact that Doom is, by temperament and happenstance, a loner. By one of those coincidences that seem to happen with amazing frequency in the comics, Doom and a young Reed Richards arrive at State University on the same day. Richards offers to share a dormitory room with Doom, which Doom rejects out of hand: "I have no wish to share a room with anyone! I desire privacy!" Doom is eventually expelled from the school for "conducting forbidden experiments," the last of which causes an explosion that disfigures his face. Still in search of "forbidden secrets," Doom journeys to Tibet, where he joins a monastery. There he crafts his trademark gray faceplate and armor and assumes the persona of Dr. Doom.[24]

Using his scientific genius and advanced technologies, Doom somehow assumes control of Latveria, which he employs as a base of operations for his more grandiose plans. Doom rarely thinks small: although he occasionally acts for financial gain, most often he hopes to gain forbidden wisdom and/or world domination. These themes again demonstrate the importance of the group, which can act as a check on the individual members. Like Doom, the members of the Fantastic Four possess incredible powers—Mr. Fantastic, a formidable intellect to boot—but by acting as a group, they can turn their awesome talents to "good" ends. Doom, unhindered by peers, demonstrates the dangers of unchecked individuality.

Dr. Doom and the Fantastic Four thus neatly encapsulate the tensions between the individual and the organization as expressed in the early 1960s. Doom, the solitary genius—the individual—is consistently bested by the group. The message is perfectly clear: a group, working together, will trump the individual, no matter how talented. Moreover, it seems more than coincidental that the group—at least the Fantastic Four—is portrayed as "good": the public, for the most part, respects and even admires the Fantastic Four. Doom, in contrast, is quite clearly "bad," hated and feared even by his own subjects.

Whether Stan Lee and the other creators of the Fantastic Four intended their comic to promote the benefits of the organization seems doubtful. Nonetheless, the success (and continuing success) of the series suggests that the comic clearly hit a nerve and resonated with its audience. Though not the first comic to feature of group of superheroes— remember that Lee came up with the idea in response to the appearance of a new group comic from DC Comics—it was, without a doubt, the most successful (at least until the appearance a number of years later of the X-Men, also created by Lee and the Marvel staff).

If, as suggested by Bradford W. Wright in *Comic Book Nation*, the most successful comics are those with which the audience most clearly identifies, the success of the Fantastic Four hints that the readership was captivated by the group. Its successes, failures, squabbles, and everything else make the Four accessible. This group dynamic and accessibility made the Fantastic Four unique for their time: the members were flawed and, despite their superpowers, human. Yet, notwithstanding their problems, the quartet remained together and, more important, found success by acting as a cohesive group. They represented an organization much like that critiqued by William H. Whyte in *The Organization Man*.

And so in the end, the Fantastic Four conveyed a subversive message that might well have appalled Ralph Hopkins's *Flannel Suit* comic-crusading workaholic and self-made man. His real-world counterparts eventually gained the sort of control they sought over the moral message of comics, but at the same time, they set the stage for an attack on the very values that they held dear. The Fantastic Four might have followed the comic code, but their not-so-subtle critique of unfettered individuality might have been, in the long run, even more subversive than any mere lurid image.

## NOTES

1. Sloan Wilson, *The Man in the Gray Flannel Suit* (New York: Simon & Schuster, 1955), 167–68.

2. Bradford Wright, *Comic-Book Nation: The Transformation of Youth Culture in America* (New York: The Johns Hopkins University Press, 2003), 83.

3. For a full account of the formation of the Comics Magazine Association of America, see Wright, *Comic-Book Nation*, especially chapters 4–6.

4. For more on the origins of the Fantastic Four, see Wright, *Comic-Book Nation*, 204–7. See also Shirrel Rhoades, *A Complete History of American Comic Books* (New York: Lang, 2008), 78–80; Les Daniels, *Comix: A History of Comic Books in America* (New York: Outerbridge and Dienstfrey, 1971), 137–40.

5. Wright, *Comic Book Nation*, 204–5.

6. Rhoades, *A Complete History*, 79.

7. Wright, *Comic Book Nation*, 205, 207.

8. William H. Whyte Jr., *The Organization Man* (New York: Simon & Schuster, 1956).

9. David Reisman, *The Lonely Crowd* (New Haven, CT: Yale University Press, 1950); C. Wright Mills, *White Collar: The American Middle Classes* (Oxford, England: Oxford University Press, 1951), and *The Power Elite* (Oxford, England: Oxford University Press, 1956). There are myriad useful histories of the 1950s; though quite different, two of the most useful are David Halberstam's *The Fifties* (New York: Random House, 1993) and Karal Ann Marling's *As Seen on TV* (Cambridge, MA: Harvard University Press, 1994).

10. For a discussion of Western films and the 1960s, see Tom Engelhardt, *The End of Victory Culture* (Amherst: University of Massachusetts Press, 1995), and Richard Slotkin, *Gunfighter Nation: The Myth of the Frontier in Twentieth-Century America* (New York: Harper Perennial, 1992).

11. "The Fantastic Four Meet the Skrulls from Outer Space," *Fantastic Four #2* (Marvel Comics, 1962).

12. Whyte, *The Organization Man*, 383–84.

13. "The Menace of the Miracle Man," *Fantastic Four #3* (Marvel Comics, 1963), 6, 11.

14. "The Menace of the Miracle Man," 15–16.

15. "The Menace of the Miracle Man," 23.

16. Whyte, *The Organization Man*, 134–35.

17. "The Mad Thinker and His Awesome Android," *Fantastic Four #15* (Marvel Comics, 1963), 12.

18. Whyte, *The Organization Man*, 226–27.

19. Whyte, *The Organization Man*, 205.

20. Whyte, *The Organization Man*, 151.

21. "The Frightful Four," *Fantastic Four #36* (Marvel Comics, 1965); "Defeated by the Frightful Four," *Fantastic Four #38* (Marvel Comics, 1965).

22. "The Brutal Betrayal of Ben Grimm," *Fantastic Four #41* (Marvel Comics, 1965); "To Save You, Why Must I Kill You?" *Fantastic Four #42* (Marvel Comics, 1965); "Lo! There Shall Be an Ending," *Fantastic Four 43* (Marvel Comics, 1965).

23. "The Fantastic Origin of Doctor Doom," *Fantastic Four Annual #2* (Marvel Comics, 1964), 2.

24. "The Fantastic Origin of Doctor Doom," 5–9.

# ELEVEN

# Seen City

*Frank Miller's Reimaging as a Cinematic "New Real"*

Christina Dokou,
University of Athens

In a lecture entitled "Hellenism and Hollywood: From Aristotle to Alexander (Payne)," Twentieth Century Fox CEO Jim Gianopulos predicted that the upcoming film *Avatar*, shot in RealD, would change the way that we watch movies forever.[1] Although the film indeed became a huge blockbuster that unleashed a steady stream of 3-D/RealD movies in its wake, what is argued here is that the ushering to a new historical era of hyperreal cinematic experience—with all its glorious potential but mostly with disturbing ramifications—is probably better signaled by another film, released in 2005: *Frank Miller's Sin City*, codirected by Frank Miller and Robert Rodriguez.[2] The reasons for this claim are primarily found in the hybrid nature of this film, transferring as it is Miller's homonymous comic book hit series to the silver screen within the larger context of contemporary culture, which is primarily—overwhelmingly—visual–digital: "We live in a world saturated with screens, images and objects, all demanding that we look at them," claims visual culture theoretician Nicholas Mirzoeff, with the qualification that "at the same time, scholars of visual culture remind us that there is no such thing as a visual medium because all media are necessarily mixed. That is why the field is properly called visual culture."[3] Borrowing the term *visuality* from Thomas Carlyle's 1841 conservative and "autocratic" conceptualization of the Hero as he "who alone could visualize History" and combining it with W. J. T. Mitchell's work in recent decades on pictures and the pictorial construction of the field of human interactions since the digital revolution, Mirzoeff considers visuality—the mode of seeing, being seen, and negotiating sight, look, spectacle, appearance, image, imagination, and all such affiliated variables as more than a mere matter of vision (reduced to text)—the dominant currency of human interaction and political actualization since modernity. Hence, visuality, as "that which renders the processes of History visible to power," becomes an apposite tool here for the examination of the historicocultural ramifications of *Sin City*'s creation, in terms of its form and content, as well as the way that these—cum underlying ideologies—function. [4] *Sin City* is seen as a case emblematic of how twenty-first-century Western society has shifted from a mere emphasis on the (technology-enhanced) visual image to a relocation of its imagined collective self in the virtual, the pure simulacrum. We are no longer just looking at ourselves in the mirror of presumed reality, trying on costumes and making faces; we are *through* the looking glass, questioning the very physics of mirroring itself and, by extension, the traditional humanitarian social ethics founded upon such a conception of *physis*.

A film about a comic book is a fitting conduit to such an investigation. Comics and film are joined by their mutual essentially hybrid textual–pictorial nature, on one hand, and their front-row location as indicators (and perhaps promulgators) of sociocultural changes, on the other. In the wake of a long and heated history of definitions, Hillary Chute defines comics as

> a hybrid word-and-image form in which two narrative tracks, one verbal and one visual, register temporality spatially. Comics moves forward in time through the space of the page, through its progressive counter-point of presence and absence: packed panels (also called frames) alternating with gutters (empty space). [5]

It is by now a commonplace to remark the similarity between this definition and the frames or cells of conventional "pictures," while an artist's choices in rendering an action scene or moving from frame to frame resemble the positioning and motion of the director's camera or a reader's (conscious) eye. Furthermore, critics such as Aaron Meskin, summing up the long and bitter debate on whether comics "deserve" the status of literature, "suggest that the way out of this impasse is to recognize that comics are a hybrid art form that evolved from literature and a number of other art forms and media"—and that it is precisely the comics' pictoriality that accords them separate status as "autographic" (i.e., art whose content is ineluctably fixed on its original created form/image). [6]

As far as innovation goes, while television has been the main disseminator of images in modern culture, no medium has displayed so clearly the best and worst of visual politics as cinema. The silver screen has been an ideal breeding ground for experiments testing the limits of our relationship with the image and the suspension of disbelief en masse, as opposed to our domestic, more privatized (and often less selective) television viewing. Since film's early days, there have been avant-garde filmmakers (mostly European) whose art—from the German expressionism of Robert Wiene's *The Cabinet of Dr. Caligari* to Sergei Eisenstein's soviet montage in *Battleship Potemkin* to Louis Buñuel's surrealism in *Un Chien Andalou* or Peter Kubelka's trilogy of "metric" films—exposes, challenges, transcends, and overcomes the culturally coded distinction between (*a*) text inviting the imagination, in relative creative freedom, to "clothe" with pictures the assumptions of the reader's interpretive faculties and (*b*) image, offering those pictures (moving ones, in the case of film) ready-made to viewers, forcing them to the position of a more passive participants despite their active contribution of some degree of identification process. Such films function as dense "hypertexts" that must not just be experienced, viewed, or enjoyed but painstakingly thought about and analyzed, often from equally valid alternative angles and by methods reserved for print (i.e., multiple reviewings, juxtaposition of image to text), for their layers of meaning to unfold. Modern auteurs such as Wim Wenders, Gus Van Sandt, and Teo Angelopoulos and experimenters such as Eija-Liisa Ahtila, Sharon Lockhart, and even Guy Debord have also sought to overturn mainstream cinematic narrative techniques, mostly by playing with time depiction, montage, and mixed media and/ or by eschewing "realism" in dialogues, thus slowing down the viewers' instantaneous perceptions to the pace of a slow plodding through (e.g., a text of poetry or a particularly dense and tricky picture puzzle). A small but significant role in this endeavor was played by cartoon films, whose medium (animation) allowed for far more wild creative freedom than that of the live camera or what early, primitive *trompe l'oeil* effects could allow. Although assigned, sometimes affectionately, to the category of "whacky," Tex Avery's visual gags, for example, pushed the envelope on mimesis like nothing else, while scholars such as Tom Klein reveal how early animators of children's cartoons camouflaged, inside their lowbrow creations, experiments in avant-garde surrealism or abstract expressionism.[7]

Similar guerilla innovativeness is noted by Chute in the entire history of comics, whose early-twentieth-century production (*a*) "influenced and was influenced by avant-garde practices, especially those of Dada and surrealism," then (*b*) proceeded to artistic "wordless novels" that "responded to contemporary culture and anticipated the elaboration of genres and the mixture of high and low modes we recognize in present-day fiction," then (*c*) became a speculum of "the seismic cultural shifts" of America in the 1950s, 1960s, and 1970s, marrying modernism to massproduced pop through underground comics, and (*d*) culminated in highest-caliber art, such as Art Spiegelman's Pulitzer Prize–winning graphic Holocaust memoir, *Maus I* (1986) and *Maus II* (1991). Thus, "comics—as a form that relies on space to represent time—becomes structurally equipped to challenge dominant modes of storytelling and history writing," at the same time it reflects with uncanny faithfulness the Occidental zeitgeist.[8] Indeed, the category of comics proper, as a species of art whose reputation and nature have been organically tied to historical changes and their corresponding shifts in cultural perceptions since modernity, often serves as a prime indicator of cultural wars. Their increasing inclusion in curricula; their creative "intrusion" into other, "serious" kinds of writing (e.g., Scott McCloud's famous *Understanding Comics*, a seminal study written in comic book form); their proliferation and economic evolution from a cheap amateur hack industry into a number of multinational conglomerates with huge net profit margins and impact; and their pop dissemination and thematization in other forms of art, from the paintings of Roy Lichtenstein to Tim Kring's NBC television series *Heroes* (2006–2010) and Michael Chabon's Pulitzer Prize–winning novel *The Amazing Adventures of Kavalier and Clay* all suggest that comics discourse has become a major cultural currency in our visually oriented culture, affecting its ways of cognition and production while maintaining a strong conceptual hold on children, teens, and young adults: its main readership.[9] Elaine Martin sums it up:

> The phenomenal growth of graphic novels—a veritable tsunami—in the past decade, but particularly in the past five years, would indicate that the genre is here to stay. It would seem to attest to fundamental changes, at least in western cultures: first, an increasingly visual orientation due to the internet and second, the increasing interpenetration of popular culture and high culture.[10]

In the same vein, Stephen Tabachnick and Lisa Zunshine, among others, underline the advantages of using graphic novel versions to teach canonical literature to students.[11] Pop culture critic Andrew Ross extends to comics his argument for the mutually beneficial, if antagonistic, relationship between pop and highbrow, with the former providing dissemination routes and vigor and the latter, legitimation and innovation, noting that their huge influence over the minds of America's youth long preceded their induction into mainstream art/literature.[12]

Not surprising, then, given such ties of kinship, there has been in recent years an increasing number of films based on comic books, usually of the superhero variety (*Superman, Batman, Spiderman, Daredevil, X-Men, Iron Man, Thor, Hulk, The Fantastic Four, Green Lantern*, etc.) but also graphic novels such as Alan Moore's *The Watchmen* and John Wagner and Vince Locke's *A History of Violence* or limited series such as Mark Millar's *Wanted*. Comics, in turn, have been upgraded culturally from a mass youth- or fan-oriented medium to popular entertainment for all ages and (eclectic) tastes, allowing for even better, more innovative work in the field. Combining that recent trend with what he identifies as the easily seductive power of the comic book, critic Douglas Wolk may not be wrong in claiming, "If there's such a thing as a golden age of comics, it's happening right now."[13] Also, this cross-fertilization has prompted a new and vigorous field of scholarly interest: adaptation studies for comic-to-film projects.[14]

As they say, however, the devil is in the details, and in terms of visuality, it is important to note the differences between each of the two media's modes of mise-en-scène for action—which, for Mirzoeff, is always an action "of violence and displacement," a conflict of civilizations in the historical sense.[15] Daniel Gronsky's historical analysis of the comic-book film, for example, alerts us to the easy co-opting and commercialization of innovation in youth culture: "Thus, the rise in production of comic book films over the last decade is a result of both the rise in status of youth culture and the willingness of cultural gatekeepers to adopt elements of this subculture in order to maintain hegemony."[16] It is a process, however, that requires analysis if we are to understand and use the caveat, especially since "moving image literacy becomes important, not only as a tool to create stable artworks, but as a means of communication in a social system increasingly dominated by new media."[17] Following a formalistic route, Chute notes that, unlike film, "comics doesn't blend the visual and the verbal . . . but is rather prone to presenting the two non-synchronously," forcing a "disjunctive" reading/looking experience on the reader.[18] It follows that film for Chute must necessarily offer an intellectually diminished, less involved experience, unless it should go against its own conventions consciously. It is precisely this filmic "diminishing" that is under investigation here, for the way it is effected determines, to a large extent, its effects on the comics medium and, most important, on the sociocultural sensibility of audiences. David Rodowick sums up the interactive potential:

> Because of contemporary life is immersed in an audiovisual and information culture, cinema's ways of working through the relations of image concept have become particularly significant tour strategies for seeing and saying. . . . However, cinema's history of images and signs is nonetheless both the progenitor of audiovisual culture and perhaps the source of its unfounding as simulacral art.[19]

Still, scholarly unfounding does not necessarily entail demoting in the field of cultural exchanges. The simulacrum, as conceptualized by Jean Baudrillard's 1981 *Simulacra and Simulation*, may be a self-concealing unreality, but like all Foucaultian forms of power, it is also creative.[20] Theoreticians from Max Horkheimer and Theodor Adorno to Roland Barthes and Arthur Kroker may alert us to the mind/humanity-shrinking power of the moving, virtual, pop culture image but at the same time cannot but recognize, with varying degrees of despair, its hegemony.[21] Perhaps the very fakeness and precariousness of the digital image is a virtue if it makes it the most powerful and appropriate—ironically "au-thentic"—sign of a historical age hailed as "virtual," a paradox noted by Mirzoeff:

> In the past half century, the potentially deceptive and misrepresenta-tive capacities of visualized media of all kinds have been exposed over and again. Yet we find . . . globalization, meaning the means of delin-eating social totality formed by global capital, is mediated by images.[22]

Alternatively, Kristen Daly hails digital cinema production and repro-duction "as a cultural form in a time of changing rituals where we are reworking the symbolic reality and the communities in which we exist and interact."[23] Thus, besides Disney short animated films reshaping de-finitively the way that generations of American children see and under-stand their culture's founding legends, who today has not heard the phrase, usually from the lips of a teenager, that one has not read the book but "has seen the movie" or is "waiting for the movie to come out"—consolidating in one phrase the power of unreality entertainment with the real juggernaut of commercial interests? It is important that the crea-tive process never be seen as a semantic void, where the only thing that exists is the proliferating joy of a postmodern "free-for-all"; instead, the media (which are the message?) involved in the shape of global indus-tries and the formal modes of transformation affect both the end product and the reproducers or receptors of it.

The importance of the medium becomes apparent when considering the nature of the innovativeness of the Rodriguez and Miller's *Sin City*, a loose collection of stories about a corrupt desert metropolis named Basin City (read: Sin City), where dark, dangerous, but sentimental heroes such as Marv, Dwight, and Hartigan clash with the monstrously evil city bosses (the Roark family) over naked damsels in distress (mostly armed prostitutes). While *Avatar* is an interpretation of an original script, never before imaged, and subsequent Miller digital imaging (DI) adaptations—such as *300* or *The Spirit*—take more liberties with the original comics source toward more visual and thematic verisimilitude, *Sin City* is cited by all concerned as the most faithful rendition of a comic onscreen to date, a "Type One" adaptation with almost no intermedium interven-tion.[24] "Almost every sequence uses the original panels as storyboard, and a combination of make-up, CGI and lighting effects transforms the cast into the images of their on-the-page originals,"[25] to a point where the term *adaptation* becomes inaccurate, and we are speaking about a "reim-aging," a virtual repetition in motion of the images in the art of Frank Miller's comic series:

> For Type One adaptations, the representational aspects of the visual style must be maximized, the filmed version should match, as closely as possible, the visual style of the comic books. Ideally, all that should change is the addition of motion. *Sin City* (2005, dir. Robert Rodriguez)

is the definitive example of the Type One adaptation approach in terms
of both narrative representation and ideological interpretation; indeed,
it is one of a only a few examples available.[26]

Smith goes on to note how the film's faithfulness to the comic "literally
broke Hollywood rules. Calling the film a 'translation' rather than an
adaptation, co-director Robert Rodriguez attempted to mimic—virtually
shot by shot—the distinctive angles, visual tone and color schemes of
Frank Miller's graphic novel stories."[27] This breaking of rules refers to
the fact that Rodriguez had to quit the Directors Guild of America to
establish Miller, a nonprofessional, as codirector, but it also describes
accurately how such a reimaging, or "translation," redefines in a historical sense our understanding of film: not an onscreen depiction of a "true
to life" story any longer but a different medium with its own dominant
rules on visuality/reality and the need for adaptation for any "still" text/
image entering its realm.

Rodriguez's decision, then, at first glance, seems to equate the static
comic panel with the moving pictures. As *Sin City* actor Clive Owen
enthused, "everyone has the same objective . . . to bring Frank Miller's
comics to life. Literally."[28] It is a relation, to be sure, made possible, on
one hand, by Miller's own styling of his comic in terms of image and
action after a movie genre, namely film noir. There are panels in the
comic where action repeats itself from different characters' points of
view, such as parallel shots in a film, while the close-ups, use of shadows,
and the male characters' uniformly trench-coated appearance and internal macho monologue are homage to hard-boiled. [29] However, this
"translation," or for Gronsky, "the extreme end of the evolution of the
comic book film," would not have been made possible with such faithfulness if it were not for the potential of CGI (computer-generated imagery)
and new DI, green-screen technologies: as Aylish Wood's analysis of the
film's digital innovations shows, "the technological choices made for *Sin
City* by Rodriguez pushed the limits of digital post-production, making
the image accessible to manipulation at increasingly micro-levels."[30]
Wood's extensive analysis of the film's image semiotics underlines not
only the mind-blowing potential of DI but, most important, the resulting
*un*reality of *Sin City*, as opposed to other comic-based or CGI-saturated
films that strive for visual plausibility.[31] It was, furthermore, an unreality
sought after by Rodriguez, who apparently wanted the world of the film
to be not (like noir) a fictional rendition of a historical era but an allusion
to a digital utopia: as Jeff Jensen notes (and quotes), "Rodriguez had been
a *Sin City* fan since the beginning. Looking at the books again in 2003, he
saw the potential for another *Matrix*, perhaps, 'one of those visual turning points, where people would see movies in a different way.'"[32] But is
it the unreality of the film that is the "different" element here? Fiction and
films have dealt in unreality even before Aristotle made his famous bid

for "probable impossibilities" being preferable to "improbable possibilities" in his *Poetics*.[33] Moreover, the audience would see nothing new in a
moving comic, a cartoon. Or is it that here the claim to probability or
possibility is never relinquished, because it was never there to begin
with, and in fact a different claim is being made of the viewer, that the
suspension of critical judgment be total and unre(a)lated?

What is for certain is that *Sin City* allows us to see Miller's comic in a
different, new, amoral way and that, as with all translations, something is
lost/betrayed/gained in the process. DI-aided fanboy Rodriguez though
he may be, the medium that he uses dictates partly what happens to the
comic when it begins to move. Or, as Rodowick puts it, following Thierry
Kunzel, "the fiction film produces an ideological reading forged ultimately by its technological conditions of presentation. However, the task of a
textual reading is con-founded by the code of movement through which
the film constitutes itself as spectacle."[34] Most important is the eradication of the comics gutter, which allows for seamless movement from one
panel/frame to the next at twenty-four frames per second, or the digital
equivalent thereof: "comic books traditionally require a bit more from the
reader in terms of connecting events which occur between panels," Gronsky notes. "In a film, however, the panel becomes the entire frame, and
that relationship is lost. Frames can only follow one another sequentially."[35] The result is that the speed of processing is not only controlled but,
in a sense, goes out of control for the viewer: our eye literally cannot
follow the sequence change—hence, the illusion of motion. Summing up
the observations of comics legend Will Eisner, Smith explains that the
result is less involvement for the thinking viewer:

> But for Eisner, the key difference between comic books and films is
> relegated to the modes of reception; comic books may be read at the
> pace chosen by the reader whereas films dictate the viewer's rate of
> speed. Such an immersion into a filmic reality of invisible artifice pro-
> vides the pacing and *mise-en-scene* to guide the viewer, whereas in com-
> ic books a different kind of active reading—participation on the part of
> the reader within the text—is dependent on the reader's chosen pace
> for a complete absorption of the text. Both mediums require active
> participation on the part of the audience, but the speed of engagement
> is creator-controlled for film and reader-controlled in comics.[36]

In addition to the speed, the spatiality of the comics page is reduced to a
seemingly inexorable linearity when transferred to film, and this is what
happens in *Sin City* too.[37] Miller's famous style—with the bold graphics,
spreading large on the page, overlapping, or playing games with the
lettering of the sounds—is an invitation to the reader to read the comic
interactively, choosing his or her path from panel to panel or which detail
to foreground. True, Miller is not one of those artists who pack a panel
(like Joe Sacco) or create carnivalesque centerfold vistas (like George Per-

ez), instead preferring impressive single close-ups or action shots: a review of the *Sin City* comic notes that "one does not linger on individual
panels for long but moves fairly swiftly through the story line of comple-
mentary visuals and script."[38] Nevertheless, the spatial play is there for
the having, as Gronsky's analysis of a key visual instant shows.[39] In the
film, however, despite the startling visual renditions of Miller's *individual*
panels, the *cluster* effect(s) of panel arrangement is lost to a uniform and
relentless sequence. Speaking semantically, we see the word but miss the
syntax—where, for linguistics since Saussure, Lacan, and Derrida, the
unit's meaning is ultimately deferred. This has a double effect: what Mirzoeff calls a "banality of images" in which the thematic and ideological
content of the image is "overwhelmed by the sheer image flow."[40] Most
important, though, Mirzoeff notes that, as the work of Jacques Rancière
has shown, this banality has a direct political impact regarding the construction, in the individual consciousness, of the historical event as important: the filmic effect is like having a policeman directing witnesses
away from the event with the "move on, nothing to see" attitude.[41] So,
even though Jones claims that "film tends to be inductive in the sense
that the spectator moves from specific imagery to general thoughts and
feelings" and, thus, "what strikes the spectator first is always the sensual
perception, which is only later contextualized and processed through
additional, higher-level cognition," one wonders whether the hypothetical *Sin City* spectator will be moved to contextualize the titillating on-
slaught of violent and/or sexist images further than recognizing the
amazing similarity to the visually arresting comic with its already thin
layer of underlying cogitation.[42] Notably, Ang Lee's 2003 adaptation of
Marvel's *The Incredible Hulk* used CGI to retain the comic's paneled look,
an innovation that gave an eloquent visual push to the film's main idea:
the multiple, intrusive underlying dimensions of even the most "innocent" and "unattached" academic science. However, Lee's artistic stunt
turned *Hulk* into a box office flop because the multipaneled screen dis-
tracted fans from being pleasantly absorbed in the action.[43] At the same
time, then, that *Sin City* audiences are overwhelmed by the miracle of a
living comic-book image—for it is not so much that the comic book is
brought to life but that, thanks to DI, the filmic "reality" is made cartoon-
like, as if that were possible to exist—they are also motioned (literally) to
disregard this as anything more than a momentary distraction, as a bear-
er of any ethical, ideological, or thematic signification. Like the too-wily
Oedipus, we interpret the cinematic Sphinx's image only to go blind to
the crime.

A few astute critics have also noted that, even though DI would allow
it, Rodriguez did not transfer onscreen the onomatopoeic banners (like
*BLAM* for gunshot or *KA-BOOM* for explosion) that are every comic
book's staple.[44] Arguably, as experience shows, similar attempts have
resulted either in tongue-in-cheek, "parodic" camp, such as the 1960s'

*Batman* television series with Adam West, or in monumental failures, such as Julie Taymor's 2011 adaptation of *Spider-Man* into a Broadway musical.[45] The transmedium transference, as noted before, draws some impassable lines if one aims for plausibility, and in his critique of *Spider-Man*, Daniel Mendelsohn wisely locates the musical's failure in its inability to balance comics–mythic unreality, the demand for verisimilitude from an audience weaned on superheroes and special effects, and the postmodern invitation for "unmasked" theatrical aesthetics.[46] It is understandable, then, that Rodriguez would sacrifice this visual impossibility to the effect of unity of action and plausibility. However, besides giving up on the opportunity for a potentially truly innovative integration of comics and film as media, what is lost here is what Chute calls the "double vision" elicited by the comic book's page containing "'nonsynthesized' narratives of words and images" that "may mean differently," even, from one another, complicating the narrative semantics.[47] The stripping away of the page's two-dimensional hybridity, image and text, ironically leaves the film even flatter, creating a "realism" that looks possible but not structurally interesting or cogitatively nourishing—that is, unable to generate questions of theme or ideology in terms of its form. The crowds exiting the multiplex are not encouraged, then, to carry off with them any messages relevant to their socioethical education, as the hypervisual denudes image into its lowest possible denominator: a gaudy surface. Rodriguez himself seems to be unaware of this irony, as his concern with verisimilitude is at the same moment laced with an understanding—correct as an instinct yet perhaps ideologically blind or indifferent—that this "realism" must spring from unreality: "I never got tired of the books looking that way," he says in an interview, "and you need that degree of stylization for the story to work: if you shot it straight up it wouldn't make sense. It's not about camera tricks, it's about setting up a world that's consistent—you have to enter that world and feel you're really there."[48] One must envelop an audience in unreality to sustain its suspension of disbelief. Yet there are worlds of difference among suspension of disbelief regarding the conventional stage or the poetic license of a hyperbolic plot; the unreality of destroying the suspension of disbelief by avant-garde techniques; and the acceptance of a cartoon reality as valid. The former two present themselves as *signifiers* for what could happen (a condition for generating the Aristotelian "pity and fear") or caution us away from false identifications by critiquing the signifying process, while the latter, by ridding itself of the double vision (a precondition, as we know from biology, for depth perception), presents itself as the *signified*, a Real conflated with its own sign: Miller's book (like *The Matrix*, where the "truth" lies behind the machine-generated world simulation that humans experience).[49] A live-action *WHAK* would suggest, for example, that the violence inflicted by a punch is unreal within the cartoonish context of conflict between hero and bad guys, which can be enjoyed in perspective because, there, nobody ever gets permanently hurt or dies, as Umberto Eco has shown in his famous analysis of the comic book's iterative scheme in "The Myth of Superman."[50] Take that iterative (comics, noir, or both) convention away, and the remaining enjoyment of the violence that Miller's indestructible heroes gleefully disseminate, a pleasure founded on real pain and death, becomes a disturbing lesson in sociopathic thinking.

There are two more points of divergence that, in terms of visuality, become significant: story selection and color. Rodriguez does not film the entirety of the *Sin City* stories, choosing instead only books 1, 3, and 4, plus a single "short" story from book 6 that serves as the opening shot (and is alluded to at the end). This means that elements that establish continuity among the various stories in the comic lose their linkage to significance in the film. Dwayne's relationship with Gail, for example, devoid of its background—even such a flimsy and schematic one as exists in Miller's stories—appears arbitrary and irrational. Thus, we are invited to either take the world of the film for granted despite its unrealistic feel or legitimize it by deferring the claim to "real" onto its relationship with the "complete" book, again establishing a relationship of signification between a sign/signifier and a "Sign"/signified. This point brings us to the use of color, which, as Gronsky points out, diverges from the comic and becomes problematic in terms of the film's ideological visuality. While Miller uses color sparingly, to emphasize the narrative importance of an element (i.e., the skin of the Yellow Bastard or Dwight's shoes), Rodriguez arbitrarily adds color to other individual objects that have (in the film version) no narrative import but just look pretty when colored inside a black-and-white narrative.[51] While this makes the film more visually arresting, it clouds the line separating violence from its aestheticizing or places aesthetics in general over (and in separation from) meaning.

A final element that the film medium adds and that was noted by practically all reviews but whose import has not perhaps been duly explored is the star-studded cast assembled by Rodriguez for this project, which puts specific faces (with genre expectations) on the comic book characters. Most commercial reviews focus on the sexual appeal of the female protagonists (Jessica Alba, Rosario Dawson, etc.) or on this or that actor's quality of interpretation, taking the cast as a indication of Rodriguez's praiseworthy commitment to the project of bringing Miller's comic to life. All personal opinions aside, the fact is that each male star— Mickey Rourke, Bruce Willis, Clive Owen—could well carry a major motion (action) picture on his own and has successfully done so in the past. Even actors appearing for a few minutes onscreen, such as Michael Clarke Duncan, Josh Hartnett, Rutger Hauer, and Powers Boothe, come preendowed with considerable acting fame, to the effect that the film feels more like a night at the movie awards rather than a character- or plot-based noir. In a comic, we may recognize a character from his or her costume or some caricature/nonhuman feature (a yellow trench coat, a hypertrophic nose, or metallic animal claws), but the actual human features of one's face are up to the reader's imagination, activating that apparatus in the brain that makes a real-life equivalency out of a sketch or painting. But here, the image is literally *in your/one's face*, so, in one more way, visuality (the authority of the star's image) overwhelms content. Furthermore, to the degree that our mind, as Mark Seltzer notes, works on the basis of a "graphic unconscious," imprinting prior associations to cogitate on new data, the actor factor leads audiences to take the film's quality in good faith by virtue of reference not to the actual acting in this film (whose Manichean characters and over-the-top dialogue would make the staunchest thespian despair) but on each star's preestablished reputation.[52]

Iterative convention, not actual quality, once more becomes the measure in a closed, self-referential system. And even though star power is fuel for the majority of films, the DI melding of recognizable actual faces and CGI distortion/prosthetics (Benicio del Toro's nose, Rourke's scarred face, Duncan's golden eye) so blends the dividing line between actual and virtual that it does not allow the viewer to see monstrosity as a representational convention but rather as a facet of a truer-than-life, grim and gritty "reality" whose mark the heroes/villains bear. "The presence of quasi-recognizable human beings here emphasizes the absence of any real emotions or relationships," claims a reviewer, and it can be argued that the observation is true for the audience as well.[53] At the same time, however, since "intertextuality can be used to provide a more complete conception of a character within the comic text and, especially within a film adaptation of that text," the reference of the film's dramatis personae to the comic, on one hand, and to their own star value, on the other, acts as a potent drug for audiences, leading them to grant the film's ideology unquestionable authority.[54] One could even extend the argument to the use of Quentin Tarantino as guest director of a small sequence or Miller's name on the codirectorial credits, which authenticates for the fans the film as "genuine," regardless of whether "genuine" here is only a self-referential nod toward Tarantino-esque innovations on the hard-boiled genre or Miller-esque idiosyncracies of surreal pencilwork and outrageous plots, "a stylized, self-contained fantasy work . . . calculated to astonish rather than convince."[55] This accords with Mirzoeff's description of how Carlyle imagined his Hero:

> In his lectures *On Heroes*, Carlyle argued that only the Hero had the vision to see history as it happened, a viewpoint that was obscured for the ordinary person by the specters and phantasmagorias of emancipation. . . . Visuality was, then, the clear picture of history available to the Hero as it happens and the historian in retrospect.[56]

Rodriguez's slavish reimaging of Miller's comic vision, then, casts Rodriguez in the role of the historian–scribe and Miller in the role of the Hero, or at least the visionary speaking through his heroic avatars. But is it a vision of history they offer, the real as it happens, or a vision of visuality as a purely personal act with total(itarian) control over cognition of whatever Real may be out there? And are we not thus moving from a Disneyfication of history toward a *de*cognition (if I may be allowed the neologism) of history itself as a social concept, along with its related ethics?[57] Ironically, the Hero's totalizing and crystal-clear vision is reduced here to the ruminations of "private eyes," who substitute a panoptical understanding with an all-encompassing self-absorption.

The implications of the medium hybridization process, especially regarding its visual politics, described earlier in the translation of Miller's work on film become even more serious if one considers the other constituent part of this seamless Chimera: the comic. As Wolk observes, comics are "such an immediate art: so seductive, so easy to sink into and get carried away by, so un-hungry for explanation," only to caution us that "easy pleasure and simple pleasure aren't the same thing. It's worth thinking about how that immediacy and seduction . . . work."[58] Indeed, Frank Miller is, without question, one of the most seductive comic book creators in the commercial field, with brilliant artistic innovations and a hard-boiled approach that brought life to moribund or jaded superhero titles, such as Marvel's *Daredevil* (1979) or DC Comics' Batman in *The Dark Knight Returns* (1986): "Next to the *Aliens* franchise, Frank Miller's *Sin City* is Dark Horse Comics' most successful series," notes Michael Lavin in his overview of its publications, adding that "*Sin City*'s real claim to greatness lies in Miller's intense, innovative artwork."[59] The trademark of this art is stark visuals, with exaggerated depictions of beauty (for women) or musculature (for men) inscribed by hard lines and abstract surfaces playing chiaroscuro tricks, imprinting more than drawing an item on the surface of the page. It is an art that looks persistently two-dimensional, while often the effect with intelligent comics would seem to go the other way or, alternatively, use abstraction only to counteract the superhero-dictated codes of predictable and easily consumable physical perfection, as Zunshine notes:

> Graphic narratives have been evolving a visual vocabulary for conveying to readers information about the level of sociocognitive complexity they are about to encounter. For instance, in many cases the volume of physical action and emotional intensity on the cover is inversely related to the level of sociocognitive complexity of the story. Static human figures with relatively neutral facial expressions (see the covers of *American Splendor, Asterios Polyps, Epileptic, Blankets, Embroideries, Ghost World, Logicomix, Maus, Persepolis, Shortcomings,* and *Stitches*) signal action turned inward.[60]

Miller appears also to turn inward with his superhero stories, engaged in making them more gritty and psychologically intense, suggesting a realism that was heretofore lacking in this medium. However, his aim is clearly not to take the reader's mind away from the graphics but instead to substitute the instantaneous appeal of the image for any content and exonerate the latter by virtue of the former, the same way that Roland Barthes sees politicians using photography for instant, thought-eradicating electorate appeal.[61] This seduction is particularly essential since Miller specializes in making superhero protagonists absorbing by painting them anew as immensely gifted creatures but also more or less insane and above morality (like *Sin City*'s Marv). Thus, Miller, by virtue of the autographic nature of comics, has trained his fans for decades to respond to his stylized expressionistic visuals as if they were a suprareal cognizant vision of the world that must supercede all other "ordinary" considerations, as if he were truly Carlyle's Hero. The implications of totalitarianism in such a mind-set—and its accompanying propaganda art—are not lost to critics of graphic narrative, especially given the visual similarity between the Nazis' physically perfect Aryan *Übermensch* and the genetically godlike Superman: "the two graphic media whose images make up the visual memory of the twelve-year Reich [are] . . . cartoons and cinema. Both are intimately linked to the aesthetic vision and historical legacy of Nazism."[62]

Intimations of totalitarian spirit are also found in Miller's idiosyncratic coloring of *Sin City*, or lack thereof: in its almost exclusively black-and-white pages, the eye is infrequently surprised, as noted earlier, by splashes of coded primary colors. More than one critic has noted that the key trick in the film, taken directly from the comic's visuals, involves "gushes of blood appearing as glowing white" (or, in the case of *That Yellow Bastard*, banana yellow), especially in the film's "most ultra-violent sequences."[63] Although black-and-white has been the favorite mode of underground comix creators, delivering some acclaimed graphic novels, in Miller the use of black-and-white to accentuate facial close-ups and intensity of body action recalls Mirzoeff's observations on the totalitarian implications of the color white, linked as it was to a wrong perception of Graeco-Roman plastic aesthetics and, subsequently, to Aryan supremacism and "the Modernist aesthetic of flatness."[64] It is certainly no accident that the shurikens frequently used by a key character in both *Sin City* versions—Miho, the mute ninja prostitute (?!)—are swastika shaped.

This brings us to the characters themselves, which are, frankly, puerile hard-boiled caricatures with a Manichean black-and-white code of ethics and driven by extreme and unfounded emotional swings. Not surprising, it is the more scholarly critiques that confound the film, while commercial reviewers rave at the action or the naked flesh (dis-)splayed: giving credit to the superb stylization, Steven Aoun nevertheless delivers a scathing feminist analysis of the film—true also for the comic—as "a relatively safe place for the male id to keep abreast of itself or flip the bird to civilized society," while the "moral compass or point of view" just tends to revolve around the direction that someone's penis might be pointing in.[65] Alternatively focusing on what is lost in the filmic translation, Lisa Schwarzbaum notes,

> Rodriguez/Miller's screen version, fleshed out by eager-to-play-along stars . . . warps those characters into alienating—or worse, laughable— avatars of violence and sexual humiliation [that end up sounding] like Guy Noir parodies from Garrison Keillor—when spoken out loud with broad sneers rather than read, nestled on the page amid the crackle and pop of the illustrations.[66]

The observation is significant in pointing out the key role of comic reader implication in the process of creating not only meaning but quality as well. (Self-)Questioning may be almost a humanities cliché since the early twentieth century, but it also keeps one's faculties trained and in healthy engagement with the world. Characters as adamantly sure about themselves or as unthinking as Miller's Dwight or Marv or Miho offer no incentive for participation, just consumption through audience identification, and the effect is exponentially exacerbated when the fast-paced filmic action allows no time for rumination.

To this, we must add the observation that Miller's characters in *Sin City*, despite their being identified uniformly as derived from noir, function less as hard-boiled detectives and more like indestructible superheroes. [67] While the fedora and trench coat are a noir staple, in *Sin City* everyone wears some kind of uniform, from Dwight's red Converse sneakers to Marv's obsession with trench coats (which all the male characters wear, rain or shine). All but two of the women wear uniforms: the prostitutes dress up in various costumes suggestive of both superhero garb and sexual role-play (a conflation of the ethical and the unethical that accords with the film's amorality discussed here), and Nancy wears a stripper's cowgirl outfit. Most important, while noir or hard-boiled heroes bleed if you prick them, volume 4 has Hartigan, the aged hero with a severe heart condition who resists by sheer willpower the effects of hanging long enough to break a window, snatch a shard with his bare legs, and, contorting, cut himself loose from the noose![68] Dwight survives being beaten, run over, shot twice, and thrown out the window.[69] Manute, another villain, survives an eye-gouging beating, explosions, defenestration, katana stabs, and six bullets in the chest.[70] The hulking Marv of volume 1 receives a hail of bullets and incredible beatings; he gets run over twice; and even the electric chair cannot kill him at first. Roark Jr. even grows a new set of genitalia![71] While the film does boost the plot's claim to "realism," its base material treats human bodies as indestructible and with unlimited raw potential for violence and suffering, reducing the perception of humanity to an episode of *Tom and Jerry*. Violence becomes an excuse for cruel slapstick laughter, which, as it "echoes the inescapability of power," according to Horkheimer and Adorno, desensitizes the modern audience toward the loss of human empathy and the acceptance of a cinematic condition of pictured superhumans whom they must blindly idolize and emulate.[72]

Finally, the sense of inescapable, albeit artificial, "reality" to which the Rodriguez–Miller audiences are seduced is made even more imperative by the setting of the story, Basin/Sin City, depicted by Miller as a synecdoche of hell: eternal darkness visible; urban dereliction turning upon itself; forbidden neighborhoods and claustrophobic, labyrinthine, or centrifugal architecture; a "relentless confining and framing—by frames within frames within frames," symbolically locking the characters into asphyxiating dead-ends: "Whether redolent of heaven or hell, these claustrophobic chambers expressionistically evoke the controlling desires and fears of each of the heroes."[73] Alternatively, the only country spot in the film, the Roark family farm, is depicted as the nexus of ultimate evil, pushing viewers back into the city as the only viable choice. It is interesting that in the film, Rodriguez chose only the stories where the main characters die or are sucked into Sin City's underworld for good and not, for example, volume 7, where Wallace escapes from "Hell" in the end (as the title goes). This editing of plot strengthens this sense of inescapability from this reality, suggesting its visualized omnipotence and lack of alternatives—ironically, the only thing that this "reality" would have in common with, say, the Foucaultian conception of actual modern society as a carceral.[74] Daly, speaking about films with a spatial rather than temporal arrangement, explains how making Sin City the film's inescapable focus works to disorient in terms of visuality:

> [Spatial] movies . . . provide an excess cognitive stimulation, a surplus of characters and plots, along with the excess of aural and visual stimulation. In place of the norms of narrative reception in the cinema, these types of movies do not expect the viewer to completely understand the complicated, interconnected plots. He or she is supposed to be left slightly dazed and confused.
>
> In these movies, numerous characters and events are intertwined not causally, but by coincidence and their navigation of the space. Characters cross and double-cross because they exist together spatially. This is more like a video game.[75]

From Tom and Jerry to video games then, Sin City's blend of DI virtual and noir grittiness functions like a potent drug that keeps audiences hooked and believing. Furthermore, the heroes depicted die defending a certain grotesque status quo, making sure that the laws of violence remain respected by friends and foes: most characteristically, Dwight stages an all-out war of prostitutes versus the Mob, only to keep the "Old Town," the bastion of self-governed prostitution, exactly as it is![76] This resonates with Gronsky's observation about the insidious agenda behind comics' seeming subversiveness:

> Because the comic book, and the superhero genre in specific, is both a product of youth culture but also non-threatening to the dominant cultural hegemony (in that it generally lacks subversive elements and serves to reinforce culturally dominant themes such as the concepts of good and evil, right and wrong, and the overall infallibility of the system), it becomes a site of shared ground between the oppositional forces, and allows for a continued negotiation between the two.[77]

This, in terms of *Sin City*'s heroes, for Gronsky, means that "although the film acknowledges that these men may have certain admirable qualities, it also makes it explicit that behavior such as theirs will not be tolerated. . . . Ultimately the power of the dominant hegemonic structure is reaffirmed."[78] Considering how totalitarian ideologies are essentially reactionary, despite often adopting a "revolutionary" façade, this social message for audiences would be homeostasis, if not outright atavism: after all, in a virtual "reality," no real harm is ever done and no real progress expected.

What is then the result of this virtual blend of comic and film or, rather, animation of comic as an impossibly visualized live-action film? As theoreticians from Jacques Derrida and Michel Foucault to Judith Butler have shown us, it is rather the performative repetition of the sign—the proliferation of its discourses and not some innate value of it—that legitimates its existence as what we conventionally accept as "real."[79] Thus, the panel-by-panel reimaging of Miller's comic onscreen enhances his prestige as "probably comic books' biggest marquee name right now" to the status of not just a classic but the unalterable sign, the center of signification as posited by Derrida in "Structure, Sign, and Play," "which arrests and grounds the play of substitutions" by being itself ultimate meaning, transcendental.[80] At the same time, the impossibly visible outcome of the blend of comic and DI, something that looks and yet is not anything like real life, indeed posits the reference base for the film in the realm of the hyperreal, the transcendental. The game of self-referentiality originates, in fact, in Miller's comic, where the action, by virtue of its containment in space, periodically loops and reloops to the same moments, seen through different people and from different angles, for no apparent reason.[81]

However, the enlivening repetition onscreen in a medium with a long history of adaptations of other media and immense mass dissemination increases the repetition effect exponentially, even excessively, considering that, as Jones's study has shown, audiences who read a comic book first and then see the film derive an increased sense of "telepresence" (hence, movie impact) from the latter.[82] As one exasperated critic put it, "call me an insensitive non-fangirl, but if the sacred works of Jane Austen can stand up to free-wheeling reinterpretation, then so, too, can heavy-breathing pages about trussed-up little girls and a vile-smelling cartoon pervert known as Yellow Bastard."[83] It is also notable that while "the film is caught within popular culture's vicious cycle of eternal returns or law of diminishing returns," ever since *Sin City*, Miller's status as an Author/ity has risen to unparalleled levels: as a critic notes about the subsequent Milleriad, "in the case of *300*, the hand [that] audiences felt was really Miller's, since whenever Snyder made a creative decision, he asked himself, What would Frank do?"[84] One finds the parody of "What would Jesus (one of Western culture's transcendental signifieds) do?" in the case of art and creativity more than disconcerting. It cancels history as we know it, positing an envisioning of life or a film/fiction/comics tradition from which each creator can borrow freely, the searing stamp of one man's mode of interpretation to be followed blindly.[85] A critic observes,

> Movies may have been seen at their outset as something like amber cubes of captured reality, but over a century's accumulation later, what they are in toto is history . . . a torrential parallel history intersecting at haphazard intervals with reality as it's lived, while reflecting, opposing and infiltrating it in unpredictable ways.[86]

In Rodriguez and Miller's copying, stunning (in both senses) interpretation, one sees not so much opposition or reflection but surrender to an image mirroring something that however does not and cannot exist—a simulacrum of the fourth order, pure virtuality as delineated by Jean Baudrillard.[87] To the extent that "the seeing machine is also a personation machine" that "links processes of objectification, identification and representation to what might be called the making of persons . . . the intricated matters of . . . seeing and seeing oneself," visuality becomes the pathway to the individual viewer's indoctrination into another order of reality.[88] In other words, the entertainment industry consolidates its powers of seduction over the audience, while the loss of a sense of the "real" as an ethical or heuristic yardstick (even an aspiration) is counted as an acceptable side loss.

Thus, we reach the true innovation of *Frank Miller's Sin City* in terms of cinematic history, its positing of a hyperreality visualized in impossible terms as the New Real, to which no alternative is given and all roads of cinematic and comic rhetoric converge with no detour allowed.[89] DI was used here not to simulate a world that does not exist but to simulate one that, we are *shown*, is possible—is in fact a world that lurks out there, as is the premise of noir, except we, ordinary people, have no intimation of it and must rely on the Hero's all-seeing "private eye" to visualize it for us as well. Only this time, the gritty societal underbelly of noir is the DI green-screen virtuality. It is, more important, a world circumscribed by the dubious comic-book politics of Miller's heroes (especially), attuned—as is the case with many celebrated comic-book artists/authors, from Alan Moore to Rick Veitch—to the teenage boyhood mentality of their reading audiences, with all its raw and agonizing questions of adolescence, its sexist gender stereotyping, its absolutist romanticism and ideological Manichean extremism, its inexperienced lack of empathy regarding issues of hard-core and hard-boiled violence, totalitarianism, and vigilantism yet energized by sensitive and volatile sensibilities. What is affirmed as Real is what modern Western cultural or educational expectations hope can be overcome by a growing awareness, on the part of their young readers, of the complexities or "real life," which in turn should allow them to mature out of their teen ideological awkwardness. Channeling, however, this "reality" through a medium so popular and, as noted by Bertold Brecht, so influential in its brutal simplicity as to sway even him despite his awareness, "his radical politics," and "his radical aesthetics" handicaps the process, especially within a culture where the illusion of virtuality steadily replaces the illusion of conventional actuality.[90] Two of the most acclaimed comic creators caution us to the persuasive power of comics: "Cartoons," Art Spiegelman observes, "have a way of crawling past our critical radar and getting right into the id. It may be that their reductive diagrammatic qualities echo the way the brain sorts information," or, as Jones explains, because we respond to the comic-book message twice, in accordance to its hybridity: once in terms of the text and once unconsciously, in terms of the body language and facial expressions depicted.[91] Alan Moore corroborates this in the following info-snippet: "Pentagon studies in the 1980s demonstrated that comic strip narrative is still the best way of conveying understandable and retainable information," which explains why, as Andrew Ross notes, comics were largely used for anticommunist propaganda.[92] If one adds to that the results of Knulst and van den Broek's study on the relationship of comics readers to general and fiction reading, which classifies them statistically as predominantly male, adolescent, of medium-low educational level and having the steepest decline in reading, one understands how the closed walls of Sin City become an eloquent metaphor for the lack of critical perspective of the majority of fans of Miller's work in its various influential reimagings.[93] Faced with this new set of visual politics, where to visualize conflict is to realize its possibility, perhaps Andreas Huyssen's words of caution, in his analysis that ties the art of *Maus* to the *Bilderverbot*, the Hebrew injunction against graven images, ring truer than ever.[94] The dangerous seduction of *Sin City* lies, indeed, in its realization of false idols that, like Moloch, consume our critical eye/I into their own "immense reality show."[95]

## NOTES

1. James Gianopulos, "Hellenism and Hollywood: From Aristotle to Alexander (Payne)," lecture, "Great Ideas" talk series of the Stavros Niarchos Foundation, Athens Megaron Hall, Greece, November 25, 2009.

2. *Frank Miller's Sin City*, directed by Frank Miller and Robert Rodriguez (2005; New York: Dimension Films, 2005), DVD.

3. Nicholas Mirzoeff, *An Introduction to Visual Culture*, 2nd ed. (London: Routledge, 2009), 1.

4. Mirzoeff, *An Introduction to Visual Culture*, 5, 6.

5. Hillary Chute, "Comics as Literature? Reading Graphic Narrative," *PMLA* 123, no. 2 (2008): 452.

6. Aaron Meskin, "Comics as Literature?" *British Journal of Aesthetics* 49, no. 3 (2009): 219; for the summary of the debate, see 223–24 and 232–33.

7. Michael Cieply, "That Noisy Woodpecker Had an Animated Secret," *New York Times*, April 10, 2011, C1.

8. Chute, "Comics as Literature?" 455.

9. Scott McCloud, *Understanding Comics: The Invisible Art* (New York: Kitchen Sink Press, 1993); Michael Chabon, *The Amazing Adventures of Kavalier and Clay: A Novel* (London: Harper Perennial, 2000).

10. Elaine Martin, "Graphic Novels or Novel Graphics? The Evolution of an Iconoclastic Genre," *The Comparatist* 35 (May 2011): 178.

11. Stephen E. Tabachnick, "The Graphic Novel and the Age of Transition: A Survey and Analysis," *English Literature in Transition, 1880–1920* 53, no. 1 (2010): 3–28; Lisa Zunshine, "What to Expect When You Pick Up a Graphic Novel," *SubStance #124* 40, no. 1 (2011): 114–34.

12. Andrew Ross, *No Respect: Intellectuals and Pop Culture* (London: Routledge, 1989), 128.

13. Douglas Wolk, *Reading Comics: How Graphic Novels Work and What They Mean* (Philadelphia: Da Capo Press, 2007), 10.

14. See Benjamin Smith, "Spandex Cinema: Three Approaches to Comic Book Film Adaptation" (master's thesis, University of Central Oklahoma, 2009).

15. Mirzoeff, *An Introduction to Visual Culture*, 6.

16. Daniel Gronsky, "Frame to Frame: A Historical Analysis of the Evolution and Propagation of the Comic Book Film" (PhD diss., University of Connecticut, 2008), 7.

17. Kristen Daly, "Cinema 3.0: How Digital and Computer Technologies Are Changing Cinema" (PhD diss., Columbia University, 2008), 33.

18. Chute, "Comics as Literature?" 452.

19. David Norman Rodowick, *Giles Deleuze: Time Machine, Post-contemporary Interventions* (Durham, NC: Duke University Press, 1997), 202.

20. Jean Baudrillard, *Simulacra and Simulation*, trans. Sheila Faria Glaser (Ann Arbor: University of Michigan Press, 1994).

21. See, for example, Max Horkheimer and Theodor Adorno's 1947 "The Culture Industry" from *Dialectic of Enlightenment: Philosophical Fragments*, trans. Edmund Jephcott, ed. Gunzelin Schmid Noerr (Palo Alto, CA: Stanford University Press, 2002), 94–136; Roland Barthes's "The Romans in Films" (26–28) and "Photography and Electorate Appeal" (91–93) from *Mythologies*, trans. Annette Lavers (New York: Farrar, Straus and Giroux, 1972); and Arthur Kroker's *SPASM: Virtual Reality, Android Music and Electric Flesh* (New York: St. Martin's Press, 1993) and the collection edited by him and Marylouise Kroker, *Critical Digital Studies: A Reader* (Toronto: University of Toronto Press, 2008).

22. Mirzoeff, *An Introduction to Visual Culture*, 14.

23. Daly, "Cinema 3.0," 199.

24. Smith, "Spandex Cinema," 26.

25. Kim Newman, "*Sin City* Review," *Sight & Sound* (June 2005): 72.

26. Newman, "*Sin City* Review," 27.

27. Newman, "*Sin City* Review," 28.

28. Jeff Jensen, "Spring Movie Preview: *Sin City*," *Entertainment Weekly* 807 (February 14, 2005), http://www.ew.com/ew/article/0,,1026704,00.html.

29. Frank Miller, *Sin City*, vol. 7, *Hell and Back* (Milwaukie, OR: Dark Horse Comics, 1999), 98, 106.

30. Gronsky, "Frame to Frame," 203; Aylish Wood, "Pixel Visions: Digital Intermediates and Micromanipulations of the Image," *Film Criticism* 32, no. 1 (2007): 72.

31. Wood, "Pixel Visions," 87–91.

32. Jensen, "Spring Movie Preview."

33. Aristotle, *Poetics*, 24.2, trans. S. H. Butcher, http://classics.mit.edu/Aristotle/poetics.3.3.html.

34. David Norman Rodowick, "Review: The Figure and the Text," *Diacritics* 15, no. 1 (1985): 36.

35. Gronsky, "Frame to Frame," 197.

36. Smith, "Spandex Cinema," 19–20.

37. Chute, "Comics as Literature?" 454, sees this spatiality as "the way temporality can be traced in complex, often nonlinear paths across the space of the page," but one could argue that it is not only temporality that is interpreted thus but other elements as well (pictorial irony, moods, etc.).

38. Peter Goggin, "Review: *Sin City Volumes 1–4: The Hard Goodbye; A Dame to Kill For; The Big Fat Kill; That Yellow Bastard*," *Journal of Adolescent & Adult Literacy* 49, no. 5 (2006): 447.

39. Gronsky, "Frame to Frame," 198.

40. Mirzoeff, *An Introduction to Visual Culture*, 14.

41. Mirzoeff, *An Introduction to Visual Culture*, 14.

42. Matthew T. Jones, "Found in Translation: Structural and Cognitive Aspects of the Comic Art to Film" (PhD diss., Temple University, 2008), 18–19.

43. *Hulk* (widescreen 2-disk special edition), directed by Ang Lee (2003; Universal City, CA: Universal Studios, 2007). For a critique that sums up the audiences' reactions, see Erik Sofge, "In Defense of *Hulk* (Yes, the Ang Lee One)," *Slate*, June 17, 2008, http://www.slate.com/id/2193478/.

44. Luke Arnott, "*BLAM!* The Literal Architecture of *Sin City*," *International Journal of Comic Art*, 10 no. 2 (2008): 398.

45. Smith, "Spandex Cinema," 15–16.

46. Daniel Mendelsohn, "Why She Fell. Review of *Spider-Man: Turn Off the Dark*," *New York Review of Books*, May 12, 2011.

47. Chute, "Comics as Literature?" 459.

48. Mark Olson, "Interview: Robert Rodriguez," *Sight & Sound* 15, no. 6 (2005): 16.

49. *The Matrix*, directed by Andy Wachowski and Larry Wachowski (Burbank, CA: Warner Home Video, 1999).

50. Umberto Eco, "The Myth of Superman," trans. Natalie Chilton, in *The Critical Tradition: Classic Texts and Contemporary Trends*, 2nd ed., ed. David H. Richter (Boston: Bedford Books, 1998), 870–73.

51. Gronsky, "Frame to Frame," 200.

52. Mark Seltzer, "The Graphic Unconscious: A Response," *New Literary History* 26, no. 1 (1995): 21–28.

53. Todd McCarthy, "Reviews: Through a Toon Darkly," *Variety*, March 28, 2005, 45.

54. Jones, "Found in Translation," 84.

55. Newman, "*Sin City* Review."

56. Mirzoeff, *An Introduction to Visual Culture*, 92.

57. For the term *Disneyfication* (or *Disneyization*), see Sharon Zukin, *The Cultures of Cities* (Oxford, England: Blackwell,1996), 128; the idea of Disneyland as a semantic mode of debunking the historical, however, can be traced to French thinker Louis Marin, in his *Utopics: Spatial Play*, trans. Robert A. Vollrath (Atlantic Highlands, NJ: Humanities, 1984).

58. Wolk, *Reading Comics*, 16.

59. Michael R. Lavin, "A Librarian's Guide to Dark Horse Comics," *Serials Review* 24, nos. 3–4 (1998): 88.

60. Zunshine, "What to Expect," 126.

61. Barthes, *Mythologies*, 92–93.

62. Thomas Doherty, "Art Spiegelman's *Maus*: Graphic Art and the Holocaust," *American Literature* 68, no. 1 (1996): 72. Doherty's thesis that the animal-based art of *Maus* precisely deconstructs Nazi propaganda of Jews as "vermin" while opposing the Nazi visuality (i.e., aesthetic–ideological) criterion of the physical perfected form is also echoed by Chute, discussing Spiegelman's art as "abdicating aesthetic mastery" (459) and Sacco's "formalism" as resisting "easy consumption" (460) in "Comics as Literature?"

63. Newman, "*Sin City* Review," 72.

64. Mirzoeff, *An Introduction to Visual Culture*, 103; for the whole discussion on whiteness, see 104–7.

65. Steven Aoun, "DVD Reviews: *Sin City*," *Metro Magazine: Media and Education Magazine* 149 (2006): 237.

66. Lisa Schwarzbaum, "Frankly Speaking," *Entertainment Weekly* 814 (April 8, 2005), 44.

67. On Miller's relation to and influences by noir and hard-boiled, see Graham Fuller, "Colour Me Noir," *Sight & Sound* 15, no. 6 (2005): 12–16; Christopher Pizzino, "Art That Goes Boom: Genre and Aesthetics in Frank Miller's 'Sin City,'" *English Language Notes* 46, no. 2 (2008): 115–28; Heidi MacDonald, "Miller's Double Noir: 'Sin City' and 'Batman Begins,'" *Publishers Weekly*, March 7, 2005, 40–43; Rachel Hodges, "*Sin City* Takes Film Noir to the Depths of Mediocrity," *Static and Feedback: Movies*, http://www.staticandfeedback.com/Movies/0105sinr.html; Brian D. Johnson, "Hard-Boiled Burlesque," *MacLean's*, April 4, 2005, 50–52.

68. Miller, *Sin City*, 4:179–83.

69. Miller, *Sin City*, 2:109–21.

70. Miller, *Sin City*, 3:107.

71. Miller, *Sin City*, 4:170.

72. Horkheimer and Adorno, *Dialectic of Enlightenment*, 112.

73. Fuller, "Colour Me Noir," 14, 16.

74. See Michel Foucault's "The Carceral," in *Discipline and Punish: The Birth of Prison*, trans. Alan Sheridan (New York: Vintage, 1995).

75. Daly, "Cinema 3.0," 192.

76. Miller, *Sin City*, vol. 3.

77. Gronsky, "Frame to Frame," 7–8.

78. Gronsky, "Frame to Frame," 183.

79. Jacques Derrida, *Of Grammatology*, trans. Gayatri Chakravorty Spivak, corrected ed. (1967; Baltimore: The Johns Hopkins University Press, 1997); Michel Foucault, "Truth and Power," in *Power/Knowledge: Selected Interviews and Other Writings , 1972–1977*, ed. Colin Gordon (London: Vintage, 1980), 109–33; Judith Butler, *Gender Trouble: Feminism and the Subversion of Identity* (New York: Psychology Press), 1990.

80. Wolk, *Reading Comics*, 173; Jacques Derrida, "Structure, Sign, and Play in the Discourse of the Human Sciences," in *Writing and Difference*, trans. Alan Bass (London: The University of Chicago Press, Routledge and Kegan Paul, 1978), 289.

81. See Miller, *Sin City*, 2:167 and 2:172, where the action repeats the events of 1:50–51 and 1:54–55.

82. Jones, "Found in Translation," 204–6. Interestingly, films alone did not differ in telepresence level from the experience of only reading the comic, proving that it is the repetition that is significant here (let alone a reimaging such as Rodriguez's).

83. Schwarzbaum, "Frankly Speaking," 44.

84. Aoun, "DVD Reviews," 239; Rebecca Winters Keegan, "Batman's Half Brothers," *Time* 171, no. 26 (June 30, 2008), 59.

85. Gronsky, "Frame to Frame," 182, for example, links the success of the *Sin City* film (but also an underlying reason for Miller's choice of form) to the increased aggression and fear caused by the Iraq War, in the same way that film noir in the 1940s fed into the "combination of militarism and social unrest" of the World Wars. However, the focus on Miller's text as itself being the ultimate sign to replicate, the way that it is done in the film, obscures/cancels the complex substratum of cultural interplay.

86. Michael Atkinson, "Season of the Witch-Hunt," *Sight & Sound* 21, no. 5 (2011): 92.

87. Baudrillard, *Simulacra and Simulation*.

88. Seltzer, "The Graphic Unconscious," 21.

89. In anecdotal support of the argument that the film popularity and verisimilitude–comic absolutism combination does have the power to change our perceptions of reality, it was both amusing and depressing to witness how, after the airing of Miller's *300*, the tourist district of Plaka, in Athens, was flooded with imitation "Leonidas" shields and helmets—that is, with a design copied from those in the film/comic, which tourists eagerly bought as "authentic" representative items of antiquity!

90. Mirzoeff, *An Introduction to Visual Culture*, 191.

91. Art Spiegelman, *Tijuana Bibles: Art and Wit in America's Forbidden Funnies, 1930s–1950s* (New York: Simon & Schuster, 1997), 5; Jones, "Found in Translation," 71–72.

92. Spiegelman, *Tijuana Bibles*, 5; Ross, *No Respect*, 19.

93. Wim Knulst and Andries van den Broek, "The Readership of Books in Times of De-reading," *Poetics* 31 (2003): 223–28.

94. Andreas Huyssen, "Of Mice and Mimesis: Reading Spiegelman with Adorno," *New German Critique* 81 (Autumn 2000): 76.

95. Jean Baudrillard, *Screened Out*, trans. Chris Turner (London: Verso, 2002), 153, quoted in Daly, "Cinema 3.0," 221.

# TWELVE

# The Zombie Apocalypse

*A Fictional State of Nature?*

Faiz Sheikh,
University of Leeds

The fictional world of *The Walking Dead*, a comic book series written by Robert Kirkman and published by Image Comics, allows the scholar to illustrate many of the themes and concepts around the state of nature and the first steps toward state formation from this condition of anarchy. Such illustration "brings to life" much of this political theory and allows academics to explore the assumptions made by social contract theorists. While social contract theory does not necessarily equate to an actual account of the origins of societies, their assumptions about the nature of human behavior inform the basis of many of the foundations of international politics—principally, that of anarchy in the international system. The assumptions around human nature and the state of nature can be analyzed in the context of *The Walking Dead*.

In the world of *The Walking Dead* comics, society has crumbled in the wake of a zombie "infection." The nature of this infection is never revealed, but as people die, they reanimate as flesh-eating zombies. Governments have been unable to control the infection, and now the majority of the world's population are zombies. The story in *The Walking Dead* follows a band of human survivors as they struggle to carve out an existence on the outskirts of Atlanta. The story follows the group as it leaves its initial camp to settle in a prison near the town of Woodbury. After a conflict with other human survivors at the prison, the group then takes a long trip to Washington, DC, where, rumor has it, a remaining government stronghold exists. The stronghold proves to be false, but the group discovers a human society walled off in a few blocks of a DC suburb.

Society after the zombie infection has become "premodern," regressing down the scale of modernity and peace, essentially entering Thomas Hobbes's state of nature. The political philosopher Thomas Hobbes is best renowned for *Leviathan*, an ambitious reflection on the origins of society and state, published in the aftermath of the English Civil War. Hobbes's state of nature was equally fictional as the world of *The Walking Dead*, and being fictional, its base assumptions cannot be tested. With reference to the social contract, we have to be told about the essential nature of man; plausible though a "state of nature" may be, we cannot prove its existence.

The first part of this chapter tests the fundamental questions of the state of nature in an accessible, nonabstract manner, through the analysis of *The Walking Dead*. For the purpose of brevity, the chapter focuses primarily on Hobbes's state of nature. This section seeks to answer such basic questions as, Does the state of nature actually exist? Is consent a central part of creating society? Is sovereignty vested in the majority or in an individual?

The second part of the chapter asks to what extent using comics to elucidate political theory is a useful learning tool in the politics classroom. While educators now feel comfortable to use film and documentaries as a tool in classrooms, in combination with more traditional textbook methods of teaching, the comic form is often overlooked. When zombies are used to teach politics, as attempted by Daniel Drezner and Robert Blanton, methods adhere with textbook style of teaching, using a core book focusing on zombies to teach, in these cases, international relations.[1] With reference to the narrative-based teaching method used by Thomas Juneau and Mira Sucharov in teaching the Israel–Palestine conflict, this chapter inquires the extent to which the same method can be used to teach the state of nature.[2]

## THE STATE OF NATURE: FACT OR FICTION?

The state of nature is a concept describing a world with no overarching authority; people exist individually without political institutions governing them.[3] Many scholars have posited what a state of nature might look like and how individuals in such a world would form into societies and states. David Boucher and Paul Kelly observe that in engaging with social contract theory, there is no singular tradition that can take the name. Rather, there is a multitude of traditions emerging from that concept. Social contract theories are versatile, and they can be used "to create society; civil society; a sovereign; procedural rules of justice; or morality itself."[4] There is a long line of contractarian theorists, from the classical origins of Thomas Hobbes, John Locke, and Jean-Jacques Rousseau to the more modern articulations of John Rawls. It is Hobbes, however, who is most applicable to the world of *The Walking Dead*.

Hobbes's social contract—and the state of nature he describes as its starting point—is the most potent imagining of this world, one that continues to inform the way that states operate in international relations. Mark Heller remarks that "the state of nature is a convenient metaphor for the fragmentation of authority among states."[5] However, Hobbes's theories on the state of nature, which inform theories on the anarchy of the international system, are not paradigm theories, as they cannot be tested.[6] Rather, Hobbes creates a fictional world, seeking to "justify obedience to political authorities by grounding it in the rational acts of rational agents."[7] Hobbes famously describes his state of nature as thus:

> In such condition, there is no place for industry; because the fruit thereof is uncertain; and consequently no culture of the earth; no navigation, nor use of the commodities that may be imported by sea; no commodious building; no instruments of moving, and re-moving, such things as require much force; no knowledge of the face of the earth; no account of time; no arts; no letters; no society; and which is worst of all, continual fear, and danger of violent death, and the life of man, solitary, poor, nasty, brutish, and short.[8]

Hobbes appeals to our imagination to create this world, and he tantalizes our intellect to believe that the decisions of people in this state of nature are those of rational individuals. Daniel Drezner observes that when Hobbes wrote the aforementioned, "zombies were either on his mind or outside his door."[9]

Robert Kirkman's ongoing comic book *The Walking Dead* is a grounded look at the lives of survivors of a zombie apocalypse. It is distinct from the superhero comics of the major comic publishers, as it deals with adult content, with the depiction of reanimated corpses being the most obvious clue that this is a series not intended or suited for children. Beyond the obvious though, *The Walking Dead* is at times a hard read, dealing with such issues as sexual violence, cannibalism, adultery, insanity, and murder. It is not a book for the light-hearted, as the author delights in looking at, in his own words, "how people react when pushed to extremes."[10] The series remains relevant to this discussion with the *context* that this human drama unfolds.

Drezner explains that "most of the zombie cannon . . . concludes that the natural response to the rise of the living dead would be sheer panic, leading to genuine anarchy."[11] The world of *The Walking Dead* is no exception. The synopsis found on the back of the trade paperbacks of the comic summarizes this context in succinct yet equally vivid language as Hobbes:

The world we knew is gone. The world of commerce and frivolous necessity has been replaced by a world of survival and responsibility. An epidemic of apocalyptic proportions has swept the globe causing the dead to rise and feed on the living. In a matter of months society has crumbled, no government, no grocery stores, no mail delivery, no cable TV. In a world ruled by the dead, we are forced to finally start living.[12]

The context of *The Walking Dead*, then, is sufficiently akin to Hobbes's description of the state of nature to justify our comparison. While Hobbes describes a world with no arts, letters, or society, Robert Kirkman describes a world with no television, no mail, and no government. More so, in Hobbes's world people live in continual fear of violent death at the hands of their neighbors; in Kirkman's world, people live in continual fear of the zombie infestation and, later in the series, their neighbors.

The worlds of Hobbes and Kirkman are entirely fictional, yet both attempt to show the reader that the actions of those individuals within them are the actions of rational people. In this way, we can use the latter and its narrative examples to analyze the assumptions of the former. The benefit of analyzing one fictional world through the lens of another may not be immediately apparent. However, the fact that they are both works of fiction does not acknowledge the differences between them. While Hobbes's aim is a political piece of writing, in which he indulges the imagination only as much is necessary to make his point, Kirkman is writing a piece of ongoing fiction. As such, one world—Hobbes's world—is not a world in which we live; it is far more abstract: a world glimpsed from the outside looking in. There is no one within Hobbes's world whom we recognize as anything beyond the lowest common denominator of human being. The people in *The Walking Dead* comic book are ones whom we identify with far more than the individuals in Hobbes's description.

The extensive stories found within the comic cover societal breakdown, the immediate scramble for survival, the first grouping of strangers into some sort of society, and the eventual growth of that community. This study engages with stories and characters from the midway point of this grand narrative, around the time in which individuals begin to come together in this state of nature/zombie apocalypse. As the characters begin to form societies, we see if this happens in the same way that Hobbes theorized it would, how they might differ, and why. An essential part of any group dynamic revolves around the issue of leadership, and it is governance and sovereignty that are the center of discussion in this chapter.

## THE LEGITIMACY OF GOVERNMENT: ILLUSTRATING HOBBES'S ABSOLUTE SOVEREIGN

If all humans are equal, what agreement can legitimize government — can legitimize some other equal acting on our behalf and ruling over us? In modern society, this is a moot point. We are born into societies that do not ask our permission to govern us. For those born into a democracy, it is the will of the people that gives those in power the right to govern, although "the will of the people" did not and cannot ask an infant for permission to rule. Similarly, citizens who vote for the losing party do not necessarily consent to being governed by the winners. The idea of consent as a legitimizing tool for government is a theoretical one; in practice, it is far easier to point to Max Weber's notion of the monopoly of legitimate force as the method of securing government. For Weber, a state can be called as such when an authority within it (a government) has unchallenged use of legitimate force within its borders.[13] There is no moral theorizing as to the worth of individuals or where sovereignty is vested within this state. Contractarian theorists ask not how, in reality, to legitimize government but rather how to posit an ideal.[14] If government needed the consent of the governed, how is this achieved? In answering the question, social contract theory finds it difficult to reconcile the theory of consent to government and the practice of being born into and never being asked to consent to the method of government that you find yourself in. It is at this juncture that *The Walking Dead* can help us.

As previously discussed, in the world of *The Walking Dead* we are shown a society in complete collapse. This is a world where individuals are no longer bound by any abstract notion of nationhood or even more concrete notions of ethnicity or culture. Here is a world so dangerous that to care for such simplistic concerns in the face of the imminent danger of zombies would threaten your survival. In such a condition, people are entirely selfish and consumed with their survival to such an extent that meeting a stranger, even meeting a friend in this postapocalyptic world, must be met with caution. Is this new person a threat? Will this person try to steal your food while you sleep? The assumption that a fellow human being, by virtue of not being a zombie, is a boon to your survival is naïve. In such a world of hyperindividuality where nothing can be assumed, people have to actually be *asked*, actually have to *consent* to any form of authority acting on their behalf. Such an individualistic position is one that has received much criticism from socialist and communitarian theorists. Macpherson's famous socialist critique of Hobbes and others accuses these theories of grounding themselves in a notion of the individual that is intrinsically bound to notions of capitalism.[15] As with Hobbes, however, while Macpherson's critique is argued thoroughly, as it rests on a notion of human nature that is not falsifiable, it cannot be proven or disproven. Here *The Walking Dead* is the perfect place to test the assumptions of social contract theories that are often so abstract that they are dismissed out of hand as bearing no real-world relevance.

Hobbes's classic social contract claims that people in the state of nature have three options: to remain in the state of nature; to group under a government with limited and divided power; or to group under a government with unlimited power, vested in an individual sovereign.[16] For Hobbes, the first and second are false choices, as neither removes an individual entirely from the state of nature. If not removed from the state of nature, according to Hobbes, these individuals can never live a happy and fulfilled life. Only the third choice—to put unlimited power into the hands of one individual sovereign—truly removes society from the perils of the state of nature. Hobbesian people empower their sovereign by obeying his commands. This sovereign reigns as such because he is committed to the safety of his subjects. Those people need obey their sovereign as long as they believe it is conducive to their safety.[17]

In the three principal societies depicted in *The Walking Dead*, all ostensibly place the powers of sovereignty in one individual.[18] In the original band of Atlanta survivors, Rick Grimes is the unofficial leader. Before the zombie infection, Rick was a police officer. He travels with his young son and wife and always has their safety in mind with action that he takes. In the town of Woodbury, the Governor is in charge. He is a cruel and authoritarian individual who is deeply disturbed. He keeps his infected zombie daughter alive by feeding her with the remains of his political enemies. Finally, in the Washington community, Douglas Munroe is the leader. Douglas is an ex-congressman who lives in the Washington community with his wife and son. The experience of the Washington community is the least developed in the comic, yet it is the one that seemingly agrees most with Hobbes's account of sovereignty, so we begin there.

## WASHINGTON AND DOUGLAS MUNROE

The leader of the Washington community, Douglas Munroe, is the furthest away from an absolute sovereign as seen in any of the groups encountered in *The Walking Dead*. The Washington community established itself early on in the zombie infection, erected walls and defenses, and, by drawing on solar-powered facilities, became a self-sufficient community of around fifty people. As opposed to complaining about survival issues such as the zombies, safety, or the need to secure food, the inhabitants of this community grumble about the lack of hot water: "half the houses here can't get hot water and we don't have enough power to run lights all the time."[19] From Kirkman's portrayal of this community, it never entered the state of nature as the Woodbury or Atlanta groups experienced; while the rest of the world crumbled around them, these inhabitants found ways to prevail.

As this group slowly realizes that it lives in more danger than originally thought, it moves from a devolved, semidemocratic government into a more autocratic one. Rick—leader of the Atlanta group, which at this point has been accepted into the Washington community—emerges as its leader. Douglas Munroe mentions that the Atlanta group and Rick in particular are exactly what the Washington group needs to survive in the future.[20] Eventually, when danger reaches the gates of this community, Douglas Munroe actually relinquishes his powers as leader to Rick, under the auspices of keeping the community safe. As a separate group of armed men, still living in the state of nature/zombie-infected world, seek to forcibly impose themselves on the Washington community, that society creates a sovereign with the power to keep them *safe*, consistent with Hobbes's notion of sovereignty.[21] Adding further credence to Hobbes's argument, the Washington community does not appear truly safe until that *absolute* sovereign is appointed. The full nature of this absolute sovereign—and the veracity of Hobbes's expectations of him—is examined in the next section, regarding the Atlanta survivors.

## THE ATLANTA SURVIVORS AND RICK GRIMES

The original Atlanta survivors briefly discussed the nature of leadership; Dale, an older man, talks to Rick, effectively giving him permission to lead the group. Dale says, "We need someone to look up to . . . to make us feel safe. . . . I talked to everyone earlier. . . . We think that someone is you."[22] In this dynamic, the emphasis is explicitly put on *safety* as a primary legitimizing factor for the passing of one's sovereignty to another, for the formation of some kind of authority, or government. This process is precisely the reason that Hobbes theorized would be the case. Hobbes concluded that if individuals are concerned primarily with their own survival, then they would empower another to act on their behalf, only if that person could provide greater security as a result. However, for Hobbes, this sovereign must have absolute power. For Hobbes, complete control is the only way to truly provide safety.[23] Indeed, Rick proceeds to govern all aspects of the group's survival: he is the diplomat of the group, the logistics officer, the general, the town planner, the law enforcement, and everything in between. That he is capable of carrying out all these functions gives credence toward considering him absolute sovereign. It can be argued that in a community any larger than the handful of people that make up the Atlanta group, an absolute sovereign is impossible, as that leader would be forced to delegate his authority to state bodies to govern effectively. In delegating authority, the sovereign is no longer absolute. This is not a problem for Rick, but it is observed later that the Governor of Woodbury may not qualify as an *absolute* sovereign for this reason.

By following Rick's story of leadership of the Atlanta survivors, we can see that the absolute sovereign is an impossible feat. Despite the explicit consent of the Atlanta group given to Rick to lead, ostensibly giving him the power of absolute sovereign, he is not. As leader, he is legitimate in his rule as long as he provides safety to the group. In volume 10 of *The Walking Dead*, after the group suffers a series of catastrophes, Dale (the same character who gave Rick consent to lead earlier) decides to break from the group. Dale blames Rick for bringing the group into danger, and in doing so, Dale feels that his interests and safety would be best served by reclaiming his decision-making powers from Rick and leaving.[24]

The reliance of Hobbes's absolute sovereign on the consent of the ruled is the fundamental failure of Hobbes's social contract, as highlighted by Jean Hampton. For Hampton, as the ruler only holds power as long as people obey his commands, the subjects, not the sovereign, determine whether or not he will continue to hold power, much in the way that it is Dale who decides whether he will continue to obey Rick. In this way Rick, the sovereign, is not an absolute. Dale's choice to obey is beyond Rick's power to influence. Hampton goes on to say that this failure in Hobbes's contract means that such a group can never secure peace, according to Hobbes, as it can never secure an absolute sovereign.[25]

## WOODBURY AND THE GOVERNOR

The community at Woodbury and its leader, the Governor, serve as principal antagonists for a sizable duration of Kirkman's ongoing comic. The reader thus does not get a sense of the organizational structure within the community except for what the protagonists, the Atlanta group, observe. Despite this change in perspective, it is easy to single out the Governor as the leader of this group. But is the Governor an absolute sovereign?

None of the inhabitants of Woodbury ever refer to the Governor by his actual name, as they are all in awe or fear him. His control of those closest to him, those who help him govern effectively, is strictly through fear and a strong belief that the Governor knows what is best for the safety of the community. Such delegation to an inner circle is necessary, as the Woodbury community is far larger than the Atlanta community, consisting of more than one hundred people. Such delegation brings into question whether the Governor is an absolute sovereign or not, as he relies on others to govern effectively. But there are greater flaws in the Governor's leadership than his lack of direct control over all aspects of his community, as highlighted in the following paragraphs.

Those outside this inner circle, the majority of Woodbury, are in awe of and respect the Governor. He relies on manipulation as his primary method of control. The Governor explains, "You gotta keep people *occu-*

*pied* or they'll *turn* on you."[26] To these ends, he establishes a blood sport in a local dirt track stadium to placate his population. By including zombies in the sport, the arena also serves as a reminder to the population of the dangers outside Woodbury.

As the only broker of safety in the community, those he cannot control through manipulation he controls by the threat of removal—the intimidation of putting an individual back into the state of nature lures possible deviants back into the fold. Much like Rick's consent to govern in the Atlanta group, the Governor rose to leadership because of his capacity to keep people safe.[27] Unlike Rick, the Governor is not at the mercy of his followers' choice to obey. Rather, should followers in Woodbury believe that what he is doing is not in their best interests, the Governor would bring physical harm to the dissidents. As one such discontented individual explains, "what do you think he'd *do* to anyone who opposed him? I hate the son of a bitch but I can't *do* anything."[28]

So the Governor is not Hobbes's absolute sovereign, as he provides only partial safety. The citizens of Woodbury are safe from zombies but not from the Governor's whims. As such, they are not removed from the state of nature in the same way that the Atlanta group is (at times). In fact, this disconnect between ruler and ruled leads to the Governor's demise and that of his community. As he does not act with the consent of his people, when at last he needs to marshal his community to some great feat, it rebels and kills its leader.[29]

The experiences of these three communities highlight not the shortcomings of Hobbes's conclusions but the shortcomings of his premises. Hobbes argues that an absolute sovereign is the only way to guarantee safety and escape the anarchical world of the state of nature. Similarly, Hobbesian theorists posit that the only way to secure world peace is one overarching state. However, in the narrative put forward in *The Walking Dead*, such an authority is shown to be an impossible feat. If we can reject the very premise of Hobbes's peace, we can begin to refute many of the other assumptions that form the basis of anarchy in the international system. Indeed, such rejection of these assumptions, taken by too many as irrefutable facts, is the starting point of much constructivist theory on international relations.

## TEACHING HOBBES THROUGH COMIC BOOKS

By using the ongoing narrative of *The Walking Dead*, as a world within which to test the abstract assumptions that Hobbes makes on human nature, societal formation, and sovereignty, we have illustrated some of the strengths and weaknesses of his account of society and state. The question remains, can *The Walking Dead* be used in classroom settings to the same effect as it has been used in this chapter? Similar to Jason Dittmer's observations on the comics of the major publishers, Marvel and DC Comics, *The Walking Dead* may not be "primarily intended as political texts . . . [yet it does] have political content."[30] The challenge to the educator, then, is to tease out this political content and make it useful.

As illustrations are widely accepted and utilized in society to enhance understandings of abstract concepts, so too are they used in education; indeed, "cartoons have been used in modern educational materials for at least 75 years."[31] However, there are many types of cartoons, many categories of illustration and, indeed, comic books. The comic book specifically has pedagogical merit because of its ability to present "brutal and down-to-earth accounts of complex issues, including a strong tone of social critique."[32] Thomas Juneau and Mira Sucharov talk at length about the merits of this intimate perspective in teaching the Israel–Palestine conflict. For them, the use of a narrative approach—that is, "one that focuses on the experience of political actors in understanding and framing their actions"—helps students who read these books to put aside any political prejudice when discussing such a volatile topic.[33] As Juneau and Sucharov elucidate, "by being immersed in the kind of storytelling that graphic novels present, and being forced to confront the 'frame' of the narrative, students are also helped to set aside whatever political biases they may hold."[34]

The themes around social contract and the state of nature are profoundly different from the themes found in studying the Israel–Palestine conflict, though in both instances there is a need to identify the political themes in, sometimes, a not overtly political text. However, in the case of Hobbes, the benefit is not in helping the students to look past issues of morality but to immerse them in the abstract world of Hobbes's state of nature and see the decisions of individuals in this state of nature from the perspective of the people making the decisions. In this way, *The Walking Dead*, like the comics that Juneau and Sucharov use to illustrate their subject, shows aspects of the subject matter that more conventional tools sometimes cannot.

This different and valued perspective comes at a price. *The Walking Dead* is a serialized, ongoing comic that has no discernible end. Due to its ongoing nature, there are now over one hundred issues of the comic, compiled into seventeen volumes. These are a lot of material to ask students to read, and while it is possible to select only the story arcs and character moments that bear relevance to the state of nature, as done in this chapter, this is to the detriment of the approach put forward by Juneau and Sucharov. For them, the character development and intimacy gained from following a story from beginning to end is how one can step into another's shoes and gain the other's perspective. Selecting only sections of the comic to read maintains a perspective of being on the outside looking in, which already exists with Hobbes's account of the state of nature.

ZOMBIES IN THE CLASSROOM: SOMETHING TO CHEW OVER

The work of Thomas Hobbes has had a lasting influence in the political theory of the Western world, and his state of nature is frequently invoked to explain anarchy in the international system. While the social contract has fallen out of favor in political theory, excluding the revival by John Rawls in the 1970s, many of the presumptions that underpin such theories permeate into the modern world. Furthermore, these theories, including that of Hobbes, rest on unfalsifiable assumptions on the basis of human nature.

Robert Kirkman's *The Walking Dead* comic book is a world in which various communities have sprouted in the aftermath of a zombie outbreak that has plunged the world into a "state of nature" situation. The inhabitants of the Woodbury community are never removed from this condition: although their leader, the Governor, provides them security from the zombie menace, they are no better off, because he terrorizes whom he wishes, when he wishes. As such, the citizens of Woodbury are only partially safe and therefore only partially removed from the state of nature. The Washington community, initially led by Douglas Munroe, is shown to not be truly safe until it vests authority in an "absolute sovereign," to use Hobbes's terminology. Only with this absolute sovereign, who can make decisions with impunity, is the community made safe and removed from the state of nature. While the Washington scenario seemingly corroborates Hobbes's assumptions on the conditions necessary for society to form, the experience of the original Atlanta survivors, led my Rick Grimes, undermines this assumption. Rick is given permission to lead the Atlanta group explicitly because of his ability to keep the group *safe*, just as Hobbes surmised. However, Hobbes's assumption that the absolute sovereign is the only method to escape the state of nature is troubled by the Atlanta group's experiences. Hobbes's absolute sovereign is never truly absolute, as the character Dale in *The Walking Dead* demonstrates when he chooses to leave the Atlanta group. Rick, the ostensibly absolute sovereign, cannot guarantee Dale's obedience, and in this way, his power is limited. In the ways outlined here, *The Walking Dead*, as a "lived in" world, is able to illustrate the otherwise unprovable assumptions of Hobbes's notions of sovereignty in the social contract.

While *The Walking Dead*'s length may make it unsuitable for the narrative-based approach to teaching in the political science classroom, the first volume alone makes an excellent introduction to the state of nature. It is short, approximately one hundred pages, and helps put readers into the mind-set of a world with no infrastructure or political organization. *The Walking Dead* helps to place readers into the world of hyperindividuality that is the cornerstone of Hobbes's state of nature. However, beyond this introduction to the state of nature, the length of *The Walking Dead* and its serial nature do not make it an appropriate tool for the classroom. A discussion that begins to delve into the intricacies of Hobbes's theory through the medium of *The Walking Dead*, as attempted in this chapter, requires much work on the part of the instructor to tease out the political themes found within, though it is not an impossible task. The narrative-based approach is capable of giving readers an alternate perspective and can be pursued to more success with other, more overtly political comic books.

## NOTES

1. Daniel Drezner, *Theory of International Politics and Zombies* (Princeton, NJ: Princeton University Press, 2011), and Robert G. Blanton, "Zombies and International Relations: A Simple Guide for Bringing the Undead into Your Classroom," *International Studies Perspectives* 14, no. 1 (2013): 1–13.

2. Thomas Juneau and Mira Sucharov, "Narratives in Pencil: Using Graphic Novels to Teach Israeli–Palestinian Relations," *International Studies Perspectives* 11, no. 2 (2010): 172–83.

3. Robert Grafstein, "The Significance of Modern State of Nature Theory," *Polity* 19, no. 4 (1987): 529.

4. David Boucher and Paul Kelly, "The Social Contract and Its Critics: An Overview," in *The Social Contract from Hobbes to Rawls*, ed. D. Boucher and P. J. Kelly (London: Routledge, 1994), 2.

5. Mark Heller, "The Use and Abuse of Hobbes: The State of Nature in International Relations," *Polity* 13, no. 1 (1980): 32.

6. Nicholas Onuf, *World of Our Making: Rules and Rule in Social Theory and International Relations* (Columbia: University of South Carolina Press, 1989), 14.

7. Alexander J. McKenzie, "Group Dynamics in the State of Nature," *Erkenntnis* 55, no. 2 (2001): 180.

8. William Molesworth, ed. *Leviathan, or the Matter, Form, and Power of a Commonwealth Ecclesiastical and Civil in The English Works of Thomas Hobbes of Malmesbury* (London: Scientia Verlag Aalen, 1966), 3:113.

9. Drezner, *Theory of International Politics and Zombies*, 13.

10. Robert Kirkman, "Letter Hacks," *The Walking Dead #70* (2010).

11. Drezner, *Theory of International Politics and Zombies*, 71.

12. Robert Kirkman, *The Walking Dead: Days Gone Bye* (Berkeley, CA: Image Comics, 2004).

13. Sam Whimster, *The Essential Weber: A Reader* (London: Routledge, 2004), 137.

14. Boucher and Kelly, "The Social Contract and Its Critics," 2.

15. Crawford Brough Macpherson, *The Political Theory of Possessive Individualism*, 8th ed. (Oxford, England: Oxford University Press, 1979), 3.

16. Gregory Kavka, "Hobbes's War of All against All," in *The Social Contract Theorists: Critical Essays on Hobbes, Locke, and Rousseau*, ed. Christopher Morris (Lanham, MD: Rowman & Littlefield, 1999), 5.

17. Jean Hampton, "The Failure of Hobbes's Social Contract Argument," in *The Social Contract Theorists*, 54–55.

18. There is a fourth society of cannibals depicted in issues 62–66, but that society has only a passing reference.

19. Kirkman, *The Walking Dead #70*, 17, panel 3.

20. Kirkman, *The Walking Dead #70*, 21, panel 1.

21. Morton A. Kaplan, "How Sovereign Is Hobbes' Sovereign?" *Political Research Quarterly* 9, no. 2 (1956): 390–91.

22. Robert Kirkman, *The Walking Dead: Miles behind Us* (Berkeley, CA: Image Comics, 2004), 7, panel 5, original emphasis.

23. Kavka, "Hobbes's War of All against All," 5.

24. Robert Kirkman, *The Walking Dead: What We Become* (Berkeley, CA: Image Comics, 2009), 133, panel 5.

25. Hampton, "The Failure of Hobbes's Social Contract Argument," 54–55.

26. Robert Kirkman, *The Walking Dead: The Best Defense* (Berkeley, CA: Image Comics, 2006), 67, panel 4.

27. Kirkman, *The Walking Dead: The Best Defense*, 105, panel 4.

28. Kirkman, *The Walking Dead: The Best Defense*, 104, panel 6, original emphasis.

29. Kirkman, *The Walking Dead: The Best Defense*, 146, panel 1.

30. Jason Dittmer, "The Tyranny of the Serial: Popular Geopolitics, the Nation, and Comic Book Discourse," *Antipode* 39, no. 2 (2007): 247.

31. Larry Dorrell, Dan Curtis, and Kuldip Rampal, "Book-Worms without Books? Students Reading Comic Books in the School House," *Journal of Popular Culture* 29, no. 2 (1995), http://0-gateway.proquest.com.wam.leeds.ac.uk/openurl?ctx_ver=Z39.88-2003&xri:pqil:res_ver=0.2&res_id=xri:lion&rft_id=xri:lion:ft:abell:R01288533:0.

32. Juneau and Sucharov, "Narratives in Pencil," 172.

33. Juneau and Sucharov, "Narratives in Pencil," 173.

34. Juneau and Sucharov, "Narratives in Pencil," 179.

# THIRTEEN

## *Logicomix* and the Enunciatory Apparatus

### Beatrice Skordili,
### Independent Scholar

While politics and history have often lurked even in the crassest of commercial comics, recent developments in the graphic novel have put it in the service of an overtly subjective rendition of history. *Persepolis* and *Palestine,* as well as the precursor of this kind of graphic text, *Maus,* are, in a sense, personal documentaries in graphic form. In these texts, history is treated without pretense to objectivity, since the medium bespeaks its mediation and subjective bias. This is more or less true even in the case of *The 9/11 Report,* since whatever "objective" or consensual version of history is "reported," it is still mediated by the graphic medium and obviated by the diachronic semantics of the genre (simplification, selectivity, and reification).[1]

A rather unexpected *New York Times* best seller, *Logicomix,* by Apostolos Doxiadis, Christos Papadimitriou (concept, story, and script creators), Alecos Papadatos (character designer and artist), and Annie Di Donna (colorist)—plus Anne Bardy (visual researcher and letterist)—has unique features as a graphic novel in the ways that it organizes the use of narrative voice/persona and in the role that space plays in it.[2] Over and against a mostly univocal genre, *Logicomix* appears to want to institute a kind of dramatic chorus as the very mode of its narration, thereby placing (at least part of) its enunciatory apparatus in view, as a way to mediate its relationship to history. As a result of its manifest enunciatory apparatus, a number of issues are raised: the value and validity of the novel's narrative premise about a correlation between madness and logic, its theoretical and working relationship with mathematical history and "truth," and, finally, the role and operations of a seemingly overt enunciatory apparatus.

The narration of *Logicomix* comes in the form of Chinese box narratives, each one enveloping the other. At the core lies the history of the development of logic in the fruitful years of the first half of the twentieth century, presented as a personal narrative by Bertrand Russell: mathematician, philosopher, and pacifist. This narrative places the development of logic squarely within the problematic of human decision in the face of insanity.

Russell's narration resembles closely the type of subjective retrospective narrative that we encounter mostly in other graphic novels. Russell tells his story in the context of a lecture at an (unnamed) American university on September 4, 1939, the day that Britain enters the Second World War. A group of antiwar protesters advocating noninvolvement in the war for the United States asks Russell, famous for his pacifism in World War I, to join them. In lieu of an answer, he invites them to attend his lecture "The Role of Logic in Human Affairs."

In it, Russell unfolds a narrative of his childhood as an orphan in the house of his ex–prime minister grandfather and stern grandmother, a childhood menaced by dark secrets: his parents' fall from grace with his grandparents (they were involved in a ménage à trois "with a sickly young man"), their disappearance and that of his sister (they had died in fact), and his uncle's madness (his uncle is kept hidden under the same roof with Russell).[3]

To quell his fears about a genetic predisposition to madness, the young Russell flees into the apparent nomological orderliness of mathematics.[4] His studies in mathematics, however, reveal the unsound foundations of this seemingly pristine science. Under the influence of fellow student George Moore, he decides to pursue logic as a way "to set the house of mathematics in order."[5] Buoyant in his newfound faith in logic, Russell also merrily disregards his grandmother's dire warning that his bride of choice, Alys, carries in her background the taint of insanity, and he proceeds with what was to be the first of a series of ill-advised liaisons in his long life.

His encounter with Alfred Whitehead sends Russell, in search of knowledge and direction, on a continental tour with his new bride to visit Gottlob Frege and George Cantor, two of the people whose theoretical contributions afford hope of a resolution to the inherent problems of mathematics. These encounters, however, seem to bring Russell face-to-face with his old fears: Frege, whose *Foundations of Arithmetic* Russell will eventually disprove, is decidedly odd. The shock, however, is that Cantor, whose invention of set theory is logic's brightest development at the time, is confined to an asylum. Russell nearly has a breakdown of his own at this discovery. Still, he moves on to his next destination, Paris, where the International Congress of Mathematics is taking place along-side the famous International Exhibition. The year is 1900, and in the shadow of the newly built Eiffel Tower, a monumental event is taking place—at least for mathematicians: David Hilbert delivers an address calling for the solution of some of the greatest unsolved problems in mathematics, laying out the work for the new century (and beyond, as it turns out), also making the famous claim that in mathematics, there can be "no *ignorabimus*" (no "we shall not know"). Russell discovers in this phrase confirmation for his foundational project. Soon, he makes his first major contribution to logic and mathematics, Russell's paradox, which according to *Logicomix* destroys both logic and set theory "with one stone."[6]

Russell and Whitehead devote a decade on the *Principia Mathematica* to establish proper foundations for mathematics through logic, eschewing the need for axioms, thereby taking 362 pages to prove that $1 + 1 = 2$.[7] The work is not nearly finished when Ludvig Wittgenstein walks into Russell's life as a student and starts poking holes into his system. While Russell goes to prison as a conscientious objector (presumably because war is utter irrationality), Wittgenstein conceives his *Tractatus Logico-philosophicus* in the front line of battle, moving away from building a self-consistent system of logic and toward establishing a logical correspondence with reality. Finally, Kurt Gödel comes along to put a tombstone on the foundational quest with his incompleteness theorems, *proving* that there are unprovable statements in mathematics—indeed, that the opposite of Hilbert's Paris pronouncement holds—and using Whitehead and Russell's *Principia* to do it.

Faced with the impossibility of an incontrovertible system of logic by which to make judgments, Russell suggests at the end of his lecture that each person should exercise his or her judgment responsibly and ethically according to the circumstances: there are no readymade answers for war or any other decision in human affairs.

As presented in *Logicomix*, Russell's quest for the foundations of mathematics has a meaningful psychological motivation in the fear of insanity, with the solemn proviso that, in this context, insanity needs to be understood as an extreme form of irrationality. This fear is what invests the Russell figure with interiority and provides the thrust of narrativity in an otherwise dry and difficult topic. This is also what endows the quest with the poignancy of classical tragedy.

Obviously, this bias skews the presentation of the nit and grit of Russell's life and the development of logic. Some degree of biographical accuracy with respect to Russell's life is maintained, at least in terms of the broad strokes, but when it comes to his encounters with history (mathematical history, that is), great liberty has indeed been taken. By fiat of poetic license, events are invented, and encounters that took place on only the intellectual plane are now transferred to the physical plane:

Russell's meetings with Frege and Cantor and his presence at Hilbert's "no *ignorabimus*" address or Gödel's "incompleteness" lecture are in fact fictive.[8] Frege's insanity, which is shown in a later encounter with Russell, is also certainly exaggerated, as is Russell's single-minded devotion to the foundational quest for so many years.[9] Furthermore, although Russell lectured at various American universities in 1939 and apparently addressed the issue of U.S. involvement in World War II, there is no record of a lecture on this topic on September 4 or at another time.[10]

Most of the departures from "historical truth" are well documented either by the authors within the text, who admit openly that they are interested in creating a novel rather than documenting actual history, or by careful reviewers; they are also dealt with, in an afterword titled "*Logicomix* and Reality" and in the "Notebook" section at the end.[11] In fact, for a text that confesses quite frankly that it aims to be a "novel," it takes extraordinary pains to discuss and remark on the kind of license that it takes with historical truth.[12]

What is striking, however, is that this license with historical truth, which is justified by narrative coherence and thrust, is done to favor a narrative premise of a tenuous nature, one that fails to adhere to logical principles: that logicians are prone to one or another form of madness. As anyone with a modicum of common knowledge in psychology can deduce, insanity is not a misguided use of reason; it is not irrationality. This is why you cannot reason anyone out of their psychopathologies. In fact, when it comes to paranoia, one might legitimately argue that one of its most telling traits is an extravagant application of logic to incorporate meaningless quotidian details into one grand system of explanation—a system, albeit, built around a stubborn psychopathological kernel.[13]

As opposed to the abusive application of reason that spawns conspiracy theories, common sense is the acceptance of a generous portion of meaninglessness and irrationality in life, something that both Russell and the authors seem to suggest at the end of the novel. And while Russell's conclusion is pretty straightforward, as it puts the burden of decision not on logic but on the ethical being, the authors do suggest something a little less pedestrian: that the form of the logicians' "insanity" is that "[logicians] eventually confused their reality with their maps"—meaning, obviously, mental maps.[14] However, given that this is left unexplained, all that I, at least, can infer is that their logical systems failed to account for and deal with the noise (impurities, wrinkles) of the real world, as Papadimitriou's nighttime adventure in downtown Athens demonstrates (which we will discuss later). However, even this explanation fails to account for anything beyond irrationality.

The narrative premise as origin of the project is attributed both within and outside the novel to a comment made by Gian-Carlo Rota in *Indiscrete Thoughts*:[15]

> It cannot be a complete coincidence that several outstanding logicians
> of the twentieth century found shelter in asylums at some time in their
> lives. Cantor, Zermelo, Gödel, Peano, and Post are some.[16]

One might deduce from the style of this statement that this is a kind of
thesis to be developed in expository form or at least to be followed by one
or more biographical sketches of the logicians mentioned. Nothing of the
sort! It is in a memoir on the mathematicians that lectured in Princeton's
Fine Hall when Rota was a student there, and not a single person from
the list above is mentioned. Oddly, none of the three Princeton mathematics professors that Rota actually discusses had anything more patho-
logical than idiosyncrasies, and they were certainly not institutionalized.

As can be judged by the brief summary given here, apart from Cantor,
there is little trace of the list of "mad" logicians provided by Rota to be
seen in *Logicomix*: Peano makes a brief appearance but only to comment
on "Russell's paradox."[17] Gödel is important in the text; however, his
paranoid refusal of food for fear of poisoning, which essentially killed
him, falls outside the chronological scope of the novel; it is mentioned,
however, within. Hilbert loses a son to insanity.[18] Also, some sort of
psychological instability is implied in Wittgenstein. By dint of an effective stategy of stringing together personal and familial cases of insanity
(as well as idiosyncracies) of plot characters with biographical information on real persons mentioned but not represented in the text, the authors manage to create the sense of an impressive array of logicians with
various degrees of aberrant behavior in the tone set by Rota's statement;
they do not seem, nevertheless, to be able to articulate a necessary and
sufficient statement correlating foundational work in logic and madness.

The authors' initial metanarrative articulation of the narrative premise
is that the people dealt with in *Logicomix* "became logicians from madness," which is not further explained as against Papadimitriou's admoni-
tion to Apostolos not to reveal the "whodunit" of the plot.[19] Near the end
of the novel, however, Doxiadis does come up with the more sophisticated "less tortured characters [who] would not have found this price [the
price for absolute certainty; i.e., obsessive and tortuous work] worth pay-
ing."[20] When Papadimitriou interjects this time that "there are many psychotics, but only one," he is not allowed to proceed, because he is interrupted by events in the metanarrative.[21] Presumably, he is about to offer
the name of an outstanding logician with a history of mental illness —
Cantor or Gödel, perhaps? The implicit argument then must be that there
is no preponderance of logicians among psychotics, even if there is a
presumed preponderance of psychotics among logicians. In one of his
two reviews of the novel, Paolo Mancosu, a Berkeley colleague of Papadimitriou, does offer some evidence to debunk even the latter claim: by his
calculation, sixty-six logicians did foundational work on mathematics between 1900 and 1935, and out of these, only four have documented peri-

ods of mental illness, an approximate 6 percent, which matches the rate in the general population.[22] In lieu of a clear narrative premise on the relationship between foundational work and madness, the book appears to contend that it is partly the collective insanity of war (particularly, the world wars) that provides the motivation for Russell's quest for certainty, starting with his encounter with a half-insane Crimea War amputee as a child.[23] The vehicle of the novel, in other words, permits a certain interpretation of history to be presented as fiction since history itself, being far too contingent, will not accommodate the interpretation easily.

This interpretation of history is one that essentially casts Russell as a tragic hero who, through hubris, finds himself on an impossible quest: to establish solid foundations for mathematics. Indeed, from beginning to end, parallels of classical tragedy are drawn for the quest, and they become quite explicit just as the *Logicomix* team heads toward the dress rehearshal of Aeschylus's classic play *Oresteia*.[24] These parallels find an unexpected explanation, beyond the madness theme, also in the common format of accounts of mathematical history.

Leo Corry has pointed out in an immensely interesting article, which expands on an argument made by Yehuda Elkana on the poetics of histories of mathematics, that the tendency of many historians (especially of popular accounts) as well as creators of mathematical fiction is to produce narratives that borrow their structure from ancient Greek drama, which equates "fate . . . with the order of nature" and which lends to scientific discovery an air of inevitability. Both Elkana and Corry base their discussion of this attitude on *Science and the Modern World*, written by none other than Alfred North Whitehead, Bertrand Russell's collaborator and a major figure in *Logicomix*. [25]

Corry, following Elkana, proposes that the form most suited to accounts of scientific discovery is "epic theatre" because, as Elkana states,

> epic theater, in order to make its point, purposefully avoids historical facts that the audience is aware of, lest they lapse into the tragic mood of knowing what is inevitably coming. Life is unpredictable and events can go in any direction, therefore life is unsensational. What is true of historical inevitability also holds for psychological inevitability, and this, too, is avoided.[26]

Let us note in passing that in contrast to what Elkana calls for in historical accounts, *Logicomix* goes out of its way to include seminal events, such as Hilbert's and Gödel's lectures, even manufacturing Russell's presence there. By contrast, scientific history in "epic theater" mode does not present events as though driven toward an inexorable conclusion, whether by a certain "fiat of nature" to unveil itself or by a psychological penchant to perform a certain kind of work. Very clearly then the "foundational quest" as motivated by "the fear of madness" or by "a certain kind of personality," as Doxiadis states in an interview, falls within the "Greek drama" rather than the "epic theater" mode.[27]

Whitehead very carefully differentiates between the "unhappiness" of the tragic hero's end in Greek tragedy and "the remorseless working of things," "their inevitableness," but Doxiadis does not: in the heat of an argument with Papadimitriou about the ending of *Logicomix*, he claims that the quest is essentially a tragedy because it ends in failure (i.e., Godel's incompleteness theorems) and because all of the people involved have unhappy ends.[28] It is clear, therefore, that Doxiadis's view of the quest conflates the unfolding of character with that of the science; thereby, not only does it impose a tragic view on the scientific history, but also implicitly, though inextricably, it associates the unhappy end of one with the other. It is as though the tragic flaw, the taint of insanity, of the foundational quest heroes did not just drive them toward an arduous pursuit of certainty; rather, it predisposed them to undertake a task that was certain to fail.

Papadimitriou's side of the argument, which is implied at several points in the novel but comes out strongly at the end, is that if "the meaning is in the ending," a different demarkation of the duration of the quest and the designation of a different hero would render the quest a comedy or at least provide it with a happy ending: decide that the "real hero" of the quest is the computer and push the story ten years ahead to include the work of Alan Turing (Papadimitriou's favorite logician) and John Von Neumann, who are the "right people," and the true goal of the quest becomes apparent—to put "the tools of reason . . . at everybody's fingertips" and to lead to the Internet, which is "our prime hope for peace, democracy and freedom!"[29] Since Papadimitriou's argument involves words such as "right" and "real," it is clear that he does not view the story of the quest as any more contingent than Doxiadis; he simply wants to do away with the "unhappy" view of events, not the "dramatic" one. Indeed, the *Oresteia* that the protagonists of the metanarrative are about to watch is his example of a "happy" ending in Greek drama: the play ends with the birth of democracy in Athens, when the goddess Athena places the fate of the matricide Orestis, who is a supplicant to the city to escape the scourging of the Erynies, in the hands of the citizens.[30] Thereby, Papadimitriou responds to all of Doxiadis's possible counterarguments about the nature of the quest and about the "unhappiness" of Greek tragedy.

Also, by mentioning Turing's involvement in cracking the codes of the Nazi Enigma machine and its subsequent effect in winning World War II as a "happy" outcome of the foundational quest, Papadimitriou, in effect, addresses the novel's framing device of war, which is utilized to increase the efficacy of the insanity premise in the novel. In this fashion, he manages in the end to win discursively the argument that he has been losing in terms of plot development throughout the novel, as Russell's story of events seemingly unfolded according to Doxiadis's view rather than his own. The presentation of the *Oresteia* with its happy ending of peace and reconciliation among humans and gods grants his side of the argument a kind of metaphoric satisfaction; but there is also some visual gratification, as though Papadimitriou is given "the last word," when the last page of the main text carries the words "the end" on the screen of a laptop computer. This is complemented by a visual pun of sorts, a kind of pseudo-anamorphosis, on the book's cover, which shows within a fade-in iris an isolated detail, an image of Russell starting a cascade of dominoes: the effect of Russell's intent look, the raised finger, and the sound effect, "click," is to create the momentary illusion that he is in fact hitting a key on a computer.[31]

But to return to the point that I was making about mathematical history and fiction, it is clear that Doxiadis and Papadimitriou both subscribe to a view of the history of foundational work in mathematics that falls essentially into the category of "classic drama" as involving an inevitability of outcome. What is truly astounding, though, is that a version of Corry's paper on the poetics of mathematical history and fiction was originally presented at the first "Mathematics and Narrative" conference organized by "Thales + Friends," a group interested in promoting discussion and awareness of issues pertaining to the relationship between mathematics and narrative, of which Doxiadis is a founding member.[32] Also present at the conference, which took place in 2005 just as work on the *Logicomix* was beginning, were Papadimitriou and Papadatos, two more *Logicomix* people. Furthermore, Corry's paper also discusses, among others, Doxiadis's earlier mathematical novel *Uncle Petros and the Goldbach Conjecture*. All in all, I find it extremely unlikely that the *Logicomix* team, Doxiadis in particular, was not aware of Corry's claims, as his paper is included among the conference papers on the "Thales + Friends" website.[33]

A number of possibilities emerge, then, about the way that the creators of *Logicomix* handled the mode of presentation of the history of mathematics in the novel: either they did not associate Corry's argument with their own work and proceeded in the "Greek drama" mode without considering the possibility that they might be falling prey to a sort of "intentional fallacy" provoked by Rota's comment—it is, afterall, the dominant mode of presenting scientific fiction; or, they chose to disregard Corry's argument as being counternarrative, something that appears corroborated by Doxiadis's insistence on producing a captivating story, which he views as motivated by character and not by the unfolding of the development of ideas.[34] Or—more likely—they considered that whatever infractions were made at the level of main narrative, whether against the proper mode of presenting scientific history or against historical accuracy, were corrected by the presentation of historical fact and the dialectic of different viewpoints in the metanarrative.[35]

The metanarrative consequently affords a way for the *Logicomix* team to create a compelling fiction imbued with inevitability (rather than contingency) and not to violate historical and scientific accuracy—to have their cake and eat it too. It is to the metanarrative, therefore, that we should turn to understand what is really at issue in this novel.

The metanarrative, which is the outer shell of *Logicomix*'s Chinese box narration, is rendered as a number of meetings between Papadimitriou, the Berkeley-based computer science professor, and the rest of the Athens-based *Logicomix* team (Doxiadis, Alecos, and Annie, plus the researcher Anne), in effect the human components of the enunciatory apparatus of the novel. As a result, the enunciatory apparatus—understood as a mobile agglomerate of psychic structures, material conditions, pragmatics of reception, intertextual and paratextual references, generic conventions, stylistic choices, and discourses involved in the production of a text and, important for me, made present within the textual universe figuratively or otherwise—is given in this particular text a most realistic representation.

During their meetings, Papadimitriou and other team members take walks around the historic center of Athens, meet at the production headquarters, and attend rehearsals of the *Oresteia*. This perambulatory approach to narrative provides a physical correlative to the "foundational quest" of the main narrative.[36] The purpose of the meetings, as they are presented in the metanarrative, is partly, as we have seen, to reach a kind of consensus about the amount and handling of biographical, historical, and scientific information.

We have already addressed the questions of biography and history. Now, as concerns the foundational quest itself, an effort is clearly made to render concepts and developments with fidelity but without going into much detail. As Corry points out with great prescience,

> whereas we may discern in mathematics in fiction (as in fiction in general) intended departures from the historical record through the literary aims pursued by authors, it is much more difficult to imagine similar moves away from the "mathematical record."[37]

Indeed, the intentional, or even the unintentional, falsification of mathematics seems to run against a kind unspoken prohibition that is not in place for history. This is, then, another significant reason for the existence of the metanarrative: to allow the enunciatory apparatus of the novel to negotiate an accurate presentation of the science without turning Russell's narrative into a graphic exposition of ideas.

Not surprising, therefore, Papadimitriou is instrumental in introducing most of the scientific theory in the text as against Doxiadis's avowed protestations that "mathematics and comics, like oil and water, don't ever *mix*."[38] Despite the careful framing of Russell's narrative as not "Logic for Dummies," the text flirts on occasion with the format of such books, which have proliferated over the last few years with great success.[39] Indeed, reviewers have hailed *Logicomix* as an excellent and captivating introduction to the ideas involved in this branch of philosophy.[40] However, in the metanarrative, Papadimitriou and Doxiadis nearly have a falling out when Papadimitriou suggests that they "put a few things on computers" at the end of Russell's tale: Doxiadis angrily responds that "Christos would like [them] ideally to write a comic book 'Theoretical Computer Science for Morons,'" to conclude that "obviously [their] aims diverge."[41] But this is more of a disagreement to do with the temporal scope of the novel as outlined here—the anxiety about the indeterminacy of genre arising, as I understand it, from the fact that quazi-Aristotelian unities (action and character) would be breached in this case.[42] Doxiadis, in fact, grudgingly acquiesces when Papadimitriou provides a definition of logic, or explicates the liar's paradox; but *Logicomix* also contains beautiful graphic renditions of Boolean algebra, Cantor's infinity, Russell's paradox, algorithms, and Wittgenstein's understanding of the relationship or language and reality.[43] Through these means, *Logicomix* does manage to have its cake and eat it too; in other words, it succesfully introduces elements of "a graphic guide to Logic" in the unfolding of a graphic novel—and it must be said that these logical "vignettes" greatly enhance the appeal of the novel, as the reader (already familiar with the format of, say, the Pantheon Books *For Beginners* series) feels invited into the adventure of ideas.[44]

These departures from narrative flow, while beautifully integrated into the text, are nevertheless clear breaks with the verisimilitude of Russell's narration, which is why they are always announced via the metanarrative, even when they involve Russell as a character.[45] This is then another way in which the metanarrative organizes the transmission of information by disclosing the apparatus, rather than assimilating it and submerging it to achieve a more "conventional" narrative feel.

The metanarrative is, as I have suggested, the space in which a kind of "documentary truth" appears to reside, as it becomes a testament to the struggle, not so much to present a/the truth, but to do justice (perhaps a higher justice) to the material that goes into the novel—a veritable quest in its own right. However, it is not the only record of "the making of" *Logicomix*; there is, in fact, also a film documentary available on the *Logicomix* website. *Logicomix: One Page at a Time—The Creation of a Graphic Novel* indeed shows Doxiadis and Papadimitriou strolling on Dionysiou Areopagitou Street in the shadow of the Acropolis or working at the production studio with Papadatos, Di Donna, and Bardy much as their counterparts do in the metanarrative.[46] We even catch a glimpse of Manga, the dog, Doxiadis's sidekick in the novel, who is indeed the spitting image of his comics' equivalent.

The documentary, however, introduces yet another layer of mediation in the reception of the text, paratextual this time. Obviously made for marketing purposes, this is not an ordinary run-of-mill home-camera recording; it is a fully produced film with credits, music, script, camera man, director, and producers. It is also made in English and later subtitled into Greek, a fact that shows the degree to which the international launch of *Logicomix* was anticipated well ahead of the novel's first (Greek) publication—this is also corroborated by the fact that the novel was originally written in English.[47] Doxiadis, who has had a significant career as director of feature films, does not even direct it himself. As a supplement to the "realism" of the metanarrative, the documentary affords a glimpse into the physical production process more hinted at than shown in the novel, with its focus on the dialectic of choices. The impression left, however, by the documentary is so similar to that of the metanarrative that the film appears to have almost been created, not to show how the comic was made, but to offer a preview of the novel or even to afford a glimpse of the tantalizing similarity of the real people with the characters. The documentary then by default functions as a guarrantor of the "realism" of the presentation of the enunciatory apparatus in the metanarrative, as against the constructedness of the graphic rendition of history and biography in the main narrative.

Should the metanarrative be understood then as a sort of comic-book version of what might well have been a film documentary? The fact that Doxiadis addresses the reader on occasion as if on camera suggests something of the sort. However, while "documentary truth" might very well reside in spirit in the metanarrative, there are indications that other processes are at work.

One of the clearest indications is offered by the presentation of the city of Athens, which is the location of the "first narrative" in Gerard Genette's sense (the present time of the narrating instance).[48] The locale in which the characters move has undergone subtle but significant changes. In the beginning of the novel, Doxiadis apparently emerges with Manga from a house in the general direction of Lycabetus Hill to meet Papadimitriou outside the Presidential Residence on Irodou Attikou Street. However, as they start talking about the novel, Doxiadis and Papadimitriou begin climbing a hill, which can only be Philopappou, since they find themselves eventually overlooking the Acropolis without any indication of a break either in the narration or in the conversation: to get there from the Presidential Residence, however, they would have had to pass by some of the most striking landmarks of Athens, the National Garden, the Kallimarmaro (the first modern Olympics stadium), the remains of the temple of Zeus, and perhaps—depending on the route—the Acropolis. Needless to say, a good half hour should also have elapsed in between.

Then, the view itself from Philopappou, while spectacular—a view of Acropolis with Athens spreading around it and the Saronic Gulf in the distance—is an impossible view, as the Acropolis and the sea lie on oppo-

site sides of Philopappou Hill. In fact, the distinctive pointed top of Lycabetus Hill, which should be on the right in the distance, is also missing. A
possible explanation for this strange rearrangement of the city's topography is that the visual researcher Bardy—following patterns of research
shown in the metanarrative—opted for a wonderful nineteenth-century
engraving of the view of the Acropolis from Philopappou Hill, offering a
near-identical perspective to that in the novel, which has a rather indis-
tinct flat area in the general vicinity where Papadatos has drawn the sea
and a very faint outline of Lycabetus Hill in the distance.[49]

A more conscious reason for this change in topography is implicitly
given in "Logicomix and Reality," where the authors offer a quote by El
Greco (Dominikos Theotokopoulos) about the freedoms taken for aesthetic reasons with Toledo's cityscape in "Storm over Toledo" as a metaphor for their approach to historical fact. This serves beautifully as a
literal explanation for the changes in Athenian topograhy in the novel:
the view combining the Acropolis and the sea, since it does not exist,
would have had to be invented. A scenic approach, in fact, prevails
throughout the text: Doxiadis and Papadimitriou are seen emerging from
Philopappou Hill (walking around its lovely paths amid olive trees) or
nearby into Dionysiou Areopagitou Street (a pleasant pedestrian street
and the best real estate in Athens) in the shadow of the Acropolis, following a route that takes them past the ancient theater of Herodes Atticus
and that of Dionysus to end up in a charming traditional Athenian house
in the vicinity of Plaka (the preserved traditional part of Athens) or the
Metro.[50] Invariably, they also emerge from or end up in one of the brand
new metro stations of Athens, eschewing the use of cars—whose intrusion is ubiquitous in Athens. Once Doxiadis even surfaces from the
Acropolis station, Manga in tow, though dogs are not allowed in the
metro (unless in carry cases).[51] Even when Papadimitriou and Anne get
lost at night in downtown Athens around Omonia Square, an area popu-
lated by illegal immigrants, prostitutes, and con artists, what we see is
not a squalid run-down image of a city but a mysterious labyrinthine
underworld that naturally ushers the characters into the darkness of the
rehearshal of the Oresteia with its dog-headed Erynies panting for
Orestes's blood.[52] There is, therefore, evidence here of an attempt to win-
dowdress Athens but not to offer the international reader an idealized
image (as they decidedly elide touristy places); it is, I believe, to reclaim a
landscape much abused but well loved.[53] This reappropriation also bespeaks another truth about *Logicomix*; it is a book of which Athens is an
integral component: the *location* situates the *occasion* for the emergence of
the book (the quest of the metanarrative) and thereby separates it from all
other possible graphic renditions of the foundational quest or Bertrand
Russell's work.[54]

Besides being an index to a dramatic mode of understanding both
main narrative and metanarrative, the *Oresteia* performs, therefore, an-

other important function: it re-marks a vital element of the enunciatory apparatus of the novel, since the Athenian turf, which is given pride of representation throughout, receives retroactive justification as the *locus* of drama *par excellence*.[55] With this last piece of the puzzle in place, the unlikely conjunction of a mostly Greek group of people (with international histories and connections, though) meeting in Athens, Greece, to create a novel about a mostly Northern European development in philosophy/ science with little reference to ancient Greek philosophy (and logic's first philosopher, Aristotle) introduces yet another twist in the issue of representation within the text: the ideological framing of the discourse of the novel both affirms and contradicts the dominant national discourse of placing ancient Greece as the origin and ultimate truth of all human (and, in a sense, philosophical) questions.[56] Within the context of the "Thales + Friends" project of theorizing and promoting the development of mathematical fiction (which numbers a relatively large Greek contingent with international careers), *Logicomix* appears in the new light of spearheading an intellectual niche for modest national pride for modern natives. The novel, it seems, is a way to address the symptomatology of the national complex: the presumed pervasive underachievement of modern Greeks as against the superiority of their ancient ancestors.

Another indication that the metanarrative is not a mere documentary transcription of the team's meetings comes from the way that the authors are presented. Despite the centrality of Papadimitriou in the mise-en-scène of the novel, it is really Doxiadis who provides the narrative voice and/or focalization in the text. In fact, *Logicomix* begins with Doxiadis addressing the readers as if on camera on his way to meet Papadimitriou, who is not made privy to the fact that he is being "filmed" so to speak (though, a few pages later, in the "whodunit" incident, he is obviously aware of the "camera."[57] This is not a device insisted on in the text, but it introduces a "documentary" effect at the level of the metanarrative that implies veracity, as we have seen. At the same time, the metanarrative dehisces into two more Chinese boxes: Doxiadis's narration and the story of the "making of" *Logicomix*. Although unobtrusive—since the narrating instance can be, and in this particular case is, submerged by the visual presentation in a graphic novel—Doxiadis's narration resurfaces when, for the narrative to include events to which he was not present, he is required to read a letter by Papadimitriou "on camera," concerning the story of Papadimitriou and Anna's nighttime adventure in the commercial downtown. The narrating instance makes its final appearance at the end of the novel when Doxiadis, in an aside, directly addresses the reader to relegate final word on the topic of the novel to Aeschylus's play.[58]

This is not to suggest that Papadimitriou does not break the fourth wall now and then, but these occasions are very brief and somewhat implicit.[59] The established mode of narration is, in fact, that Doxiadis "narrates" Papadimitriou. This mirrors the actual production of enunciation: Doxiadis and Papadimitriou coauthored the story, but Doxiadis, being a director, essentially scripted and storyboarded the whole thing with the help of Papadatos. In fact, as Doxiadis states in *Logicomix: One Page a t a Time* and in his radio interview with Fitch, he was specific about angles of vision, shots, and mise-en- scène, and he playacted all the parts, indulging, as he intimates, in a director's fantasy of exercising complete control over the final product.[60] Note, then, that this means that in all the heated arguments between Doxiadis and Papadimitriou, Doxiadis has also been "acting" Papadimitriou's part; indeed, in the documentary, we get a glimpse of just such a moment when Christos has his outburst about the "happiness" of the story's ending.[61] Ultimately, at the level of enunciation, this radically destabilizes the metanarrative's pretence to any kind of "documentary truth."

While, therefore, the purpose of the metanarrative is to reconcile the difference of views between the two authors by bringing it forth to representation, at the same time, a peculiar effect is produced by dimly discerning Doxiadis as the master pappeteer: Papadimitriou's "voice," as opposed to his views, becomes impossible to detect. The locus of the emanation of the voice within the text, already split between two authors with divergent views, becomes a question.

In graphic texts, the markers of enunciation are obscured, since things such as angles of vision and visual information provide an ostensibly external point of reference for the action of the story that is relatively absent in a verbal text where characters by necessity move in a world of the narrator's own description.[62] Additionally, the very constructedness of presentation in a graphic novel betrays the retrospective nature of narration, even when there is a present time referent in it, as is the case with the metanarrative.

In *Logicomix*, the retrospective form of narration, the constitutive split in enunciation, and the elusive locus of narration ultimately eschew the position of a univocal subject of enunciation. The subjective position shifts from a person to a primitive form of subjectivity, the seed form of focalization, the time- and placeholder of the narrating instance. This simply locates the point of emergence of narration as modern-day Athens.

A corollary to this is the fact that the unnamed university where Russell delivers his lecture turns out to be the Univeristy of California, Berkeley, Papadimitriou's institution—the telltale signs being the images of Sather Gate and Sproul Hall.[63] As though by inherent necessity, the occulted locus of enunciation of Papadimitriou's voice finds a concrete correlative in the main narrative, displaced and figured as the location of the emergence of Russell's voice. Thus, Berkeley, understood as a placeholder for Papadimitriou voice, is represented as narrated by Athens, a subtle mirroring of the actuality of the enunciatory apparatus.

The impossible view of the Acropolis from Philopappou Hill that the two authors of *Logicomix* gaze at as they discuss how to shape their novel, then, is a figuration of the enunciatory apparatus in the novel; indeed, it stands for the primal scene of its inception. For, while the enunciatory apparatus operates in almost materialist fashion comprising all the elements and processes that go into making a work, it invariably projects a virtual stand-in within the work, a figure for the emergence of the elusive subject of enunciation (which is work specific, however much tied to an actual author) and the work at the same time. This figuration is structured, as I have already indicated, along the lines of the Freudian "primal scene," the matrix of fantasy, since it involves an impossible (and/or forbidden) view, the presence of the subject at the scene of its inception.[64] This impossible view is invariably depicted as a view from above (sometimes also a vision of the heavens).[65] It is thus indicative of the function of this particular image in the novel that, while in reality one can see the Acropolis from Philopappou at eye level at best, in *Logicomix* it is decidedly seen from above.

The content of the scene, understood as the primal scene of the subject of enunciation of the novel—the view of the Acropolis from above—essentially reveals the relation that structures the work as a whole: as the perceived pinnacle of ancient Greek achievement, the Acropolis constitutes the posited origin of the authors (so goes the symptomatology of the national complex) in their endeavor. At the same time, it epitomizes the essence of the accomplishment that they are striving for: their future anterior as subject of enunciation.[66] The fact that almost the entire metanarrative takes place under the shadow of the Acropolis and indeed culminates at the ancient theater right at its foot, then, is no accident: the metanarrative is fundamentally organized by the subjective–objective structure of the gaze. Once being posited as origin and future anterior of the subject, in the view from Philoppapou, Acropolis becomes the visual point of reference that oversees and measures the success of the quest in the metanarrative. This structuring figure then captures and attempts to resolve the quandary of the national complex through the creative act.[67] *Logicomix* is indeed a textbook example of the emergence of the figure for the subject of the enunciatory apparatus in a work.

The novel contains kindred figures in Russell's narration: One is when Bertie has a kind of apocalyptic vision of communion with nature via Shelley's "Alastor" as he decides to face his fear of irrationality.[68] Another is an odd moment in Hilbert's "no *ignorabimus*" address, as Russell conceives of his "foundational quest": he looks up, and we see what appears to be a vision of a bright star or sun, which as the panels pan out, turns out to be the ceiling of the Sorbonne—the graphic medium, by its nature, facilitating a *trompe l' oe il* confusion between painting and actual vision.[69]

After taking all these issues of enunciation into consideration, the original impression, augmented by the inclusion of the performance of the *Oresteia*, that *Logicomix* puts the enunciatory apparatus in an unmediated dramatic form on the stage of representation is belied by the mode of narration: a series of Chinese boxes that enfold not only Russell's narrative but also Papadimitriou's voice and those of the other contributors (Papadatos and Di Donna, even Bardy).[70] At the same time, there is naturally the presupposition that Doxiadis, who chooses for his counterpart Doxiadis the figure of the "clown" (the metanarrative is rife with scenes of his antics), exercises his directorial control in the direction of honesty (rather than realism)—also, because his version of events is presumably subject to the ongoing approval of the other team members on whom he is dependent (the graphic medium intervening again in peculiar ways in the enunciatory apparatus with respect to historical accuracy).[71] Is Doxiadis then "spoken" by his collaborators even as he speaks them? Ultimately, the staging of the enunciatory apparatus becomes a figure of infinite regress.

It appears, therefore, that the supervening of history within this graphic novel puts great pressure on the enunciatory apparatus. Thus, it proliferates mechanisms to satisfy the requirements of fiction and historical fact: narrative logic and the contingency of history. These mechanisms in turn unfurl a manifold of dynamics and processes, usually submerged under the necessity for integration.[72] This integration is complicated by the need to handle the particular characteristics of graphic enunciation—verbal and visual.[73] The visual aspect is immediate (since it is given to be seen) and mediated (since the graphic medium signifies its own opacity). Hence, a device becomes necessary to negotiate and represent this opacity as against the "reality" of historical or personal fact. In the most sophisticated of graphic novels, this device is very characteristic: In *Maus*, it is the choice of animal figures (mice, cats, and dogs) to represent people, responding to a kind of *bilderverbot* interdiction against realistic representation of the Holocaust, as Andreas Huyssen points out in his excellent discussion "Of Mice and Mimesis."[74] In *Persepolis*, the stylized approach to visuality (with repetitive motifs) also re-marks the distance from reality. In *Palestine*, it is pronounced visual distortions that indicate the subjective point of view combined with extensive personal narrative in textual form. Contrast this with the degree of immediacy produced by *The 9/11 Report*, whose images almost recall digitized photographs and which does not possesses any device to indicate mediation except the proviso that it is not a rendition of history but an official document, the congressional 9/11 report.

*Logicomix* stages the whole question of mediation as an integral part of its presentation; but while it does an impressive job of rendering this issue, thereby attempting to put it to rest, it also introduces further layers of mediation in the metanarrative. In the end, though it bespeaks transparency, the metanarrative is in actuality as constructed as the main story. The staging of the enunciatory apparatus in this unique graphic form ultimately short-circuits representing (enunciation) and represented (utterance) while laying bare a complex of issues of representation that are often cloaked by the very instance of representation itself.

## NOTES

1. Marjane Satrapi, *Persepolis: The Story of a Childhood* (New York: Pantheon, 2003), and *Persepolis 2: The Story of a Return* (New York: Pantheon, 2004); Joe Sacco, *Palestine* (Seattle, WA: Fantagraphics, 2001); Art Spiegelman, *Maus: A Survivor's Tale—My Father Bleeds History* (New York: Pantheon, 1986) and *Maus II: A Survivor's Tale—And Here My Troubles Began* (New York: Pantheon, 1991); Sid Jacobson and Ernie Colón, *The 9/11 Report: A Graphic Adaptation* (New York: Hill & Wang, 2006).

2. Henceforward, I use the first names of the creators of *Logicomix* to refer to their personas inside the text and last names for their real-life counterparts.

3. Apostolos Doxiadis, Christos Papadimitriou, Alecos Papadatos, and Annie di Donna, *Logicomix: An Epic Search for Truth* (New York: Bloomsbury USA, 2009), 68.

4. A mad uncle is what the text volunteers, but there were actually more instances of madness in the Russell family, including Russell's elder brother, who is mentioned in only the metanarrative as one of the things that the team decides to cut out of Russell's story, although he was instrumental in introducing Russell to mathematics. Further down the family line, Russell's son was diagnosed as schizophrenic, and his daughter (Russell's granddaughter) committed suicide. Doxiadis et al., *Logicomix,* 77, 281.

5. Doxiadis et al., *Logicomix,* 113.

6. Doxiadis et al., *Logicomix,* 152, 168.

7. Doxiadis et al., *Logicomix,* 185.

8. Doxiadis et al., *Logicomix,* 345.

9. Paolo Mancosu, "Book Review: *Logicomix* by Apostolos Doxiadis, Christos H. Papadimitriou, Alecos Papadatos, and Annie di Donna," *Journal of Humanistic Mathematics* 1, no. 1 (2011): 144–45; Richard Zach, "Logic and Madness," *Logblog,* September 30, 2009, http://www.ucalgary.ca/rzach/blog/2009/09/logic-and-madness.html; Apostolos Doxiadis and Christos Papadimitriou, "Bertrand Russell: Lover, Husband, Mathematician, and Comic Book Hero," interview by Bill Casselman, *Notices of the American Mathematical Society* 57, no. 11 (2010): 1478.

10. Apostolos Doxiadis and Christos Papadimitriou, "Bertrand Russell," 1477.

11. Doxiadis also confesses to Alex Fitch a dislike for historical novels; "Apostolos Doxiadis' *Logicomix,*" interview, Panel Borders, Resonance Radio London, December 3, 2009; see Mancosu, "Book Review," 144–46; Jim Holt, "Sunday Book Review: Algorithms and Blues," *New York Times,* September 27, 2009, BR14. "Notebook" contains biographies of major logicians and philosophers, as well as descriptions of key philosophical concepts mentioned in the text.

12. Doxiadis et al., *Logicomix,* 345. In the same vein, Doxiadis states to Alex Fitch that *Logicomix* serves "the God of fiction not the god of history"; "Apostolos Doxiadis' *Logicomix .*"

13. That said, it should be noted that both Frege's anti-Semitic disquisitions and Cantor's messianic ravings, as presented in the novel, involve a psychopathological abuse of logic.

14. Doxiadis et al., *Logicomix,* 217.

15. Doxiadis et al., *Logicomix,* 14; Doxiadis and Papadimitriou, interview by Casselman, "Bertrand Russell," 1477.

16. Gian-Carlo Rota, *Indiscrete Thoughts,* ed. Fabrizio Palombi (Boston: Birkhäuser, 1997), 4.

17. With hindsight, one may detect a hint of Peano's mental disturbance in the fact that he is shown furiously walking around in circles, exclaiming "Non, é possibile"—a behavior associated with catatonic excitement (this is symptom of the schizophrenia–psychosis spectrum of disorders); but this may also be an ordinary reaction to something that turns one's belief system on its head. Doxiadis et al., *Logicomix*, 169.

18. Doxiadis et al., *Logicomix*, 281–82, 303.

19. Doxiadis et al., *Logicomix*, 24.

20. Doxiadis et al., *Logicomix*, 203; Doxiadis and Papadimitriou interview by Casselman, "Bertrand Russell," 1478. This suggests, as Doxiadis states elsewhere, that "a certain kind of personality was drawn to the task of foundational work."

21. Doxiadis et al., *Logicomix*, 204.

22. Mancosu, "Book Review," 150.

23. Doxiadis et al., *Logicomix*, 64.

24. Doxiadis et al., *Logicomix*, 303.

25. Leo Corry, "Calculating the Limits of Poetic License: Fictional Narrative and the History of Mathematics," *Configurations* 15, no. 3 (2007): 195–226; Yehuda Elkana, "The Myth of Simplicity," in *Albert Einstein: Historical and Cultural Perspectives*, ed. Gerald Holton and Yehuda Elkana (Princeton, NJ: Princeton University Press, 1982), 205; Alfred North Whitehead, *Science and the Modern World (Lowell Lectures, 1925)* (New York: MacMillan Press,1925), 15. In fact, the quote I offer is a close paraphrase of Whitehead's words.

26. Elkana, "The Myth of Simplicity," 208.

27. Doxiadis et al., *Logicomix*, 78; Doxiadis and Papadimitriou interview by Casselman, "Bertrand Russell," 1478.

28. Whitehead, *Science and the Modern World*, 15; Doxiadis et al., *Logicomix*, 308.

29. Doxiadis et al., *Logicomix*, 303, 305; Doxiadis and Papadimitriou interview by Casselman, "Bertrand Russell," 1478. Papadimitriou utilized the ideas of Turing in a novel of his own, *Turing: A Novel about Computation*. As Papadimitriou states in a common interview, "my special interest in this story is summarized in the last pages, namely, the amazing reversal that turned the spectacular failure of the foundations quest into the advent of the computer." In the same interview, Papadimitriou indicates that at the time that Doxiadis proposed the project to him, Martin Davis's *Engines of Logic* had come out, a book that was instrumental in motivating him to get involved in the *Logicomix* project. Davis's account indeed sets the chronological parameters of the quest along the lines that Papadimitriou advocates and must be considered, in a way, the text that underwrites Christos's attitude in the metanarrative.

30. Orestes kills his mother to avenge the murder of his father, Agamemnon, whom Clytemnestra kills to avenge the (presumed) sacrifice of her daughter Iphigenia to obtain propitious winds for the Greek fleet on its way to Troy.

31. Doxiadis et al., *Logicomix*, 237. This is not the first cover of the book, the Greek edition, nor is it the only cover of subsequent editions; however, it is the cover used in most international editions. The image comes from the text and offers kind of visual homologue to the news of an escalating First World War. It strikes me, nevertheless, that this is a visual pun only to the degree that it invokes *schemata* naturally arising in the mind of our generation, accustomed as we are to images of persons in front of computers, though it is clearly anachronistic for Russell's time.

32. Mykonos, Greece, July 12–15, 2005.

33. Also consider that Doxiadis, speaking a few days after the end of the conference in an interview on the "Thales + Friends" website, makes special mention of the historians of mathematics present at the conference and shows great awareness of issues in mathematical history. "Thales and Friends—Apostolos' Interview," Thales + Friends, http://www.thalesandfriends.org/en/index.php?option=com_content&task=view&id=48&Itemid=83&phpMyAdmin=rcOunTMVHvdSvjLzdNr45lZ-X09.ematics. The conference website actually offers a link to Corry's paper on his personal website (http://www.tau.ac.il/~corry/publications/articles/Narrative/main.html); but it is an already reworked version, prepared for publication, so there is

no way to know how deeply Corry delved into issues of historiography in the original (conference) version.

34. Doxiadis et al., *Logicomix*, 22–23, 98, 201–3.

35. There is probably another context here as well, as Martin Davis, whose *Engines of Logic* was important for Papadimitriou, also presented a paper at his conference, and his main concern appeared to be the historical accuracy of *historical*, not fictional, accounts of mathematics. It is therefore likely that the *Logicomix* team was more concerned about what fault Davis might find with their work, rather than Corry.

36. It is also reminiscent of ancient perambulatory modes of philosophizing—notably in Plato's *Phaedrus*, which is essentially one long walk, but also in Aristotle's Peripatetic (walking) School of Philosophy (something of a misnomer though, since it was meant to indicate the place of meetings for the school as the promenade—the *Peripatos*—of ancient Athens).

37. Corry, "Calculating the Limits of Poetic License," 214.

38. Doxiadis et al., *Logicomix*, 200.

39. Doxiadis et al., *Logicomix*, 12.

40. Mancosu, "Book Review," 147–50; Paolo Mancosu, "[Review of *Logicomix*, by A. Doxiadis, C. Papadimitriou, A. Papadatos, and A. di Donna]," *Bulletin of Symbolic Logic* 16, no. 3 (2010): 419–20. This is true even of Mancosu, who has nevertheless raised a few issues about the accuracy of both the mathematics and the logic.

41. Doxiadis et al., *Logicomix*, 200.

42. S. H. Butcher, *Aristotle's Theory of Poetry and Fine Art* (New York: Dover, 1951), 288–301. It should be noted that the three unities are entirely an imaginative extrapolation from Aristotle's *Poetics* by later—first Roman and then Renaissance—scholars. S. H. Butcher, celebrated English translator and commentator of the *Poetics,* notes that the only unity explicitly put forward by Aristotle is the unity of action.

43. Doxiadis et al., *Logicomix*, 99, 166, 101–9, 126–29, 164–65, 240–42, 248–50, 256–57. With respect, now, to the last set of references, it should be noted that the presentation of the ideas in the *Tractatus*—the only theory introduced by Apostolos—is actually one of the faults that Mancosu finds with *Logicomix*.

44. Although varied in how successfully the graphics are integrated into the presentation of ideas, the Pantheon Books *For Beginners* series contains real gems, such as Richard Appignanesi and Oscar Zarate's *Freud for Beginners*. I frankly believe that without the innovations and success of such books, *Logicomix* would not have been possible. Pantheon, let us not forget, is the publisher of Art Spiegelman, Marjane Satrapi, and Chris Ware (among others), some of the most important graphic novelists of our time. It therefore seems to me that Apostolos is (justifiably) worried more about the similarity to this series than to the Wiley *For Dummies* one or, I will add, the Icon Books *Introducing* series.

45. Doxiadis et al., *Logicomix*, 100.

46. *Logicomix: One Page at a Time—The Creation of a Graphic Novel*, directed by Alexis Kardaras (Athens: Apostolos Doxiadis & Pan Entertainment), online video, http://www.*logicomix*.com/en/index.php?option=com_content&view=article&id=90&Itemid=62&phpMyAdmin=F42cngRU%2CPpk9DnEBgIsHy%2CFVk3.

47. "Apostolos Doxiadis' *Logicomix*," interview by Fitch.

48. Gerard Genette, *Narrative Discourse: An Essay in Method*, trans. Jane E. Lewin (Ithaca, NY: Cornell University Press, 1980), 48.

49. Doxiadis et al., *Logicomix*, 221. An image of an engraving by R. Brandand—of an earlier picture by Wolfensberger (no first name provided) included in a travel memoir by G. N. Wright, *The Rhine, Italy, and Greece* (London: Fisher)—was available on the Internet at the time of *Logicomix*'s production (however, the book was digitized only in 2009 by the Internet Archive). This comes as a great surprise, since the *Logicomix* website in the "Behind the Scenes" section claims great accuracy for the locations shown—especially for Russell's European tour, for which they conducted on-site research and provide panel to picture comparisons. http://www.*logicomix*.com/en/index.php?option=com_content&view=article&id=91&Itemid=30.

50. The name of the street of the presidential residence, where the protagonists first meet, and that of the ancient theatre, which they pass by so many times and where they eventually end up for the dress rehearsal of the Oresteia, is the same (despite following different conventions in being converted into English). This unspoken—since the names are never mentioned—"metaphor" lends the metanarrative a kind of formal completeness that is lacking given the abrupt shift to the drama in the end. Christos even remarks on the "cuteness" of the studio, on first being taken there. Doxiadis et al., *Logicomix*, 25. The *Logicomix* website, however, in the "Behind the Scenes" section admits that the studio is "not quite as quaint," http:// www.*logicomix*.com/en/index.php?option=com_content&view=article&id=91&Item-id=30.

51. Doxiadis et al., *Logicomix*, 217.

52. The journey to the Underworld is, of course, a common *topos* of quest narratives.

53. This type of graphic reappropriation of a cityscape, of creating a psychogeogra-phy, is apparently an emerging feature of graphic novels. I am thinking here of Eliza-beth Ho's discussion of Alan Moore's *From Hell*, which describes a similar process of reappropriation of tourist London in Moore's graphic novel via the re-marking of occult territories of violence, which according to Ho follows the model of Iain Sin-clair's discursive psychogeographies in *Lights Out for the Territory*; "Postimperial Landscapes: 'Psychogeography' and Englishness in Alan Moore's graphic novel *From Hell: A Melodrama in Sixteen Parts*," *Cultural Critique* 63 (2006): 109. In *Logicomix*, it is not violence but the traditional recreational walk in downtown Athens and around the Acropolis that re-marks a familiar Athenian territory, a *habitus*. Needless to say, this is a territory eroded by cars (illegally parked everywhere), rising crime in certain areas, but mostly through the appropriation of open urban spaces by increasing numbers of the world's disenfranchised—illegal immigrants who peddle, beg, scavenge, prosti-tute themselves, or simply live in the downtown. The unimpeded, unselfconscious walk of chatting friends is now perhaps mostly possible in the elliptic landscape described by Apostolos and Christos's walks around Athens.

54. In fact, Icon Books published in 2011 *Introducing Bertrand Russell*, obviously banking on *Logicomix*'s success.

55. There is, however, also another subtext for the use of the *Oresteia*: the appear-ance of a three-page comic in the manner of the metanarrative by the *Logicomix* team (reduced now to Doxiadis, Papadatos, and Di Donna) presenting Lévi-Strauss's struc-tural analysis of myths via the *Oresteia* should be seen as another step in the direction of developing a mathematical (formal) approach to narrative—only now Apostolos and Alecos become the sparring partners. This piece in fact announces the *Oresteia* as Papadatos's next graphic project about the "birth of Democracy," which raises serious questions about the seeming "fortuity" of the inclusion of the play in the novel and about who is "speaking" Christos, when he expounds about the play in precisely the same terms. See Apostolos Doxiadis, Christos Papadimitriou, Alecos Papadatos, and Annie di Donna,"Exclusive Claude Lévi-Strauss Cartoon," *Financial Times*, February 27, 2010.

56. Aristotle contributes a basic definition of logic and is otherwise mentioned only in relation to poetics. Doxiadis et al., *Logicomix*, 99, 201, 265.

57. Doxiadis et al., *Logicomix*, 14, 24.

58. Doxiadis et al., *Logicomix*, 306.

59. Doxiadis et al., *Logicomix*, 24, 27, 274.

60. "Apostolos Doxiadis' *Logicomix*," interview by Fitch.

61. Actually, "glimpse" is a bit of a misnomer, as Doxiadis's "impersonation" of Christos is heard off camera.

62. Of course, most graphic novels, with their univocal subjective retrospective nar-ratives, graphically underscore the subjective nature of their narrative. I am thinking here of Laura R. Micciche's discussion of the spatial distortions produced by the sub-jective narrative of rape in Debbie Drechsler's "Daddy's Girl." Micciche, "Seeing and Reading Incest: A Study of Debbie Drechsler's 'Daddy's Girl,'" *Rhetoric Review* 23, no.

1 (2004): 5–20. This is not to say that even in these highly subjective accounts, there is not a surplus of visual information that exceeds a narrator's grasp. It is mostly in comic books that we find characters moving in a seemingly neutral background—think, for instance, of Hergé's *Tintin* , whose *claire ligne* style is adopted in *Logicomix*. Note, however, that although *Logicomix* uses the rather neutral *claire ligne* that Fitch suggests is most suited to the presentation of historical narratives and does not utilize "subjective" visuals except in Russell's narrative (in moments of crisis), Adelheid R. Eubanks, in her discussion of the novel, suggests that the metanarrative provides graphic analogues of the problematic of narrative choices in the way that Apostolos and Christos pick their way among the paths of Philopappou Hill and the lanes of Plaka when they discuss narrative development in their walks. "Apostolos Doxiadis' *Logicomix*," interview by Fitch. Adelheid R. Eubanks, "*Logicomix*: From Text to Image/from Logic to Story," *The Comparatist* 35 (2011): 182–97.

 63. This is, in fact, an anachronism since Sproul Hall was not built until 1941; Sproul is nevertheless the appropriate place for an antiwar protest because it was the site of all Berkeley protests in the 1960s and 1970s.

 64. It is an impossible view because the subject is located on both sides of the gaze; it is forbidden because it involves the time paradox of the very existence of the subject.

 65. This is not the place to elaborate the full theory of the figurations of the enunciatory apparatus, contained in my doctoral dissertation "Destroying Time" (which figurations are not limited to the "view from above"); however, I offer a couple of examples by way of illustration: Adam and Archangel Michael surveying human history in Milton's *Paradise Lost* or Combray emerging out of Marcel's teacup in the "madeleine incident" in Proust's *Á la Recherche du Temps Perdu*.

 66. I speak of "the subject," not "the subjects," of enunciation—the point bears repeating—because I am not referring to Doxiadis and Papadimitriou but to the subject of enunciation posited in the future anterior by the work itself: the subject that will have come into existence upon completion of the work.

 67. One should read the team's three-page comic commissioned by *Publisher's Weekly* for its "Why I Write" column, "Why (We) Write: a Modern Greek Tragi-comedy," as a sort of admission of the type of desire suggested by my analysis of the "primal scene" in *Logicomix*. In it, each of the four creators of the novel indicates (tongue in cheek) his or her motivation as an early desire for the highest possible achievement in his or her field (a Pulitzer Prize, an Oscar in animation, a theorem with one's own name, a great work of art). Indeed, in the simultaneously published Greek version for *Kappa* magazine of *Kathimerini* newspaper, the phrase "wish fulfillment" is rendered in Greek as απωθημένο, that is, "repressed wish," which accords better with what I have been trying to describe. Apostolos Doxiadis, Christos Papadimitriou, Alecos Papadatos, and Annie di Donna, "Why (We) Write: A Modern Greek Tragi-comedy," *Publishers Weekly*, December 21, 2009, 30–32; Apostolos Doxiadis, Christos Papadimitriou, Alecos Papadatos, and Annie di Donna, "Γιατί Γράφουμε: Μια Σύγχρονη Ελληνική Τραγι-κωμωδία," *Kappa* 342 (December 20, 2009): 32–34.

 68. Doxiadis et al., *Logicomix*, 85.

 69. Doxiadis et al., *Logicomix*, 152. In fact, no such ceiling exists in the Richelieu Amphitheater, which is the location (based on several visual clues) of Hilbert's lecture; the ceiling of this—and other major old Sorbonne amphitheaters—is indeed glass. This alone bespeaks intentionality. (Furthermore, the characteristic mythological mural of the amphitheater, of which only the far-right corner is shown, has also undergone a peculiar change, with a raised arm being transformed into a horn—as though copied from a bad picture.) *Logicomix* contains other figurative moments, such as a vision of the human predicament (the figure from Edvard Munch's *Scream* before a vortex with a human skeleton) precipitated by Evelyn Whitehead's near-death experience (235); however, these are not to be confused with figurations of the enunciatory apparatus, which may in fact not be as images very figurative per se.

 70. Significantly, in the paratext accompanying the novel's international success, Anne Bardy—so important (as a persona) in the story's development since she pro-

vokes the team's attendance of the *Oresteia*—is not mentioned. Harking back to Jacques Derrida's understanding of the Freudian *darstellung*, "Freud and the Scene of Writing," in *Writing and Difference*, trans. Alan Bass (Chicago: University of Chicago Press, 1978), 196–231.

71. In his radio interview with Fitch, Doxiadis states that as work progressed, the team members became "typecast" as "the skeptic," "the clown," and "the nerd"— Alecos, Apostolos, and Christos, respectively, by my take—and that the metanarrative is a reflection of this.

72. Roughly, this is a process that corresponds to the Freudian primary and secondary processes: the secondary (ego) processes operate in the text to integrate everything into a univocal, smooth, logically and temporally organized whole; the primary (unconscious) processes reveal the traces of the original nonintegrated multiplicities that shape the work. The secondary processes enfold the primary processes but do not efface them; they persist as figures, peculiarities, and contingencies within the text. In a text such as *Logicomix*, where some of the requirements of integration are relaxed, the primary processes are often very prominent, which does not annul the apparent effort to integrate them in some fashion.

73. The development of theoretical tools to discuss graphic novels, especially in terms of mimesis, would greatly benefit by an examination of how Gerard Genette's categories of "narrative of events" and "narrative of words" can be adapted to discuss graphic narrative discourse. "Frontiers of Narrative" in *Figures of Literary Discourse*, trans. Alan Sheridan (New York: Columbia University Press, 1982), 131–33.

74. Andreas Huyssen, "Of Mice and Mimesis: Reading Spiegelman with Adorno," *New German Critique* 81 (autumn 2000): 65–82. Note also that at the moment when the issue of representation arises in *Maus II*, with the enormity of the success of *Maus I*, the mouse shifts from persona to mask.

# Bibliography

## PRIMARY SOURCES

Adel Manufacturing Company. "Mother, When Will You Stay Home Again?" Advertisement. *Saturday Evening Post*, May 6, 1944, 99.

Agrimbau, Diego. "Argentina a los pies de Astérix." *Sudestada*, July 2008, 14–15.

"Aides Relieve Nurse Shortage." *Life Magazine* 12, no. 1 (January 5, 1942): 32–35.

*Alexander the Great*. Directed by Robert Rossen. Los Angeles, CA: United Artists, 1956.

Athos 6. "Organisation." *Patrouille de France*. June 23, 2011. http://www.patrouilledefrance.net/index.php?option=com_content&view=article&id=24&Itemid=94.

*Batman*. No. 84. New York: DC Comics, 1954.

"Behind the Scenes." *Logicomix*. http://www.logicomix.com/en/index.php?option=com_content&view=article&id=91&Itemid=30.

*Ben-Hur: A Tale of Christ*. Directed by Fred Niblo. Los Angeles, CA: Metro Goldwyn Mayer, 1925.

Blum, Alex A. *Treasure Island*. New York: Berkley, 1949.

Brubaker, Ed, and Greg Rucka. *Gotham Central*. New York: DC Comics, 2003–2006.

Burroughs, Edgar Rice. *The Jungle Tales of Tarzan*. New York: Cosimo Books, 2005.

Butcher, S. H., trans. *Poetics*, by Aristotle. http://classics.mit.edu/Aristotle/poetics.mb.txt.

Byrne, John, Bill Mantlo, Scott Lobdell, et al. *Alpha Flight*. New York: Marvel, 1983–1994.

Carlin, Mark, ed. *Superman in the 50s*. New York: DC Comics, 2002.

Carroll, Andrew, ed. *War Letters: Extraordinary Correspondence from American Wars*. New York: Washington Square Press, 2001.

*César*. Directed by Marcel Pagnol. Marseille, France: Les Films Marcel Pagnol, 1936.

Coste, Philippe. "Ce que les Américains pensent des Français." *L'Express* June 22–28, 2011, 58–62.

Dales, Douglas. "6 State Bills Seek Comic Book Curbs." *New York Times*, February 20, 1952.

Doctorow, E. L. *City of God: A Novel*. New York: Random House, 2000.

Doxiadis, Apostolos, Christos Papadimitriou, Alecos Papadatos, and Annie di Donna. *Logicomix: An Epic Search for Truth*. New York: Bloomsbury USA, 2009.

"DSK arrest a setup." *Mail Today*, July 5, 2011.

*El Informador*. Guanajuato, Mexico.

*El Nacional*. Mexico City, Mexico.

Englehart, Steve. *Millennium*. New York: DC Comics, 1988.

———. *The New Guardians*. New York: DC Comics, 1988.

*The Flag Code*, 36 U.S.C. § 10.

Four Vagabonds. "Rosie the Riveter." *The War Years*. CD. Intersound, 1943. See figure 10.

Fox, Gardner, and Joe Gallagher. "A Cure for the World." *All Star Comics* #22. New York: DC Comics, 1945.

———. "The Justice Society Fights for a United America!" *All Star Comics* #16. April/May 1944. New York: DC Comics.

Fox, Gardner, Sheldon Mayer, and Sheldon Moldoff. *All Star Comics #11*. New York: DC Comics, 1942.

Fox, Gardner, and H. G. Peter. *All Star Comics #11*. New York: DC Comics, 1942.

*Frank Miller's Sin City*. Directed by Frank Miller and Robert Rodriguez. DVD. New York: Dimension Films, 2005.

General Electric. "Who Said This Is a Man's War?" Advertisement. *Good Housekeeping*, October 1942, 82.

Gold, Mike, ed. *The Greatest 1950s Stories Ever Told*. New York: DC Comics.

Goscinny, René, and Albert Uderzo. *Astérix aux Jeux Olympiques*. Paris: Editions Dargaud, 1968.

———. *Astérix chez les Belges*. Paris: Editions Dargaud, 1979.

———. *Astérix chez les Bretons*. Paris: Editions Dargaud, 1966.

———. *Astérix chez les Helvètes* . Paris: Editions Dargaud, 1970.

———. *Astérix en Corse*. Paris: Editions Dargaud, 1973.

———. *Astérix en Hispanie*. Paris: Editions Dargaud, 1969.

———. *Astérix et Cléopâtre*. Paris: Editions Dargaud, 1965.

———. *Astérix et le chaudron*. Paris: Editions Dargaud, 1969.

———. *Astérix gladiateur*. Paris: Editions Dargaud, 1964.

———. *Astérix le Gaulois*. Paris: Editions Dargaud, 1961.

———. *Astérix légionnaire*. Paris: Editions Dargaud, 1967.

———. *La serpe d'or*. Paris: Editions Dargaud, 1962.

———. *La Zizanie*. Paris: Editions Dargaud, 1970.

———. *Le Cadeau de César*. Paris: Editions Dargaud, 1974.

———. *Le Devin*. Paris: Editions Dargaud, 1972.

———. *Le domaine des Dieux*. Paris: Editions Dargaud, 1971.

———. *Le tour de Gaule d'Astérix*. Paris: Editions Dargaud, 1965.

———. *Obélix et Compagnie*. Paris: Editions Dargaud, 1976.

*The Greatest 1950's Stories Ever Told*, edited by Mike Gold. New York: DC Comics, 1990.

Gripper Fasteners, Scovill Manufacturing Company. "It's No Fun . . . but It's Patriotic!" Advertisement. *Good Housekeeping*, March 1942, 175.

Heinberg, Allan. *Young Avengers*. New York: Marvel, 2005–2006.

*Histoire de France en Bandes Dessinées*. 24 vols. Paris: Larousse, 1976–1978. Hereafter, *HFBD*.

*HFBD* 1. "De Vercingétorix aux Vikings." Larousse, October 1976.

*HFBD* 5. "Les Croisades." Larousse, February 1977.

*HFBD* 7. "La chevalerie." Larousse, April 1977.

*HFBD* 10. "Louis XI, François 1er." Larousse, July 1977.

*HFBD* 17. "Napoléon." Larousse, February 1978.

*HFBD* 15. "La Révolution." Larousse, December 1977.

*HFBD* 20. "La Commune, la IIIeme République." Larousse, May 1978.

*HFBD* 23. "La second guerre mondiale." Larousse, August 1978.

*HFBD* 24. "1942–1974." Larousse, September 1978.

*Histoire et Bande Dessinée, Supplément Bédésup*. 10 (October 1979).

*Hulk*. Directed by Ang Lee. DVD. Universal City, CA: Universal Studios, 2007.

*Hulk Magazine #23*. 1980.

Jacobson, Sid, and Ernie Colón. *The 9/11 Report: A Graphic Adaptation*. New York: Hill & Wang, 2006.

———. *After 9/11: America's War on Terror (2001– )*. New York: Hill & Wang, 2008.

Jergens Lotion. "You Were Coming Home, Dear." Advertisement. *Ladies Home Journal*, January 1944, 43.

Johns, Geoff, Grant Morrison, Greg Rucka, and Mark Waid. *52*. New York: DC Comics, 2006–2007.

"The Judgement on DSK." *Wall Street Journal*, August 25, 2011, 16.

Kane, Bob, Bill Finger, et al. *Batman*, New York: DC Comics, 1939–2011.

Kanigher, Robert, Ross Andru, and Mike Esposito. "Top Secret." *Wonder Woman #99*. New York: DC Comics, 1958.

Kanigher, Robert, and Joe Kubert. "A New Kind of War!" *Our Army at War #104*. New York: DC Comics, 1961.

Kanigher, Robert, and H. G. Peter. "Peril in Paradise Island." *Sensation Comics #42*. New York: DC Comics, 1945.

———. *Sensation Comics #48*. New York: DC Comics, 1945.

Kirkman, Robert. *The Walking Dead #70*. 2010.

———. *The Walking Dead*. Vol. 1, *Days Gone Bye*. Berkeley, CA: Image Comics, 2004.

———. *The Walking Dead*. Vol. 2, *Miles behind Us*. Berkeley, CA: Image Comics, 2004.

———. *The Walking Dead*. Vol. 5, *The Best Defense*. Berkeley, CA: Image Comics, 2006.

———. *The Walking Dead*. Vol. 10, *What We Become*. Berkeley, CA: Image Comics, 2009.

*La Jornada*. Mexico City, Mexico.

"L'après-DSK." *Le Monde*, May 21, 2011, 24.

Lee, Stan, and Dick Ayres. "Fighting Side-by-Side with . . . Captain America and Bucky!" *Sgt. Fury and His Howling Commandoes #13*. New York: Marvel Comics, 1963.

Lee, Stan, and Jack Kirby. *The Essential Fantastic Four*. Vol. 1, *Fantastic Four #1–#20 and Annual #1*. New York: Marvel Comics, 2005.

———. *The Essential Fantastic Four*. Vol. 2, *Fantastic Four #21–#40*. New York: Marvel Comics, 2006.

———. *The Essential Fantastic Four*. Vol. 3, *Fantastic Four #41–#63 and Annual #1–#4*. New York: Marvel Comics, 2007.

Lee, Stan, Jack Kirby, et al. *X-Men*. New York: Marvel, 1963–2011.

Lee, Stan, Jack Kirby, Jim Shooter, et al. *Hulk*. 1962–2011.

"Les Oncle Paul." *Tout le Journal de Spirou*. http://www.toutspirou.fr/Lesonclepaul/lesonclepaul.htm.

Listerine. "Put It There, Sister!" Advertisement. *Good Housekeeping*, June 1944, 3.

*Logicomix: One Page at a Time. The Creation of a Graphic Novel*. Directed by Alexis Kardaras. Athens: Apostolos Doxiadis and Pan Entertainment. http://www.logicomix.com/en/index.php?option=com_content&view=article&id=90&Itemid=62&phpMyAdmin=F42cngRU%2CPpk9DnEBgIsHy%2CFVk3.

*Lucky Luke*. Directed by James Huth. DVD. UGC, 2010.

Lysol Disinfectant. "Mother Keep House Clean the Way Uncle Sam Does." Advertisement. *Good Housekeeping*, April 1942, 69.

Mangels, Andy. "Out of the Closet and into the Comics: Gays in Comics. The Creations and the Creators: Part I." *Amazing Heroes #143*. June 15, 1988.

———. "Out of the Closet and into the Comics: Gays in Comics. The Creations and the Creators: Part II." *Amazing Heroes #144*. July 1, 1988.

Marble, Alice. "Wonder Women of History." *Wonder Woman #1*. New York: DC Comics, 1942.

Marston, William Moulton, et al. *Wonder Woman*. New York: DC Comics, 1941–2011.

Marston, William Moulton, and Frank Godwin. "The Unbound Amazon." *Sensation Comics #19*. New York: DC Comics, 1943.

Marston, William Moulton, and H. G. Peter. "The Adventure of the Beauty Club." *Wonder Woman #6*. New York: DC Comics, 1943.

———. "America's Wonder Women of Tomorrow!" *Wonder Woman #7*. New York: DC Comics, 1943.

———. "Battle for Womanhood!" *Wonder Woman #5*. New York: DC Comics, 1943.

———. *Comic Cavalcade #1*. New York: DC Comics, 1942/1943.

———. *Comic Cavalcade #3*. New York: DC Comics, 1943.

———. "Danny the Demon Had Plans!" *The Big All-American Comic Book*. New York: DC Comics, 1944.

———. "Grown-Down Land." *Sensation Comics #31*. New York: DC Comics, 1944.

———. "Introducing Wonder Woman." *Wonder Woman #8*. New York: DC Comics, 1941–1942.

———. "The Masked Menace!" *Sensation Comics #16*. New York: DC Comics, 1943.

————. "Racketeers Kidnap Miss Santa Claus!" *Sensation Comics #38*. New York: DC Comics, 1945.
————. "The Return of Diana Prince." *Wonder Woman #9*. New York: DC Comics, 1942.
————. "The Secret Weapon!" *Wonder Woman #7*. New York: DC Comics, 1943.
————. *Sensation Comics #1*. New York: DC Comics, 1942.
————. *Sensation Comics #2*. New York: DC Comics, 1942.
————. *Sensation Comics #3*. New York: DC Comics, 1942.
————. *Sensation Comics #4*. New York: DC Comics, 1942.
————. *Sensation Comics #5*. New York: DC Comics, 1942.
————. *Sensation Comics #6*. New York: DC Comics, 1942.
————. *Sensation Comics #9*. New York: DC Comics, 1942.
————. *Sensation Comics #17*. New York: DC Comics, 1942.
————. *Sensation Comics #21*. New York: DC Comics, 1943.
————. *Sensation Comics #23*. New York: DC Comics, 1943.
————. "Villiany, Incorporated!" *Wonder Woman #28*. New York: DC Comics, 1948.
————. *Wonder Woman #2*. New York: DC Comics, 1942.
————. *Wonder Woman #3*. New York: DC Comics, 1943.
————. *Wonder Woman #4*. New York: DC Comics, 1943.
————. *Wonder Woman #5*. New York: DC Comics, 1943.
————. *Wonder Woman #12*. New York: DC Comics, 1945.
————. "Wonder Woman Is Dead!" *Sensation Comics #13*. New York: DC Comics, 1943.
————. "Wonder Woman's Last Battle." *Wonder Woman #179*. New York: DC Comics, 1968.
————. "Wonder Woman's Rival." *Wonder Woman #178*. New York: DC Comics, 1968.
Martin, Jacques. *Alix l'intrépide*. Paris: Editions Le Lombard, 1956.
————. *C'était à Khorsabad*. Paris: Editions Casterman, 2006.
————. *Iorix le grand*. Paris: Editions Casterman, 1971.
————. *La griffe noire*. Paris: Editions Le Lombard, 1959.
————. *La tiare d'Oribal*. Paris: Editions Le Lombard, 1958.
————. *La tour de Babel*. Paris: Editions Casterman, 1981.
————. *Le dernier Spartiate*. Paris: Editions Casterman, 1966.
————. *Le dieu sauvage*. Paris: Editions Casterman, 1969.
————. *Le fils de Spartacus*. Paris: Editions Casterman, 1974.
————. *L'enfant grec*. Paris: Editions Casterman, 1979.
————. *Le Prince du Nil*. Paris: Editions Casterman, 1973.
————. *Les légions perdues*. Paris: Editions Casterman, 1962.
————. *Le spectre de Carthage*. Paris: Editions Casterman, 1976.
————. *Le sphinx d'or*. Paris: Editions Le Lombard, 1956.
————. *Le tombeau étrusque*. Paris: Editions Casterman, 1967.
————. *L'Ile maudite*. Paris: Editions Le Lombard, 1957.
————. *Roma, Roma* . Paris: Editions Casterman, 2005.
*The Matrix*. Directed by Andy Wachowski and Larry Wachowski. DVD. Burbank, CA: Warner Home Video, 1999.
Miller, Frank. *Sin City*. Vol. 1, *The Hard Goodbye*. Milwaukie, OR: Dark Horse Comics, 1991.
————. *Sin City*. Vol. 2, *A Dame to Kill For*. Milwaukie, OR: Dark Horse Comics, 1993.
————. *Sin City*. Vol. 3, *The Big Fat Kill*. Milwaukie, OR: Dark Horse Comics, 1994.
————. *Sin City*. Vol. 4, *That Yellow Bastard*. Milwaukie, OR: Dark Horse Comics, 1996.
————. *Sin City*. Vol. 5, *Family Values*. Milwaukie, OR: Dark Horse Comics, 1997.
————. *Sin City*. Vol. 6, *Booze, Broads, and Bullets*. Milwaukie, OR: Dark Horse Comics, 1998.
————. *Sin City*. Vol. 7, *Hell and Back*. Milwaukie, OR: Dark Horse Comics, 1999.
Milligan, Peter. *John Constantine, Hellblazer*. New York: DC Comics, 1988–1993; Vertigo, 1993–2011.
Mitterrand, Frédéric. *La Mauvaise Vie*. Paris: Editions Robert Laffont, 2005.

Moore, Alan, David Lloyd, Steve Whitaker, et al. *Promethea: Book 5.* Illustrated by J. H. Williams III. La Jolla, CA: America's Best Comics, 2005.

———. *V for Vendetta.* New York: DC Comics, 2005.

Mora, Victor, and Raffaele Marcello. *Taranis, Fils de la Gaule.* Vols. 1–2. Paris: Editions Vaillant, 1980–1981.

———. "Taranis, fils de la Gaule: A l'abordage!" *Pif Gadget* 498 (October 1978): 17–26.

———. "Taranis, fils de la Gaule: Complot contre César." *Pif Gadget* 510 (January 1979): 19–28.

———. "Taranis, fils de la Gaule: Dans la gueule du loup." *Pif Gadget* 495 (September 1978): 17–26.

———. "Taranis, fils de la Gaule: Le bracelet de Taranis." *Pif Gadget* 648 (August 1981): 13–27.

———. "Taranis, fils de la Gaule: Le poignard des sacrifices." *Pif Gadget* 536 (July 1979): 37–47.

———. "Taranis, fils de la Gaule: Le premier choc." *Pif Gadget* 438 (August 1977): 21–30.

———. "Taranis, fils de la Gaule: Le rendez vous des marécages." *Pif Gadget* 643 (July 1981): 21–30.

———. "Taranis, fils de la Gaule: Le retour de Taranis." *Pif Gadget* 617 (January 1981): 25–40.

———. "Taranis, fils de la Gaule: Les hommes bleus." *Pif Gadget* 526 (April 1979): 37–46.

———. "Taranis, fils de la Gaule: Piège pour une légion." *Pif Gadget* 481 (June 1978): 12–21.

———. "Taranis, fils de la Gaule: Un message pour Vercingétorix." *Pif Gadget* 404 (December 1976): 43–54.

Nabisco, National Biscuit Company. "And I'm No Part-Time Wife!" Advertisement. *Good Housekeeping*, July 1946, 74.

Nabisco, National Biscuit Company. "There's a War Job in My Kitchen." Advertisement. *Good Housekeeping*, September 1942, 101.

*New York Times.* "Anti Comics Drive Reported Waning." January 21, 1950.

*New York Times.* "Comic Books Held Aids to Education." April 3, 1956.

*New York Times.* "Health Law Urged to Combat Comics." December 4, 1951.

*New York Times.* "Juvenile Delinquency Seen on Increase; Quaker Official Blames New Comic Books." June 24, 1948.

*New York Times.* "Obscene Books Ban Pushed at Albany." March 4, 1953.

*New York Times.* "Psychiatrist Charges Stalling Tactics on Legislation to Control Comic Books." January 24, 1950.

*New York Times.* "Urges Comic Book Ban." September 4, 1948.

Olson, Mark. "Interview: Robert Rodriguez." *Sight & Sound* 15, no. 6 (2005): 16.

Pepperell Fabrics. "Wanted: Housekeepers to Help the Army and Navy." Advertisement. *Ladies Home Journal*, August 1943, 66.

Pennac, Benacquista, and Achdé. *Cavalier Seul.* Vol. 5, *Les aventures de Lucky Luke d'après Morris.* Givrins, Switzerland: Lucky Comics, 2012.

———. "Cavalier Seul (episode 1/6)." *Spirou*, September 26, 2012, 5–12.

———. "Cavalier Seul (episode 6/6)." *Spirou*, October 31, 2012, 14–18.

Pond's Cold Cream. "She's Engaged! She's Lovely! She Uses Pond's!" Advertisement. *Good Housekeeping*, June 1943, 65.

Prost, Jean, and Alain Pelletier. "A Propos de 'Il Était une Fois Lugdunum.' (T. 1 de l'Histoire de Lyon en Bande Dessinée)." *Histoire et Bande Dessinée, Supplément Bédésup* 10 (October 1979): 23–34.

Rolfe, J. C., trans. Suetonius: The Lives of the Twelve Caesars . Loeb Classical Library Edition, 1913–1914. http://penelope.uchicago.edu/Thayer/E/Roman/Texts/Suetonius/12Caesars/Julius*.html.

Rucka, Greg. *Batwoman: Elegy.* New York: DC Comics, 2009–2010.

Sanderson, Peter. "The Big Switch." *Amazing Heroes* #76. 1985.

Satrapi, Marjane. *Persepolis: The Story of a Childhood*. New York: Pantheon, 2003.
———. *Persepolis 2: The Story of a Return*. New York: Pantheon, 2004.
Schiff, Jack, Win Mortimer, and Eric Kachelhofer. "Institutional Ad: The World of Adventure in Books." In *The Greatest 1950s Stories Ever Told*, edited by Mike Gold. New York: DC Comics, 1990.
Secretaría de Educación Pública. *Episodios Mexicanos*. 68 vols. Mexico City, Mexico: Consejo Nacional de Fomento Educativo, 1981.
———. *México: Historia de un Pueblo*. 20 vols. Mexico City, Mexico: Editorial Nueva Imagen, S.A. and Consejo Nacional de Fomento Educativo, 1980.
Secretaria de Educación Publica, Departamento de Archivo Histórico y Reprografía, Director General de Publicaciónes y Bibliotecas, México City. File 9211/1. Letter from Javier Barros to Miguel Limon. November 16, 1979, 5.
Secretaria de Educación Publica, Departamento de Archivo Histórico y Reprografía, Subsecretaria de Cultura y Recreación, Director General de Publicaciónes y Bibliotecas, México City. File 9190/26. Report sent May 17, 1979, from Max Molina Fuente to Francisco Serrano. "Marco de Referencia: El Concepto de Educación Permanente."
Siegel, Jerry, Joe Shuster, et al. *Superman*. New York: DC Comics, 1932–2011.
*Spartacus*. Directed by Stanley Kubrick. Los Angeles: Universal Pictures, 1960.
Spiegelman, Art. *Maus: A Survivor's Tale. My Father Bleeds History*. New York: Pantheon, 1986.
———. *Maus II: A Survivor's Tale. And Here My Troubles Began*. New York: Pantheon, 1991.
Tangee Lipsticks. "War, Women, and Lipstick." Advertisement. *Ladies Home Journal*, August 1943, 73.
Tezuka, Osamu. *Astro Boy*, edited by Frederik I., Schodt. Milwaukie, OR: Dark Horse Comics, 2002.
Vaughan, Brian K. *Runaways*. New York: Marvel, 2003–2009.
Watson, Paula. "All Guts for Old Glory, One Person's Choice for Woman of the Century Is: Rosie the Riveter." Editorial. *Dallas Morning News*. December 29, 1999, K4656.
Weisinger, Mort, George Papp, et al. *Green Arrow*. New York: DC Comics, 1941–2011.
Wells, Zeb. *Civil War: Young Avengers/Runaways*. New York: Marvel, 2006.
Wertham, Frederic. "The Comics . . . Very Funny!" *Saturday Review of Literature*, May 29, 1949, 6–10.
———. *Seduction of the Innocent*. New York: Main Road Books, 2004.
Woodbury Facial Soap. "Contact." Advertisement. *Ladies Home Journal*, February 1945, 91.
Yann and Oliver Schwartz. *Gringos Locos*. Marcinelle: Dupuis, 2012.
———. "Gringos Locos (episode 1/6)." *Spirou*, November 30, 2011, 5–15.
———. "Gringos Locos (episode 6/6)." *Spirou*, January 4, 2012, 12–15.
Zimmerman, Ron. *Rawhide Kid: Slap Leather*. New York: Marvel, 2003.

## SECONDARY SOURCES

Agulhon, Maurice. "Le Mythe Gaulois." *Ethnologie Française: Revue Trimestrielle de la Société d'Ethnologie Française* 28, no. 3 (1998): 296–302.
Ahamed, Naseer, and Saurab Singh. *Kashmir Pending*. New Delhi: Phantomville, 2007.
Albarrán, E. J. "Comino Vence al Diablo and Other Terrifying Episodes: Teatro Guiñol's Itinerant Puppet Theater in 1930s Mexico." *The Americas* 67 (2011): 355–74.
Alberelli, Christian. "Du Roman à la Bande Dessiné: Scenario pour une Adaptation." In *L'Histoire . . . par la Bande. Bande Dessinée, Histoire et Pédagogie*, edited by Odette Mitterrand and Giles Ciment, 23–34. Paris: Syros, 1993.
Anderson, Lucia. "Rosie the Riveter: Rear-Guard Support That Shattered the Male-Only Mindset." *American Legion Auxiliary National News* 87, no. 1 (2007): 8–10, 12, 14.

Aoun, Steven. "DVD Reviews: Sin City ." Metro Magazine: Media & Education Magazine 149 (2006): 237–39.

Aristotle. *Poetics*. Translated by S. H. Butcher. http://classics.mit.edu/Aristotle/poetics.3.3.html.

Arnott, Luke. "*BLAM!* The Literal Architecture of *Sin City*." *International Journal of Comic Art* 10, no. 2 (2008): 380–401.

Arrouye, Jean. "Bandes à Part." *Histoire et Bande Dessinée, Supplément Bédésup* 10 (October 1979): 116–17.

Atkinson, Michael. "Season of the Witch-Hunt." *Sight & Sound* 21, no. 5 (2011): 92.

Aziza, Claude. *Guide de l'Antiquité Imaginaire*. Paris: Editions Belles Lettres, 2008.

Babic, Annessa Ann. "Buying and Selling a Piece of the American Pie: Uses and Disuses of Patriotic Consumption." In *The Globetrotting Shopaholic: Consumer Products, Spaces, and Their Cultural Places*, edited by Annessa Ann Babic and Tanfer Emin Tunç, 13–29. Newcastle upon Tyne, England: Cambridge Scholars Press, 2008.

Barthes, Roland. *Mythologies*. Translated by Annette Lavers. New York: Farrar, Straus and Giroux, 1972.

Bartra, Armando. "The Seduction of the Innocents: The First Tumultuous Moments of Mass Literacy in Postrevolutionary Mexico." In *Everyday Forms of State Formation: Revolution and the Negotiation of Rule in Modern Mexico*, edited by Gilbert Michael Joseph and Daniel Nugent, 301–25. Durham, NC: Duke University Press, 1994.

Baudrillard, Jean. *Screened Out*. Translated by Chris Turner. New York: Verso, 2002.

———. *Simulacra and Simulation*. Translated by Sheila Faria Glaser. Ann Arbor: University of Michigan Press, 1995.

Baumet, Philippe. "Le Top 10 des Gadgets de Pif." *La Revue Schnock*, May 11, 2011. http://larevueschnock.com/?p=155.

Beaulieu, Jean-Philippe. "Astérix et les Romains: De la Psychoanalyse à la Sociologie." *Romance Notes* 32, no. 2 (1991): 169–77.

Bell, Anthea. "Translator's Notebook." In *The Signal Approach to Children's Books*, edited by Nancy Chambers, 129–39. Metuchen, NJ: Scarecrow, 1981.

Blanton, Robert G. "Zombies and International Relations: A Simple Guide for Bringing the Undead into Your Classroom." *International Studies Perspectives* 14, no. 1 (2013): 1–13.

Bosser, Frédéric. "Uderzo: Souvent Copié Jamais Égalé." *dBD*, December/January 2009–2010, 15–26.

Bouchard, Gilbert. *L'Histoire de la Haute Savoie en BD*. Grenoble, France: Glénat, 2002.

Boucher, David, and Paul Kelly. "The Social Contract and Its Critics: An Overview." In *The Social Contract from Hobbes to Rawls*, edited by D. Boucher and P. J. Kelly, 1–34. London: Routledge, 1994.

Bourque Dandridge, Eliza. "Producing Popularity: The Success in France of the Comics Series 'Astérix le Gaulois.'" Master's thesis, Virginia Polytechnic Institute and State University, 2008.

Bové, José, and François Dufour. *The World Is Not for Sale*. Translated by Anna de Casparis. Interview by Gilles Luneau. London: Verso, 2001.

Brooks, David, and Jim Cason. "Reconstruir el Imaginario Colectivo, Meta Constante: Paco Ignacio Taibo." *La Jornada*. November 14, 2004. http://www.jornada.unam.mx/2004/11/14/044f2con.php?origen=.

Brooks, Edward Jr., trans. Caesar's Commentaries on the Gallic War . Chicago: Farquhar and Albrecht, 1896.

Bruno, Pierre. "Chronique culture jeune. Pif Gadget : qu'est-ce qu'un périodique progressiste pour la jeunesse?" Le français aujourd'hui 2, no. 161 (2008): 127–32.

Bruscino, Thomas. *A Nation Forged in War: How World War II Taught Americans to Get Along*. Knoxville: University of Tennessee Press, 2010.

Bryman, Alan. "Global Implications of McDonaldization and Disneyization." In *McDonaldization: The Reader*, edited by George Ritzer, 319–23. Thousand Oaks, CA: Pine Forge Press, 2006.

———. "McDonald's as a Disneyized Institution." In *McDonaldization: The Reader*, edited by George Ritzer, 54–82. Thousand Oaks, CA: Pine Forge Press, 2006.

Butcher, S. H. *Aristotle's Theory of Poetry and Fine Art*. New York: Dover, 1951.

Butler, Judith. *Gender Trouble: Feminism and the Subversion of Identity*. New York: Psychology Press, 1990.

Camp, Roderic Ai. *Intellectuals and the State in Twentieth-Century Mexico*. Austin: University of Texas Press, 1986.

Campbell, Bruce. ¡*Viva la Historieta! Mexican Comics, NAFTA, and the Politics of Globalization*. Jackson: University Press of Mississippi, 2009.

Cappe, Jeanne. *Contes Bleus et Livres Roses*. Bruxelles, Belgium: Editions des Artistes, 1940.

Casselman, Bill. "About the Cover: Bertrand Russell. Lover, Husband, Mathematician, and Comic Book Hero." *Notices of the American Mathematical Society* 57, no. 11 (2010): 1477–78.

Cassou-Yager, Hélène. "Astérix: A Bouillon Cube of French History, Gaullist Politics, and French Attitudes and Prejudices towards Other Countries." In *Selected Proceedings: 32nd Mountain Interstate Foreign Language Conference*, edited by Gregorio Martín and Javier Herrero, 85–92. Winston-Salem, NC: Wake Forest University, 1984.

Castellar, Georges, et al. *Missiles et Sous-Marins: Le Conflit des Malouines*. Paris: Larousse, 1984.

Chabon, Michael . *The Amazing Adventures of Kavalier and Clay: A Novel*. New York: Harper Perennial, 2000.

Chute, Hillary. "Comics as Literature? Reading Graphic Narrative." *PMLA* 123, no. 2 (2008): 452–56.

Cieply, Michael. "That Noisy Woodpecker Had an Animated Secret." *New York Times*, April 10, 2011, C1.

Clark, Andrew. "Imperialism in Astérix." *Belphégor: Littérature Populaire et Culture Médiatique* 4, no. 1 (2004): 1–11.

Coogan, Peter. *Superhero: The Secret Origin of a Genre*. Austin, TX: Monkey Brain Books, 2006.

Corry, Leo. "Calculating the Limits of Poetic License: Fictional Narrative and the History of Mathematics." *Configurations* 15, no. 3 (2007): 195–226.

Coste, Philippe. "Ce que les Américains pensent des Français." *L'Express*, June 22–28, 2011, 58–62.

Costello, Matthew J. *Secret Identity Crisis: Comic Books and the Unmasking of Cold War America*. New York: Continuum, 2009.

Couperie, Pierre, et al. *Bande Dessinée et Figuration Narrative*. Paris: Musée des Arts Décoratifs, 1967.

Coville, Jamie. "United States Senate, Subcommittee of the Committee on the Judiciary, to Investigate Juvenile Delinquency." http://www.thecomicbooks.com/clendenen.html.

Covo-Maurice, Jacqueline. "Lecturas para el pueblo: Novelas mexicanas ilustradas." In *Prensa, Impresos, Lectura en el Mundo Hispánico Contemporáneo: Homenaje à Jean-François Botrel*, edited by Jean-Michel Desvois, 239–249. Pessac Cedex, France: PILAR, 2005.

Cowen, Tyler. *In Praise of Commercial Culture*. Cambridge, MA: Harvard University Press, 1998.

Crépin, Thierry. *Harro sur le Gangster! La Moralisation de la Presse Enfantine 1934–1954*. Paris: CNRS, 2001.

Crépin, Thierry, and Thierry Groensteen, eds. "*On tue à Chaque Page!" La Loi de 1949 sur les Publications Destinées à la Jeunesse*. Paris: Éditions du temps, 1999.

Cultures & Questions qui font débat. "Alix, une série culte de Jacques Martin." http://culture-et-debats.over-blog.com/20-categorie-92056.html.

Daly, Kristen. "Cinema 3.0: How Digital and Computer Technologies Are Changing Cinema." PhD diss., Columbia University, 2008.

Daniels, Les. *Comix: A History of Comic Books in America.* New York: Outerbridge and Dienstfrey, 1971.

———. *Wonder Woman: The Life and Times of the Amazon Princess.* San Francisco: Chronicle Books, 2000.

David, Peter. "When You Wish upon a Northstar." February 14, 1992. http://www.peterdavid.net/index.php/2004/11/23/when-you-wish-upon-northstar/.

Davis, Martin. *Engines of Logic: Mathematicians and the Origin of the Computer* . New York: Norton, 2001.

Delesse, Catherine, and Bertrand Richet. *Le Coq Gaulois à l ' Heure Anglaise: Analyse de la Traduction d ' Astérix.* Arras, France: Artois Presses Universitaires, 2009.

———. "Une histoire marquée par la suspicion." Interview by Jean-Michel Demetz. *L'Express*, June 22–28, 2011, 66–68.

Demetz, Jean-Michel. "Deux siècles d'amour vache." *L'Express* June 21–28, 2011, 58.

Derrida, Jacques. "Freud and the Scene of Writing." In *Writing and Difference*, translated by Alan Bass, 196–231. Chicago: University of Chicago Press, 1978.

———. *Of Grammatology.* Corrected edition. Translated by Gayatri Chakravorty Spivak. Baltimore: The Johns Hopkins University Press, 1997.

———. "Structure, Sign, and Play in the Discourse of the Human Sciences." In *Writing and Difference*, translated by Alan Bass, 278–94. Chicago: University of Chicago Press, 1978.

Dierick, Charles, ed. *Le Centre Belge de la Bande Dessinée.* Bruxelles, Belgium: Dexia, 2000.

Dinter, Martin T. "Francophone Romes: Antiquity in *Les Bandes Dessinées*." In George Kovacs and C. W. Marshall, edited by *Classics and Comics*, 183–92. New York: Oxford University Press, 2011.

Dittmer, Jason. *Projections of War: Hollywood, American Culture, and World War II.* New York: Columbia University Press, 1999.

Doherty, Thomas. "Art Spiegelman's *Maus*: Graphic Art and the Holocaust." *American Literature* 68, no. 1 (1996): 69–84.

Dorrell, Larry, Dan Curtis, and Kuldip Rampal. "Book-Worms without Books? Students Reading Comic Books in the School House." *Journal of Popular Culture* 2 (1995). http://0-gateway.proquest.com.wam.leeds.ac.uk/openurl?ctx_ver=Z39.88-2003&xri:pqil:res_ver=0.2&res_id=xri:lion&rft_id=xri:lion:ft:abell:R01288533:0.

———. "The Tyranny of the Serial: Popular Geopolitics, the Nation, and Comic Book Discourse." *Antipode* 39, no. 2 (2007): 247–68.

Douglas, Susan. *Where the Girls Are: Growing Up Female with the Mass Media.* New York: Three Rivers Press, 1994.

Dovetto, Joseph, and Raymond Roge. "La Croisade Contre les Albigeois dans la Bande Dessinée." *Histoire et Bande Dessinée, Supplément Bédésup* 10 (October 1979): 36.

Doxiadis, Apostolos. "Apostolos Doxiadis' *Logicomix*." Interview by Alex Fitch. *Panel Borders.* Resonance Radio London, December 3, 2009.

———. "Thales and Friends—Apostolos' Interview." *Thales + Friends.* http://www.thalesandfriends.org/en/index.php?option=com_content&task=view&id=48&Itemid=83&phpMyAdmin=rcOunTMVHvdSvjLzdNr45lZ-X09.ematics.

Doxiadis, Apostolos, Alecos Papadatos, and Annie Di Donna. "Exclusive Claude Lévi-Strauss Cartoon." *FT Magazine*, February 27, 2010. http://www.ft.com/intl/cms/s/2/5284373a-1f94-11df-8975-00144feab49a.html#axzz1i6RPblnw.

Doxiadis, Apostolos, and Christos Papadimitriou. "Bertrand Russell: Lover, Husband, Mathematician, and Comic Book Hero." Interview by Bill Casselman. *Notices of the American Mathematical Society* 57, no. 11 (2010): 1477–78.

Doxiadis, Apostolos, Christos Papadimitriou, Alecos Papadatos, and Annie di Donna. "Why (We) Write: A Modern Greek Tragi-Comedy." *Publishers Weekly*, December 21, 2009, 30–2.

———. *Logicomix: An Epic Search for Truth.* New York: Bloomsbury USA, 2009.

———. "Γιατί Γράφουμε: Μια Σύγχρονη Ελληνική Τραγι-κωμωδία." *Kappa (Kathimerini)* 342 (December 20, 2009): 32–34.

Drezner, Daniel. *Theory of International Politics and Zombies*. Princeton, NJ: Princeton University Press, 2001.

du Chatenet, Aymar, and Caroline Guillot. *Goscinny: Faire rire, quel métier!* Paris: Gallimard, 2009.

Duhamel, Alain. *Le Complexe d'Astérix*. Paris: Gallimard, 1985.

Dusseau, Brigitte. "Un accord financier confidentiel clôt l'affaire DSK à New York." *Public Sénat*, October 12, 2012. http://www.publicsenat.fr/lcp/politique/un-accord-financier-confidentiel-cl-t-laffaire-dsk-new-york-337715.

Eco, Umberto. "The Myth of Superman." Translated by Natalie Chilton. In *The Critical Tradition: Classic Texts and Contemporary Trends*, 2nd ed., edited by David H. Richter, 866–77. Boston: Bedford Books, 1998.

"Editorial." *New York Times*, January 24, 1992, A28.

Eerden, Bart. 2009. "Anger in *Astérix*: The Metaphorical Representation of Anger in Comics and Animated Films." In *Multimodal Metaphor*, edited by Charles J. Forceville and Eduardo Urios-Aparisi, 243–64. Berlin: Mouton de Gruyter, 2009.

Eisler, Benita. *Private Lives: Men and Women of the 1950s*. New York: Franklin Watts, 1986.

Eisner, Will. *Comics as Sequential Art*. Tamarac, FL: Poorhouse Press, 1985.

Elkana, Yehuda. "The Myth of Simplicity." In *Albert Einstein: Historical and Cultural Perspectives*, edited by Gerald Holton and Yehuda Elkana, 205–51. Princeton, NJ: Princeton University Press, 1982.

Emad, Mitra C. "Reading Wonder Woman's Body: Mythologies of Gender and Nation" *Journal of Popular Culture* 39, no. 6 (2006): 954–84.

"Émoi en France, Astérix fait la publicité de McDonald's." *LeDevoir*, August 20, 2010). http://www.ledevoir.com/culture/actualites-culturelles/294661/emoi-en-france-asterix-fait-la-publicite-de-mcdonald-s.

*The Encyclopedia of Comic Book Superheroes*. Vol. 2. Edited by Michael Fleisher. New York: Macmillan, 1976.

Engelhardt, Tom. *The End of Victory Culture*. Amherst: University of Massachusetts Press, 1995.

Eubanks, Adelheid R. "Logicomix: From Text to Image / From Logic to Story." *The Comparatist* 35 (2011): 182–97.

"Exhibitions: Luis A. Jimenez." Plains Art Musuem. http://plainsart.org/exhibits/the-white-album-the-beatles-meet-the-plains/barfly/.

Faludi, Susan. *Stiffed: The Betrayal of the American Man*. New York: Perennial, 2000.

Faur, Jean Claude. "Bande Dessinée ou Histoire? Caligula dans l'Imagerie Populaire." In *Histoire et Bande Dessinée, Supplément Bédésup* 10 (October 1979): 17–25.

Feuerhahn, Nelly. "Astérix et les pirates: Une Esthétique du naufrage pour rire." *Ethnologie Française: Revue Trimestrielle de la Société d'Ethnologie Française* 28, no. 3 (1998): 337–49.

Filippini, Henri. "Les quatre vies de Lucky Luke." *dBD*, Novembre 2009, 32–36.

Filippini, Henri, et al. *Histoire de la Bande Dessinée en France et en Belgique*. Grenoble, France: Glénat, 1984.

Flora, Cornelia Butler. "Roasting Donald Duck: Alternative Comics and Photonovels in Latin America." *Journal of Popular Culture* 18 (summer 1984): 163–183.

Forceville, Charles. "Visual Representations of the Idealized Cognitive Model of Anger in the Astérix Album *La Zizanie*." *Journal of Pragmatics: An Interdisciplinary Journal of Language Studies* 37, no. 1 (2005): 69–88.

Foucault, Michel. *Discipline and Punish: The Birth of Prison*. Translated by Alan Sheridan. New York: Vintage, 1995.

———. *The History of Sexuality*. Vol. 1, *An Introduction*. Translated by Robert Hurley. New York: Random House, 1990.

———. "Truth and Power." In *Power/Knowledge: Selected Interviews and Other Writings, 1972–1977*, edited by Colin Gordon, 109–33. London: Vintage, 1980.

Freidan, Betty. *The Feminine Mystique: Twentieth Anniversary Edition*. New York: Dell, 1983.

Frémon, Yves. "La colonne trajanne, une BD de Pierre." La rubrique en trop, January 15, 2011. http://www.cablechronicles.com/wp-content/uploads/2011/01/La-colonne-Trajanne-article.png.

Frevert, Ute, and Anne Schmidt. "Geschichte, Emotionen und die Macht der Bilder." *Geschichte und Gesellschaft* 37, no. 1 (2011): 5–25.

Fuller, Graham. "Colour Me Noir." *Sight & Sound* 15, no. 6 (2005): 12–16.

Furey, Emmett. "Homosexuality in Comics, Part II." *Comic Book Resources News*, July 17, 2007. http://www.comicbookresources.com/?page=article&id=10809.

———. "Homosexuality in Comics, Part IV." *Comic Book Resources News*, July 19, 2007. http://www.comicbookresources.com/?page=article&id=10809.

Gaudreault, André. *Du littéraire au filmique*. Paris: Nota Bene, 2005.

Genette, Gerard. "Frontiers of Narrative." In *Figures of Literary Discourse*, translated by Alan Sheridan, 127–44. New York: Columbia University Press, 1982.

———. *Narrative Discourse: An Essay in Method*. Translated by Jane E. Lewin. Ithaca, NY: Cornell University Press, 1980.

Gerstle, Gary. "Pluralism and the War on Terror." *Dissent Magazine*, spring 2003. http://www.dissentmagazine.org/article/?article=502.

Gianopulos, James. "Hellenism and Hollywood: From Aristotle to Alexander (Payne)." Lecture given as part of the "Great Ideas" talk series of the Stavros Niarchos Foundation, Athens Megaron Hall, Greece, November 25, 2009.

Goggin, Peter. "Review: *Sin City Volumes 1–4: The Hard Goodbye; A Dame to Kill For; The Big Fat Kill; That Yellow Bastard*." *Journal of Adolescent and Adult Literacy* 49, no. 5 (2006): 446–48.

Gould, Chester. *The Dick Tracy Casebook: Favorite Adventures, 1931–1990*. Edited by Max Allan Collins and Dick Locher. New York: St. Martin's Press, 1990.

Goscinny, René, and Albert Uderzo. *Astérix and the Golden Sickle*. Translated by Anthea Bell and Derek Hockridge. Vol. 2 of *Astérix*. London: Hodder & Stoughton, 1975.

———. *Astérix and the Great Crossing*. Translated by Anthea Bell and Derek Hockbridge. Vol. 22 of *Astérix*. London: Hodder & Stoughton, 1976.

———. *Astérix le gaulois*. 6th ed. Vol. 1 of *Astérix*. Paris: Hachette, 1999.

———. *La grande traversée*. 6th ed. Vol. 22 of *Astérix*. Paris: Hachette, 1999.

———. *La serpe d'or*. Vol. 2 of *Astérix*. Neuilly-sur-Seine, France: Dargaud, 1962.

Grafstein, Robert. "The Significance of Modern State of Nature Theory." *Polity* 19, no. 4 (1987): 529–50.

Griswold, Robert L. *Fatherhood in America: A History*. New York: Basic Books, 1993.

Groensteen, Thierry. *La Bande Dessinée en France*. Paris: adf, 1998.

———. *La Bande Dessinée, Mode d'emploi*. Bruxelles, Belgium: Les impressions nouvelles, 2007.

———. *The System of Comics*. Jackson: University of Mississippi Press, 2007.

Gronsky, Daniel Gaines Edward. "Frame to Frame: A Historical Analysis of the Evolution and Propagation of the Comic Book Film." PhD diss., University of Connecticut, 2008.

Guadalupe Jiménez Codinach, Estela. "Historia e Historieta Episodios Mexicanos." In *Los Intelectuales y el Poder en México: Memorias de la VI Conferencia de Historiadores Mexicanos y Estadounidenses . Intellectuals and Power in Mexico: Papers Presented at the VI Conference of Mexican and Unites States Historians*, edited by Roderic Ai Camp, Charles A. Hale, and Josefina Zoraida Vásquez, 781–94. Mexico City: El Colegio de México; Los Angeles: UCLA Latín American Center, 1981.

———. Interview by Melanie Huska, digital recording, Mexico City, Mexico, July 20, 2005.

Gustav-Wrathall, John Donald. *Take the Young Stranger by the Hand: Same-Sex Relations and the YMCA*. Chicago: University of Chicago, 1998.

Gustines, George. "Straight (and Not) Out of the Comics." *New York Times*, May 28, 2006.

Hajdu, David. *The Ten-Cent Plague: The Great Comic-Book Scare and How It Changed America*. New York: Farrar, Straus and Giroux, 2008.

Halberstam, David. *The Fifties*. New York: Random House, 1993.

Hampton, Jean. "The Failure of Hobbes's Social Contract Argument." In *The Social Contract Theorists: Critical Essays on Hobbes, Locke, and Rousseau*, edited by Chisrtopher Morris, 1–22. Lanham, MD: Rowman & Littlefield, 1999.

Hartman, Susan M. *The Home Front and Beyond: American Women in the 1940s*. Boston: Twayne, 1982.

Hayes, Joy Elizabeth. "National Imaginings on the Air: Radio in Mexico, 1920–1950." In *The Eagle and the Virgin: Nation and Cultural Revolution in Mexico, 1920–1940*, edited by Mary Kay Vaughan and Stephen E. Lewis. Duke University Press Books, 2006.

———. *Radio Nation: Communication, Popular Culture, and Nationalism in Mexico, 1920–1950*. Tucson: University of Arizona Press, 2000.

Heller, Dana A. "Memory's Architecture: American Studies and the Graphic Novels of Art Spiegelman." In *Teaching the Graphic Novel*, ed. Stephen E. Tabachnick, 155–62. New York: MLA, 2009.

Heller, Mark. "The Use and Abuse of Hobbes: The State of Nature in International Relations." *Polity* 13, no. 1 (1980): 21–32.

Helper, Allison. "'And We Want Steel Toes Like the Men': Gender and Occupational Health During World War II." *Bulletin of the History of Medicine* 72, no. 4 (1998): 689–713.

Herman, David. "Multimodal Storytelling and Identity Construction in Graphic Narratives." In *Telling Stories: Language, Narrative, and Social Life*, ed. Deborah Schiffrin, 195–208. Washington, DC: Georgetown University Press, 2008.

Herner, Irene. Interview by Melanie Huska, Mexico City, Mexico, November 19, 2009.

Herner de Larrea, Irene. *Mitos y Monitos: Historietas y Fotonovelas en Mexico*. Mexico City, Mexico: Editorial Nueva Imagen, 1979.

Higson, Andrew. "Representing the National Past: Nostalgia and Pastiche in the heritage Film." In *Fires Were Started: British Cinema and Thatcherism*, 2nd ed., edited by Lester D. Friedman, 91–109. London: Wallflower, 2006.

Hilbish, D. Melissa. "Advancing in Another Direction: The Comic Book and the Korean War." *War, Literature and the Arts: an International Journal of the Humanities* 11, no. 1 (1999): 209–27.

Hinds, Harold E., and Charles M. Tatum. *Not Just for Children: The Mexican Comic Book in the Late 1960s and 1970s*. Santa Barbara, CA: Greenwood Press, 1992.

Ho, Elizabeth. "Postimperial Landscapes: 'Psychogeography' and Englishness in Alan Moore's Graphic Novel *From Hell: A Melodrama in Sixteen Parts*." *Cultural Critique* 63 (spring 2006): 99–121.

Hodges, Rachel. "*Sin City* Takes Film Noir to the Depths of Mediocrity." *Static and Feedback: Movies*. http://www.staticandfeedback.com/Movies/0105sinr.html.

Holt, Jim. "Sunday Book Review: Algorithms and Blues." *New York Times*, September 27, 2009, BR14.

Honey, Maureen. *Creating Rosie the Riveter: Class, Gender, and Propaganda during World War II*. Amherst: University of Massachusetts Press, 1984.

Hoppenstand, Gary . "Pulp Vigilante Heroes, the Moral Majority and the Apocalypse." *Twentieth-Century Literary Criticism* 214 (2009).

Horkheimer, Max, and Theodor Adorno. *Dialectic of Enlightenment: Philosophical Fragments*. Translated by Edmund Jephcott. Edited by Gunzelin Schmid Noerr. Palo Alto, CA: Stanford University Press, 2002.

Humansïdes Associés. "Ce Que Cachent Les Abysses . . . Cathago." http://www.bedetheque.com/serie-3850–BD-Histoire-de-France-en-bandes-dessinees.html.

Huyssen, Andreas. "Of Mice and Mimesis: Reading Spiegelman with Adorno." *New German Critique* 81 (Autumn 2000): 65–82.

Isaac, Jules. *Histoire de France*. Paris: Hachette, 1922.

Jensen, Jeff. "Spring Movie Preview: *Sin City*." *Entertainment Weekly* 807 (February 14, 2005). http://www.ew.com/ew/article/0,,1026704,00.html.

Johnson, Brian D. "Hard-Boiled Burlesque." *MacLean's*, April 4, 2005, 50–52.

Jones, Gerard. *Men of Tomorrow: Geeks, Gangsters, and the Birth of the Comic Book*. New York: Basic Books, 2005.

Jones, Matthew T. "Found in Translation: Structural and Cognitive Aspects of the Comic Art to Film." PhD diss., Temple University, 2008.

Juneau, Thomas, and Mira Sucharov. "Narratives in Pencil: Using Graphic Novels to Teach Israeli-Palestinian Relations." *International Studies Perspectives* 11, no. 2 (2010): 172–83.

Kaminski, Matthew. "DSK's Fall from Grace." *Wall Street Journal*, November 1, 2011, A17.

Kaplan, Morton A. "How Sovereign Is Hobbes' Sovereign?" *Political Research Quarterly* 9, no. 2 (1956): 389–405.

Karaboudjan, Laureline. "Astérix vaut-il mieux qu'un Big Mac?" *Des bulles carrées: Le blog BD de Laureline Karaboudjan*, August 17, 2010. http://blog.slate.fr/des-bulles-carrees/2010/08/17/asterix-vaut-il-mieux-quun-big-mac/.

Karon, Tony. "Why Courts Don't Deter France's Anti-McDonald's 'Astérix.'" *Time*, February 15, 2001. http://www.time.com/time/world/article/0,8599,99592,00.html.

Kauffman, Judith. "Astérix: Les Jeux de l'humour et du temps." *Ethnologie Française: Revue Trimestrielle de la Société d'Ethnologie Française* 28, no. 3 (1998): 327–36.

Kavka, Gregory. "Hobbes's War of All against All." In *The Social Contract Theorists: Critical Essays on Hobbes, Locke, and Rousseau*, edited by Christopher Morris, 1–22. Lanham, MD: Rowman & Littlefield, 1999.

Keegan, Rebecca Winters. "Batman's Half Brothers." *Time* 171, no. 26 (June 30, 2008).

Kessler-Harris, Alice. *Out to Work: A History of Wage Earning Women in the United States*. Oxford, England: Oxford University Press, 1982.

Kincheloe, Joe L. *The Sign of the Burger: McDonald's and the Culture of Power*. Philadelphia: Temple University Press, 2002.

Knulst, Wim, and Andries van den Broek. "The Readership of Books in Times of Dereading." *Poetics* 31 (2003): 213–33.

Kroker, Arthur. *SPASM: Virtual Reality, Android Music and Electric Flesh*. New York: St. Martin's Press, 1993.

Kroker, Arthur, and Marylouise Kroker. *Critical Digital Studies: A Reader*. Toronto: University of Toronto Press, 2008.

Kuhn, Betsy. *Angels of Mercy: The Army Nurses of World War II*. New York: Antheneum Books, 1999.

Lacoste, Jean Hervé. "Les Maîtres du Château de Bonaguil et Leurs Problèmes." *Histoire et Bande Dessinée, Supplément Bédésup* 10 (October 1979): 44–50.

"La Cultura de la Imagen." Parte III. *Gaceta UNAM*, 12.

Lavin, Michael R. "A Librarian's Guide to Dark Horse Comics." *Serials Review* 24, nos. 3–4 (1998): 76–94.

Lefèvre, Jean-Philippe. "Spéciale Albert Uderzo, le dernier des géants." In *Un Monde de Bulles*, 29 minutes, July 14, /2011. http://www.publicsenat.fr/vod/un-monde-de-bulles/speciale-albert-uderzo,-le-dernier-des-geants/69227.

Lefort, Gérard and Mathieu Lindon. "Jacques Martin classé Alix." *Libération*, September 5, 1996. http://www.liberation.fr/livres.0101192729–jacques-martin-classe-alix.

Lenner, Lorry. "Introduction to the Letters." In *An Officer and a Lady: The World War II Letters of Lt. Col. Betty Bandel, Women's Army Corps*, edited by Sylvia J. Bugbee. Lebanon: University Press of New England, 2005.

Lent, John A, ed. *Pulp Demons: International Dimensions of the Postwar Anti-comics Campaign*. Madison, WI: Farleigh Dickinson Press, 1999.

"Le Tandem Alix/Enak et la Rumeur de l'Homosexualité: un Duo Libre, Fier et Esthétiquement Réussi." Le Site Non-Officiel d'Alix l'Intrépide. http://www.tcomt.fr/Sitealix/Dossiers/07Interview/interview04.html.

Levard, Olivier. "Publicité pour Mac Do: Astérix se défend." *MYTF1News*, August 18, 2010. http://lci.tf1.fr/economie/entreprise/2010-08/publicite-pour-mac-do-asterix-se-defend-6040857.html.

Lindenmeyer, Kristie. *The Greatest Generation Grows Up: American Childhood in the 1930s*. Chicago: Ivan R. Dee, 2005.

Lindon, Mathieu. "Alix hic et nunc." *Libération*, December 19, 2002. http://www.liberation.fr/livres/0101434651-alix-hic-et-nunc.

"Lorg: 'Gringos Locos, c'était du caviar et on nous a servi du poisson pané.'" Interview with Laurent Gillain. *Expressbd*, January 18, 2012. http://expressbd.fr/2012/01/18/lorg-gringos-locos-c-etait-du-caviar-et-on-nous-a-servi-du-poisson-pane/.

Loyo, Engracia. "Popular Reactions to the Educational Reforms of Cardenismo." In *Rituals of Rule, Rituals of Resistance: Public Celebrations and Popular Culture in Mexico*, edited by William H. Beezley, Cheryl English Martin, and William E. French, 247–60. Wilmington, DE: Scholarly Resources, 1994.

MacDonald, Heidi. "Miller's Double Noir: 'Sin City' and 'Batman Begins.'" *Publishers Weekly*, March 7, 2005, 40–43.

Macpherson, Crawford Brough. *The Political Theory of Possessive Individualism*. 8th ed. Oxford, England: Oxford University Press, 1979.

Maguet, Frédéric. "Astérix, un mythe? Mythogénèse et amplification d'un stéréotype culturel." *Ethnologie Française: Revue Trimestrielle de la Société d'Ethnologie Française* 28, no. 3 (1998): 317–26.

Maier, Charlotte. *Weiter-höher-schneller, Verkehrsgeschichte auf Marken und Medaillen*. Munich: Deutsches Museum, 1987.

Mancosu, Paolo. "Book Review: Logicomix by Apostolos Doxiadis, Christos H. Papadimitriou, Alecos Papadatos, and Annie di Donna." *Journal of Humanistic Mathematics* 1, no. 1: 137–52.

———. "[Review of *Logicomix*, by A. Doxiadis, C. Papadimitriou, A. Papadatos, and A. di Donna]." *Bulletin of Symbolic Logic* 16, no. 3 (2010): 419–20.

Marchetto, Marisa Acocella. *Cancer Vixen*. New York: Knopf, 2006.

Marin, Louis. *Utopics: Spatial Play*. Translated by Robert A. Vollrath. Atlantic Highlands, NJ: Humanities, 1984.

Marling, Karal Ann. *As Seen on TV*. Cambridge, MA: Harvard University Press, 1994.

Martin, Elaine. "Graphic Novels or Novel Graphics? The Evolution of an Iconoclastic Genre." *The Comparatist* 35 (May 2011): 170–81.

May, Elaine Tyler. *Homeward Bound: American Families in the Cold War Era*. New York: Basic Books, 2008.

Maza, Miriam Martínez, Jorge Tlatelpa Meléndez, and David Zamora Díaz. *Las Historietas en Las Colecciones de Las Bibliotecas Publicas Mexicanas*. Mexico City, Mexico: Colegio Nacional de Bibliotecarios y Universidad Autónoma de Baja California Sur, 1993.

McAllister, Matthew P., Edward H. Sewell Jr., and Ian Gordon, eds. *Comics and Ideology*. New York: Lang, 2001.

McCarthy, Todd. "Reviews: Through a Toon Darkly." *Variety*, March 28, 2005.

McClintock, Anne. *Imperial Leather: Race, Gender, and Sexuality in the Colonial Conquest*. New York: Routledge, 1995.

McCloud, Scott. *Understanding Comics: The Invisible Art*. New York: Kitchen Sink Press, 1993.

McDevitte, W. A., and W. S. Bohn, trans. The Gallic Wars: Julius Caesar's Account of the Roman Conquest of the Gauls . CreateSpace, 2012.

"McDonald's Takes on Astérix." *BBC News*, December 20, 2001. http://news.bbc.co.uk/2/hi/entertainment/1721029.stm.

McKenzie, Alexander J. "Group Dynamics in the State of Nature." *Erkenntnis* 55, no. 2 (2001): 169–82.

"Mejor Reparto de los Bienes Culturales." *El Informador* (Guanajuato), June 20, 1980, 3A.

Mendelsohn, Daniel. "Why She Fell. Review of *Spider-Man: Turn Off the Dark*." *New York Review of Books*, May 12, 2011.

Meskin, Aaron. "Comics as Literature?" *British Journal of Aesthetics* 49, no. 3 (2009): 219–39.

Micciche, Laura R. "Seeing and Reading Incest: A Study of Debbie Drechsler's 'Daddy's Girl.'" *Rhetoric Review* 23, no. 1 (2004): 5–20.

Miller, Ann. *Reading Bandes Dessinées: Critical Approaches to French Language Comic Strip.* Chicago: University of Chicago Press, 2007.

Minery, Jean-Frédéric. "La BD et les villes de France et DOM/TOM." http://www.bedetheque.com/serie-13296–BD-Histoire-des-villes-Collection.html.

Ministère de l'Éducation Nationale. *Les Bandes Dessinées: Histoire, Langage, Mythes.* Bordeaux, France: CRDP, 1978.

Mirzoeff, Nicholas. *An Introduction to Visual Culture.* 2nd ed. London: Routledge, 2009.

Mitterrand, Odette, and Giles Ciment, eds. *L'histoire . . . par la Bande. Bande Dessinée, Histoire et Pédagogie.* Paris, Syros, 1993.

Molesworth, William, ed. *Leviathan, or the Matter, Form, and Power of a Commonwealth Ecclesiastical and Civil.* Vol. 3 of *The English Works of Thomas Hobbes of Malmesbury.* London: Scientia Verlag Aalen, 1966.

Moore, Alan. *The Watchmen.* New York: DC Comics, 1986–1987.

*New Original Wonder Woman.* "The Man Who Could Move the World." Video, 46:17, 1977. http://www.thewb.com/shows/wonder-woman/the-man-who-could-move-the-world/fef55001-89f5-42ea-8dff-37225ab9c8f9.

*New Original Wonder Woman.* "Pilot: The New Original Wonder Woman." Video, 70:53, 1976. http://www.thewb.com/shows/wonder-woman/pilot-the-new-original-wonder-woman/b6dad16f-4e16-41f0-8534-590f88ef6c44.

Newman, Kim. "*Sin City* Review." *Sight & Sound* (June 2005): 72.

Nora, Pierre. "Between Memory and History." In *Realms of Memory,* edited by Lawrence D. Kritzman, translated by Arthur Goldhammer, 1–20. New York: Columbia University Press, 1996.

Nyberg, Amy Kiste. *Seal of Approval: The History of the Comics Code.* Jackson: University of Mississippi Press, 1998.

Olivès, Michel. "Jacques Martin, le créateur d'Alix, est mort." *Têtu,* January, 22, 2011. http://www.tetu.com.actualites/culture/jacques-martin-le-createur-dalix-est-mort-16373.

Onuf, Nicholas. *World of Our Making: Rules and Rule in Social Theory and International Relations.* Columbia: University of South Carolina Press, 1989.

Oremus, Will. "The Crisis in a Nutshell: 'A Rutting Chimpanzee.'" May 17, 2011. http://www.newyorker.com/online/blogs/newsdesk/2011/05/the-crisis-in-a-nutshell-a-rutting-chimpanzee.html.

Ory, Pascal. "Historique ou historienne?" In *L'Histoire . . . la Bande. Bande dessinée, Histoire et Pédagogie,* edited by Odette Mitterrand and Giles Ciment, 96. Paris: Syros, 1993.

Palagret, Catherine-Alice. "Publicité comparative: Avantage au parc Astérix face à Disneyland." *Archéologie du futur / Archéologie du quotidien.* July 23, 2011. http://archeologue.over-blog.com/article-publicite-comparative-avantage-au-parc-asterix-face-a-disneyland-80043470.html.

Parker, Martin. "Nostalgia and Mass Culture: McDonaldization and Cultural Elitism." In *McDonaldization Revisited: Critical Essays on Consumer Culture,* edited by Mark Alfino, John S. Caputo, and Robin Wynyard, 1–18. Westport, CT: Praeger, 1998.

Pasamonik, Didier. "C'est officiel: Didier Conrad est le prochain dessinateur d'Astérix." *Actua BD,* November 10, 2012. http://www.actuabd.com/C-est-officiel-Didier-Conrad-est.

Peeters, Benoît. *Lire la Bande Bessinée.* Barcelona: Novoprint, 1998.

Perez, Damien. "Bienvenido a los gringos!" Interview with Yann. *Spirou,* November 30, 2011, 4.

———. "Voyage en air de famille." Interview with Wilbur and Conrad. *Spirou,* April 25, 2012, 4.

Perrout, René. *Trésors des Images d'Epinal.* 1912. Strasbourg, France: Gyss, 1985.

Pinet, Christopher. "Astérix, Brassens, and Cabu: The ABC's of Popular Culture." In *Popular Traditions and Learned Culture in France: From the Sixteenth to the Twentieth Century*, edited by Bertrand, Marc, 275–86. Saratoga, CA: Anma Libri, 1985.

Piquard, Michèle. "La Loi Du 16 Juillet 1949 et la Production De Livres Et Albums Pour la Jeunesse." In *L'Image Pour Enfants: Pratiques, Normes, Discours*, edited by Annie Renonciat, 219–35. Rennes, France: PUR/La licorne, 2007.

Pizzino, Christopher. "Art That Goes Boom: Genre and Aesthetics in Frank Miller's 'Sin City.'" *English Language Notes* 46, no. 2 (2008): 115–28.

Poirier, Agnes. "Le Scandale DSK: The Accusation That Dominique Strauss-Kahn Sexually Assaulted a Maid Has Launched a Wave of Soul-Searching among the French Political Class." *Toronto Star*, May 19, 2011, A27.

Porret, Michel, ed. *Objectif Bulles: Bande Dessinée et Histoire*. Geneva: Georg, 2009.

Ratier, Gilles. *Avant la Case: Histoire de la Bande Dessinée Francophone du XXe Siècle Racontée par les Scenarists*. Sangam, 2005.

"Raymond Poivet." *Office de Tourism du Chambresis*. http://www.tourisme-lecateau.fr/page-10102-raymond-poivet.html.

Reisman, David. *The Lonely Crowd*. New Haven, CT: Yale University Press, 1950.

Reitberger, Reinhold, and Wolfgang Fuchs. *Comics: Anatomy of a Mass Medium*. Boston: Little, Brown, 1970.

Renonciat, Annie, ed. *L'image pour Enfants: Pratiques, Normes, Discours*. Rennes, France: PUR/La licorne, 2007.

Rhoades, Shirrel. *A Complete History of American Comic Books*. New York: Lang, 2008.

Riley, John. "DSK Gets Passport Returned." *Newsday*, August 26, 2011, A18.

Ritzer, George. "An Introduction to McDonaldization." In *McDonaldization: The Reader*, edited by George Ritzer, 4–24. Thousand Oaks, CA: Pine Forge Press, 2006.

Rizzo, Johanna. "ZAP! POW! BAM!" *Humanities* 27, no. 4 (2006): 28–29.

Robinson, Lillian S. *Wonder Woman: Feminisms and Superheroes*. New York: Routledge, 2004.

Rochfort, Desmond. *Mexican Muralists: Orozco, Rivera, Siqueiros*. San Francisco: Chronicle Books, 1993.

———. "The Sickle, the Serpent, and the Soil: History, Revolution, Nationhood, and Modernity in the Murals of Diego Rivera, José Clemente Orozco, and David Alfaro Siqueiros." In *The Eagle and the Virgin: Nation and Cultural Revolution in Mexico, 1920–1940*, edited by Mary Kay Vaughan and Stephen E. Lewis, 43–57. Durham, NC: Duke University Press, 2006.

Rodowick, David Norman. *Giles Deleuze: Time Machine, Post-contemporary Interventions*. Durham, NC: Duke University Press, 1997.

———. "Review: The Figure and the Text." *Diacritics* 15, no. 1 (1985): 32–50.

Roffat, Sébastien. *Disney et la France: Les Vingt ans d'Euro Disneyland*. Paris: Editions L'Harmattan, 2007.

Rose, Lloyd. "Comic Books for Grown-Ups." *Atlantic* 258, no. 2 (2004): 77–80.

Ross, Andrew. *No Respect: Intellectuals and Pop Culture*. New York: Routledge, 1989.

Rota, Gian-Carlo. *Indiscrete Thoughts*. Edited by Fabrizio Palombi. Boston: Birkhäuser, 1997.

Rouvière, Nicolas. "Astérix et les Pirates ou l'Obsession Que le Pire Rate: La Conjuration d'un Naufrage de l'Histoire." In *Témoignages de l'Après-Auschwitz dans la Littérature Juive-Française d'Aujourd'hui: Enfants de Survivants et Survivants-Enfants*, edited by Annelise Schulte, 151–68. Amsterdam: Schulte Nordholt, 2011.

———. *Astérix ou les lumières de la civilisation*. Paris: Presses Universitaires de France, 2006.

Rubenstein, Anne. *Bad Language, Naked Ladies, and Other Threats to the Nation: A Political History of Comic Books in Mexico*. Durham, NC: Duke University Press, 1998.

———. Personal communication with Melanie Huska, July 2005.

Samuel, Henry. "Quelle Horreur! Astérix Surrenders to McDonald's." *The Telegraph*, August 18, 2010. http://www.telegraph.co.uk/news/worldnews/europe/france/7952441/Quelle-horreur-Asterix-surrenders-to-McDonalds.html.

Samuels, Maurice. *The Spectacular Past: Popular History and the Novel in Nineteenth Century France*. Ithaca, NY: Cornell University Press, 2004.

Schlund-Vials, Cathy J. "Crisis of Memory: Memorializing 9/11 in the Comic Book Universe." *Modern Language Studies* 41, no.1 (2011): 12–25.

Schwarzbaum, Lisa. "Frankly Speaking." *Entertainment Weekly* 814 (April 8, 2005).

Screech, Matthew. "A Hero for Everyone: René Goscinny's and Albert Uderzo's Astérix the Gaul." In *Masters of the Ninth Art: Bandes Dessinées and Franco-Belgian Identity*, 75–94. Liverpool, England: Liverpool University Press, 2005.

———. *Masters of the Ninth Art: Bandes Dessinées and Franco-Belgian Identity*. Liverpool, England: Liverpool University Press, 2005.

Seltzer, Mark. "The Graphic Unconscious: A Response." *New Literary History* 26, no. 1 (1995): 21–28.

Skidmore, Max J., and Joey Skidmore. "More Than Mere Fantasy: Political Themes in Contemporary Comic Books." *Journal of Popular Culture* 17, no. 1 (1983): 83–92.

Slotkin, Richard. *Gunfighter Nation: The Myth of the Frontier in Twentieth-Century America*. New York: Harper Perennial, 1992.

Smith, Benjamin. "Spandex Cinema: Three Approaches to Comic Book Film Adaptation." MA thesis, University of Central Oklahoma, 2009.

Sofge, Erik. "In Defense of *Hulk* (Yes, the Ang Lee One)." *Slate*, June 17, 2008. http://www.slate.com/id/2193478/.

Spiegelman, Art. *In the Shadow of No Towers*. New York: Pantheon, 2004.

———. *Tijuana Bibles: Art and Wit in America's Forbidden Funnies, 1930s–1950s*. New York: Simon & Schuster, 1997.

Sringhall, John. "Horror Comics: The Nasties of the 1950s." *History Today* 44, no. 7 (1994): 10–13.

Stamp, Shelly. *Movie-Struck Girls: Women and the Motion Picture Culture after the Nickelodeon*. Princeton, NJ: Princeton University Press, 2000.

Steinem, Gloria. "Introduction." In *Wonder Woman*. New York: Holt, Rinehart and Winston, 1972.

———. "Introduction." In *Wonder Woman: Featuring Over Five Decades of Great Covers*, edited by Amy Handy and Steven Korté. New York: Abbeville Press, 1995.

Stéphany, Pierre. *Histoire de la Belgique au Fil de la BD de 1830 à Nos Jours*. Bruxelles, Belgium: Versant Sud, 2005.

Stoll, Andreas. *Astérix ou l'épopée Burlesque de la France*. Paris: Presses Universitaires de France, 1978.

Sultan, Abdul, and Partha Sengupta. *The Believers*. New Delhi: Phantomville, 2006.

Szasz, Ferenc M., and Issei Takechi. "Atomic Heroes and Atomic Monsters: American and Japanese Cartoonists Confront the Onset of the Nuclear Age, 1945–80." *Historian* 69, no. 4 (2007): 728–52.

Tabachnick, Stephen E. "The Graphic Novel and the Age of Transition: A Survey and Analysis." *English Literature in Transition, 1880–1920* 53, no. 1 (2010): 3–28.

Tomblin, Barbara Brooks. *GI Nightingales: The Army Nurse Corps in World War II*. Lexington: University Press of Kentucky, 2003.

Torres, Alissa. *American Widow*. Illustrated by Sungyoon Choi. New York: Villard, 2008.

Uderzo, Albert. *Astérix and the Falling Sky*. Translated by Anthea Bell and Derek Hockridge. Vol. 33 of *Astérix*. London: Orion Books, 2006.

———. *Le ciel lui tombe sur la tête*. Vol. 33 of *Astérix*. Paris: Albert René, 2005.

———. *Uderzo se raconte*: Stock, 2008.

Vanderwood, Paul J. *The Power of God against the Guns of Government: Religious Upheaval in Mexico at the Turn of the Nineteenth Century*. Stanford, CA: Stanford University Press, 1998.

Varma, Pavan K. *The Great Indian Middle Class*. New Delhi: Penguin Books, 1998.

Vaughan, Mary K. *Cultural Politics in Revolution: Teachers, Peasants, and Schools in Mexico, 1930–1940*. Tuscon: University of Arizona Press, 1997.

Verdaguer, Pierre. "Le Héros national et ses dédoublements dans San-Antonio et Astérix." *French Review* 61, no. 4 (1988): 605–14.

Vessels, Joel. *Drawing France: French Comics and the Republic.* Jackson: University of Mississippi Press, 2010.

Vidal, Albert Barrera. "Les Relations Franco-Allemandes dans la BD D'Expression Francaise, ou L'Histoire Revue et Non Corrigée." *Histoire et Bande Dessinée, Supplément Bédésup* 10 (October 1979): 86–94.

Vidal, Guy, Anne Goscinny, and Patrick Gaumer. *René Goscinny: Profession. Humoriste.* Paris: Dargaud, 2007.

Vines, Lois Davis. "Teaching Belgian Cultural Connections with Astérix." *French Review: Journal of the American Association of Teachers of French* 81, no. 6 (2008): 1224–38.

Walker, Nancy. *Shaping Our Mothers' World: American Women's Magazines.* Jackson: University Press of Mississippi, 2000.

Weatherford, Doris. *American Women and World War II.* New York: Facts on File, 1990.

Whimster, Sam. *The Essential Weber: A Reader.* London: Routledge, 2004.

White, Hayden. "Introduction: Historical Fiction, Fictional History, and Historical Reality." *Rethinking History* 9, nos. 2/3 (2005): 147–57.

———. "The Question of Narrative in Contemporary Historical Theory." *History and Theory* 23, no. 3 (1984): 1–33.

Whitehead, Alfred North. *Science and the Modern World: Lowell Lectures, 1925.* New York: MacMillan Press, 1925.

Whyte, William H. *The Organization Man.* New York: Simon & Schuster, 1956.

Wilkie, J., et al., eds. *Statistical Abstract of Latin America.* 38 vols. Los Angeles: UCLA Latin American Center Publications, 1962–2002.

Wilson, Sloan. *The Man in the Gray Flannel Suit.* New York: Simon & Schuster, 1955.

Witek, Joseph. *Comic Books as History: The Narrative Art of Jack Johnson, Art Spiegelman and Harvey Pekar.* Oxford: University of Mississippi Press, 1989.

Wolk, Douglas. *Reading Comics: How Graphic Novels Work and What They Mean.* Philadelphia: Da Capo Press, 2007.

Wood, Aylish. "Pixel Visions: Digital Intermediates and Micromanipulations of the Image." *Film Criticism* 32, no. 1 (2007): 72–94.

Wright, Bradford. *Comic-Book Nation: The Transformation of Youth Culture in America.* New York: The Johns Hopkins University Press, 2003.

Wright, G. N. *The Rhine, Italy, and Greece.* London: Fisher.

Zach, Richard. "Logic and Madness." *Logblog,* September 30, 2009. http://www.ucalgary.ca/rzach/blog/2009/09/logic-and-madness.html.

Zukin, Sharon. *The Cultures of Cities.* Oxford, England: Blackwell,1996.

Zunshine, Lisa. "What to Expect When You Pick Up a Graphic Novel." *SubStance* 40, no. 1 (2011): 114–34.

# Index

# About the Contributors

**Annessa Ann Babic,** PhD, is revising her next work—a full-length manuscript ("Undoing Glory: Gendered Constructions of Patriotism in Twentieth Century U.S. Society, 1917–1972"). Some recent works, of many, include "What Lies Beneath: Jasper Johns' Flag (1954–1955) as a Mirror for the Changing Face of Postwar Patriotism," in *The Theme of Cultural Adaptation in American History, Literature and Film: Cases When the Discourse Changed* (2009), and "Eastern Eyes for Western Goods, Western Eyes for Eastern Markets: Consumer Goods, Popular Culture, and National Identity," in *The Transnational Turn in American Studies: Turkey and the United States* (2012). Also, "Wandering Eyes for Turkish Delights upon an Asian and Middle Eastern Axis: Cultural and Travel Appeals for Turkey" is set for publication in *Asia and West*. Additionally, she is the recipient of numerous grants and fellowships and a two-time teaching fellow. She has published on topics as varied as terrorism in the post–September 11 age to American patriotism and has presented at conferences outside her field and around the globe. In addition to academic pieces, she has contributed to *Lupus Now* (a magazine for Lupus patients and those seeking material on the disease) and *The Lupus Magazine.*

**Henri-Simon Blanc -Hoàng,** PhD, began his teaching career in 1994 and since 2007 has taught Spanish, French, Latin American literature, and Afro-Francophone studies at the Defense Language Institute in Seaside, California. Blanc-Hoàng's research interests include film studies, postcolonial/national and globalization studies, and graphic novels and science fiction studies. He regularly contributes articles to the World Film Location book series. For this publication, he wrote features on science fiction films set in Las Vegas, contemporary ethnic cinema produced in Marseille, and war/spy/political movies set in Prague. Blanc-Hoàng will also have chapter on masculinity in twenty-first-century Spanish films, which will be published as part of another anthology. He is now working on a new article on science fiction in the Latin American graphic novel.

**Guillaume de Syon,** PhD, teaches history at Albright College, Reading, Pennsylvania, and is a research associate in the history department at Franklin & Marshall College, Lancaster, Pennsylvania. He is the author of *Zeppelin! Germany and the Airship, 1900–1939* (2002) and *Science and Technology in Modern European Life* (2008). His research focuses on the cultural history of technology, the history of travel in Germany, and facets of

European popular culture. In the realm of comics, he has published articles on the perception of aerospace in the Francophone comic tradition.

**Christina Dokou**, PhD, is an assistant professor of American literature and culture at the Faculty of English Language and Literature of the National and Kapodistrian University, Athens, Greece. She has published articles and anthology chapters on comparative literature (myth in modern literature), American folklore, pop Americana (comics and the graphic novel), and gender studies (androgyny). She is the coeditor of two anthologies: *The Periphery Viewing the World* (2004) and *The Letter of the Law: Literature, Justice and the Other* (2013).

**Lynda Goldstein**, PhD, teaches contemporary culture studies, primarily in film, drama, and literature, at Penn State Wilkes-Barre. Her research interests have mostly focused on feminist and queer issues, but increasingly, perhaps as a result of aging, questions of history and memory have come to the fore in the classroom and her research.

**Melanie Huska**, PhD, received her doctorate in history from the University of Minnesota in 2013. Her research examines the ways in which the Mexican state borrowed popular culture forms for public history initiatives, including historically themed comic books and soap operas, to shift public opinion in the transition to neoliberalism in the 1980s and 1990s. She is revising her dissertation, "Entertaining Education: Teaching National History in Mexican State–Sponsored Comic Books and *Telenovelas*, 1963 to 2000" into a book manuscript. She is currently a visiting assistant professor at Oberlin College.

**Kara Kvaran**, PhD, is a native of southeastern Michigan. In 2004, she received her bachelor's degree in history from Eastern Michigan University. She continued her studies in American history and feminist theory at Purdue University and was awarded her master's degree in 2006 and her doctorate in 2011. She joined the University of Akron women's studies program in 2012 as a full-time college lecturer. Dr. Kvaran's research interests lie at the intersection of modern American popular culture and gender. Her work explores music, film, and literature and its connection to gender history—specifically, how American society creates and frames notions of masculinity and femininity through media. Her dissertation, which she is currently revising into a manuscript, is titled "Gendered Underground: Men, Women, and American Punk Rock, 1965–1995." She is currently working on a socioeconomic analysis of slasher films and an article on Wonder Woman, gender, and foreign policy.

**Peter W. Lee** is a doctoral candidate at Drew University, where he focuses on American cultural history and youth history. Among his publications, he has contributed to The Ages of Superman , Comic Books and the Cold War, 1946–1962 , Web-Spinning Heroics: Critical Essays on the History and Meaning of Spider-Man , Comic Books, and American Cultural History—An Anthology , and the Critical Survey of Graphic Novels: Heroes and Superheroes reference set. His work has also appeared in Thymos: The Journal of Boyhood Studies , The Bright Lights Film Journal , and Studies in Medievalism . His dissertation concentrates on boyhood and children's identity construction as portrayed in films during the early Cold War.

**James C. Lethbridge,** a New Jersey native, is a graduate of Bloomfield College. He is enrolled in the College of Graduate Studies at the University of Toledo, where he is pursuing his master of arts in philosophy, with which he will study medieval philosophy and dabble in theology, history, and literature.

**Annick Pellegrin** graduated from The University of Sydney with a bachelor of arts (languages) (honours) in 2009, with majors in French, Spanish, Italian, and linguistics. She is a doctoral candidate between the French and Spanish departments at The University of Sydney. Her dissertation, "(Not) Looking Together in the Same Direction," is a comparative study of "Latin American" self-representation and the Franco-Belgian gaze on "Latin America" in a selection of comics. She has presented papers on Franco-Belgian and "Latin American" comics in Australia, Mexico, Argentina, and the United Kingdom, which led to some of her work being published in *European Comic Art* and *Literature and Aesthetics*.

**Micah Rueber,** PhD, graduated from Mississippi State University in 2010. After serving as a postdoc at Auburn University, he joined the faculty at Mississippi Valley State University in 2012. His primary focus is the history of the United States from 1877 to 1945. He has written and presented on a variety of topics, but his emphasis is on agricultural and technological history. He is currently working on two projects: the first involving governmental programs aimed at reducing disease among African Americans living in Mississippi during the 1930s and 1940s and the second, a history of the reintroduction of whitetail deer to Mississippi in the 1950s and 1960s.

**Faiz Sheikh** is a doctoral student in the School of Politics and International Studies at the University Leeds, England. His research focuses on the international relations of political Islam, looking at the interaction of international relations theory with Islamic theology. He is a member of the British International Studies Association, the British Society for Middle Eastern Studies, and the Zombie Research Society.

**Beatrice Skordili,** PhD, is revising her dissertation, "Destroying Time: Topology and Taxonomy in *The Alexandria Quartet.*" It proposes, through a critique of classic narratology (specifically, Gerard Genette's *Narrative Discourse*), a topological approach to narrative that lays emphasis on the operations of the enunciatory apparatus. She has taught as an adjunct professor in the United States and Greece. She is working, at present, in secondary education, awaiting better professional opportunities. She has published articles in *Surfaces* (Canada), *Agora* (Canada), and *In-Between* (India) and encyclopedia pieces in the *Routledge Encyclopedia of Postmod-*

*ernism* and *The Encyclopedia of Travel and Exploration*. Her interests, besides narrative theory, include psychoanalytic and poststructuralist theory and the twentieth- and twenty-first-century novel.

CPSIA information can be obtained at www.ICGtesting.com
Printed in the USA
BVOW07*1245031213

R5538100001B/R55381PG337649BVX1B/1/P